D1289174

From the Land of Shadows
The Making of Grey Owl

Donald B. Smith

Western Producer Prairie Books
Saskatoon, Saskatchewan
1990

Copyright © 1990 by Donald B. Smith
Western Producer Prairie Books
Saskatoon, Saskatchewan

First paperback printing 1991

All rights reserved. No part of this publication may be reproduced, stored
in a retrieval system, or transmitted, in any form or by any means,
electronic, mechanical, photocopying, recording, or otherwise, without the
prior written permission of the publisher or, in the case of photocopying
or other reprographic copying, a licence from the Canadian Reprography
Collective.

Cover photograph: detail of a photo of Grey Owl taken by W. J. Oliver,
at Riding Mountain National Park, June 1931. Glenbow Archives,
Calgary/NA–4868–213.
Cover design by John Luckhurst/GDL
Edited by Bob Beal

The publisher wishes to acknowledge the support received for this
publication from the Canada Council.

Printed and bound in Canada
10 9 8 7 6 5 4 3 2 99 98 97 96 95 94 93 92 91

Western Producer Prairie Books is a unique publishing venture located
in the middle of western Canada and owned by a group of prairie
farmers who are members of the Saskatchewan Wheat Pool. From the
first book in 1954, a reprint of a serial originally carried in the weekly
newspaper, *The Western Producer,* to the book before you now, the
tradition of providing enjoyable and informative reading for all Canadians
is continued.

Canadian Cataloguing in Publication Data

Smith, Donald, B., 1946–

From the land of shadows

Includes bibliographical references.
ISBN 0–88833–347–1

1. Grey Owl, 1888–1938. 2. Conservationists—
Canada—Biography. 3. Novelists, Canadian (English)
—20th century—Biography.* I. Title.

E90.G75S45 1990   639.9'092   C90–097010–3

*To Agnes
and in memory of
Dawn and Johnny*

My thanks to Agnes Belaney Lalonde for permission to quote from Grey Owl's letters, and to the repositories that have carefully preserved her father's writings. In particular, I thank the Macmillan Archive, The William Ready Division of Archives and Research Collections, McMaster University Library, Hamilton, Ontario; the Charles Scribner's Sons Archive, Princeton University Library, Princeton, New Jersey; and the National Archives of Canada.

To quote from the writings of William A. Deacon, H. Lovat Dickson, Hugh Eayrs, Conrad Foster, Lloyd Roberts, Betty Somervell, and Geoffrey Turner, I thank the trustees of their respective estates. I am also grateful to H. A. R. Cawkell, Vince Crichton, Ken Conibear, Marilyn Legge Godfrey, Ferg Legace, Stuart MacDougall, and Jack Shadbolt, for permission to quote from their manuscripts, and correspondence with me, about Grey Owl.

The description of W. J. Oliver's initial meeting with Grey Owl in 1931 first appeared in *Sunday. Calgary Herald Magazine,* on September 18, 1988. The account of Grey Owl's near-exposure—in March 1937—as Archie Belaney, the husband of Angele Belaney of Temagami, Ontario, was included in an article on Grey Owl in the *Globe and Mail* on April 12, 1988. The review of Grey Owl's visit to Peterborough, Ontario, in March 1938, was first published in the Peterborough *Examiner,* April 19, 1988.

Contents

MAPS AND ILLUSTRATIONS

MAPS

ILLUSTRATIONS

Following page 25

Following page 93

"Side by side with modern Canada lies the last battleground in the long drawn out bitter contest between civilisation and the forces of nature. It is a land of shadows and hidden trails, lost rivers and unknown lakes, a region of soft-footed creatures going their noiseless ways over the carpet of moss, and there is silence, intense, absolute and all-embracing."

The opening lines of Grey Owl's first published article, "The Passing of the Last Frontier," *Country Life*, March 2, 1929, p. 302.

1   The Modern Hiawatha

The audience took their seats for the afternoon performance. The theatre darkened. A gramophone, unseen behind the platform, played classical music. Then a lone spotlight revealed a tall, dark, hawk-faced man, clad in moccasins and buckskins, with a single eagle feather in his hair. He walked across the stage as if it were forest moss under his feet. The opening bars of Beethoven's "Moonlight Sonata" played until the spotlit figure raised his hand, saluting the audience of 1,400 people with the Indian greeting "How Kola." [1]

Three days before, the Hastings edition of the *Evening Argus* announced the talk on December 2, 1935, by the "modern Hiawatha." "Grey Owl is an Indian. His father, however, was a Scotsman, who served as a Government Scout at Fort Laramie, in Wyoming, under the celebrated 'Buffalo Bill'—Colonel Cody. His mother was an Apache Indian. From his earliest years he led the life of a plains Indian, and hunted and trapped with the braves. He was adopted by the Ojibways, and learned the lore of the wild." Both the *Argus* and its rival, the *Observer*, ran his photo.

The "Red Indian" looked and acted exactly as his audience in the English seaside resort of Hastings imagined he would. The British press had already commented on his poise and dignity. Shortly after his arrival in Britain, the London *Times* reported: "A picturesque figure in Indian dress, with the thoughtful face of the philosopher, Grey Owl comes as the friend of nature." He spoke in an earnest, concerned way about the wilderness and talked, the Manchester *Guardian* reported, "with the true nasal twang of the Canadian Indian." Later the London *Sunday Express* commented: "There never came a Redder Red Indian to Britain." [2]

The child of nature began, standing with his hand uplifted. "I speak with a straight tongue. I will tell you only what is true. I have come from very far to speak to you and because you have come to hear me the sky is very bright." [3] He said he crossed the Atlantic as "a spokesman for that vast, inarticulate, rapidly dwindling army of living things, our co-dwellers in the Land of Shadows, our kin of the Last Frontier." [4] On one shoulder he wore a maple leaf embroidered in shiny beads, the symbol of his adopted country; on the other, a beaver, the symbol of his crusade to preserve the North's forests, lakes, and its wildlife. [5]

Widely known for his articles, books, and movies with his tame beaver, Grey Owl had completed one-third of his triumphant lecture tour of the British Isles when he appeared at Hastings. It began on October 17, 1935, with his arrival on the *Empress of Britain* from Montreal. One of the journalists who interviewed him wrote: "It was as refreshing to meet Grey Owl, when the *Empress of Britain* docked at Southampton tonight, as it is to wake up on a fine morning in the country after a year's confinement in the city. No sentimentality about it, simply the most unaffected lecturer I have ever met. His one ambition is to gain increasing public sympathy for wild life of every kind." He looked such a happy, cheerful man. He told the reporter: "I'm a round peg in a round hole." [6]

From Grey Owl's first weeks in London, the tour exceeded all expectations. After he spoke at the *Sunday Times* annual book exhibition on November 7, the London *Observer* called him "the favourite author of the show." The *Sunday Graphic & Sunday News* said his lecture "easily topped the bill." [7]

It quickly became difficult to hear Grey Owl speak, unless you arrived early. The day before he lectured at the *Sunday Times* book exhibition, Mrs. L. Day attended his 3 o'clock talk at Harrod's department store on Brompton Road in London.

> We went early and found a very large hall being prepared to hold about five or six hundred people. We went to get lunch, determining to return early to get good seats near him, but to our disgust when we got back just after two, the hall was more than half full and we had to sit a long way back. A few minutes later it was packed full and still the people came and came, though they could not get in. Then a notice was given out, saying that he had consented to give another talk following on this one, for all the crowd which could not get in then. [8]

The Cambridge *Review* analyzed his technique when he spoke at the Guildhall in the university town, two days after his lecture at the book exhibition. "This was an excellent lecture. . . . Perhaps the things which most struck one about the lecture were Grey Owl's personality and delivery. His pleasant, deep voice held the attention of his audience without effort, and even the longest story seemed all too short." [9]

Grey Owl drew people from all sectors of British society to his lectures, including the cultural elite. Sir Sydney Cockerell, the director of the Fitzwilliam Museum at Cambridge University, heard him speak twice. He later wrote his brother, T. D. A. Cockerell, one of the United States' most eminent biologists: "There was on each occasion a good smattering of

University bigwigs—Sir J. J. Thomson, Prof. G. I. Taylor, Seward, Thomas, etc. After a fortnight of great success at the Polytechnic in London he is absolutely at home on the platform and he instantly wins the heart and attention of his audience. . . . We all think him absolutely first class." After the afternoon lecture Sir Sydney invited Grey Owl back to his house for tea with the Sewards and Mrs. G. M. Trevelyan, wife of the famous English historian. Grey Owl's originality and his dedication to his cause, Sir Sydney claimed, was "parallel to Colonel T. E. 'Lawrence' who was born in the same year, 1888." It was high praise indeed for Grey Owl to be compared to the legendary Lawrence of Arabia, the great advocate and fighter for Arab independence whom Sir Sydney had known well. [10]

Grey Owl's renown had preceded him to Britain. When Sir Sydney, for instance, called on Rudyard Kipling and stayed for lunch and tea in late September 1935, he spoke about the famous writer, Grey Owl. Britain's first Nobel prize winner for literature (1907) replied that he had already heard of him. Rudyard Kipling and his wife were both interested in the man. [11]

Much of the "modern Hiawatha's" appeal came from the freshness of his subject. Grey Owl's books and talks gave Britons glimpses of the vast surviving forests in northern Canada, and of the beasts and birds within them. England had destroyed its "virgin woodland wilderness" a thousand years earlier. [12]

Immediately before his talk at Hastings' White Rock Pavilion on December 2, Grey Owl spoke in Edinburgh. A moment of special pride came when he made known that his father was of Scottish ancestry. Grey Owl loved the still wild Scottish landscape. With all his engaging naiveté he told his audience: "I would like to have explored these hills before the settlers reached them." [13]

A luncheon was held for Grey Owl at Edinburgh's Caledonian Hotel, a magnificent hotel just below Edinburgh Castle. Three special guests attended: the Earl of Minto and Lady Minto, and Lady Haig. [14] The Earl of Minto's father served as Governor-General of Canada from 1898 to 1904. His mother, through an American ancestor, was a descendant of the early seventeenth century Virginian settler John Rolfe and the Indian princess, Pocahontas. [15] Lady Haig was the widow of Earl Haig, commander of the British Empire's forces in the final years of the First World War. Lady Haig had previously met another distinguished Canadian, Chief Buffalo Child Long Lance, at the Calgary Stampede in 1925.[16]

After his last lecture in Edinburgh on November 30, Grey Owl left for Sussex on England's southeast coast. He kept up the relentless pace of the tour. So anxious was Grey Owl to fill his two lecture appointments in Hastings that he appeared against doctor's orders. It had rained steadily for three weeks in Britain [17] and Grey Owl had a severe cold. But he insisted on speaking in the town where two former friends still lived, "two maiden ladies, well over middle age, very sweet and kind," who had entertained him when he was convalescing from injuries suffered at the front during the Great War. [18]

After his words of greeting from the Hastings stage, Grey Owl showed "Pilgrims of the Wild," an eleven-minute film about his life with his wife, Anahareo, at his home in distant Saskatchewan. The film had been shot at Beaver Lodge, in Prince Albert National Park, in September 1935, a month before Grey Owl left Canada for Britain. [19] It showed him and his beautiful Indian wife canoeing, portaging, and calling the beaver.

The film took its title from Grey Owl's autobiography published the previous year. In this moving account the former trapper told the story of how he had decided to abandon the hunt and to work instead for the conservation of the beaver and all wildlife. Nearly a decade earlier Anahareo had convinced him to adopt two orphaned beaver kits, and while they raised them his attitude toward wildlife changed. Instead of contributing to the extermination of the beaver, he now worked for the salvation of the endangered species. The National Parks Branch of Canada had made him a guardian of the wildlife at Prince Albert National Park in Saskatchewan. There he wrote *Pilgrims of the Wild,* and his new children's book, *The Adventures of Sajo and her Beaver People.*

While his silent film ran, the lecturer moved to and fro across the front of the screen recounting tales of his beloved northern Canada. He told stories about wildlife—particularly about those intelligent, hard-working animals he lived with: the beaver, Canada's national animal. He talked directly to his audience, and used no notes. His animated dialogue and his second, third, and fourth films magically transported his listeners from the narrow streets of Hastings to the vast, unbroken Canadian forests. The *Evening Argus* commented on "his arresting personality, his deep sincerity and rare sense of humour." [20]

During the Great War, twenty years earlier, Hastings had been a temporary home to thousands of Canadians. The Canadian Army used it as a convolescent centre. [21] Many Hastonians had met Canadians before, and they had heard them talk about their country, but few Hastonians had heard of Grey Owl's Canada. In his lectures he spoke with a simple, direct earnestness about "the Beaver People, the Indian, the North, harsh, savage, yet beautiful." [22]

Among his audience sat two soberly-dressed elderly ladies in their mid-seventies, enthralled by his films, and engrossed by his every word. Ada and Carrie Belaney lived as recluses in their comfortable red-bricked terraced house on Wellington Road, off Milward Road, just below the ruins of Hasting's old Norman Castle, about half-a-kilometre from the sea. At the very beginning both ladies made eye contact with the speaker. As the Misses Belaney later recalled: "Grey Owl walked on the stage and seemed to scan the audience until he came to us. Then he smiled and gave a little bow to us." [23]

After Grey Owl's presentation, the Misses Belaney anxiously waited for the autographing session to end. Long lines of admirers had formed to shake hands with him, to talk to him, and to obtain the author's signature on the frontispiece of their newly purchased volumes. After each performance local booksellers sold 100 to 300 copies of his three books. [24] Only after the last autograph-seeker left could Grey Owl and the Misses Belaney finally talk, for the first time since the war. Ada and Carrie "had a long chat with him in the hall, after which we met and had a light meal at the Queen's Hotel before he returned to the White Rock Pavilion for his second lecture." [25]

The visitor enjoyed meeting the Misses Belaney again. A few months later, from Prince Albert National Park, he would write Norman Gray, manager of the White Rock.

Dear Sir.—You may recollect that I (Grey Owl the Indian) lectured in your fine hall during last winter on beavers, Indians, Canadian wild life, etc., with moving pictures.

I have very happy memories of Hastings, and also have not a few pleasant reminiscences of war days when I was convalescent at Hastings before being shipped back to Canada, having served as a sniper in the 1st Canadian Division.

All this may not interest you particularly, as you only saw me for an afternoon and an evening, but I am giving you these details to establish my identity, and to give you a guarantee that I am not one of those crank letter writers that are the bane of my own existence; and I would not trouble you without a definite reason.

Would you please be kind enough to look up the directory and find the address of the Misses Belaney (Miss A. and C. Belaney) and send it to me. They are good friends of mine and entertained me both during the war days and again at the time of my lecture.

They are two maiden ladies, well over middle age, very sweet and kind, and the address seems to me to be around a "Millward-road" or a "Millward-crescent," but am not sure.

I would be very much obliged if you would go to the trouble of ascertaining their address for me and send it to me. I cannot send you a stamp, of course, which I regret, but will be in England in 1937 and will redeem the debt of honour at that time.

Should you be unable to locate these ladies, perhaps if you would ring up the White Rock Hotel (I think that was the name); it is straight south from the Albert Memorial, occupying a corner on the sea front near where some big yachts go out on short trips into the Channel, and has a sunken road in front of it. They may remember me and, again, maybe they won't.

Thanking you, I am,
Yours truly,
GREY OWL [26]

It had been an extraordinary sight. Two elderly ladies dressed very much like the elderly Queen Victoria, dining with the world-famous Indian writer, lecturer, and defender of the Canadian beaver, [27] in what was then Hastings' largest and most prestigious hotel. It is not known if he was in his stage costume or if he changed before leaving the White Rock Pavilion for the hotel. But even in his ordinary clothes, the tall, hawk-faced man, with his long hair in braids, would have attracted attention. Offstage he wore a red shirt, his new blue serge suit, a large Mexican hat, a black hanky around his neck, and moccasins. [28] His dress advertised his true self, for as he wrote in *Pilgrims of the Wild*, "houses and clothes not unusually reflect the personality of those who occupy them." [29]

At their table at the Queen's Hotel—perhaps the most public place in all of Hastings—this strange trio shared the most private information. What merriment they had. For a few moments Ada Belaney, the stern-faced one, forgot the painful arthritis in her hands. [30]

In reality, Grey Owl's letter, written several months after their meeting, only hinted at the true bond linking together these three individuals. It consisted of far more than a number of meetings, in Grey Owl's words, "when I was convalescent at Hastings before being shipped back to Canada, having served as a sniper in the 1st Canadian Division." The visitor could duplicate the cultured, upper-middle-class accent of the two elderly English ladies before him. Other surprises followed. Instinctively he seemed to have the same table manners as they did. After a studied gaze you could notice an astounding physical resemblance. All three had the same hawk-like face.

The link between Grey Owl and these two ladies dated back to the moment of his birth. On the frontispiece of his first book, *The Men of the Last Frontier*, published in 1931, Grey Owl included this inscription to Ada Belaney, without naming her: "Dedicated as a tribute to my aunt, whom I must thank for such education that enabled me to interpret into words the spirit of the forest, beautiful for all its underlying wildness." [31]

Ada had shaped her nephew Archie Belaney, inspired him, prepared him. When he was but a young child she recognized the intelligent boy's unique understanding of wild animals and had encouraged him. Now she and Carrie admired their nephew's transformation into a North American Indian, completed, in Ada's words, "so that he could carry on his work among the Red Indians more easily and naturally." [32] The boy that these two ever-devoted ladies loved and raised as if he were their own son also felt a strong attachment to them, one so strong that Grey Owl would risk his exposure as Archie Belaney just to see them.

In one of the most poetic passages in *Pilgrims of the Wild*, Grey Owl wrote that his real life began in northern Canada.

> The feel of a canoe gunnell at the thigh, the splash of flying spray in the face, the rhythm of the snowshoe trail, the beckoning of far-off hills and valleys, the majesty of the tempest, the calm and silent presence of the trees

that seem to muse and ponder in their silence; the trust and confidence of small living creatures, the company of simple men; these have been my inspiration and my guide. Without them I am nothing. [33]

This statement, however, is only partially true. Grey Owl could not completely escape from his past. The key to his creativity and his genius lies in his childhood in England. A combination of circumstances led him to enter into a fantasy world of his own making, one which would totally devour him. Incidents in his English past and his later experiences in Canada both helped to make this gifted individual into one of the most effective champions of the Canadian wilderness in this century. As a popularizer in the 1930s of Canada's forests, lakes, rivers, and wildlife, Grey Owl had no equal.

2   The Belaneys

"Please, please do not use that awful 'Archibald', it is a name wished on me by a misguided and patriotic Scotch aunt, a high-sounding, pretentious cake-eating epithet, just 'Grey Owl', please." So wrote Grey Owl to a correspondent in the 1930s, adding that "Archie is bearable, but Archibald no."[1] With that one statement the man known to his correspondent as "Archie Grey Owl" revealed a frustration of his childhood. As if she were trying to bring their deceased father back to life to keep her worthless brother in check, Ada had insisted on calling her brother's son, "Archibald."

Archie Belaney's namesake—his paternal grandfather—was born in 1822 into an ambitious Scottish farming family. His grandfather's father rose from the status of a farm labourer to become a merchant (grocer) in Ayton, a small town just north of the Scottish-English border. The Belaney family[2] greatly valued education, and independence. While three brothers stayed to help their father at his store and on the farm, three others, Robert, James, and Archibald, left for England.

Robert became the most distinguished of the six brothers, and as a spokesman for animal rights an example for the future Grey Owl. Destined for the ministry, Robert had entered Edinburgh University in 1821 at the age of seventeen, and had later attended Cambridge University, where he obtained an M.A. degree. After becoming an Anglican clergyman, he converted in 1852 to the Roman Catholic Church. As a Roman Catholic priest he brought the Jesuits to Glasgow and later introduced the Servite Fathers to London.[3]

The defence of the Roman Catholic Church and animals' rights were Father Belaney's two major preoccupations as a writer. Vigorously he opposed vivisection. The vivisectionist's object, he wrote in *Vivisection viewed under the light of Divine Revelation* (1877), was "not to kill at all; but to put animals on the rack and to keep them there for the sake of scientific discoveries, alive, as long as possible, writhing in agony, as

Christians were wont to be kept in the times of pagan persecution, when the object was to extinguish them and their religion with them."[4] Ada and Carrie Belaney kept their uncle's books in the family's library,[5] where Archie probably at least leafed through them. Since Robert lived to 1899 (he was believed to be the oldest living Roman Catholic priest in England in the late 1890s), Archie might well have visited him at his London home with his aunts.

If Robert, the oldest of the six brothers, can be said to have achieved the greatest fame, James Cockburn Belaney, the second oldest, obtained the greatest infamy. He became a physician, and practised at North Sunderland, just south of Berwick-upon-Tweed, in northeastern England.[6] An avid sportsman, he championed the sport of falconry, and wrote a book on the subject, *A Treatise Upon Falconry in Two Parts*, in 1841. He had one falcon with whom he travelled over 3,000 kilometres.[7] After that date, however, family members preferred to try to forget him. In 1844 he was tried at London's Old Bailey for fatally poisoning his wife, the wealthy daughter of a local merchant family. When the court acquitted him (a travel guide published in the year of Archie's birth recounts) a crowd, convinced of his guilt, burned down his home. James Cockburn Belaney fled and took up residence in Bordeaux, France.[8]

Archie quite likely knew about the family's black sheep. He wrote this suggestive passage in *Pilgrims of the Wild* (1934), in reference to a beaver kit he and Anahareo tried to revive: "She fell asleep or into a coma and her heart action nearly ceased, and I suddenly remembered a case of opium poisoning I had seen, or heard of, or read about somewhere. I told Anahareo to rub her, rub her hard over the whole body, to massage the hands and feet, to keep her awake at all costs."[9]

Archibald Belaney, the third son to leave Scotland for England, went to London where he became a prosperous merchant and shipbroker.[10] At thirty-four, he married Julia Jackson at London's St. Marylebone Church, the place of worship of one of the richest parishes in England.[11]

Julia Jackson, then twenty-five, had been raised by her uncle, George Stansfeld Furmage, a wealthy wholesale grocer, after Julia's parents died when she was quite young. Through her maternal grandmother, a Stansfeld, a prominent family from Halifax in Yorkshire, Julia could claim direct descent from Alfred the Great.[12] Her uncle, a man with high social and business standing, commissioned a fine oil portrait of his niece. The painting, which showed her as a young woman in her first ballroom dress, hung in the Belaney homes in Hastings.[13]

Like his two oldest brothers, Archibald had a strong literary interest. Between the birth of his son, George Furmage (named after his wife's uncle) in 1857, and his second child, Carrie, born in 1859, he composed a nearly two-hundred-page epic poem, *The Hundred Days of Napoleon*, in 1858. As the prelude says, he wrote the poem as "a song of triumph in Britannia's praise," a celebration of the Duke of Wellington's victory over Napoleon at the Battle of Waterloo. One of the Belaney family's most treasured momentos was a green and gold copy of the poem, and a letter from Queen Victoria's secretary acknowledging its receipt.[14]

Julia Belaney became a widow in 1865, only four years after the birth of her third child, Ada. Her husband's sudden death at forty-three left her as a single parent with three children, all under ten. Anxious to have a male family head, she lavished all her attention on her son, George. Much of her substantial fortune went to him, first to pay for his expensive public school education. George began his life with much promise, this typical upper-middle-class Englishman, well-dressed, cultured, and a keen games-man. George looked very much the sporting man he was. He stood 6'3", usually wore tweeds, had very dark hair, dark brown eyes, and a slight military moustache.[15] Julia and her daughters worried, though, about George's complete lack of self-discipline.[16] He always wanted to enjoy himself and could never sit still. While clever, handsome, and charming, her son had no profession. When he was about twenty, his mother approached Sir Frederick Huth, a wealthy London tea merchant who had married her second cousin. Sir Frederick agreed to take the young man on as a tea-taster.[17]

Julia's love for her only son was excessive. Throughout his childhood she spoiled him, and this continued when he was a man. While exacting and firm with her two daughters, she gave in to George's every request. When the apprentice tea-taster asked his mother to set him up as a tea merchant on his own in 1879, she did so. "George Furmage Belaney & Co., Tea & Coffee Merchants," at 2 Talbot Court, off Gracechurch Street in London, lasted less than a year before folding.[18] To his sisters' dismay, the spendthrift George had just gone through yet another sizeable slice of their mother's diminishing fortune.

Julia again missed the signals and continued to spoil her son. George loved to hunt, and after his business failed he proposed a big game expedition to South Africa with a friend. Wanting to help him break out of his depression, and to stop his heavy drinking, she agreed to pay for it. George went, and he brought back with his trophies a black servant. As his mother could not financially support another servant, she had to let him go. George found the African a job in a circus.[19]

By his mid-20s the restless George had become a constant trial to his mother and his two sisters. But the worst was yet to come. At the age of twenty-four he married the fifteen-year-old daughter of a Suffolk innkeeper. Rose Hines was already pregnant with his child, Rose Ethel Belaney, who arrived six months after their marriage in 1881. The baby only lived a year and a half. Her grandmother recorded the death in May, 1883, as her own daughter had left her native Suffolk village. Nothing more is known about Rose Hines. George himself had vanished.[20]

George kept his first marriage a secret from his mother and his sisters.

That was but one of his deceptions. He was reminded of his mother's opposition to any marriage on his part when he brought Elizabeth Cox, believed to be the daughter of a racehorse breeder in Kent, to meet his mother. With all his considerable charm, the favoured child asked Julia for financial support if they married. To his surprise, she refused. "Not until he had made a career for himself," she said. Yet, as before, her spirit soon collapsed, and with more of Julia Belaney's money (and some from the estate of Elizabeth's grandmother), George and Elizabeth left for the United States, taking Elizabeth's younger sister, Kittie, with them. George bought land that contained an established orange grove at Bridgeport, near Palatka in central Florida.[21]

It is not known if George ever actually married Elizabeth, but several months after Elizabeth's death early in 1886 he did marry her 15-year-old sister. A Justice of the Peace married them on November 27, 1886, at Federal Point, near Bridgeport.[22] By the time she became pregnant in early 1888, George's capital had so diminished that he hastily sailed back to England. In England he had left Rose Hines, his first wife, and had abandoned Rose Ethel, his first daughter. Now he gave up Gertrude, believed to be his daughter by Elizabeth, to a couple at Bridgeport to look after.[23]

Julia Belaney met her wayward son and his pregnant child-bride in a London hotel in the summer of 1888. George arrived drunk.[24] Although greatly distraught, Julia, then in her early 60s, invited the couple to her and her daughters' new home in Hastings, a fashionable English seaside town.[25] Julia and her daughters made arrangements to rent a small terrace house on neighbouring St. James' Road for the birth in September.

Once the shock passed, Julia and her two unmarried daughters accepted the fact of a baby's imminent arrival, and they waited eagerly. Ada and Carrie, in their late twenties, nearly double Kittie's age, made baby clothes and bought bedding and other baby supplies.[26] Although George told Kittie not to say she was Elizabeth's sister (this was a complication as English law still forbade a man to marry his deceased wife's sister),[27] Ada and Carrie saw through the cover-up and deduced that the quiet girl was indeed Elizabeth's sister or cousin.[28]

A doctor, assisted by a nurse, delivered the child between ten and twelve on the morning of September 18. Julia became Granny Belaney. Ada and Carrie brought over to 32 St. James' Road a beautiful swaying cot-basket and the carefully prepared baby clothes they had made.[29] The choice of names for the boy indicates Kittie's influence in the Belaney family: zero. The Belaneys named the baby after Julia's late husband, Archibald, and selected as his middle name Stansfeld, in honour of Julia's uncle and benefactor, George Stansfeld Furmage.

Scarcely two months later, after George, Kittie and little Archie had moved to rented lodgings nearby, the baby was baptised at the neighbouring Christ Church, Blacklands.[30] For the ceremony he wore a robe that had been in the family for several generations. Ada was his godmother.[31] Within two years, Carrie and she, in effect, replaced Kittie as his mother.

Julia and her daughters decided to take Archie into their home shortly after George and Kittie (who was expecting her second child) moved to the seaside resort of Deal in neighbouring Kent around 1890. Here George apparently made an honest attempt to recover from his chronic alcoholism. He stopped drinking and studied to become a typesetter. The reformation was short-lived. Again George became morose and moody and began drinking heavily. He experienced the DTs, and had to be hospitalized for a spell. Just before Kittie gave birth to her second child, the Belaney sisters acted. They took Archie back to Hastings to live with them and Granny. They had little confidence in Kittie's ability to raise Archie, particularly now that she had a second son.[32]

Ada and Carrie loathed George, who had swallowed up almost all the family fortune with his public school education, failed business, African big game expedition, land investments in Florida, and his drinking. Then the devil had the nerve to name his second son "Hugh Cockburn Belaney," the middle name being taken from that of James Cockburn Belaney, the accused wife-murderer.

The family took Archie away and several years later went a step further. After more lapses on his part, even his mother realized that George could not be reclaimed. He must leave England. The family's solicitors in London advised the wayward son that his mother would allow him an income sufficient for his needs, only if he lived abroad. If he ever returned and tried to communicate with Kittie, her special allowance, as well as his, would end instantly. Kittie signed the agreement.[33]

Archie occasionally saw his mother. Kittie and Hugh had an open invitation to visit the Belaneys at Hastings, and in the summers, particularly before Archie entered Grammar School at the age of eleven, she and Hugh did so. Did Archie, though, ever see his wastrel father?[34] Ada and Carrie tried to prevent it. But he might have seen him once or twice when George came begging to his mother, perhaps at the time he convinced his elderly mother to hand over to him items of the family silver.[35]

Charles Belaney, one of Archibald Belaney's brothers who had initially stayed on the family farm in Scotland, later moved to Canada. He died in 1890, but several of his children still lived in Manitoba before the First World War. The future Grey Owl's Canadian cousins have one family story about George Furmage Belaney. Sometime between 1905 and 1910, the ne'er-do-well called on them at harvest time in the Brandon Hills. Wilmot McComb, the son of George's first cousin, Jessie Belaney McComb, remembered the visit many years later. He asked George about life in England. George replied: "I really don't know much about it. I've been abroad for several years."[36] George's first cousin, Maggie Belaney, never forgot the visitor's departure. George asked for a horse and wagon to go into Brandon one night and came back in a drunken stupor. Upon his return he fell right off the wagon and his cousins had to drag him into the house. He also tried to steal some money from the family. They sent him packing and never saw him again.[37] Apparently he died somewhere in the United States shortly after this. His wife Kittie believed that he had been "killed in a drunken brawl in America."[38]

Deprived of a father, a mother, and all his grandparents except for Granny Belaney, Archie was raised by his Aunt Ada. A photograph of Archie at the age of three shows a well-fed, handsome boy in sailor costume, with the name of a British battleship on the cap-ribbon. Three or four years after the portrait was taken, the Belaneys moved to an attractive home, 36 St. Mary's Terrace, on the West Hill—with a fine view of the town and of the sea.[39]

Ada had complete charge of Archie and stressed obedience and excellence, just as she did with the collie dogs she bred. Her Spartan rules allowed no pampering, no special favours from her mother or from sister Carrie. When Archie practised the piano each morning, she stood beside him with a small cane, ready to lash his knuckles if he made a mistake.[40] Ada wanted to raise an exceptionally well-disciplined child. Her plan backfired somewhat as her nephew rebelled against her system. Archie later told Anahareo, in the mid-1920s (without giving away his aunt's and his own English origins): "I used to get a kick out of doing what I knew would have horrified her."[41] Or, as he wrote Anahareo on May 16, 1934, "my aunt spoiled my childhood, and made a kind of a devil out of me."[42]

Determined to make sure that her nephew would not turn out like his worthless father, Ada exercised total control over him at home. In his room she posted signs such as "DO NOT FORGET TO CLEAN YOUR TEETH." She even supervised his dressing. Kittie said, "he was always dressed like a child on show." Until he was eight, Ada herself taught Archie at home: English, music, geography—all subjects—even carpentry, which she loved.[43] Archie was originally left-handed but Ada forbade him to touch a pen or pencil with his left hand.[44]

Archie attended a small Anglican church school from age eight to eleven and there increased his familiarity with the Bible, so evident in his books. When he wanted to describe in his last book, *Tales of an Empty Cabin* (1936), how he became a conservationist, he wrote, "ultimately I laid aside my rifle and my traps and like Paul, worked for the betterment of those whom I had so assiduously persecuted."[45] In *Tales of an Empty Cabin* he referred to Esau's sale of his birthright to his brother Jacob for a mess of pottage (Genesis xxv). "The well-known business deal that Jacob put over on Esau still works as well as ever, it would seem."[46] The influence of the psalms is shown in his choice of the Hebrew word *Selah* to end his preface to the special edition of his first book, *The Men of the Last Frontier,* published for his second British tour:

And so, once again, England, I greet you.
I have spoken. Selah.
September 1937   GREY OWL[47]

While rather straitlaced in many areas—insisting, for example, that "Archibald" wear his Eton suit and even white gloves for church on Sunday—Ada later relaxed the rules a little. She loved animals, collie dogs in particular, and she allowed Archie to keep his own menagerie. When Archie was eleven, the family moved to a larger home, Highbury Villa, on St. James' Road, by chance almost directly opposite the small, terraced house in which he was born. It was a strange choice. Highbury was a dark, gloomy building, surrounded by trees,[48] at the end of a cul-de-sac. It was much larger than their previous house on St. Mary's Terrace and a little closer to the Hastings Grammar School, which Archie entered that same year, 1899. At Highbury Villa Ada let Archie keep his pets on the top floor, his rabbits, snakes, and mice. Recognizing that he had "a natural affinity with wild creatures,"[49] she encouraged him.

Even after a serious accident, Ada did not forbid Archie his menagerie. After the boy began grammar school, one of his adders bit him, and he had to be rushed to hospital to have the poisonous puss drained from his swollen finger. Despite this near-fatal encounter and the fact that sister Carrie hated them,[50] Archie still captured poisonous snakes, and Ada allowed the boy to keep them, after he had defanged them.

On two other occasions Archie came close to death. At age nine and again at eleven he developed pneumonia, an often-fatal disease before the development of antibiotics forty years later. A nurse had to be hired to help look after him. Throughout his illnesses the young boy showed great courage when in pain. After his second recovery Ada constantly worried about his chest and after hearing the least cough questioned him about it.[51] She knew how much the menagerie meant to him and, no doubt remembering his suffering while ill with pneumonia, she allowed him to keep it.

With his animals Archie created a secret refuge. At home with his aunts he had no friends. Apart from the short visits of his mother and his brother Hugh in the summer months, he was an only child. The boy had grown accustomed to his solitude and was not afraid of being alone. Alienated from his own immediate world, Archie loved to study animals. They did not make any demands of him, or judge or evaluate him, as Aunt Ada did.

Archie created his own world and even peopled it with an imaginary father. He wanted so much to have a real father, at home with him. Once his father (or perhaps his grandmother or aunts who said it was from George) bought him a miniature Mexican ranch, with little adobe houses, stables, and carved wooden horses. The young boy would take two of the human figures and imagine that one was his father and the other himself. He would spend hour upon hour moving them around playing out his fantasy that they both worked together on the ranch.[52] Years later he would tell an acquaintance in Canada that he had "spent the better part of three years on the trail with my father," before travelling over the "Canadian Wilderness" from 1906 to 1932.[53] He had, but only in his mind.

As a young boy Archie brought much joy to the Belaney household. Ada built her life around him. She hoped that after he completed grammar school he might study to become a doctor or take up another of the professions.[54]

When he entered the grey- and red-towered Hastings Grammar School in the fall of 1899, the second phase of Archie's boyhood began. He escaped for long periods from Ada's supervision and control. The snobbish Ada approved of the school that, if not high enough for the sons of the gentry who were sent off to public schools, was at least socially respectable for the middle class. In the medium-sized seacoast town, class divisions were clear-cut. Often on the way home from school, the rougher types from the Old Town (the fish boys) waylaid the Grammarians, cap snatching and fighting with them.[55]

Class-conscious Ada wanted her nephew among the right sort, the children of the professional classes and the well-to-do tradespeople. Archie himself, however, would come to accept the Ojibwa Indians' viewpoint over that of his aunt. "They consider every man equal, since every man comes into, and goes out of the world in the same way."[56] In his own words, Archie wanted to live in a community where "the manner of a man's speech, where he comes from, his religion, or even his name are matters of small moment and are nobody's business but his own."[57]

During his first four years at the Grammar School, Archie studied English, Religious Knowledge, French, History, Geography, and a new subject, Science, which had just been introduced into the school curriculum.[58] He mixed little with the other students in class, or afterwards. The shy, withdrawn boy, ashamed of having been abandoned by his parents, lived largely in his own world. Creatively he invented new parents for himself. He so wanted his missing father that he created a fictitious one, a western plainsman who had married his mother, an Apache Indian woman. This void, this irritation, he worked upon quietly, exactly as an oyster does a grain of sand, creating out of it years later a beautiful pearl, his fabulous story of his own origins.

3   Young Archie

At the Hastings Grammar School, Henry Hopkin became Archie's best friend.[1] Seventy years later Henry recalled that he was the only one of the approximately one hundred boys [2] with whom Archie really talked. "Hopkin" and "Belaney," as the masters called them, were only six months apart in age. Both boys had no father at home. Henry's father (a heavy-drinking veterinarian) and his mother had divorced, leaving Henry with his mother in Hastings, while his father fought in the South African (Boer) War in the Army Veterinary Corps. A large annual allowance, though, allowed them to live quite comfortably in the seaside town.

The fact that neither boy had a father at home no doubt drew them together. But in socially-conscious Edwardian England, Archie endured another stigma. He had no mother at home, either. "Young as he was there seemed to be a mystery about him," Henry recalled. Archie never talked about his father. On his visits to tea at Highbury Villa, Henry found just his friend's two maiden aunts and his elderly grandmother. In the cruel, coarse way of teenage schoolboys, some of Archie's schoolmates speculated which aunt was, in fact, his mother.[3] Archie protected himself by retreating into books, solitary games, and the rich fantasy world he had created.

At school the other boys regarded Archie as strange, for he took no interest in organized team sports like football (soccer) or cricket. Con Foster, two years younger than Archie, was in the same form at school from 1902 to 1904. Years later he recorded this memory of him. "I remember him well because he ran the Belaney gang, who played at Red Indians all the time, and I led the opposition gang, a rather amorphous body which regarded it as childish. The chief activities of his gang consisted of war-whooping round the school fields, carrying something they alleged were tomahawks, with a few feathers stuck in their hair."[4] Even at this early age Archie rebelled against everything that was organized.

Con Foster also recalled Archie's fanatical love of animals. He kept lizards, frogs, hedgehogs, and beetles, and took special delight in snakes, which occasionally he carried with him from the schoolyard into the class-room. Desperately the boy craved attention, and the respect of his school-mates. "Not dangerous if you know how to handle them," he boasted, as he brought a brown snake, whose fangs he had drawn, out of his pocket.

To Foster and others he once revealed his "secret": he had "Red Indian" blood in his veins. They laughed at him because he looked so obviously English. "Most of the boys thought he was a bit cracked. We used to call him 'The Squaw Man' when we got sick of his tales, because we had heard that was a term of contempt among Red Indian chiefs."

Archie loved to go off on solitary walks to look for plants and wild animals. Ada recalled that he went alone because "other people walked too heavily and frightened the animals away."[5] Sometimes Henry accompanied him when he went to look for snakes at Fairlight Glen on the East Hill, just beyond the town.

Others recalled Archie's love of wildlife. Frank Sparkes, an older student, knew him at the Grammar School in 1899–1900. "You used to see him up in the St. Helen's Woods crawling about under the branches, and he reckoned he could get within an inch or two of a bird or other wild creature and not be detected by it."[6] St. Helen's Woods, about a kilometre north of Highbury Villa, became Archie's favourite hideaway.

Hastings Grammar School masters taught the students their imperial heritage. They ingrained in their charges the idea of the superiority of British civilization and of Christianity. Britain had not merely the right but also the duty to rule one quarter of the world. Britain must carry "the white man's burden" of civilizing inferior races. At least one student did not fully agree. On account of his reading outside of school, "Belaney" idealized the dark-skinned, non-Christian North American Indians. He had never met one, or even seen one, but he had books about them. In the margins of these books he sketched feathered braves in buckskins—youthful drawings very similar to those he later used to illustrate his books.[7] He longed to live amongst the noble red men of James Fenimore Cooper's and Henry Wadsworth Longfellow's imaginations.

Archie particularly liked Cooper's novels and also had a lifelong love of Longfellow's poem *Hiawatha*.[8] One of his favourite passages described Chibiabos, the Indian he emulated on his forays in St. Helen's Woods:

> Where he passed, the branches moved not;
> Where he trod the grasses bent not,
> And the fallen leaves of last year
> Made no sound beneath his footsteps.[9]

Henry Hopkin recalled that " 'playing Indians' was his passion, and he had a vast store of knowledge on the subject gathered from books."[10]

Archie probably also read a number of the twenty-odd volumes of animal stories and nature essays by Ernest Thompson Seton, the innovative nature writer and artist who in 1898 had published his first book, *Wild Animals I Have Known*. It quickly became one of the most widely read bestsellers of all time. In 1903 Seton published his famous *Two Little Savages. Being the Adventures of Two Boys who Lived as Indians and What They Learned*.[11]

In his books Seton pioneered what has become known as the realistic animal story. Instead of presenting animals talking and thinking like humans, as Jack London and Rudyard Kipling did, Seton attempted to view life from the animal's perspective. The English-born writer, who was raised in Canada but later lived in the United States, tried to depict animal lives and personalities as they actually were. He helped millions gain a new respect and concern for the rights of wild animals. Throughout his work Seton condemned western man's belief that by right he must dominate nature. As he wrote in his "Note to the Reader" in *Wild Animals I Have Known*:

> I hope some will herein find emphasized a moral as old as Scripture—we and the beasts are kin. Man has nothing that the animals have not at least a vestige of, the animals have nothing that man does not in some degree share.
>
> Since, then, the animals are creatures with wants and feelings differing in degree only from our own, they surely have their rights. This fact, now beginning to be recognized by the Caucasian world, was first proclaimed by Moses and was emphasized by the Buddhist over two thousand years ago.[12]

Archie certainly read Seton's works, for as Grey Owl he showed a familiarity with them. In his last book, *Tales of an Empty Cabin* (1936), Grey Owl, for instance, included this note: "Ernest Thompson Seton once wrote to the effect that an animal is able to divine instantly man's intentions toward him."[13] Earlier, an American reviewer of his *Pilgrims of the Wild* saw Seton's influence in this book, which he said "is written with a simplicity and charm that make it a compound of Ernest Seton Thompson and St. Francis of Assisi."[14] One of the books Archie had in his library as a boy appears to have been *Two Little Savages,* a gift from his brother Hugh.[15]

Archie might well have patterned his future life on *Two Little Savages*. The very first paragraph of the book about two farm boys, Yan and his friend Sam, who both undertake to understand the rituals and customs of various Indian tribes, sounds like a script of Archie's own future life. "Yan was much like other twelve-year-old boys in having a keen interest in Indians and in wild life, but he differed from most in this, that he never got over it. Indeed, as he grew older, he found a yet keener pleasure in storing up the little bits of woodcraft and Indian lore that pleased him as a boy."[16]

A highlight of Archie's youth came on August 20, 1903, when he saw Buffalo Bill and his Wild West Show in Hastings. To accommodate the entourage of 800 people, the organizers built a huge canvas town. That day Hastonians saw "Indians of the type familiarised by the illustrations which grace the covers of the penny 'blood and thunder' publications, Mexican cowboys, handy-men, and cavalry of many nations, herded together in orderly confusion, if such a term is permissible, and the demonstrations they gave of feats of horsemanship, sharp-shooting, lassoing, and other accomplishments born of long practice in far parts of the world, were indeed a revelation." [17]

As the time approached when Archie had to consider a career, his aunts hoped his passion for wildlife and Red Indians would subside. It did not. He had no desire to attend university or to prepare himself for a profession, but he stayed at school until the summer after he wrote his Cambridge Junior, or junior matriculation, examinations in December 1903. [18]

At the grammar school Archie excelled in certain subjects. He won a school prize for French in 1903 and did well in Chemistry. Of the seven Hastings Grammar School boys writing the Cambridge Junior exams in December 1903, he obtained the highest mark in English. The first section of the exam was on English grammar and the second on Shakespeare's *Julius Caesar.* He tied with Con Foster for highest mark in Religious Knowledge. Archie did well in French, but he had only a pass in History and Geography and failed Latin, Mathematics, and Experimental Science. [19] Overall he passed, but his record was not extraordinary and Aunt Ada allowed him to leave school the following July.

Part of Archie's problems at the school stemmed from his poor relations with his teachers. They could not understand or reach him. Con Foster, thirty-five years later, still vividly recalled the future Grey Owl in the classroom. "He was intelligent but, as Reptiles and Red Indians were not school subjects, never high in his form. The masters were not fond of him—there were one or two unauthorised and explosive chemistry experiments as well as the wandering hedgehogs and snakes." [20]

During Archie's last year or so at the school his friendship with Henry Hopkin fell off somewhat. Henry discovered girls, and his interest in Archie's Indian games decreased accordingly. In a revealing note in one of his journals written in the early 1930s, Grey Owl hinted at why he stayed away from women at this stage. "Owing to aunts teaching disliked women (or owing to being turned down)." [21] His addition in brackets, "or owing to being turned down," is very revealing. His aunts had sternly warned him not to become involved with girls at his young age and, at the same time, the insecure Archie feared being rejected by women.

George McCormick, two-and-a-half years younger than Archie, became his closest friend after he left the grammar school, just two months before his sixteenth birthday. The McCormicks, a warm and friendly family, lived at Preston Lodge on Quarry Road, across the passageway from Highbury Villa. George McCormick had accompanied him to Buffalo Bill's Wild West Show.[22]

Margaret McCormick never forgot how she had first met her brother's older friend. A wild sou'wester raged from the English Channel, beating and thudding against Preston Lodge. Suddenly, above the roar of the wind and rain, came the hooting call of an owl. "It's old Archie," said George to his brothers and sisters gathered around the big table where they did their homework. Out he rushed, to return with a tall, slim boy, strikingly handsome, with acquiline features, his lank dark hair wet with rain.[23]

With Archie's help and direction, George and the older McCormick children, exactly like Yan and Sam in *Two Little Savages*, built a wigwam in their garden, covering it with painted blankets. Archie, in George's words, "absolutely worshipped the outlook and behaviour of the North American Indians."[24] George and his older brothers and sisters slept in the wigwam during the summer. They loved frying potatoes and cooking bacon and eggs for breakfast in the backyard of Preston Lodge.

Archie used to come to the McCormick house with his pockets full of snakes. This was a great hit. The McCormick children loved animals and kept cats, rabbits, a dog and Billy, a tortoise.[25] The snakes, however, did cost Dora McCormick one friendship. One afternoon Mrs. McCormick had some friends for tea and while the children made their bows in the drawing room, one lady, in horror, saw Archie re-arranging a large snake in his pocket. She never visited again.[26]

Margaret McCormick remembered how Archie helped them out with a growing problem. Once, some neighbours started a chicken run close to the McCormicks' fence. This attracted large grey rats to feed on the scraps left for the hens. Archie set out to solve the problem. He sat patiently at a window on the first floor of Preston Lodge and shot each rat unerringly as it appeared. "He said it was more humane than poison," and it was more fun for him. The thundering noise led Mrs. McCormick to intervene. She asked him to try something a little quieter.[27]

During the young McCormicks' school holidays, Archie rose before the sparrows. He sneaked out of his own room by sliding down the drainpipe, then climbed up to the McCormick's second-storey ledge and through the window of George's and his brother Jim's bedroom. "Come on old-timer," he would say to George, "we're off." Sometimes Jim accompanied them to Guestling, Winchelsea, Fairlight, or Pett. Ada thought Archie was still up in his room.[28]

The boys walked ten, twelve, maybe twenty kilometres into the country, possibly coming back with a big basket of mushrooms, or perhaps they would capture some snakes, a brownish-coloured female adder or the greyer-coloured male.[29] George recalls that he and Jim "had to go out in very good Indian style. We had to lope along like an Indian, never slouch." The area south of the railway from Hastings to Rye in the east, down to the sea, became their stomping ground.

Seventy years later George still remembered one of their adventures. They had gone to Fairlight, an unspoilt stretch of the Sussex coast just east of Hastings. By the sea the cliffs rose up a hundred metres and more. At a spot near the Haddocks's coast-guard station, the two boys saw a split-off rock fragment that was almost totally separated from the cliff. Without thinking, Archie suggested that with a strong shove with their feet they send it on its way. A foolish suggestion it was, for if the detached rock sliver budged, they would fall with it down a hundred metres to certain death at the base of the cliff. Fortunately it held firm and the two boys lived,[30] one to become Grey Owl, the other a major in the British Army's tank corps in India.

On these walks, Archie, often with George, crossed much of the same territory covered by the East Sussex Foxhounds. As Grey Owl, he bitterly wrote that "under no circumstances could I make peace with a medieval custom which I had always abhored."[31] Two or three days every week, from November to March, the local gentry, led by the future Lord Brassey, rode to hounds. Two of their principal meeting places were Guestling and Fairlight, both favourite locales of Archie.[32] On occasion he must have encountered the scores of scarlet-dressed riders, with their pack of yelping hounds, pursuing a single terrified fox. Years later he wrote: "Sportsmen claim that an animal that is to be killed for fun—can you imagine it?—should be given an even chance. Is that an even chance, a hundred to one, I ask you?"[33]

Archie and George used to make what Archie called a beaver dam. The idea came from Fenimore Cooper's novels (or perhaps from *Two Little Savages* which includes a chapter on this theme, complete with a drawing).[34] Through St. Helen's Woods flowed a stream fed by a number of smaller streams draining down the surrounding hills into the valley. To his surprise, the farmer just below the woods watched the big slough he used to water his stock sink lower and lower. Archie and George had, in their game, dammed the stream to allow the beaver to make their houses there. The local gamekeeper later found out what they had done and let the water out, taking Archie's beaver dam with it.[35]

Mary, the oldest of the McCormick children and younger than Archie by a year, recalled their friend as "an absolute gentleman, but you never knew what he was going to do next." He used to put his grammar school chemistry to good advantage by making gunpowder. One Sunday he buried some in the garden of Preston Lodge, lit it, and the subsequent explosion shook all the windows in the road.[36]

Archie, never known for his deference to authority, was in George's words, "a great man for explosives." He made many little "Belaney bombs" in his bedroom and set them off in the street, taking special delight in surprising local police constable Joshua Stone. The large, bulky policeman would hear the small explosions set off late at night, or early in the morning, glimpse the culprits, but never catch them. Both the mischievous Archie and his younger accomplice George were great runners and easily outpaced the overweight police constable. Ada and George's parents knew nothing of these antics.[37]

Mr. and Mrs. McCormick got on very well with Archie. Theirs was a merry unconventional household. When sons Claude and Hugh wanted to have a shortcut to brother Leslie's and Malcolm's neighbouring room on the third floor, their father simply knocked a hole in the wall. George Sr., the manager of Hastings' branch of Lloyds Bank, collected butterflies and moths, and Archie helped him capture specimens. Dora McCormick, who had taught music at a girls' school in Hastings, was an excellent pianist and singer. Archie loved to play his star piece, Blake's Grand March, on the McCormicks' piano.[38] At the McCormicks' he found love and acceptance, neither of which he had found at school.

Percy or "Bob" Overton, a good friend of Jim McCormick, was three years younger than Archie, and with Jim he saw him occasionally. As far as Bob knew, the McCormicks were Archie's only friends. Behind Archie's back, Bob and the McCormick boys' other friends laughed at him for being so different, but they admired "Belaney" for his expertise about nature.[39]

One young woman entered Archie's life about this time, Ivy Holmes, the pretty daughter of the Misses Belaney's good friend, Florence Holmes. Ivy's father died when she was two, and she had been raised by her mother in London. Florence met Ada and Carrie one summer about 1900 in Hastings through a common interest in purebred collie dogs. Ada wanted to breed her dog with the Holmes's bitch, Juno. The Holmes began coming to Highbury Villa each summer during the school holidays.[40] A photo taken of Archie at about this time shows him in his Sunday uniform, an Eton suit, with Prince, the Belaney's dog, at his feet. The thin boy of almost thirteen looks exactly as Ada wanted him to be presented, handsome and well-bred.

Archie liked Ivy and tried to impress her. Thinking she would be interested, he showed her how he fed frogs to his snakes. In the attic he sometimes did an Indian war dance for her. A few years later Archie visited the Holmeses for short periods in London at their Hammersmith home in London's West End. Using their flat as his base, he travelled around the metropolis alone, seeing the Crystal Palace, and the London Zoo at Regent's Park where he loved to watch his favourite animal, the elephant, whose intelligence he admired.[41] It was a huge city, nearly fifty times the size of Hastings, yet London with its five million people did not intimidate him. But on no account did he want to live there or in any other part of crowded England. To Ivy he spoke of wanting to go to Canada for the hunting and fishing. Ada resisted the idea. No evidence exists, yet one cannot help but suspect Ada would have been delighted if he stayed in England and eventually married Ivy, a fine girl of whom she approved.

Eventually, however, Ada reluctantly realized that she could no longer control Archie. Her plan of keeping him at school had failed. After he left in July 1904, he took a job as a clerk at a local lumber yard, Cheale Brothers, located just north of St. Helen's Woods.[42] Archie simply was becoming too independent for Ada and Carrie to handle, and certainly their mother, now eighty, could do little to help.

After Archie left school and began working at Cheale Brothers, George McCormick came to know him best. Most weekends he and George practised at the wood yard shooting Archie's derringer and throwing his knives. It was so convenient, with plenty of room for "gunnery practice," as well as a whetstone for sharpening the knives used for the rigorous knife drill. Archie had learned to throw knives and he taught George. The two boys did everything together, including poaching trout at a private fishery outside Hastings.[43]

Still the solitary Archie kept much to himself, even from his best friend. He did not feel secure enough to tell George about how badly he wanted a father, and a mother. George knew nothing at all about Archie's absent parents, whom he never mentioned apart from his father being "a bit of a black sheep" and his mother an "actress." Seventy years later George remembered Archie as a "very clean-minded chap. He used to instill in me no smut, no dirty talk, no women, nothing like that, no drink. He was very strict in that."[44] Archie merely repeated Ada's teachings to George and shared no confidences with him.

Only Ada's strong hand kept the frustrated teenager at home. One day Archie could not stand his imprisonment at Highbury Villa any longer. He decided to make himself so troublesome that Ada would welcome his departure. On this particular day he hid behind two huge potted plants at the entrance of an alcove at Highbury Villa. A statue of an eminent composer sat on a tall pedestal. From his hiding place Archie planned to tip it over so that it fell on Ada as she sat reading the paper, which she did at that same spot, at the same time, every day. The plan misfired when Archie pushed the pedestal and the bust fell the wrong way, crashing down on his own head and knocking him cold.[45]

By 1906 Ada had almost concluded that he must leave. After all, the boy could have no real future in Hastings. The town that came into fashion in the Victorian age entered a downspin during the Edwardian. From 1871 to 1901 Hastings' population had doubled to more than 60,000, but in the first years of the twentieth century the expansion ended. In the early 1900s many of the wealthy residents had moved on to more fashionable seaside towns, leaving, by 1910, 2,000 empty houses in the town.[46] In any event, Archie had no desire to stay in Hastings, bust or boom, or anywhere in Britain.

Early in 1906 Archie speeded up the process of gaining Ada's approval to leave England. With George and the older McCormick boys looking on, Archie made a little bag of fireworks. Taking a long rope with him, Archie carefully let it down the chimney into his employers' office. When lit by the large fire in the grate below, the bag exploded, nearly destroying the building. Cheale Brothers quickly discovered the culprit and fired him.[47]

Now in total exasperation, Ada relented. She accompanied him to Hammersmith, where they stayed for two or three days with the Holmeses, then they went to Liverpool where Archie, on the afternoon of March 29, 1906, boarded the SS *Canada* for Halifax. He travelled second class with the moderately prosperous group of merchants, tradesmen, and farmers, rather than third class with the majority of other passengers. After her nephew stepped on board the Atlantic steamer, Ada wrote home to her mother and Carrie. "Saw Archie off. Boat left 4 P.M."[48]

One could argue that Aunt Ada had failed in her education of Archie. She certainly had discouraged his constant rebellion against authority. His fascination with Red Indians puzzled her, and she could do nothing to divert his attention to other subjects. She wanted him to stay in England, yet he left for Canada. Still, although she had never reached his inner self, his devoted aunt had influenced his development. Only two weeks after Archie, Ada, and Carrie dined together on December 2, 1935, a London reporter interviewed him in London. He found the Indian "straight from the pages of Fenimore Cooper's 'Deerslayer',' sitting intently "studying the deep shadows thrown on the walls by the firelight, listening eagerly to a radio orchestra playing Tchaikowsky."[49] He owed to Aunt Ada his lifelong love of music. She must have smiled to hear his musical selections in his lecture, including Beethoven's "Moonlight Sonata," a piece probably practised countless times on the Belaney family piano.

Archie owed to her as well his love of language. His formidable aunt might not have understood little boys, but she knew the important of literature. She conditioned Archie to read and ingrained in him an intense respect for books. Of all the Hastings Grammar School boys writing the University of Cambridge Junior exams in 1903, he had headed the class in the combined English grammar and literature exam, even beating Con Foster, his form's scholarship student. Aunt Ada implanted in him a driving urge to one day express himself creatively through the written word.

A love of music and writing, these in themselves are considerable gifts. But to Ada, Archie owed another debt. She and Carrie had always encouraged him to report to them about what he had learned and did at school.[50] He at least left Hastings with the confidence to tell imaginative, dramatic stories, similar to those the lonely boy had told his aunts at teatime and at dinner time. Ada and Carrie had helped to develop his talents as a storyteller.

Finally, Aunt Ada succeeded in what she, Carrie, and their mother considered the most important aspect of his upbringing: Archie must act as a gentleman in public. Just a month before Grey Owl met his aunts in Hastings in 1935, Georges Vanier, a future Governor-General of Canada (1959–1967) and at the time an official at the Canadian High Commission in London, wrote to the Director of Publicity of the National Parks Branch in Ottawa: "I thought you would like to know that Grey Owl has been a great success over here in every way. All those, and they are legion—who have come in contact with him, have been much impressed by his knowledge, by his simplicity and by his manners which are instinctively those of a gentleman in spite of his long and almost continuous life in the woods."[51]

Yet all of these gifts had not touched or developed Archie's inner self. He had learned to like good music and good literature. He had excellent manners and could express himself well. Yet he held back within himself all his inner pain, his hurt, at being rejected by his parents. He needed someone with whom he could talk about his confusion and his fears. Only then could the tortured young man begin to heal his suffering and himself.

Left: *Archie Belaney at age three. From one of the English newspapers, late April 1938. The photo was obtained from the Misses Belaney.* Archives of Ontario/S14264.

Right: *Kittie Scott-Brown, Archie Belaney's mother. Photo taken in Reading, England, around 1900 when she was about thirty.* Archives of Ontario/S14237. Source: Peter Davies Co. Ltd.

Ada (on the left) and Carrie Belaney (on the right), and a young friend, about 1930. Archives of Ontario/Acc. 23090–4. Source: Ivy Holmes.

In 1938 the Misses Belaney showed Lovat Dickson, Grey Owl's publisher and biographer, this photo of Archie taken in 1901 or 1902. National Archives of Canada/PA–147585.

COMPARE THE TWO . . .

Against the horizon beyond the edge of the low range of hills that bounded a distance of full 30 miles, a heavy column of smoke rose & seemed to meet the sky where it turned & rolled off in immense cloud to the south, the smoke of a forest fire. Over all shone the sun bringing into contrast the lights & shades of hill & valley. To me this was a wonderful sight; my first glimpse of the wilderness. Even the men near me used to such sights stopped their conversation, or card playing,

Other costumes much as navvies wear in England with loose trousers, gaiters below knees also ruddy breeches or knickers.

Blanket suit. loose, with hood blankets or ... are particularly hot Belted with sash

The top part of this picture shows handwriting taken from the torn exercise book, while below it are samples of Grey Owl's handwriting from his book "The Men of the Last Frontier." Mr. Ian Maloan, handwriting expert, says it is quite likely the two specimens were written by the same person, and points to similarities in the letters "g," "y," "f," and "t."

Sunday Dispatch *(London, England), April 18, 1938.*

John Egwuna and his family, Lake Temagami, around 1905. The young woman standing by the tents on the left is Maggie Petrant. The woman sitting is splitting spruce roots for use in sewing baskets or the seams of a birchbark canoe. Archives of Ontario/S14654. Source: Mrs. Arnold Leishman.

The Fire Rangers' Hall, Bear Island, Temagami. Archie Belaney married Angele Egwuna here in August, 1910. Archives of Ontario/S15166. Source: Jim Turner.

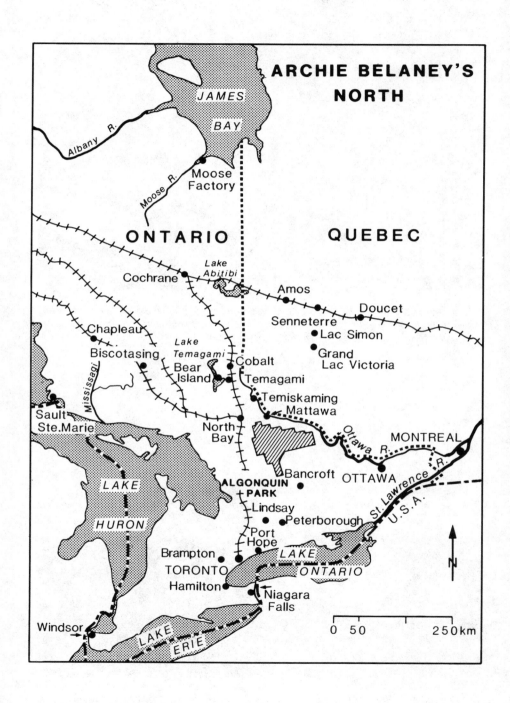

ARCHIE BELANEY'S
NORTH

JAMES
BAY

Albany R.

Moose R.

Moose
Factory

ONTARIO   QUEBEC

*Lake
Abitibi*

Cochrane

Amos

Doucet

Senneterre

Lac Simon

Chapleau

*Lake
Temagami*

Grand
Lac Victoria

Biscotasing

Cobalt

Mississagi

Bear
Island

Temagami

Temiskaming

Mattawa

Sault
Ste.Marie

North
Bay

Ottawa R.

MONTREAL

LAKE

ALGONQUIN
PARK

Bancroft

OTTAWA

St. Lawrence R.

HURON

Lindsay

Peterborough

U.S.A.

Port
Hope

N

Brampton

LAKE

TORONTO

ONTARIO

Hamilton

Niagara
Falls

0   50   250km

Windsor

*LAKE
ERIE*

Group of Ojibwa Indians on treaty payment day in 1913 at Bear Island, Lake Temagami: Chief Frank White Bear, in the centre, and second chief Aleck Paul, standing to the right next to Chief White Bear. John Egwuna appears standing second from the right, and Temagami Ned is standing at the extreme right. Angele, Archie Belaney's first wife, is standing second from left. Agnes Belaney, Archie and Angele's daughter, is the child immediately in front of her. The anthropologist Frank Speck took the photo. National Museums of Canada, Canadian Museum of Civilization/23991.

This is the earliest surviving photo of Archie Belaney in Canada. Left to right: Jimmy Sanders, Donat Legace, Archie Belaney, Raphel Legace, Marie Woodworth, Biscotasing 1913. Note Archie's moccasins. Jim Sanders was later killed while serving in the Canadian Army in the First World War. Archives of Ontario/S14531. Source: Jack Woodworth.

Chief Espagnol [Espaniel], Alex's father. He came up to Bisco from the Spanish River. Photo was taken in 1906 in Bisco during the signing of Treaty No. 9, the James Bay Treaty. The Canadian poet, and deputy superintendent of Indian Affairs, Duncan Campbell Scott, represented the Canadian government. Archives of Ontario/S7630.

Archie Belaney, probably at his aunts' home, 11 Upper Glen Road, Hollington. Compare with the second shot which shows Hugh Belaney in Archie's uniform. Both shots were probably taken on the same day in August 1915. Archives of Ontario/S14254.

Hugh Belaney in his brother's Canadian army uniform at his aunts', 11 Upper Glen Road, Hollington, near Hastings, 1915. Archie later lost his corporal's stripe for going absent without leave. Archives of Ontario /S14260. Source: Ivy Holmes.

Ivy Holmes, a photo taken in Prague, then in the Austro-Hungarian Empire, by Atelier R. Grünberger, around 1910. Ivy Holmes and Archie Belaney were married in England in 1917. Archives of Ontario/Acc. 23089–2. Source: Ivy Holmes.

Stella Brace on the left, Aunt Carrie on the right, Upper Glen Road, Hollington, near Hastings. The Misses Belaney lived here shortly before and after the First World War. Archives of Ontario/S14258. Source: Ivy Holmes.

4 Lake Temagami and Angele

An autobiographical manuscript conveys Archie's excitement as his train from Toronto left the farm country of southern Ontario. Whether the incident actually occurred or not, the excerpt highlights the impact on him of the northern forest:

> Against the horizon & beyond the edge of the low range of hills that bounded a distance of full 30 miles, a heavy column of smoke rose & seemed to meet the sky where it turned & rolled off in immense billows to the south, the smoke of a forest fire. Over all shone the sun bringing into contrast the lights & shades of hill and valley. To me this was a wonderful sight; my first glimpse of the wilderness. Even the men near me used to such sights stopped their conversation, and card playing.[1]

Thousands rushed north from Toronto in 1906 to the new silver field at Cobalt on the west (Ontario) shore of Lake Temiskaming, but not Archie. He had no interest in Ontario's equivalent of the Klondike gold field and headed instead for the wilderness on the Quebec side of the lake. He travelled on the old Canadian Pacific line which ran from the town of Mattawa on the Ottawa River to Lake Temiskaming. Thirty years later Bill Guppy recalled his first meeting at the Temiskaming station with the "decent young fellow, with such a friendly air, and so earnest about becoming a guide." The veteran woodsman took him on, and would never forget this young Englishman who had " 'individuality', a little something that made him stick out in any crowd."[2]

Archie had arrived a few months earlier in Toronto, a city which had just entered the greatest economic expansion it had ever known, as had Canada (population 5,000,000) itself.[3] Already the city of almost half-a-million people boasted what was then the British Empire's highest building, the ten-storey Traders Bank of Canada on Wellington Street.[4] The story of the city's progress, however, had little interest for Archie, who had come to Canada to live in the wilderness, near Indians. In and around Toronto the forests and the Indians had disappeared. The Mississauga Indians had abandoned their neighbouring reserve twenty kilometres to the west at Port Credit sixty years earlier. Pushed out by the pressure of settlement, they lived on a corner of the Six Nations or Iroquois Reserve, 100 kilometres to the west.[5] Archie would go northward, but first he must make some money.

The autobiographical manuscript that came to light after his death in 1938 suggests that Archie worked in Toronto in a store, perhaps Eaton's,[6] before going north. Written during the First World War, in England in 1916 or 1917, the tattered exercise book contained a vivid account of a young immigrant's experiences "working in a large departmental store of the biggest city in Ontario" selling men's ties and other "gents furnishings" across the counter. While the manuscript is now lost, one full summary of it, and some excerpts, exist. The story (with its dialogue clearly written in imitation of O. Henry, the great American short story writer) tells how the "discontented youth" dreamt "of the day when he would be able to follow a trail, camp and cook in the woods, and steer a canoe through the rapids, as skilfully as the best of the Indians." The young shop-assistant spent his time reading adventure stories about Indians. On walks through the city's ravines and the countryside on its borders he tried to imagine the wilderness. He even joined a local canoe club to learn (as he thought) how the Indians paddled.[7] Once he saved enough money, he left for the North.

That winter Archie stayed with Bill Guppy and his wife and family on Lake Temiskaming. He was so articulate and well-spoken they called him "professor." To the Guppys' delight, he was musical. After supper he played their old piano, "a wizard on the keys, rattling out tune after tune, picking up the songs we sang."[8]

The experienced woodsman also discovered that the young man already knew a surprising amount about animals, not from books but from experience. "A bird, a snake, the movements of even a little frog, would hold his attention for minutes on end. He had no fear of wild animals or of snakes, and at every opportunity would approach them as close as possible, 'freeze' near them, watch their habits, listen, and later imitate their calls pretty well." His keen eyes and ears missed nothing. But from the number of questions he asked, Bill knew that he had never trapped animals.[9]

Bill gave Archie his first lessons in trapping. He showed him his steel traps and demonstrated how to place and to set them. For the winter Bill lent him several traps and a pair of snowshoes. Archie quickly learned to snowshoe and with his long legs soon travelled speedily on them.[10]

The winter passed with Archie's days spent trapping and his evenings at the piano. After wood-chopping sessions, Bill's brothers, George and Alex, taught the young Englishman to throw a hand-axe at tree stumps outside of Bill's house. Archie was good company. The three men often stood for an hour at a time practising, and then they would switch and practise with a knife, a sport Archie already knew well.

Often after a day's trapping, Bill noticed Archie would daydream, sitting on his bunk, immersed in his own universe miles away.[11] He had always been like this, retreating when anyone came close to him. Although you would not guess as much from his exterior, he feared intimacy.

After a hearty meal and cups of steaming hot tea, Bill spoke of the Lake Temagami district, set aside in 1901 as a vast provincial government forest reserve, more than 15,000 square kilometres in size. The new railway to Cobalt and the construction of hotels had opened up Temagami to southern tourists. In 1905, Don O'Connor, a Sudbury entrepreneur, had built the Temagami Inn on Temagami Island, in the centre of the lake, about thirty kilometres or so west of Temagami Station.[12]

Once the ice left Lake Temiskaming in May, Bill, his two brothers, and Archie left for Lake Temagami. They paddled about fifty kilometres up the west side of the lake to the mouth of the Matabitchuan River, which led to the first portage on the way to Lake Temagami. The Clay Hill, or to use its other more descriptive name, the Devil's Portage, rose straight up from the river for almost 500 metres. With a heavy pack on his shoulders the young Englishman struggled manfully over a path made slippery by melting ice and snow. Years later he wrote of one difficult portage, and his remarks apply to this one: "Here the curse of Adam is fulfilled to the letter; sweat commences to pour into the eyes, down the body, dripping off the forearms." [13]

Archie's first long canoe trip through the chain of lakes linking Lakes Temiskaming and Temagami initiated him into his future career as a northern canoeman and packer. On the journey Archie passed through territory rich in animals: bear, moose, wolves, otter, and beaver.[14] He portaged and shot rapids. He had passed through one of Ontario's last extensive pine forests.

Lake Temagami, one of the largest lakes in northern Ontario, contains more than 1,200 islands and has a shoreline of 1,000 kilometres. Lake trout abounded in 1907, as did speckled trout in the streams flowing into the lake. It was surrounded by primeval stands of red and white pine forest, never touched by lumbermen. Near the geographical centre of the lake stood the Hudson Bay Company trading post on Bear Island, where the Teme-augama Anishnabai—the deep water people—a band of nearly one hundred Ojibwa Indians gathered in the summer.[15]

Until nearly a decade or so earlier, the Bear Island Ojibwa had been left largely on their own. True, a Roman Catholic missionary visited annually in the summer, as did the Indian agent, but now a deluge of newcomers came into their territory, and the Ontario government imposed all kinds of rules and regulations on the area's original inhabitants. It also leased the islands in the lake to tourists to build cottages. As Aleck Paul, the band's second chief, complained to Frank Speck, a visiting anthropologist, "If an Indian went to the old country and sold hunting licenses to the old country people for them to hunt on their own land, the white people would not stand for that. The Government sells our big game, our moose, for $50 license and we don't get any of it. The Government sells our fish and our islands and gets the money but we don't get any share."[16]

Archie would soon learn more about the Indians' anger. Only a few months before he arrived on the lake, Aleck Paul and Frank White Bear, the band's head chief, had sent a petition to Ottawa, signed by fifty band members, calling for a reserve. "We have been asking for a reserve on Lake Temagami for years . . . we do not know of any band but ourselves who have not their own reserves. We have no land that we can settle on." Among names attached to the petition were those of Michel Matthewias or Mathias, and Ned White Bear or Temagami Ned, two of Archie's first Indian friends on the lake.[17] He might well have first met Michel and Ned at the Temagami Inn that summer, as many Indians guided in the summer.

The Guppys had gone directly to the Temagami Inn. As the demand for guides exceeded the supply, they had quickly obtained jobs guiding groups of American and Canadian sportsmen and fishermen coming up from the south. But Archie had no trail experience to speak of and had to take a job as a chore-boy at the inn.[18] At the end of the summer the tourists left, the Guppys returned to Temiskaming, the Indians went back to their individual family hunting grounds, and Archie had to look for work.

Frequently Archie crossed over by canoe to neighbouring Bear Island, just two kilometres from the Temagami Inn. He loved to pass by the "smoky, balsam scented tents" of the Indians near the trading post.[19] At Charlotte McLean's, whose late father had worked for the Hudson's Bay Company, the polite young man visited and read the old Scot's British magazines.[20] He also called on Harry Woods, the Hudson's Bay Company post manager. The young Englishman, the manager later recalled, "was well educated, and always carried a little black notebook, in which he jotted down Indian words."[21] Often Archie asked for assistance, as the trader spoke Ojibwa. With the fall's arrival Archie asked for a grubstake to go trapping, adding that "he could send to the Old Country for money, but that he didn't want to."[22] Aware that Archie had almost no trapping experience, the trader turned him down.

Probably in late 1907, Archie returned to England for a brief visit with his grandmother and his aunts. An entry in one of his notebooks hints at why he returned. "Early troubles at Cobalt & Temagami & being robbed at night . . . Sickness & broke befriended by Indians."[23] Most likely he returned to obtain some money from his aunts.

Archie brought his friend George McCormick a pair of moccasins, full of the smell of smoked buckskin. George's younger sister, Margaret, recalled: "He looked more Indian than ever, leaner, if possible, and clad in a comfortable old loose suit and wide sombrero. He insisted on wearing moccasins at all times, and would swing silently along the streets with the loping gait of an Indian." On this same visit Henry Hopkin, his old grammar school friend, encountered him by chance walking on the Hastings promenade by the sea. He dated the memory to 1907 or 1908, just a year or so after he had begun to work as a journalist for the newspaper in neighbouring Bexhill. "He then disappeared out of my life all together."[24]

Archie's English visit changed his life. He came back to Canada determined to break completely with his unhappy past. A number of factors could have contributed to this decision. Perhaps Kittie, his mother, told him that she had recently heard that his father had been killed in a drunken brawl in the United States. If this was true, it would have occurred shortly after George Belaney appeared at his cousins' in Manitoba, as he visited them sometime between 1905–1910.[25] Archie never had a real father, so an imaginary one could now be substituted. Furthermore, Kittie had remarried and lived with her new husband, James Scott-Brown, their one-year-old son, Leonard, and Archie's brother Hugh (now eighteen).[26] Distant at the best of times from his mother, who had allowed his aunts to raise him, he now saw her totally preoccupied with her new baby and husband. He would create a new mother for himself as well.

By the summer of 1908 Archie had returned to the Temagami Inn, again working as a chore-boy.[27] He set out to lose the remaining traces of his English accent. He refined his story of his Indian boyhood in Mexico and the American Southwest. Instead of recognizing reality, the facts of his unhappy English childhood, Archie substituted his creative myth of a boyhood spent in the American Southwest. Tom Saville, a fellow Englishman who had married an Ojibwa girl and lived in the Temagami area, met him in 1909 and knew him there for two years or so. Years later Tom recalled: "I do not know his people, sometimes he mentioned New Mexico and the Apache people and that his people travelled with Buffalo Bill's show."[28]

Archie met Angele in the summer of 1908 at the Temagami Inn where she worked as a kitchen-helper. To gain her attention, the inn's chore-boy threw potato peels at her, which annoyed her.[29] But with sign language, a little Ojibwa, and with her few words of English, the young woman and the young Englishman began to communicate. A friendship developed, and Angele came to like him very much. She introduced him to her uncle John Egwuna and to her aunt Helen (Chief Frank White Bear's sister), who had raised her after the death of her parents. As Angele's boyfriend, Archie also met other relatives: her great-uncle Ned White Bear, a man in his early '60s, and her uncle, Michel Mathias, "Big Feather" or "Quill", a young man in his late 20s.[30]

In the autobiographical story found after his death in 1938, Archie included this reference to these two men: "Two wiry Indians, 'Both-ends-of-the-day,' aged 60, and Michael [Michel], a lithe youth in his twenties.

They were to become the 'tenderfoot's' greatest friends. He learnt to trust and rely on 'Both-ends-of-the-day' as he had trusted no white man." [31]

No wonder that "Both-ends-of-the-day," or Ned, became one of Archie's closest Indian friends—he enjoyed meeting tourists. The five-foot-tall Ned, with his mop of thick, heavy white hair, liked to seek out white visitors and practise his English. Some gave him big cigars and then took the popular Indian's picture. [32] In his first book, *The Men of the Last Frontier*, published in 1931, Grey Owl included this affectionate sketch of Ned:

> One old man of the Ojibway with the prolonged name of Neejin-nekai-apeechi-geejiguk, or to make a long story short, "Both-ends-of-the-day" . . . was a man to whom none could listen without attention, and was a living link with a past of which only too little is known. Although he died in distressing circumstances a good many years ago, I remember him well, as I last saw him; straight as an arrow and active as a young man in spite of his years, he had an unusually developed faculty for seeing in the dark, which accounts for his name, which inferred that day and night were all one to him. I recollect that he carried an alarm clock inside his shirt for a watch, and when once, at a dance, he fell asleep, some mischievous youngster set the alarm, and he created the diversion of the evening when the sudden racket within his shirt woke him up. In reality the first touch of the little urchin had awakened him, but he purposely feigned continued sleep till the alarm should go off, for he had a keen sense of humour, which Indians possess more often than they get credit for. [33]

In his third book, *Sajo and her Beaver People*, he included Michel Mathias, or Quill, as one of the children's story's characters. This note (without mentioning Temagami) appears:

> Gitchie Meegwon, or, in English, Big Feather, known as "Quill" to the white people who later entered the region, was a personal and well-loved friend of my younger days, and has long since joined the Great Majority. My first trap trail was laid under his highly efficient and somewhat stern direction. A bark canoe, made by this man, is still on exhibition at the Normal School museum on Church Street in Toronto, or was at the time of my last visit there in 1911." [34]

Archie also met, or at least heard about, another fascinating man, Dan Misabi, or "Giant," then believed to be about 100 years old. Years before he had canoed up from Georgian Bay to Lake Temagami. In his autobiographical manuscript, Archie mentioned Misabi, a man "so old that he had hunted beaver on the Don River when Toronto was a muddy village where he sold his fur." [35] From the Tema-Augama Anishnabai elders like old Misabi, Archie learned of their belief that everything around them, the animals, fish, birds, trees, and the rest of the natural world, had souls or spirits, just as human beings did. The Indian should treat everything he saw or touched with the same respect as he would a human. [36] In Misabi's youth, for instance, the old Ojibwa Indians told the young that they should avoid cutting down living trees, to save the trees from pain. When green trees were cut, the elders explained, you could hear them wailing from the ax's blows.[37] Only through their language could Archie gain a greater knowledge of the Ojibwas' closeness to nature, and he worked to become a fluent speaker.

Thanks to Angele's goodwill and patience, Archie advanced with his Ojibwa. Longfellow (using the writing of Henry Schoolcraft, a former American Indian Agent at Sault Ste. Marie, Michigan) had included about 150 Ojibwa words in a vocabulary at the end of *Hiawatha.*[38] Quickly Archie went beyond that list of words. With Angele, he practised as much as he could. He learned proper Ojibwa usage, to put the verb first before the noun.[39] Archie was a great mimic, a man who could tell an Irish story with an Irish brogue, who could duplicate the Scottish accent, and who could speak like a Cockney from London.[40] His talent for mimicry helped him to learn the language. Angele also taught him basic woodlore and how to survive in the bush.

Archie took notes on how Angele set traps and fish nets, and he made drawings. These sketches helped sharpen his powers of observation. Her uncle John liked the young *saganash* (Englishman) who took in so much, who interested himself in their way of life and in their stories. John gave him the name *ko-hom-see,* "little owl." He called him "the young owl who sits taking everything in."[41] This was indeed Archie, whose mind stored away hundreds of impressions and strange sights and packed them into his subconscious, ready for the time he could use them in his writing. The name that John Egwuna called him would surface fifteen years later in Archie's new title, "Grey Owl."

Angele's uncle used to watch for Archie crossing over to visit her at Bear Island. He was so fair that—unlike an Indian—you could see him from a long way off. John Egwuna used to say: "There's that *gitchi-saganash* (tall Englishman) coming again." You could see him for miles, "just like when you make a blaze on a tree."[42]

Eagerly Archie listened to Angele's and the Egwunas' stories and tried to remember what they told him.

He told the Egwunas tales, too. Sometimes friends came over to John's wigwam to listen cross-legged on the ground to the tales in broken Ojibwa about how the white people lived. Apart perhaps from Aleck Paul, the band's second chief who spoke English well and who had worked for several years for the Hudson's Bay Company,[43] the Temagami Ojibwa really knew very little about white people.

Frenzied activity allowed Archie momentarily to forget his past. In March 1909, for instance, he wagered that he could cross the large Algonquin Provincial Park, about 150 kilometres south of Temagami, in the dead of winter without being detected by a ranger. The rangers patrolled the park regularly to prevent poachers from trapping in the protected area. As he was still relatively new to winter travel, the rangers easily caught him—just in time to save his frostbitten legs.[44]

At some point during his first years in Temagami, he also discovered alcohol. Years later he said that "he wished all liquor tasted like ginger ale so he could enjoy the taste as well as the effect."[45] He drank for the effect. Once he went on a week-long drunk with an Indian, Baptiste Commanda. While employed to look after a prospector's camp, they found and quickly consumed "everything drinkable." On his return, the prospector fired his two drunken watchmen.[46]

Fortunately for Archie, the Egwunas invited him to spend the winter of 1909–1910 trapping with them.[47] Two decades later in elaborating on his early training by the Ojibwa Indians, he dated his adoption to 1909–1910. In a letter dated May 6, 1929, he wrote: "About twenty years ago I was formally adopted by the Ojibway Indians, and have roamed with them, starved and suffered with them on hard trails, and danced and sung with them in times of plenty."[48]

John Egwuna and his family trapped around Austin Bay, on the south arm of the lake, where the Temagami Ojibwa anticipated the federal government would eventually establish their reserve. On Bear Island the Egwunas built a wigwam, but at Austin Bay they had a log house and had cleared a little land. Very gifted with birds and animals, John had once kept at Austin Bay a pet loon and a pet deer. Near the house was a beaver pond, where the beaver came right up to Angele's uncle and other humans. Archie must have been impressed by the ease with which someone could tame a beaver.[49] Twenty years later he would do it himself.

From their base at Austin Bay the Egwunas and their guest trapped in the Egwunas' family hunting territory to the east of the lake, between Austin Bay, Shiningwood Bay, and Cross Lake. That winter Archie learned how the Temagami Ojibwa harvested their hunting territories, taking only those animals required for clothing and for food, leaving the rest to breed. They took only the increase. The Indians *farmed* the beaver most carefully, keeping count of the number of occupants, old and young, of each lodge.[50]

Finally, five years after leaving the Hastings Grammar School, Archie had a full winter's training in what he really wanted to learn. Like the two Indian children in *Sajo and her Beaver People,* his studies were: "Plant and tree life, the ways and habits of animals and how to track them; how to catch fish at all times of the year and, most important of all, how to make fire in any kind of weather, such as rain, wind or snow. They learn the calls of all the birds and beasts, and can imitate some of them very well."[51]

In the summers of 1910 and 1911 Archie worked as a guide at Camp Keewaydin,[52] an American boys' camp on the lake, northwest of Bear Island. It bore the same name as did the northwest wind in Longfellow's *Hiawatha.*

Here he became intimately acquainted with Ernest Thompson Seton's Indian lore. The camp director endorsed it, and based part of the program on *Two Little Savages* and other of Seton's books. During the summer, for example, the Manitou campers, mostly American prep school boys,[53] learned "Indian" canoemanship, fishing skills, and nature lore. The boys, aged eleven and twelve, appeared at a special Council Fire, each in "Indian garb of buckskin, made and decorated by his own hand with his own special Totem and sign."[54] All summer Archie lived in two worlds simultaneously, the make-believe Keewaydin Indian fantasy and the real Indian existence of Angele and her family.

One summer day in 1910 he asked for a short leave, and left for Temagami. Burnt brown by his exposure to the sun, with a handkerchief tied round his neck and a big felt hat tilted sideways on his head to cut some of the glare from the water, Archie paddled eastward[55] the fifty kilometres to the Temagami townsite. He went to see Arthur Stevens, the local storekeeper and Justice of the Peace. When Archie applied for a marriage license to marry Angele, he was given it.

On August 23, 1910, a visiting American minister married Archie and Angele at the Fire Ranger's Hall on Bear Island. Archie wore a handsome brown suit and brown hat, with elaborately-beaded moccasins on his feet.[56] A dance at the Lakeview House, a tourist lodge next to the hall, followed the wedding, with a large number of well-wishers, including Annie White Bear, the head chief's wife, and Tom Saville, his best man. Moses Beaucage, an Ojibwa from Lake Nipissing, played the violin that evening.[57]

The fact that Archie Belaney wanted to marry Angele in a Christian ceremony says much about his inability to escape completely from his upbringing. His inner-conservatism was previously shown by his refusal to leave home without Ada's permission. He had stayed until she agreed he could leave. Similarly, he wanted to marry Angele, who was a Christian, in a *proper* ceremony.

Angele loved her Englishman, who took such interest in Indian life and who learned some of her language. They had fun together. Long afterwards she recalled, with a smile on her face, how he would say to her, "I'll make a white woman of you, my l'Angel." And she would reply: "Oh no, Archie, I make the Indian of you!"[58] If only he could have opened up to her, Archie might have saved himself from his loneliness and alienation. He needed closeness and intimacy, something which this warm, accepting woman from another culture could have given. Even after Angele realized that Archie invented a great deal of what he told her, she still accepted him. "Maybe he not always tell the truth. But I not mind. He a good man, my man."[59] Tragically Archie missed his first opportunity in Canada of breaking down the barriers of his self-constructed prison, of telling one other human being about his shame at being abandoned by his parents, of the real pain of his childhood.

Archie certainly should not have become a father, which he did in the spring of 1911. Having no role model for a father, he had no idea even of what the part demanded. He did not know how a real family should act. The birth of their daughter, Agnes, terrified him, and within a few months he planned his escape.

On July 23, 1911, Angele took her three-month-old daughter to be baptised by Father Evain, the visiting French Roman Catholic priest. No doubt the priest had brought to her attention the inadequacies, from his viewpoint and his church's, of a marriage conducted by a Protestant minister. In his baptismal registry the missionary wrote Agnes was born "du mariage civil de Arthur Belegné et du Angele Egona." This is the first documentary reference to Archie in Canada. The French-speaking priest caught the name of the absent husband as "Arthur Belegné."[60] Archie, who had spent the summer away from his family working as a guide at Camp Keewaydin, took a more permanent leave from Angele and Agnes that fall.[61] Away from his family he let his hair grow down to his shoulders. If asked about it, he replied that he let it grow out of pride in his "connection with a race of great fighters," the Apaches.[62]

Thanks to a surviving manuscript, probably sent by his aunts to the *Hastonian*, the Hastings Grammar School magazine, more can be said of Archie's state of mind at the time. Without mentioning his wife and infant daughter left behind at Lake Temagami in the fall of 1911, the text revealingly begins: "I had intended to come home this fall, but three other fellows persuaded me that the happy hunting grounds had descended and located in the country North of the Abitabi [Abitibi] Lake, and it seemed like throwing away good money not to go, so here we are."[63]

As well as his fear of responsibility, Archie's dislike of his fellow whites' censure of his marriage led him to question it. The insecure Englishman knew that some of the tourists and rangers in Temagami for the summer scorned him for what he had done, and it affected him. The day after the wedding he met one of the rangers, who had come in to pick up his mail at the Forestry building on Bear Island, where the wedding had been held. Archie spoke to him, but the man did not even offer to shake hands with the new bridegroom. He "crowded on," kept his hand on his tumpline and passed by without stopping. The ranger regarded Archie as despicable for marrying a "squaw."[64]

At the turn of the century, many North Americans and Europeans believed that the world's races represented different stages of evolution, with the white race at the top and the dark-skinned races at the other end.[65] Archie had encountered race theory at grammar school, where Anglo-Saxondom was at the summit of the "white race." Intellectually he fought it, at least in respect to the North American Indians. But psychologically he remained in part a prisoner of his English upbringing and schooling.

Race theory permeated Canada as much as it did Britain. In 1910, for instance, William Briggs, one of Toronto's largest publishers, brought out the fourth edition of Robert J. C. Stead's *The Empire Builders and Other Poems*. The popular collection of poems included "The Mixer," a description of how the country itself turned immigrants into Canadians, "all but the yellow and brown."

> In the city, on the prairie, in the forest, in the camp,
> In the mountain-clouds of color, in the fog-white river-damp,
> From Atlantic to Pacific, from the Great Lakes to the Pole,
> I am mixing strange ingredients into a common whole;
> Every hope shall build upon me, every heart shall be my own,
> The ambitions of my people shall be mine, and mine alone;
> Not a sacrifice so great but they will gladly lay it down
> When I turn them out Canadians—all but the yellow and brown.[66]

In the excerpts from the letter published in the *Hastonian*,[67] Archie's tone is that of the superior white man. He and the other three guides from Temagami—as if it was their divine right—put out their traps without making any attempt to find out if they were infringing on Indian hunting territory. When confronted by the local chief and fifteen other men, Archie acted as the interpreter because he could "murder the beautiful flowing gutturals and meat-axe noises made by the red brother." Archie and his three white friends left, not because they had committed an injustice, but because they realized that the hostile Indians would "steal our fur and traps right along and we'd have the worst kind of trouble." From his winter with the Egwunas, Archie understood how the Ojibwa family hunting territory system worked. He knew how they considered their grounds as their private property, yet he openly violated their rules.

The excerpts from his letter reveal that Archie at this stage had second thoughts about his identification with Indians and also about his choice of trapping and guiding as a career. As he himself admitted, "I won't do any work when I can possibly get out of it."

> This thing of hunting and living in the bush generally is not what it is in books. It looks very picturesque and romantic to wear mocassins, run rapids, and shoot deer and moose, but it is not near as interesting as it seems, to be eaten up day and night by black ants, flies and mosquitos, to get soaked up with rain, or burnt up with heat, to draw your own toboggan on snowshoes and to sleep out in 60 or 70 degrees below zero.

Unfortunately—apart from this one letter—no other documentation exists on Archie in the winter of 1911–12. Clearly he did not know what to do: return to England, go back to Angele and Agnes, move to another northern Ontario community, or return to Toronto.

A very confused young man he was in the winter of 1911–12. He claimed in the letter published in the *Hastonian* that he wintered in 1911–12 with his white friends by Lake Abitibi. More likely he spent it in Toronto. Angele recalled years later that when he briefly returned to Temagami in early 1912, he told her, and she believed him, that he had walked all the way from Toronto to Temagami on the railway track.[68] He subsequently wrote in his children's book, *Sajo* (published in 1934), that he had seen Quill's birch bark canoe in 1911 at the Normal School Museum on Church Street in Toronto.[69] Without a doubt he knew Toronto well, for he has apparently modelled the large town that he mentions in *Sajo*, "a quarter of a century" ago, on Toronto. His drawing of a zoo enclosure looks distinctly like the old polar bear enclosure at the Riverdale Zoo.[70] The Toronto policemen still wore British "bobby" uniforms, as does the constable shown in one of Grey Owl's drawings. The English-speaking city in Canada was "hundreds of miles away" and directly linked by rail with Temagami. The city in *Sajo* must be based on his memories of Toronto about 1911.[71]

There is both oral and written documentation on Archie's first years in Biscotasing, Ontario, a hundred kilometres to the west, where he first appeared in the summer of 1912. He apparently accepted money each month from his aunts. Probably they had received the extra funds from the estate of their mother, who died in May 1912 and whose will was probated early that summer.[72] Ferg Legace, the son of Archie's landlady in Biscotasing, still remembered in the early 1970s how his mother would cash the monthly cheques for Archie.[73]

Now that he had some extra money, in addition to his ranger's pay and the small income he obtained from the little trapping he did, Archie forwarded some money to Angele. Sometimes it was $10, sometimes $15, and once $50. While he sent money, he never enclosed a letter with the cheques.[74] He did not know what to do: stay away or return to his Indian family. Fortunately Angele was an excellent trapper. Alone she supported herself and her daughter.

5 Biscotasing

One day in the spring of 1912 the HBC post manager's wife sent her nine-year-old daughter downstairs to bring up something for lunch from the store. Madeline Woodworth had just been reading a newspaper story about the recent *Titanic* disaster. At the foot of the stairs she had another shock. She saw a tall man in a black hat with hair down to his shoulders. "I got scared and went back upstairs. I never saw anyone with long hair like that before."[1] Archie Belaney had arrived in Biscotasing.

Located at the headwaters of the Mississagi, Spanish, Mattagami, and Groundhog rivers, Indians had long frequented Biscotasi Lake. As early as 1815 the HBC trader at Fort Mattagami to the north referred to the "Bishkitising Band."[2] Once the construction of the Canadian Pacific Railway began in the early 1880s, surveyors and clearing crews used the townsite as a base. In 1886, a special correspondent for the London *Times*, on a cross-Canada tour, described Biscotasing as "quite a busy place, upon a beautiful lake, with arms that stretch in every direction, like a double cross, giving fine vista views over the forest-bordered waters."[3] The HBC established a post there, from which canoe brigades supplied the surrounding isolated outposts.[4]

Logging developed—the pine forests coveted by the southern Ontario loggers. When the sawmill operated in the summer, the town had a steady population of about 200, dropping to 50 in the winter. The mill employed mainly French Canadians from the Ottawa Valley.[5] During the summer the village became truly multicultural, when several hundred Indians came off their trapping lines to camp near the HBC post.[6]

The Rev. John Sanders, an Indian and an Anglican clergyman, served the white Protestants in the village as well as the Anglican Indians from the north. The Ojibwa minister also visited five other Indian communities.[7] South of the village the Roman Catholic Indians gathered in the summer, served by itinerant Ojibwa-speaking Jesuit priests.

One year before Sanders' death in 1902, Charles Camsell, a future federal Deputy Minister of Mines (1920–1946), visited Bisco and described it as "a small railway village with a little frame hotel, a couple of stores, the railway station and a few log cabins."[8] Although it grew with the construction of a much larger mill in 1905, the town had no sidewalks, roads, or electricity when Archie arrived.[9]

The Ontario Forestry Branch joined the HBC, the sawmill, and the railway, becoming the village's fourth employer at the turn of the century. Every summer it hired fire rangers for the newly established Mississaga Forest Reserve, approximately 10,000 sq. kilometres in area (slightly smaller than the Temagami reserve).[10] The fifty or so rangers, working in pairs, patrolled their assigned areas taking in with them enough food to last until the fall. From 1909 to 1917 Charles Duval served as chief ranger and Archie worked under him his first three summers at Bisco.[11]

Ferg Legace, then a boy of twelve, remembered sixty years later the arrival of this colourful newcomer from Lake Temagami at his mother's boardinghouse when the fire-ranging season ended. The tall, well-mannered man "had a way of making friends with everyone he met, from an aged person to a young child . . . he was friendly to all in turn on the same level. The village people got to like him and he was often asked in different homes for a meal or to spend the evening."[12]

Later, on becoming better acquainted, the Legaces found Archie exasperating, but overall they liked him. The family remembered well his musical talent. At home they had a gramophone record player, the kind that had to be wound up with a crank. Archie would select a record he liked and play it over and over until he knew it by heart. Then he would practise on the piano until he could play the piece by ear. He played the piano at the dances.[13]

Years of running a boardinghouse had given Ferg's mother, Matilda Legace, a psychologist's insight. She realized that the long-haired newcomer from Temagami craved attention. At the dinner table she allowed him to eat with his hat on, but if he misbehaved she told him in her strong French Canadian accent: "That's enough Archie or I'll hit you over the head." Archie took the tall, heavily-built woman seriously as she had already proven how well she could deal with the unruly lumberjacks, woodsmen, and commercial travellers at her boardinghouse. On several occasions she had upended the troublemakers and tossed them out the door.[14]

In the early 1970s, several Bisco old-timers recalled their first impressions of the young man who twenty years later became world famous as Grey Owl. Colin Phillips, a trapper in his late twenties from Dorset in the Lake of Bays area of Haliburton, Ontario, knew Archie at Bisco before the First World War. From age five, Colin had trapped, first setting snares for rabbits, and was an expert at all aspects of the trapper's life.[15]

Colin's cabin stood next to the Legace's boardinghouse. He and Archie became peripherally acquainted. What surprised the professional trapper was his neighbour's inability to make things—paddles, ax-handles, his own cabin. In the bush Belaney was very observant but as a trapper, sloppy. He set his traps all over the place, but he failed to blaze his territory properly and could never find half of them. One spring he set out a number of bear traps but irresponsibly never bothered to go back and get them.[16] Much of the fur he did bring in was badly skinned and dried.[17] In short, he did not start out well in professional trapping. Archie had much to learn. He did much better at fireranging in the summer for it involved canoeing, which he loved.

Woody Cowper, who had just graduated from high school in Dundas, Ontario, near Hamilton, obtained a job as a forest ranger in the Mississaga Forest Reserve in 1912. That summer he had a good chance to observe Archie Belaney, and he never forgot him. A quarter of a century later Woody Cowper, then farming near Cobourg, Ontario, wrote a vivid sketch of Archie Belaney in his mid-twenties.

> He was considered a white man, with possibly a streak of Indian in him. He was an outstanding figure, imitating in dress and ways the Indians. He always wore moccasins. He wore his hair long, parted in the centre and down to his shoulders, but it did not look like Indian hair, being a dark brown. He kept it out of his eyes with two strands of trolling line wound around his forehead. His skin was dark, as he never wore a hat.
>
> Belaney was a hardy voyageur, and he took lots of hard trips in all kinds of rough water; sometimes he would take the canoe, while his partner, a red-headed Irishman, would walk the shore. Belaney seemed to make his home with the Indians on the Mississauga Reserve, where he was accepted by them. He was a great showman, showing off with all kinds of Indian stunts, and was an adept at throwing knives. He was in his glory when reciting original poetry, and after giving one of these pieces he would say: "That's by Bill Shakespeare, Tennyson, Browning," etc., and laugh. He seemed a remarkable, likable man, who, even in those days, wanted to hide his past. The other men put him down for a McGill man, and the rumor was that he belonged to a prominent Montreal family, but nobody appeared to know. He seemed to have Indian characteristics about some work, but when it came to a canoe trip he excelled.[18]

Frank Coryell, a Toronto businessman, hired Archie as a guide in 1913 after the fire ranging season ended. Like Colin Phillips, Coryell felt his guide's knowledge of bush skills left much to be desired, but like Woody Cowper he found him a wonderful entertainer and storyteller. On their ten-day hunting trip in the Mississaga Forest Reserve, Archie told him about "fighting Yaqui Indians in New Mexico, [and about] his father's violent death as a member of the Texas Rangers."[19]

That winter Archie came south and called on Frank Coryell at the furniture store he managed in Toronto.[20] On this trip he also visited Montreal, as he had learned that George McCormick, his boyhood friend, had emigrated from England and taken a job at the headquarters of the Royal Bank in Montreal. They had not seen each other since Archie's last visit to Hastings, about five years earlier, when Archie brought George a pair of moccasins.[21]

George explained that he left England in early April 1912. He had a "rather hectic introduction" to Canada at Halifax when, on landing, he and his fellow ship passengers learned that on the night of April 14–15 the *Titanic* collided with an iceberg 700 kilometres off the Newfoundland coast. The "unsinkable" ship went down with 1,500 crew and passengers. The day George landed, a merchant ship sailed into Halifax bringing bodies from the *Titanic*.

The meeting of the two old friends was not a success. Archie looked quite strange to the young bank clerk: long hair, large felt hat, handkerchief about his neck, buckskins, and moccasins. In George's words, "he had gone very Indian by then . . . you would have taken him for an Indian." After calling at the bank, Archie invited George to his roominghouse, a very seedy establishment near Bonaventure Station. His old friend had changed into a perfect stranger. Sixty years later George still recalled that he "gave the idea that he was hunted by some Indian tribe." When the two men parted, they did so for life. They never saw each other again.

Archie, of course, was not hunted by the Temagami Indian band nor by a single one of its members. Instead the memory of Angele and Agnes haunted him. He did not know what to do about her, or their infant daughter, and could not speak to anyone about them. In his letters home he had never mentioned his wife and child.[22] He could not talk to his aunts, or even to his best childhood friend, and he wanted to, as he had considered going back to Hastings in the winter of 1911–12. Clearly he was in a mess in 1913.

Desperately lonely, Archie began a relationship with Marie Girard (Gerrard or Jero), a Métis woman who worked as a maid at Legace's boardinghouse. The intelligent young woman spoke very good French, English, and Ojibwa. She had never attended school. At Archie's invitation she joined him on his trapline during the winter of 1913–14.[23]

In late spring 1914, Bob Wilson, a twenty-three-year-old University of Toronto student from Tilbury, just east of Windsor, Ontario, came north to work as a summer fire ranger in the Mississaga Forest Reserve.[24] Chief Ranger Duval named him and Archie travelling partners and the two men spent the next two months together. Apart from Archie's cooking—he used too much baking soda in his bannock, giving Bob constant heartburn— the young university student and the northern woodsman got on very well indeed. On the trail Archie insisted on patiently teaching Bob the Indian methods of canoeing, portaging, and camping.

Bob's long-haired canoe partner, who wore a headband, said his mother was an Apache and his father a Scot, but said nothing more about his background. "He was a most unusual personality. He had an air of mystery about him . . . uncommunicating in matters concerning himself." To play up his alleged childhood in the American Southwest, he walked bowleggedly, as if he had once been a cowboy. He made it look as if he was ready to jump on a horse.[25]

That previous winter Bob completed his second year in Arts, studying history, political science, and economics. Archie questioned him around the campfire at night about the books Bob had read and asked him about the proper spelling of words. Constantly he questioned Bob: "Do you think I could write?"

Fellow ranger Bill Draper later recorded his impressions of Archie in 1914. In the late summer, Chief Ranger Duval had sent him and Belaney, both experienced woodsmen, into the Goulais River country to the west to chase prospectors out of an area in the forest reserve closed to mining exploration. In his own right, Bill was a character. Born in England in 1878, Bill went to sea at a young age and had tattoes all over his body. On ship he loved boxing and lost the sight of one eye from a blow from an uncovered fist, as in those days heavy boxing gloves were not used. While at sea he helped smuggle ivory out of the Belgian Congo and contracted malarial fever in West Africa in 1896.

Obliged to leave the tropics, the old sailor came to Canada at the turn of the century and became a prospector in the Temagami area before moving on to Bisco. Several years before, he had employed young Archie Belaney and Baptiste Commanda as caretakers of his camp. He fired them when he came back and found them dead drunk. By the moment of his Goulais River trip with Archie, however, Bill had agreed to forget the past. Bill was understanding about this incident, as he had the habit of getting drunk himself three or four times a year. "Please excuse me, it's my birthday," he would say.[26]

Even to Bill Draper, Archie kept up his fantasy. Over the years Archie had so developed his story that even Bill Draper, a fellow Englishman, considered it plausible. Bill remembered the tale all his life.

> He then claimed that his father was a Texas Ranger and that a Mexican had killed him. Belaney in turn had shot the Mexican and had fled the country. He later told me that his mother was an Apache Indian and that his father was a Scotsman and that he was born and reared in Mexico. He used his knowledge of Spanish which he could speak a little . . . to substantiate his claims that he was raised in Mexico.[27]

Archie had an explanation for the fact that he had still a trace of an English accent when they first met. As a young man he joined Buffalo Bill's Wild West Show on its way to Britain, where he had met his father's two sisters. These two ladies, who lived "on the outskirts of London," looked after his education in England.[28]

On this Goulais River trip Archie almost gave away his fantasy when he and Bill encountered two Americans, one of whom had spent some time in Mexico. Immediately Archie began talking excitedly about a number of Mexican cities he remembered. When the American mentioned several of the districts in these same places that Archie did not know, the ranger quickly covered up his ignorance with the statement, "I was pretty young then," and said nothing more about Mexico.[29]

Bill Draper knew that Archie wanted to become a writer. He discovered this during their trip together in 1914.

> When we were travelling in the Goulais country he told me he was writing a book. That was before the war. He used excellent language in his writings and he knew his northern trails about which he was writing. I knew the trails too and he used to read the pages over to me for any little corrections that might be in order. His powers of description were marvellous and while he was reading I could just follow the trail seeing the jutting headland ahead with the clump of silver birches or the tall pine tree at such and such a place. He didn't miss a thing.[30]

Archie loved to write. On long foolscap pages he had complete authority and controlled all developments. It became a form of therapy, allowing him to escape momentarily the madness of the world he had himself created. He could write his tales for his own imaginary audience and momentarily escape thinking about his legal wife and tiny daughter, and his unhappy childhood. Alcohol also provided temporary relief from his mental torture.

Bill and Archie reached Bisco at the end of September, having only heard two weeks earlier of the world war that had begun in early August. In Bill's words, "the minute we got back to Bisco, Belaney proceeded to get drunk," and went "on a real tear."[31] Harry Woodworth, the HBC post manager who also acted as Bisco's law officer, heard of the damage the drunken Belaney had caused at the lumber company's boardinghouse.[32] He sent for Clem Jordan, the provincial policeman at neighbouring Chapleau. But before Jordan could serve his warrant, Archie had already left, supplied with food by Ferg and his sister, Célina Legace.[33] Then in mid-November he left his hiding place close to Bisco with his trapping partner from the previous winter, Marie Girard.[34]

Almost nothing is known of Archie's activities from mid-November to the following May, when he emerged in Digby, Nova Scotia, 2,000 kilometres to the east to join the Canadian Army. Frank Coryell in 1940 recalled seeing him "in the fall of 1914" in Toronto. "He was in uniform—and on his way overseas with the Canadian Expeditionary Force."[35] But this is unlikely as it appears that he remained in the bush in the Bisco area until at least January. Moreover, the only record of the enlistment of an "Archie Belaney" is that at Digby, Nova Scotia, on May 6, 1915. He gave his correct birthdate, September 18, 1888, but said "Montreal" was his place of birth.[36]

Only one reference survives which reveals where Archie was from mid-November to the end of the year: the enrolment card of John Jero at the Chapleau High School in 1932–33. On the card the birthdate of the transfer student from the Chapleau Indian School reads September 26, 1915.[37] The name of his parents does not appear, but any of the old-timers in Biscotasing could supply the details: Archie Belaney and Marie Girard.

According to three long-time Bisco residents, Archie left his girlfriend without knowing that she was pregnant, which would probably place his departure in January 1915. But perhaps he did know. Bill Draper later recalled that in 1915 Archie had written, asking him to "give money to a girl as she was in trouble."[38] Archie never saw Marie again. She died of TB shortly after giving birth to their son in the fall of 1915.[39] Edith Langevin, a warm, kindly Cree woman in Bisco whose first husband had been Andrew Sanders, a brother of the Rev. John Sanders, raised Archie Belaney's son, John Girard, or John Jero as his last name was pronounced and later written at the Chapleau Indian School.

Whatever Archie did from January to April 1915, after his departure from the Bisco area, cannot be specified for lack of documentation. Nearly twenty years later, however, he told Herb Winters, a friend in Prince Albert, Saskatchewan, that he had first enlisted in Montreal (presumably under another name), deserted, and then signed up under his real name in Nova Scotia.[40] Perhaps Frank Coryell's story of seeing him in uniform relates to early 1915, rather than to the fall of 1914. In any case, unless new evidence comes to light, no one will ever know if he first enlisted in Montreal and then deserted, or why he chose to enlist under his real name in distant Nova Scotia.

These were not pleasant months for Archie Belaney. He felt guilty about his legal wife and child. After enlisting in the army in Digby he apparently wrote Harry Woods, the HBC post manager at Bear Island, to tell Angele that "he was leaving for over-seas."[41] This note indicates a concern about her and their daughter Agnes' welfare. But he enclosed no letter for them, nor would any money follow. When he enlisted at Digby he declared himself unmarried, thus depriving Angele of any support from the federal government as the wife of an enlisted soldier.[42]

Archie kept falling deeper and deeper into personal problems of his own making, going from one crisis to another. Like his father, he dragged others with him—including now his infant son, Johnny, born just three months after he sailed in June 1915 for England with the Canadian Army.[43] With his own human affairs in such a tangled state, no wonder he loved so much the following line by Walt Whitman, the American romantic poet: "I think I could turn and live with animals, they are so placid and self-contained."[44]

By the moment of his enlistment in the Canadian Army, Archie's basic dilemma was clear. He had left England to escape his interior crisis, to flee from the memory of his abandonment by his parents and his traumatic childhood. In Hastings, Archie had held within himself his feelings of hatred for his lack of parental love. To protect himself he began his retreat from reality. He tried to handle the situation by creating stories about an imaginary childhood that never had existed and, later, by moving to a new country. In the end, however, the troubled, insecure man could not escape from the pain, the shame, the anger of his childhood. His refusal to change himself, to realize and to discuss his boyhood trauma with a supportive, caring individual, led to his continued alienation from others. Frightened and confused, he wore a mask in Canada. He wore a thousand masks, each of which he was afraid to take off.[45]

6   Archie and the Great War

James McKinnon, a farmer from Smith's Cove, near Digby, Nova Scotia, never forgot the most extraordinary-looking recruit in his company. "He was about my age, twenty-five, or maybe a year or two older. He was tall and wiry-looking, with a brown face and light eyes. But what caught everybody's attention was his hair. It hung right down to his shoulders, and all the fellows laughed. They said his first army order would be to get his hair cut. And so it was." The man said that his name was "Archie Belaney" and that he came from "out West." He carried a revolver and demonstrated his ability as a marksman by shooting sticks and cans tossed up in the air.[1]

At the Aldershot Training Camp near Kentville, Nova Scotia, the original battalion to which Archie and James McKinnon belonged, the 40th, trained together. But it was a depot battalion, one that would later be broken up to reinforce existing units. After the second battle of Ypres, in which the Canadians had more than 6,000 casualties, the frontline units badly needed reinforcements. Archie was among those taken in the first draft, which sailed for England in mid-June. He reported for duty at Shorn-cliffe near Folkestone, in Kent, next to his native Sussex. He then belonged to the 23rd Reserve Battalion.

Before the troops left Digby for Aldershot, the local town worthies attempted to promote pride and self-confidence. Archie heard the addresses given before the assembled troops and 1,000 well-wishers at the Digby Court House. The local member of parliament denounced the "war mad lord of Germany" and the "Huns." The Anglican rector of the local Holy Trinity Church reminded the men in uniform: "Remember that you are not only soldiers of the King, but that you are called upon to be soldiers of the King of Kings."[2]

None of this had any effect on Archie, who continued to live in his own fantasy world. Upon his enlistment the officer had asked if he had any "previous military experience." Confidently he replied, "yes," in the

"Mexican Scouts, 28th Dragoons." He liked the impact that his fantasy had on people. Two months later, no doubt on account of his "previous military experience," he became a lance-corporal.[3]

The repeated drill, route marching, shooting, and bayonet practice became Archie's daily concerns. Years later he claimed that he had been allowed to wear his moccasins on parade instead of the regulation army boots.[4] This is most unlikely.

British army veterans ran the Canadian Army training program in 1915. Archie disliked them, revealing his own class prejudices. Years later he wrote to a friend that in the Canadian Army he had found himself "under the yoke of Cockney Sgt. Majors who would have still, many of them, been cleaning spitoons at the Palmer House [a large Toronto hotel] only for the war, (& whose attempts at vituperation by the way, I found very inapt & unimaginative)."[5]

A photograph proves that Archie did visit his aunts shortly after his arrival in England. (To see them he went absent-without-leave and lost his stripe for this, reverting back to private.) Proudly he showed up in August 1915 at the Misses Belaney's new home, Hawkwood, on Glen Road in the village of Hollington on the northwestern outskirts of Hastings. In one shot he stands in his khaki serge jacket with his corporal's stripe on his right arm. In another photo it appears as if his brother Hugh, for fun, has put on Archie's khaki trousers, puttees (the long strips of wool that an infantryman wound up from his ankles to his knees)—*and his regulation army boots.* It was a happy visit for the Misses Belaney, who had come into hard times. They only rented the large house and to meet expenses had to operate a poultry farm there.[6]

Hastings looked so different from the time of Archie's last visit about 1908. Men in uniform marched everywhere as the British Army used the seaside resort as a victualling centre where they fed troops from the district *en route* to France. From army bases in the interior some men had a fifty-kilometre walk. Many invalided Canadian soldiers could also be seen because the Canadian Army had a convalescent hospital here.[7]

The reality of the war became apparent as the local papers replaced the pictures of departing soldiers with a whole page of the Roll of Honour, showing weekly the names of up to forty local men killed in action. Hastings would lose 1,300 men in the First World War, out of a total population of about 60,000. By the summer of 1915 tens of thousands of British soldiers had already died in battles in Flanders.

Archie learned that many of the McCormicks had enlisted. George McCormick would soon be in France. His brothers Claude and Leslie served in the Australian Light Horse (Claude would be killed on July 31, 1918), and Hugh was in the Canadian Army (he was killed September 7, 1916). Jim McCormick (next to his brother George in age), who had gone out to work in Chile before the war, had already died at sea in February 1915, while serving on the HMS *Pembroke*.[8]

Lieutenant (later Captain) Ewart Banks, a veteran of the South African War and a scouting instructor for the Canadian 23rd Reserve Battalion, met Archie at Dibgate Camp at Shorncliffe that July. Soldier Belaney made an immediate impression. "His maps and reports were so remarkable that I would show them to the colonel, then Col. F. E. [F. C.] Bowen, of Sherbrooke, Quebec, and they would be handed around to the officers in the mess."[9]

Interestingly, Archie liked Lieutenant Banks enough to tell him one of his more embroidered versions of his Indian past. Banks never forgot it and twenty years later recalled Belaney's story that "he was half Indian, and I thought, Mexican; that his brother had been killed by some follower of Pancho Villa; that he had found this out; had found who the man was and had shot him. He said he had to leave the country in a hurry and that he had made his way to Montreal, thence to the north woods of Quebec away from civilization." As the man had no trace of an English accent, Ewart believed him. For safekeeping in the large military camp, Archie asked his officer-friend to put away his two huge revolvers (with one of which he claimed to have shot the Mexican) until he was sent to the front.[10]

The lieutenant stored the six-shooters until Archie's departure in late August to join the 13th Battalion, a unit of the Royal Highlanders of Canada, known today as the Canadian Black Watch. When Ewart went to the soldier's tent to hand over the firearms he found the flap closed, and when he opened it: "Here was Belaney, with tears in his eyes, holding up a pair of kilts and telling me that an Indian could not wear women's skirts. I naturally did a little sniggering and patted him on the back. Away went Belaney to France as a Scotty."[11]

The 13th Battalion in late August 1915 occupied a sector of the front at Messines, on the southern flank of the Ypres Salient, where the Allies still held a symbolic (if small) section of northwestern Belgium. The men spent four days in the trenches, followed by an equal time out of the line in reserve in the rear area, still within range of the enemy's guns. As the official battalion history says: "The front line itself was a slimy ditch, where at best, the men sank over their ankles and where, owing to the clinging powers of the local mud, an individual, once stuck, could release himself only with the greatest difficulty."[12]

At all costs the men must hold the line. To quote a secret directive in the 13th Battalion's war diary for September 1915: "Should the enemy attack with Gas or Liquid Fire, every man must understand that all positions MUST be held."[13] In the trenches Archie became acquainted with the rattle of machine gun fire, the crack of field artillery, the wail of hurling shells. But in November came some good news for the reluctant Highland soldier. In that month the 13th Battalion switched from their mud-encrusted kilts to trousers for the winter.[14]

Several of his fellow soldiers at Messines years after the war remembered Private Belaney. As he intended, the flamboyant marksman made a lasting impression. Elmer Weedmark, then just eighteen, later recalled: "He was some character, what with his antics and tricks. He was an excellent shot and served as a sniper. I feel sure he was an Indian." Archie McWade, a twenty-three-year-old soldier from the Ottawa area, fought beside him as a sniper, and "saw him squirm up muddy hills in a way no white man could. He had all the actions and features of an Indian. . . . Never in all my life did I ever meet a man who was better able to hide when we would go out onto No Man's Land."[15]

Albert Chandler, a fellow sniper at Messines, never forgot Archie Belaney. To determine if the Germans were before them, he once put a turnip on his bayonet, with a Glengarry cap on top of it. A German soldier fired as soon as he propped it up, putting a bullet hole clean through the turnip. Chandler also recalled that Belaney and his sniping partner "drank fire-water as they called it, and then acted like half crazy metis."[16]

At Messines, Lieutenant W. E. Macfarlane, Archie's platoon commander, probably knew Private Belaney best of all. An original member of the 13th Battalion, Macfarlane had survived the Germans' chlorine gas attack on the Canadians at Ypres in late April 1915. He had then faced the next month the heavy German bombardments at Festubert and Givenchy.[17] A hardened soldier, he led patrols at night out into the no-man's-land, about one-kilometre wide, which separated the Canadians from the German trenches.[18] Nearly half-a-century later he remembered how Private Belaney "had certain Indian characteristics and did not conceal, but rather took pride in, his Indian origin."[19]

As a soldier Macfarlane regarded him as "good material," if somewhat independent. "It took a direct order to get his hair cut to regimental standard." On account of his "considerable knowledge of field craft," Macfarlane made him a sniper-observer.

> He had infinite patience and the gift of absolute immobility for long periods. His reports as an observer were short, to the point, and intelligent. Unlike many snipers he did not make exaggerated claims of 'kills.' Belaney was a dependable, if not an outstanding soldier, and I have often wished that I had had him longer under my command, to see if I could really have got 'inside' him. I never felt that I did, although I think he opened up to me more than to anyone else. . . . He held himself aloof, even from his comrades, but was not disliked or unpopular. He was just a Lone Wolf type.[20]

On January 15, 1916, Archie was wounded in the right wrist and hospitalized for two weeks. The bullet wound healed well, and he returned to his unit on February 4.[21]

In mid-March the Canadian Corps moved northward, ending their trench tour at Messines. As they came towards Ypres the more Flemish the place names became, and the more unpronounceable to the Canadians. The Canadians began to exchange places with the British V Corps, which held the southern curve of the Ypres Salient. Just before moving north, the 9th Battalion of the Royal Sussex Regiment, with its regimental motto "Nothing Succeeds Like Sussex,"[22] relieved the 13th Battalion at Red Lodge at the Messines front.[23]

Around 1905 Archie himself had belonged to the 5th Cinque Ports Battalion of the Royal Sussex Regiment. As George McCormick later recalled: "He was a stirring sight to see running along in his red uniform with his helmet on—not marching along in a soldiery manner," but "slouching along like an Indian" with a great loping stride.[24] The sixteen- or seventeen-year-old slid his foot over the road with each step, instead of lifting it.[25] But Archie missed seeing again the men of Sussex as he was then attending a sniper's course. After one month's absence, he rejoined his battalion on April 8th.[26] Back he came for the 13th Battalion's bloodiest clash since the German chlorine gas attack at Ypres the previous spring.

On March 30 the 13th Battalion moved into its new positions. Fortunately that same evening the British battalion commanders, for the first time, issued the men steel helmets, essential for deflecting shrapnel. At the beginning of the war no one had foreseen the years of trench warfare to follow, and only a year and a half later were the British Empire's troops in the field equipped with them.[27]

R. C. Fetherstonhaugh, the official historian of the 13th Battalion, with typical understatement described the troops' first days in the trenches of the Ypres Salient. "During the tour in the line there was considerable artillery activity and a general 'liveliness' that had been missing on the Messines front, where weather and ground conditions had proved the principal enemy."[28] Archie returned from his sniper's course only days before the battalion suffered heavy casualties under an intense German bombardment. His young friend Elmer Weedmark was wounded on April 17,[29] and on the night of April 18–19 a heavy shell buried and knocked unconscious Lieutenant Macfarlane, who (saved by the bottomless mud) only came to ten hours later.[30] The 13th Battalion (normally about 1000 men strong) suffered more than 170 casualties (38 killed) in the clashes in the Ypres Salient in April.[31]

On the evening of April 23 the exhausted 13th Battalion was relieved. One brief reference in the battalion war diary reported, "Pte. A. Belaney wounded."[32] No doubt it was his aunts who later provided an account of his injury to his old school magazine, the *Hastonian*. "A. Belaney is again in Hospital, having smashed a bone in his right foot. He was hit at 7 o'clock on April 23rd and 'crawled and lay till daylight next morning, when some poor chap carried me about 1½ miles under heavy shell fire'."[33] A fellow 13th Battalion sniper, Leslie Meacher, years later recalled that evening in a more simplified version. "It was at The Bluff at Ypres that one night about

8 o'clock Delaney [Belaney] left his dugout, and after about half an hour he returned dragging his rifle and one leg. He mentioned that he had trodden on a thorn or wire and had injured his foot, but on examination and after removing his long wadded rubber boot we discovered he had been shot."[34]

The accusation has been made that perhaps Archie shot himself in the foot to get himself out of the war. When contacted in 1963, Major Macfarlane ruled out the idea. Discipline, he reported, was too strict, and the commanding officer's thorough examination would have detected a self-inflicted wound.[35]

Archie never regained the complete use of his right foot as the injury had come in the central area, to the 2nd, 3rd, 4th and 5th metatarsus bones that connected the toes to the ankle.[36] Nearly twenty years later he wrote to Anahareo about it. "I'm afraid I will have to have my foot fixed, they should take off all the front part so I have no bother with it, and can walk flatfooted, and not stoop the way I do, and have an artificial piece and rubber springy sole."[37]

Archie's playful side remained intact after his injury. As nothing could be done for his foot in France at the military hospital in Boulogne, his doctors sent him to the King George Hospital on Stamford Street in London. He stayed there more than four months, then was transferred to Folkestone in the early fall, and finally to the Canadian Military Hospital in Hastings from November 1916 to March 1917, then to the London General Hospital for the removal of the 4th metatarsus and 4th toe. At the King George Hospital a Mrs. C. R. Parsons, a nurse "under whose care I spent some months," took a special interest in him, and they corresponded for years after Archie returned to Canada. "I knew him as Private Belaney. He had been wounded in the right foot. He spoke English very badly. He wrote me dozens of letters. His spelling was simply awful. No educated Englishman could spell so badly. His father, he said, was a Scotsman, and his mother an Apache Indian."[38]

What did Archie think of the war? Certainly it greatly affected him. Even on the relatively quiet Messines sector the horrors had been grotesque. Years later he told Jane Espaniel, the younger daughter of his friend Alex Espaniel at Bisco, this story. One hot night in the trenches he decided to hang up his army coat on what he thought was the branch of a tree. The next morning he saw that he had used a dead man's arm as his coatrack.[39]

At the front—particularly during his last weeks near Ypres—he had experienced the worst of trench warfare. He had killed a number of Germans[40] and, as a sniper, had seen his victims in the moment of death. Later he wrote in *Pilgrims of the Wild*:

> I had been one of those unusual people, so seldom met with in stories, who was not an officer, did not attract the attention of the higher command, entered the army as a private and left it as one. I had come back to the

woods with my efficiency much impaired, and my outlook on things generally
had been in no way improved by the job of sniper that I had held, and the
sole educational effect [of] the war had been to convince me of the utter
futility of civilization.[41]

Archie was not completely honest in his statement. Instead of rejecting
civilization after his injury, he embraced it. The war changed him. For fun
he might keep up his masquerade with strangers like the future Mrs. Parsons
(her maiden name is unknown), but now he wanted to communicate truly
with someone. After a life of solitude he apparently felt the need to end
his inward journey. When his aunts suggested that he contact Ivy Holmes,
his childhood girlfriend, he did so. They had not seen each other since
March 1906 when he and Aunt Ada spent several days with Ivy and her
mother before Archie sailed for Canada.[42]

Ivy, then twenty-six, was a very attractive, interesting woman. She had
travelled to many exotic foreign countries and learned firsthand about
different cultures. As a young girl she studied ballet in London. With her
mother's encouragement the talented girl became a professional dancer.
Ivy was escorted by Florence Holmes on her first tour abroad with an English
dance and acting troupe. The company danced and in English imitated
famous British actors. Over a period of six years they travelled to Belgium,
the Austro-Hungarian Empire, present-day Poland, Russia, Serbia, Bulgaria,
and finally, Turkey. The tour ended in 1912 after a run of three months
in Constantinople. With the outbreak of the Balkan War in 1912, Ivy, her
mother, and the troupe had to return home.

Archie, a future master of the stage himself, must have listened avidly
to Ivy's stories of travelling across Europe. In Russia she once saw a line
of men chained to each other on their way to Siberia. Of all the European
cities she visited, Ivy loved Vienna, and most of all Budapest. Her stories
about her impersonations on stage must have fascinated this veteran of
nearly a decade of presenting himself as part-Indian in Canada.

Archie had reached a turning point in his life. With Ivy he could not
claim to be an Indian—she knew his true story. But perhaps he could gain
love and the acceptance of his real self. Her entry back into his life was
as if a line had been thrown out to a man drowning in self-delusion. Would
Archie grab it and pull himself back into reality? Or was the rope still beyond
his reach?

Ivy enjoyed Archie's company. Always he was so polite, and had excellent
manners. He wore his hair short. In her presence he never drank or swore.
In many ways the man had become but a larger projection of the boy, with
the same intense love of nature and North American Indians.

As he hobbled along on crutches on their walks in London parks, or
on visits together at his aunts' at Hollington, Archie told Ivy about beavers
and the dams they built. He spoke about Biscotasing and the white water

stretches of the "Grand Discharge of Waters," as the Indians called the Mississagi River.[43] Proud of his prowess, he talked with such enthusiasm about canoeing. He made the "backwoods sound terribly attractive."[44] But he never talked about himself. A barrier always came down. How could he tell Ivy about his Indian wife and child in Canada?

Ivy encouraged him to write, as no doubt Ada did as well, and he soon sketched out several manuscripts. Genuinely he loved the forest and the life of the wilderness man. A particularly vivid passage in one of his manuscripts written at this time describes his first canoeing lessons with the Temagami Ojibwa, Big Feather (or Quill) or Michel (Michelle) Mathias. The excerpt gives a good idea of Archie's writing skills in 1917, as well as his own knowledge of, and passion for, canoeing. In a canoe he could forget the modern, confusing, man-made world around him.

> Michelle was a revelation to me. His movements when instructing me were quick and decisive; almost startlingly sudden at times, and in direct contrast to his demeanour when unoccupied. I despaired of ever learning a tenth part of what he showed me. His English was imperfect, but he was very patient and smiled indulgently at my failures. After several days I improved and made some progress. Michelle performed movements facing me in one end of the canoe. I imitated him more or less successfully at the other, each in turn. He illustrated and explained the bow stroke, long but quick, and the lightning recovery; the quick twist of the wrist and turn of the blade used in the stern to counteract the inclination of the canoe to move in circles. With a good canoeman this latter movement does not detract from the force of the stroke and is hardly noticeable, stroke and twist all occurring in exact time with the bowsman. He showed me how to make the sharp lean forward of the body at the end of the stroke do most of the work, the arms remaining stiff, and how to use the gunnell as a fulcrum to lever the paddle swiftly out of the water for the quick recover. He steered the canoe impartially from either bow, stern or middle, stood up and walked around in it with apparent care-lessness, balancing instinctively and without effort whilst doing all this. One day there was a heavy head wind, and he illustrated how the angle of the canoe against the wind and your position in it, squatting flat on your heels so as not to catch the wind, can be made to assist you, and how this position enabled a canoeman to double the most exposed point in rough weather. Every day I learnt a little more, and every night I ached all over. He taught me how to pick up and carry a canoe, no mean achievement until you get the knack. Balance seemed to be the chief requirement in all these exercises. The canoe business was strictly hard work, or at least I made it so. Michelle seemed to perform without perceptible effort what taxed my utmost strength. He produced results with the minimum of labour. I would struggle to pull the canoe around to change its direction, for a full minute, then he would take the paddle, and give a gentle twist or waft it languidly through the water, and the thing was done.[45]

In 1916–1917, Ivy brought Archie back to life after the horrors of Flanders. He wanted to become a real person, able to communicate on a human level with others. Badly he wanted to marry her, the only English girl who had known him as a boy. Yet his attempt was doomed to failure from the start. If he honestly communicated with her, how could he tell her about his legal wife and child in Canada? Once he mentioned this, she could not marry him.

On one of their walks along the Churchwood Road, just west of the Belaney's home on Glen Road, Ivy discovered the beautiful Hollington Church-in-the-Wood, located in a small forested area on the northern out-skirts of Hastings. She suggested marrying in this romantic setting, and they did so on February 10, 1917.[46] The small party assembled for the wedding dinner at the Belaneys', then the newlyweds travelled to a hotel in Battle, seven or eight kilometres away, for their honeymoon at the site of the village where William Duke of Normandy defeated King Harold of England in the famous Battle of Hastings.

Archie Belaney might best be called a man-child. So arrested had been his personal development, he had no real conception of the pain he caused others. Archie lived totally in a dream world of his own creation. He first married Ivy bigamously, and then he proposed that they settle in Canada, near Biscotasing, or only about 100 kilometres or so from his legal wife Angele and daughter Agnes. Moreover, his Métis girlfriend, Marie Girard, still presumably lived in the Bisco area.

Ivy looked forward to seeing his beloved wilderness. After his operation at the London Hospital in March 1917, Archie underwent therapy with an osteopath (or bone manipulator) in London. He "got him right" and no longer did Archie limp.[47] The couple then decided that Archie should return first to Canada (at this stage of the war wives could not yet accompany their husbands back to Canada), then once he had established himself in the northern Ontario settlement he would write to her to follow.

Adventuresome as always, and deeply in love with her husband, Ivy accepted the plan of beginning a life together in the northern Canadian forest. Archie sailed on September 19, 1917.[48] Ivy never saw him again.

7 Back to Bisco

Archie came back to Bisco confused, alienated, and physically handicapped. As his medical report prepared on May 10, 1918, reveals: "Right foot same as before. Cannot walk 1 mile on pavements without pain. Can walk 4 or 5 miles on snowshoes. Can walk a couple of miles in bush, but cannot do any packing."[1]

For several weeks in October 1917 he had been an outpatient at the old College Street hospital at College and Bay streets in Toronto. But they could do little for him. On October 26, a medical officer reported: "Patient has to walk on heel and inner surface of arch, as bearing on the ball of foot causes pain." The examining board recommended his discharge, "on account of physical unfitness. No further treatment will benefit his condition."[2]

In October 1917 the invalid soldier still considered himself as married. "Mrs. Ivy Belaney, 1 Collville Mansions, House Terrace, Bayswater, London W., Eng." appears as his wife in his "Medical History." Ivy's influence still held him in its grip, as the form prepared October 26 gave his stand on temperance as a teetotaller. Yet, surprisingly, his "address pending discharge" appears as Bisco.[3] His idea, then, appears to have been to settle with Ivy at, or near, Biscotasing—an extraordinary idea to say the least when one considers that Marie Girard, to the best of his knowledge, still lived there. Then came the thunderclap.

At some point in November he must have heard that Marie had died and that he had fathered a son, a baby named Johnny who was being raised by Mrs. Langevin. The Legaces may have first told him. (He had written them while in the army to send him a new pair of moccasins.)[4] The horrors of his return to Canada had just begun. He could not bring Ivy to the village. Totally confused, he sought out the one person he felt he could confide in—Angele.

Through the chief ranger in Temagami, he sent a message to Angele, who was then staying at Head Chief Frank White Bear's house. They met,

Angele reported twenty years later, first at Lindsay, a small town about a hundred kilometres northeast of Toronto, and again at Bancroft, farther to the northeast, where she had obtained a job at a local hotel.[5] Angele dated their meeting as having occurred when the creek at Bancroft was full of white fish, spawning, which must have been November.[6] But they only stayed a couple of days together "because he was anxious to go back to Bisco again. Anxious to go there. He wanted so bad to go." He did not stay long, in Angele's words, "because he was afraid of another person . . . he is supposed to have got a wife over there [in England]."[7]

With his world collapsing around him, Archie became a fugitive once again. He arrived by train in Bisco in late 1917, after his discharge from the army at the end of November.[8]

Archie's short relapse back into his English identity had ended. By early 1918 he had again returned to his childhood fantasy of being an Indian. We know this from an unusual letter he included in his last book, *Tales of an Empty Cabin* (1936). During his first British lecture tour he met Mrs. C. R. Parsons, the nurse who had looked after him immediately upon his hospitalisation in England in 1916. Mrs. Parsons returned to him the original letter that he had mailed to her from Canada early in 1918. In 1936, he lent it to his publisher in England, Lovat Dickson, who, at his request, printed it in *Tales of an Empty Cabin* later that year. He also later showed the letter, and identified it as his own, to J. S. Wood, the city librarian in Saskatoon, Saskatchewan, who visited him at Beaver Lodge.[9] *Anaquoness* (an Ojibway word which Grey Owl translated as "Little Hat") has signed the letter. On account of his Mexican sombrero, one of Archie's first names in the Bisco area had been Little Hat, or Anaquoness.[10]

Without acknowledging, of course, that he himself was Anaquoness, Archie included this editorial note with his letter in *Tales of an Empty Cabin:*

> This epistle was written by a North American Indian, an ex-sniper in the Canadian Expeditionary Force in France during 1915–17. It was addressed to a nurse in an English hospital where the Indian had lain recovering from his wounds, previous to being sent back to Canada for discharge. It is interesting to note the contrast, amounting almost to a conflict, between his original style and spelling, and that resulting from his attempts at self-education. The newly acquired erudition stands out rather incongruously in spots and was, happily, beyond the power of the writer to maintain throughout.

The following excerpts are selected from his letter. It seems incredible indeed that the Hastings Grammar School's top student in the Cambridge University Junior examination in English grammar and literature in 1903 could write the language of Shakespeare so abominably.

February 3rd, 1918.

Dear Miss Nurse:

Nearly four months now the Canada geese flew south and the snow is very deep. It is long timesince I wrot to you, but I have gone a long ways and folled some hard trails since that time. The little wee sorryful animals I tol you about sit around me tonight, and so they dont get tired and go away I write to you now. I guess they like to see me workin. I seen my old old trees and the rocks that I know and the forest that is to me what your house is to you. . . . Gee Im lucky to be able to travel the big woods agen. To us peple the woods and the big hills and the Northen lights and the sunsets are all alive and we live with these things and live in the spirit of the woods like no white person can do. . . . I wonder if all this means anything to you I hope you wont laugh at it anyway. It is now Seegwun when the snow is all melt of the ice and it thaw in the daytime and freeze at night, making a crust so the moose breaks through and cant run. This is the days when we have hardship and our snowshoes break through the crust and get wet an heavy an our feet is wet everyday all the time wet. The crows have come back. Between now and the break up is pleasant weather in the settlements but it is hell in the woods. White men dont travel not at all now and I dont blame him. March 20th/18 Well I lay up today all day in my camp and it is a soft moon, which is bad beleive me, so I write some more to your letter. I travel all day yestdy on the lakes in water and slush half way to my knees on top the ice. It will be an early spring. My wound is kinda gone on the blink, to hard going. . . . Say, you poor people over there gettin no meat. Dont think me mean to tell you, but we have 300lb of meat on hand now. Injuns can kill all they want for their own use. I wisht I could send you some. Hows the wee garden and the nieces coming along. Write and tell me all about them. My ears are open. . . . I will lisen to the song of a bird for a little while. Now the curtain is pulled down across the sun and my heart is black. A singing bird comes and sings an says I do this an I do that an things are so with me an I will lisen an forget there is no sun, until the bird goes, then I will sit and think an smoke for hours an say to myself, thats good, I am ony an Injun and that bird sang for me. When the morning wind rises and the morning star hangs of the edge of the black swamp to the east, tomorrow, I will be on my snowshoe trail. Goodbye.

ANA-QUON-ESS

The letter shows how much Ojibwa and nature-lore he had forgotten since he places *Seeg-wun* or Spring, "the Sap season," at the beginning of February instead of in March, when the sap truly ran.[11] When writing the word *we-o-quon-ness*, a "little hat," Archie transcribes it poorly, as "Ana-quon-ess."[12] In addition, he seems to be rhapsodizing about the songbird he allegedly heard.[13] Would songbirds themselves be back in northern Ontario by late March? It is several weeks early.[14]

Archie had forgotten a great deal, but in his letter, written as an "Injun" to his English friend, the kernel of his later environmental message surfaces: "To us peple the woods and the big hills and the Northen lights and the sunsets are all alive and we live with these things and live in the spirit of the woods like no white person can do." In another passage a revealing insight into his mind also appears. "I kill that lynx today and somehow I wisht I hadnt. His skin is only worth $10 and he didnt act cross an the way he looked at me I cant get that out of my mind."[15] His mind was already opening to an animal rights' position.

Several major worries plagued Archie in 1918, first his son, Johnny. Lacking any money himself, he left his upbringing entirely to Edith Langevin. The townspeople knew her as the "Mother of Bisco," as she acted as the village's midwife. Over the years Mrs. Langevin had delivered practically every child in Bisco. This kind-hearted Cree woman had taken charge of Johnny shortly after Marie's death.[16]

Johnny grew up until almost the age of ten not knowing who his father was. As he had been enrolled at the Chapleau Indian School in 1918, at the age of three, he only came back in summer, a time when Archie was usually away.[17] Archie never talked to him, but he thought about his son a great deal, even later telling Anahareo about him.[18] Mrs. Langevin, the boy's guardian, hesitated about identifying Johnny's father to him as she had little respect for Archie. As a staunch teetotaller herself, his drinking habits revolted her.[19]

Archie did not know what he should do about Johnny, or about Ivy, who still waited to be asked to join him in Canada. For a year or so he continued to write her regularly until he finally marshalled enough courage to tell her of his previous marriage. Naturally she then filed for divorce on the grounds of bigamy, obtaining full details of his previous marriage from Arthur Stevens, Temagami's Justice of the Peace.[20]

In the summer of 1921 a Sudbury lawyer brought the divorce papers to Archie, then working as deputy chief ranger in the Mississaga Forest Reserve. Archie appeared quite nonchalant, as lawyer J. J. O'Connor later recalled: "At the time Belaney was deputy fire ranger and the most blasphemous and kick-in-the-pants-go-to-hell individual I ever came across. He took service of the papers in his stride and was so undisturbed that he had me as supper guest in the rangers' cabin."[21] Underneath his gruff exterior, though, the blow hurt deeply, ending the only friendship he had dating back to his childhood. It also momentarily led to a break with his aunts.

Ada and Carrie viewed their nephew's treatment of Ivy and Angele as nothing less than diabolical and were furious with him.[22] What had they done wrong? When he was a boy, one of their favourite punishments had been to put him in the corner and make him read portions of the Bible.[23] But what good had that done? Despite all of their efforts the boy they had raised for fifteen years had deceived and emotionally almost destroyed their best friend's daughter.

Through Arthur Stevens the Misses Belaney obtained Angele's address and mailed several dolls and a dollhouse to daughter Agnes, then ten years old.[24] As so little evidence survives, one does not know if the aunts continued to write to Archie. He wrote them.[25]

Archie spent 1918 recuperating as best he could. He slowly regained better control over his injured right foot but a disability remained. Basically he had lost one toe completely, two partially, and had a large ball on his foot. On occasion his foot became swollen almost to twice its normal size.[26]

As always, instead of directly facing his problems and trying to resolve them, Archie escaped by retreating into his fantasy world. The summer of 1919 Archie worked on a survey party for the firm of Lang and Ross. Stuart MacDougall, a sixteen-year-old packer, kept a diary that summer. It contains a reference to a fellow packer in the party. "June 22nd, Sunday. In the evening, went up the Nagagami River in one of the canoes with Archie Belaney, from whom I am, 'Taking a course in paddling.' He is a quick-tempered Mexican half-breed."[27]

The "Mexican half-breed" had an unattractive side. "He was taciturn and morose, with a violent, almost maniacal temper." Young Stuart once heard the professed atheist "battling the wind in order to get a tree felled in a particular direction, call upon God, The Angels, and all of Heaven to come down and fight it out with him to see who was the best man." (Finally he did succeed in felling the spruce tree where he wished.) Years later Stuart still had visions of Archie at camp in the evening, "sitting around the fire, and tapping on a dish-pan in a dull, monotonous beat, singing ancient Indian songs—weird rhythmic melodies—that none of our Cree or Ojibway Indians had ever heard."[28]

Ferg Legace knew him before and after the war. Embittered by his injured foot, Archie had changed a great deal. "Village people were starting not to think so well of him on account of his drinking, and night actions of hooting and howling." Another Bisco resident, Harry Woodworth, the HBC post manager, put it this way: "He had got a lot of experience while in the army amongst men and had changed a lot. He got to be quite bold again, got drunk more often and raised more hell around Bisco than ever before."[29]

Ontario had gone dry at the end of the war, which inspired Archie to try to recall all he could of his grammar school chemistry. Back in the bush he made his own moonshine, stirring the mash (made of wheat, yeast cakes, and sugar) with a paddle, then distilling it. He generally made his brew at Whisky Lake, a few kilometres from Bisco, using for the distilling operation a fire extinguisher, gas stove, oaken barrel, water boiler, and copper tubing. Archie would put the mash-filled extinguisher in the huge water boiler on the stove, then collect the liquid in the barrel connected to the extinguisher by the copper tubing.[30] For the first couple of drinks you had to hold your nose as the moonshine smelled so awful.[31]

To attract attention Archie frequently, when in town, attended the English Church (as the villagers called the local Anglican church). He would wear his black hat in church and consciously sit in front of an angry Edith Langevin, who would pull it off his head. In a big loud voice he bellowed: "Thank you Mrs. Lange-way." Once he asked the minister during the service: "Why do you have so many nicknames for Jesus? Christ? the Nazarene? the Saviour?"[32] During another service he sat in the back cutting his fingernails until the minister called for prayers for King George V. Then suddenly the tall, long-haired, inebriated trapper shouted out: "Why pray for him? What about us poor sinners?"[33]

Johnny Jero eventually learned his true relationship to this strange man that he later called "Archie Baloney."[34] The young boy often heard his "mother" (Mrs. Langevin) talk about the weird character who lived just across the lake from them. When "liquored up" he loved to beat his drum and sing his "Indian songs" at all hours. One day in 1924 or so Johnny told Mrs. Langevin that he did not want to grow up to be like that. To Edith Langevin befell the painful task of explaining, before someone else did, that Archie Belaney was his father.[35]

Local fur buyer Jack Leve remembered him as a perfect gentleman and a wonderful conversationist, when sober. Drunk, he became a different person. Few villagers wanted to bother with him in such a state. Once in the winter Jack spotted him lying on the steps of the lumber company's store. It would have taken perhaps only a half hour more for Archie to freeze to death outside on that icy night, so Jack picked him up and threw him into the first empty room at the boardinghouse. On another occasion the fur buyer noticed him walking shakily out of his shack. Archie said:

"Jack, do you know I'm drunk?"

"So what?"

"Jack, I got drunk on shoe polish."[36]

Archie loved to play the role of Bisco's bad guy. He liked the attention his tough *hombre* role attracted from strangers. Once he stood on the station platform when a harvester train (carrying men to work on the Western Canadian harvest) ran through Bisco. Seeing the bizarre-looking, long-haired man, a harvester yelled out, "Hey there you SOB you're cheating the barber!" Archie then whipped out his knife and threw it, lodging it in the wooden strip between the two windows on the railway coach.[37] On another occasion a man stepped by mistake on Archie's moccasined foot. He jumped up yelling: "Where I come from they hang men for less. But I don't have rope, so I'll use my knife,"[38] and pretended, knife in hand, to lunge for the offender. But Jack Woodworth, Harry's son, who liked Archie a great deal, knew his bluff, as did most of Bisco. "If you said 'boo' to him, he'd run away like a scared deer."[39] Years later Ferg Legace could not recall a single occasion in which Archie actually got in a fight in Bisco.[40] For all his bluster, he hated physical conflict.

Ted Cusson, a trapping partner in the winter of 1919–1920, realized what terrible physical shape Archie was in. Every morning at the cabin he spent 30 minutes to an hour dressing his foot. Even then he could not travel overland very far. He did not have the lungs for long portages over this land of rolling hills.[41] He ate very little and in town drank everything alcoholic in sight.

As he remained an excellent canoeist, Chief Ranger Lloyd Acheson named him his deputy on the Mississaga Forest Reserve in the summers of 1920 and 1921. Here Archie was at his best, on the five three-week tours through the huge reserve, checking on the summer ranger stations situated 50 to 60 kilometres from each other.[42] Haddow Keith, a war veteran who had just completed his first year of medicine at the University of Toronto, served as a forest ranger under his supervision in the summer of 1920.[43]

The deputy chief loved the wilderness. He insisted that these town-raised college men carefully check all camping sites for fire and also work on the trails, keeping up the portages to the different lakes in their district, allowing access in case of a fire. He told them they must never drink in the woods. While he pressured them to work hard, he was fair and "really wasn't the driver or taskmaster he pretended to be." Years later Haddow remembered his boss as "a well-trained, lean, energetic man" who made a strong impression. Haddow that summer took a photo of Archie and Jim Espaniel, his Ojibwa canoe partner, on a portage.[44] In the picture one sees the genuine joy and contentment of the deputy chief in the Mississagi River country.

Ed and Lottie Sawyer and their family of six children knew him well in Bisco. Like Jack Leve, if they found him under the weather this couple, who themselves did not drink, would take him home and sober him up. For a number of summers Ed worked with Archie on the fire range. His wife, Lottie, one of the first white children to be born in the area, a woman who could skin beavers and shoot moose with a .303 rifle with deadly aim, also liked him.

The lumberman's assault on northern Ontario's remaining pine forests genuinely worried Archie. With the Sawyers, true friends of the forest, Archie spoke from the heart of his hatred of the lumbermen. He did not claim to be religious but sometimes he would write out on birchbark and post signs saying: "GOD MADE THIS COUNTRY FOR THE TREES DON'T BURN IT UP AND MAKE IT LOOK LIKE HELL" and "GOD MADE THE COUNTRY BUT MAN DESTROYED IT." Archie wanted the Canadian, or the Ontario, government to make the rugged Mississagi country, with its magnificent original stands of timber, into a park.[45]

The Sawyers saw the best, the humorous, side of Archie. An entertaining guest he was. Once at the Sawyers he disputed the theory of evolution, that man descended from monkeys. How ridiculous, he said. "Monkeys didn't drink, beat up their wives, run off."[46]

Young children, such as the Sawyer's oldest daughter, Libby, saw through Archie's rough exterior. Libby never heard him swear or act offensively. When in town drunk, or sober, he bought oranges or peanuts for the kids. He loved to play tricks on Libby, whom he called "Jidimo," the Ojibwa word for squirrel. Once on her birthday he bought her a box of candy, a big two-kilo box of chocolates with plastic violets on it. Carefully he placed the box in the middle of the path upon which he saw his young friend walking toward him. Then from his hiding place Archie gently pulled it away with a string. Once she caught on, the trickster came forward and handed over her present. Libby liked immensely this "endearing rebel."[47] Years later she said that "Archie was one of the nicest things that happened to me when I was growing up."[48]

In Bisco, Archie's best friends were the Espaniels, or L'Espagnols (French for "Spaniards"), an Ojibwa family with whom he lived for several years in the early 1920s. He considered Alex Espaniel as "a kind of adopted father of mine"[49] and, in many respects, Alex was the only real father Archie ever had. Alex's son Jim, and Jane, his younger daughter, became Archie's life long friends. Alex's father, Louis Espaniel, had run a small HBC outpost at Pogamising, just east of Bisco. Louis' grandfather, the original L'Espagnol, or "Spaniard," in some ways had been a late-eighteenth-century Spanish equivalent of Archie Belaney, a white man who had adopted an Indian lifestyle. The Spanish adventurer had joined the Ojibwa around the post of La Cloche, on the north shore of Lake Huron, after the British Conquest. He married a local Indian woman and came to lead her band.[50]

Alex was born at Pogamising on Christmas Day, 1870. Anxious that he secure a good education, Louis sent him to a Roman Catholic boarding school in Montreal. Alex studied in French and to the end of his days in Bisco loved to read Montreal's *La Presse*.[51] A good trapper, he also guided and prospected.

A generous man, he was always buying food for someone or paying for someone to go to the hospital. He welcomed Archie into his home. Alex's wife, Anny, and the Espaniels' six children found Archie excellent company. Anny Nootchai Espaniel had been raised at the Whitefish Reserve near Sudbury and as a young woman had worked as the housekeeper for several of Sudbury's doctors. Like her husband, she knew the non-Indian world well.[52]

Archie stayed with the Espaniels for two or three years and joined them for two winters at their trapping ground at Indian Lake on the east branch of the Spanish River, just above Archie's hunting ground at Mozhabong Lake.[53] In one of his notebooks Archie paid Alex this compliment: "Early days everything speedy, rip tearing speed. After I met Alex Spaniel more calm & quiet contentment, little intimate enjoyments, the appreciation of the woods in its fuller sense."[54] From the Espaniels, Archie learned the "Indian way of doing things"—which in Jim Espaniel's words "the white man calls conservation."[55] Archie must keep track of the number of lodges in his hunting territory and the age of their inhabitants. Most important of all, he must leave a pair behind in each lodge.[56]

The Espaniels helped Archie immensely over one of the most difficult periods of his life. Occasionally, in his bewilderment, he became completely irresponsible, once even to the point of using dynamite to blow up a beaver lodge. Alex soundly scolded him when he heard of this outrage and warned him he would never trap with him if he did this again. When Anny Espaniel found dynamite caps in Archie's bedroom, she kicked him out. "You can come back when you get rid of them." He did. Years later Archie sent the Espaniels a copy of *Pilgrims of the Wild* with this inscription: "To one whom I am proud to call 'Dad', & who taught me much of whatever I may know."[57]

After Grey Owl's death, Anny Espaniel recalled the long conversations Archie had with her husband at their house and the evenings when he did his writing beside the flickering oil lamp in their kitchen: "He could speak Indian but not so good when he came here to live with us after the war. He used to study my Indian prayer book to get the words right . . . Archie Belaney used to keep my husband up until 2 o'clock in the morning asking about the old days of my people. He used to take notes in a little book on everything my husband said."[58]

Archie poured his excess energy (and his loneliness) into his note-taking, and later his writing. Jim Espaniel recalled:

> He used to take notes whenever he thought of anything in the bush. We worked from 4:30 in the morning until nine at night in those days, and when Belaney was finished he would sometimes make notes in his notebook. When we came back to the house here in Biscotasing in the spring, Belaney wrote from those notes. He had nearly a packsack of material written on pad sheets when he left here. He would write so much and then roll it up and file it in the packsack.[59]

At his trapping cabin Archie also scribbled away story after story after story. Ted Cusson remembers the winter they spent together on Archie's hunting ground on Mozhabong Lake, about fifty kilometres south of Bisco. For long hours he sat on his bunk smoking his meerschaum pipe and writing.[60] Often the stories ran to thirty or forty pages. He included notes of where he went, of the animals he had seen, and of the weather that particular day.[61] He included sketches, too, of animals, trappers, and Indians. When he read books and magazines he often took notes.[62]

For one who had lived so long within himself, night held no terrors. Ted could not understand Archie's strange practice of travelling through the forest in the dark. It make him a very poor trapping partner the next day.[63] Later Archie explained in *The Men of the Last Frontier* his love of night journeying: "Few can realize, without the experience, the feeling of wildness and barbaric freedom that possesses the soul of one who travels alone in the dark, out on the edge of the world; when anything may happen, beasts of all kinds are abroad, and flitting shapes appear and disappear, dimly seen by the light of the stars.[64] Always Archie wanted to be busy because, in his words, "only high-pressure activity keeps the mind from wandering into the black abyss of introspection."[65]

In Bisco he often became, to use his own description of a man he once guided, "a human distillery."[66] He also had another demanding activity in Bisco, trying to pass as an Indian. To appear Indian he dyed his brown hair jet-black and coloured his skin brown with henna. For hours he posed in front of a mirror trying to get an Indian-looking expression on his face.[67] Whenever he saw old-time Indians like Big Otter or To-gense, he talked with them in Ojibwa.[68] Harry Woodworth often saw him at the HBC store and later commented: "Nothing made Archie Belaney prouder than to be termed a full-blooded Indian. . . . If he was standing around the store and some newcomers pointed him out as a 'real Indian' he was pleased as Punch."[69]

Archie also gave special attention to his "Indian war dance" which he introduced at Bisco. His war dance surprised the local Ojibwa and Cree for, as fur buyer Jack Leve put it, "the Bisco Indians didn't know his brand of Indian lore."[70] Archie's inspiration came, of course, from his boyhood reading of Fenimore Cooper and Longfellow. His boyhood acquaintance at the Hastings Grammar School, Con Foster, recalled an early version of it. Occasionally on the school grounds Archie and the Belaney gang "would capture some inoffensive little kid and torture him, but it was usually some pretty 'mother's darling', whose greatest agony would be that they made him late for lunch. I believe now that they only twisted his arm to make him howl loud enough to get some of us off the 'Flat', where we played football, to rescue him, so that they could have palefaces to operate against."[71]

Bisco's reaction to the war dance was honest. Some liked it. Bill Miller, a clerk at the HBC store, even old Harry Woodworth himself, the post manager, found it good fun. Jim Minnewasqua, the self-appointed chief of the Bisco Indians, joined in, as did To-gense, the brother of Sabik (Yellow Rock), an Ojibwa with known spiritual powers from the Mississagi River. Until he married in 1923, Jim Espaniel participated, as did Ferg Legace.[72] Others though, such as Edith Langevin, detested the war dances as one more excuse for more drinking. The participants headed for the high wine can, or moonshine, immediately after the dance.[73] Robert McWatch, a Cree Indian then living in Chapleau, sometimes visited Bisco. In his opinion, the knife-wielding, axe-shaking Archie Belaney was "half-crazy."[74] Many of the Anglican Ojibwa Indians from Fort Mattagami to the north (where the Rev. John Sanders had been raised) thought Archie's dance was evil, and they called him *Nottaway*, "Snake," a word they used for their traditional enemies the Iroquois Indians to the south.[75]

Usually soft-spoken (very seldom did he ever speak in a loud voice),[76] Archie became transformed in his war dance. Finally he stood at the centre.

The insecure, neglected Archie became the star. For the occasion he wore beaded moccasins, buckskins, and a headdress he made himself with turkey feathers and with red ribbons from the HBC store.[77] While he sang his war songs (all unrecognizable to the Ojibwa and Cree), he beat his drum made from a cheesebox with a deerskin covering over it. "Hi-Heh Ho! Hi-Heh, Hi-Heh, Ha! Hi-Heh, Hi-Heh, Ho! Hi-Ho, Hi-Ho, Ha!"[78] Archie chanted this as he entered at the head of his war party. The half-dozen men wore costumes made from brown cotton sold at the lumber company's store, on which Archie had painted designs and added animal teeth and skulls. The men danced with their knives or axes, whatever they had with them. Before starting out, as one participant put it, "we'd have a couple of drinks under our belt that would make you dance a lot better, at least you thought you danced a lot better with a few drinks."[79]

The big show came on May 24, 1923, Victoria Day, a celebration organized by Jack Leve, who later wrote up the day's activities for the Sudbury *Star.* The story, published on May 30, contains the first Canadian reference to Archie in print. "War Dance Given at Biscotasing. A Big Celebration Held on Victoria Day." In honour of the good queen to which his grandfather and namesake had sent his epic poem, *The Hundred Days of Napoleon,* Archie put on the greatest war dance of his life. It began at 8 P.M. after the afternoon's baseball games and canoe and foot races. They had taken a white prisoner, tied him to a pole, and now danced around him. As Jack Leve reported:

> The Chief began his death song by the beating of his drum, singing and mocking the prisoner. The chief and council then held a conversation in their own language in which they decided the fate of the prisoner. The chief then spoke in English which was a surprise to the prisoner, and explained to him that he had been educated and went through college and also told him the wrongs that the white man had done to the Indian. After this was over the fire was lit and, the entire tribe began their torture dance by beating their spears, knives and tomahawks by the flame of the fire. Then they danced around the prisoner, letting out wild yells and stabbing the prisoner with their weapons. The dance and torture lasted for about fifteen minutes after which the chief addressed the prisoner, telling him that he admired him for being a brave man and therefore let him free.
>
> Great credit is due to Mr. A. Belaney acting as chief and organizer of the performance, also to his assistant and second chief F. [Lagace].

Archie loved drama, particularly the visits of the police from Chapleau to arrest him for some misunderstanding such as a little knife-throwing down at the station.[80] Irene Shaughnessy, the new nineteen-year-old schoolteacher who arrived in the village in January 1924, soon became acquainted with the fugitive. At noon one day she came back to the boardinghouse where she stayed (Mrs. Legace had retired by this time), to find that Mrs. Kohls had made Archie a huge meal. He had his toboggan ready. Then, suddenly, a policeman appeared in sight of the boardinghouse. Off Archie went, escaping again, just in the nick of time.[81] Although now a man in his mid-thirties, Archie still was playing basically the same game that he had played as a teenager with Constable Joshua Stone in Hastings.

Shortly before this, Irene had met Archie Belaney for the first time. She had only been in Bisco a month when one day she heard the sounds of Indian drums and tramping outside. Indians! Jack Leve and two commercial travellers rushed out of their rooms. As the fur buyer quickly pushed the long-haired man in buckskins out of the boardinghouse, he protested, "Who do you think you are? the Proprietor of this Hotel, or the King of England?" While the war-like Indian and his two friends in grey blankets backed away, he pointed out that they had only come to serenade the new teacher.

The young farmgirl from near Barrie, Ontario, was terrified. Shortly afterwards, Ernestine Messervier, a Bisco girlfriend, tipped her off. Archie was harmless. Ernestine told her that he had been in the poolroom drinking and his drinking partners had put him up to it. Shortly afterwards Archie met the new schoolteacher again and this time made a very favourable impression with his piano playing and his fascinating stories. He told her all about Buffalo Bill and recounted for her the story of Custer's Last Stand.[82]

Early in April 1925 Edgar Pellow, the Justice of the Peace at Chapleau, issued another warrant for Archie Belaney. The charge read he had "unlawfully conduct[ed] himself in a disorderly manner whilst drunk at Biscotasing Railway Station."[83] Aimless, directionless and lost, Archie did not know what to do next. Suddenly, three months later he decided to leave Bisco for good and returned to Temagami, of all places. He left in early July.[84] Harry Woodworth, Bisco's unofficial law officer, did not understand why he went. He later commented: "Archie Belaney had one or two drinks too many and was 'owl hooting' at the station. It was just a plain case of being drunk. He didn't really leave town to escape the warrant, I don't think. He was going away anyhow."[85]

Two years earlier, about 1923, Archie had visited Angele, the first time he had seen her since he returned from the war. She was very ill with pneumonia, and he saw her at the hospital at neighbouring Haileybury.[86] He knew she still loved him, and the existence of this safe, sure friend probably drew him back.

While he guided in Temagami in the summer of 1925, Archie often stayed with Angele. Early the next spring, Angele would give birth to their second daughter, Flora[87] (Agnes was now fourteen). He spent his time much as he had done fifteen years earlier. His daughter Agnes recalled, "He wasn't interested in the white people." He would go and visit Aleck Paul and his family, "and sit there and listen for he could understand Indian. And he used to take notes of everything they were saying."[88]

Angele never forgot his last words to her that fall: "I go away. I will come back sometime. I like travel." She still loved him, and as she knew that he "liked to go and travel in the Indian way," she made him a new leather costume.[89] She saw him off at the train station in the fall of 1925. Angele never saw Archie again. Fifteen years after he first married her, he could not tear down the barriers of solitude that he had built around himself. He feared intimacy.

8   Anahareo

"There he stood, tall, straight, and handsome, gazing wistfully across the lake in the direction from which he had come. As he stood there with his paddle in his hand, his attitude seemed to express such yearning and loneliness that my heart quite went out to him. . . . what really set my imagination afire was his long hair and wide-brimmed hat. . . . In my imagination, this man looked like the ever so thrilling hero of my youth, Jesse James, that mad, dashing and romantic Robin Hood of America." So wrote Gertrude Bernard, or "Pony," as her friends called her, almost half-a-century after she first saw Archie Belaney in the late summer of 1925.[1] The attraction proved mutual when the thirty-six-year-old guide met the nineteen-year-old waitress at Camp Wabikon on Lake Temagami.

Although they only saw each other a few times before Pony returned to her home at Mattawa, on the Ottawa River, Archie became infatuated with her. He found the attractive Iroquois woman, half his age, "cultured, talented and personable."[2] He wanted her to join him on his new trapping grounds in northern Quebec. That winter Archie had to move to Quebec as Ontario that June had prohibited non-Indians from trapping beaver and other fur-bearing animals. Legally speaking, for all his camouflages, Archie was a non-Indian. He was not registered as an Indian under the federal Indian Act. For that matter neither was Pony. Her grandparents had left the "oppression and the poverty" of their home reserve at Oka, near Montreal, decades earlier and had lost their Indian status.[3]

Pony's mother had died when she was only four years old. Her paternal grandmother had initially raised her in Mattawa. When her elderly grandmother could no longer care for her, Pony lived with an aunt and uncle, and later joined her widowed father and her brother and sister. An adventurous young woman, she loved the outdoors, particularly her camping trips with her father and the trips in the spring to the sugar bush to collect maple sap. Bright and intelligent, she had easily become bored at grade school and had played hooky a great deal.[4] In her future husband's words, she "was not highly educated, save in that broader sense which is much to be desired, and is not always the result of schooling."[5]

Just a few weeks before she first met Archie, Pony's future had all been planned for her. Shortly after her summer job ended at Wabikon, she was off to Toronto to upgrade her education. Two wealthy American tourists at Wabikon had offered to pay all her fees at Loretto Abbey, a Roman Catholic boarding school. But the appearance of this modern desperado, with long hair, wide-brim hat, and a revolver, changed the picture. As she later wrote, "The prospect of going into the north with a real live Jesse James had set my imagination afire."[6]

Both Archie and Pony later wrote accounts of their life together from 1925 to 1931. By far Archie's classic *Pilgrims of the Wild*, his best book, is the more dramatic and better-written. But as historical records, her two volumes—*My Life with Grey Owl* (1940) and *Devil in Deerskins* (1972)[7] —rank much higher. Grey Owl's opening statement in *Pilgrims* about their courtship serves as a good example of the fictional gloss he gave his narrative. Throughout *Pilgrims* he used his considerable imaginative powers to create the impression that he had controlled the relationship from the outset. "The affair was quite wanting in the vicissitudes and the harrowing, but stirring episodes that are said to usually beset the path of high romance. The course of true love ran exasperatingly smooth; I sent the lady a railroad ticket, she came up on a pullman and we were married, precisely according to plan."[8] In reality their courtship ran totally contrary to Archie's plans, and he almost lost her to the convent school in Toronto.

As she was under twenty-one (and Wabikon did not usually hire waitresses under that age), Isobel LeDuc, the camp's social manager, had acted as her guardian during her stay there.[9] Archie approached Pony's older friend about his intentions in late September. Pony had already returned to Mattawa when a rather timid Archie knocked on Isobel's door and asked to see her privately. As she recalled thirteen years later:

> I stepped outside, and he stood before me, a bit dramatically folded his arms and sank cross legged to the grass. Then he spoke, and right from the heart his words seemed to come, simply and sincerely. . . . He wanted to know of the proposed plan for her education by a Dr. Howard and his brother, of New York, and when I explained it to him, he said he did not want to stand in the way of this, for he appreciated all it meant. He was, however, very fearful that it would take her from him entirely.[10]

Archie next made a special visit to Mattawa to see Pony and her father. Before he journeyed into his new trapping ground near Doucet, in Abitibi in northern Quebec, he also wrote her every day for two weeks. She loved the lengthy notes: "They were something like a Walt Disney picture—had everything in them from soup to nuts. One contained a lengthy story about a weasel, and all that Archie saw of that weasel was its tracks in the snow, but yet he knew all about it, including its forefathers on both sides of the family."[11]

Pony still resisted, and when Archie made his last ploy in mid-February, he did so without any certainty she would accept. Only one day before she arrived at Doucet on February 25,[12] his trapping partner, Bill Cartier, had mailed a letter from Doucet to their friend, fur trader Jack Leve, welcoming him to visit them and do some trading. Bill made no reference to a woman joining Archie on the trapline. "Just a few lines to let you know that we are still all in best of Health & hope you are the same [.The] same old Bunch of Bisco [is] in the province of Quebec trapping that is Archie Belaney & the Bear [Ted Cusson] & Bill all trapping we are making out fine here."[13]

Bill, Ted Cusson, and Jim Pichette, another trapper from Ontario, had all helped Archie build a cabin for Pony, in case she did come, and Archie had set up his tent-cabin nearby for himself. Once she arrived, Bill, Ted and Jim obligingly transferred their trapping headquarters a few kilometres away.[14] These three good French Canadian friends had even lent him money to pay for Pony's ticket.[15]

The circumstances were most unusual—a town-bred Indian woman was taught how to survive in the northern forest by a white man born in England. The first day he led her to his camp. It was a long seventy-kilometre journey, all day on snowshoes. It was tough, but she made it.[16] Originally Pony had intended just to visit briefly and then go back out again. But very soon she learned to love the way of life and the man she had come to visit. Several years later she told a reporter, "I'm very lonesome in town. It's different in the bush and I feel more at home packing and paddling."[17]

Pony fitted in so well. After only one year together Archie wrote his aunts in Hastings enclosing a beautiful photo of her, with this inscription on the back: "This is my wife Gertie, an Iroquois chief's daughter 21 years old. Tall, slim & very strong. A woman of great courage & a true partner. Well-educated, talks perfect English; everybody likes her." Archie's three years with Pony in Abitibi would be the happiest of his life.[18]

Archie found Abitibi "magnificently spectacular with its 6 or 8 feet of snow & fine timber & surroundings,"[19] but the Bisco Bunch had not come for the winter scenery. The Ontario government's trapping ban[20] had forced them east to Quebec's forested area along the Canadian National Railway in eastern Abitibi, which remained open. They had come to Doucet after hearing that marten and lynx abounded there.[21]

The Bisco Bunch, with hundreds of others, invaded the trapping grounds of the Grand Lac Victoria and Lac Simon Indians, now opened up by the new railway across Abitibi, completed only about ten years earlier. This Algonquin Indian group, who spoke a slightly different dialect of Ojibwa than did the Indians to the west, had never signed a treaty with the federal government. Their predicament was exactly the same as that of the Indians at Temagami, and exactly the same as other northern Indian groups, such as the Crees of Lubicon Lake in northern Alberta, today.

Like the Temagami Indians, the Algonquins had neither a reserve nor any recognized control over their hunting grounds. One Indian hunter in the winter of 1925–26 actually had twelve white men trapping on his family hunting territory. Disease had taken so many of the band that its approximately 180 surviving members could not protect their lands. As the white newcomers trapped an area until it became barren, to protect themselves from exploitation the Indians began to do the same.[22]

Ignace or Nias Papaté, the chief of the Grand Lac Victoria and Lac Simon band, reviewed the band's predicament in a letter written in 1927 in Algonquin to the Department of Indian Affairs. The non-Indian hunters had invaded their grounds from the newly constructed Canadian National Railway, "and as a result we have no place to go to earn for our families. When these whitemen see anything belonging to Indians in the bush they do not hesitate in taking it, although the Bible says that no man should steal. They also cause much sickness among our Indians as they make bad medicine and whiskey for them. They also set poison in the bush."[23]

Initially Archie forgot the troubles of the Indians. Smitten with Pony, he ignored all else. At night he talked to her about books and read aloud to her, as his Aunt Ada years before had done for him.[24] At Doucet he read her James Fenimore Cooper's *Last of the Mohicans* and Robert Service's poetry.[25] Anxiously he sought to please her, even suggesting that she cut off his long hair, a move Pony welcomed. (When she completed the job, though, and saw how poorly Archie looked with his boney neck and his ears sticking out, she vowed never to cut it again.)[26]

For probably the first time in his life he also began to talk about himself, his real self. He told the young woman about his painful, lonely childhood, about Angele and his early adventures in Temagami, his days in Bisco—even about Marie and their son Johnny, and about Ivy, his English wife.[27] Quickly Pony had shown herself a trusted friend. She did not criticize him, or judge him, she just listened sympathetically. After her mother died she, too, had been raised by an overbearing aunt. Archie's marital adventures also fitted in perfectly with his Jesse James image.

Momentarily Archie brought down the high barrier he had spent a lifetime building up around himself. As he later recorded of her in a notebook: "Insurmountable wall, which I never overcome, which exists really only in imagination, until [at] the last discover no wall."[28] This young woman was helping to heal him, by drawing the poison out. But he panicked and stopped. The period of full communication between Pony and Archie lasted only their first two or three years together. How close he came to admitting that he was not part-Indian, we will never know. Even with her, he would not disclose the falseness of his identity. Even with her, he could not reveal his true, inner self.

During their long conversations Pony had told him about her Iroquois background and her ancestors at Oka. She spoke about her great-great-grandfather, Chief Naharrenou, her great-grandmother, Mary Robinson, a white woman brought to Oka as a captive. Her grandmother had told her about the family's later wanderings from Oka to Mattawa. Filtering the information through his romantic imagination, Archie Indianized the name of the young woman named Gertrude Bernard. She became "Anahareo," a name he abbreviated from that of "Naharrenou." [29] Although in their correspondence he called her Gertie or Gertrude, [30] in his classic, *Pilgrims of the Wild* (1934), she was Anahareo.

Gradually, as Anahareo came to know him better, she discovered weaknesses he tried very hard to hide. Archie, she found, had surprisingly little self-confidence. He loathed conflict and if they had an argument, afterwards he "felt miserably" and "always humbly apologized, whether or not he was responsible for the discord." [31] She learned, too, of his poor health, particularly his weak heart. Occasionally he had spells of weakness (a condition he attributed to the war) when he would almost faint. [32] Already they probably both realized that his days as an active trapper were numbered.

Anahareo soon realized how sentimental Archie could be. "He always wanted to keep a piece of bone of any animal that made a particular impression on him, whether that impression was good or bad." At Bisco he had kept a trunk full of mementos, including four kilos of negatives of pictures he had taken, bits of cloth from old friends' clothing, pine cones and stones from places dear to him. Once he had paddled back thirty kilometres to find a little decorated spoon that he had been given as a souvenir the last day he served in the army. He had left it on a portage. [33]

What impressed Anahareo greatly was his sense of justice for the Indian. When the local band approached Archie to help in a court case, he immediately accepted. Two band members had been accused of burning down a trappers' shack and ruining their traps by pouring coal oil over them (no animal will go near a trap which smells of kerosene). Yet the Indians had only done so because the two white trappers had used strychnine, the winter before, as a bait for wolves and foxes. The trappers failed to retrieve the unused bait at the end of the season and many of the Indians' huskies subsequently died from eating the poison. In a courtroom in Amos, about 100 kilometres to the west, Archie argued their case, explaining the Indians' side of the incident. He pointed out that the white trappers' use of strychnine was illegal in itself. Instead of the maximum sentence of two years, the judge gave the Indians only thirty days. [34]

The Indians gave the credit for the light sentence to Archie and invited him and Anahareo to visit their encampment at Lac Simon southwest of Doucet in early June 1926. Chief Nias Papaté welcomed them. Before leaving to spend the summer as a Quebec fire ranger, manning a fire tower, Archie and Anahareo stayed at Lac Simon. At their request, the white-haired chief pronounced them man and wife on the second last day of their visit.[35]

The summer of 1926 passed quickly and happily, but the thought of another winter alone each day in a cabin appalled Anahareo. That winter she insisted that she join Archie on his trapline. The town-bred Anahareo hated what she saw. In Archie's words, "The sight of frozen twisted forms contorted in shapes of agony, and the spectacle of submissive despairful beasts being knocked senseless with an axe handle, and hung up in a noose to choke out any remaining spark of life while the set was being made ready for a fresh victim, moved her to a deep compassion."[36] Her concern slowly had its effect on Archie, gradually weakening his resolve to trap. Already he knew the beaver was becoming extremely scarce. This had forced him and the Bisco Bunch out of Ontario.

Since he arrived in Abitibi, Archie had talked with many Indians. What they told him confirmed what he had already seen in Ontario: overtrapping threatened the beaver's very survival.

> I had sat in council with the Simon Lake Ojibways and had talked with other bands from Grand Lake Victoria, Waswanipis from the Megiskan, Obijuwans from the head of the St. Maurice, wide-ranging half-breeds from far off Peribonka, they all carried the same tale. The beaver were going fast; in large areas they were already gone. Was this then, to be the end? Beaver stood for something vital, something essential in this wilderness, were a component part of it; they *were* the wilderness.[37]

Slowly, the influence of Anahareo, his own poor health, and a personal realization that Quebec would soon join Ontario in banning non-Indian beaver trapping, led him to a crossroad in his life. The passage in his letter to Mrs. Parsons about his regret at killing a lynx, written nearly ten years earlier, hints that already he was predisposed to abandoning the hunt. At this very moment his mother in England re-surfaced.

During the winter of 1926–27 Archie had again corresponded with his aunts—and mother. Shortly after Anahareo's twenty-first birthday on June 18, 1927, he had sent his aunts a striking photo of her, announcing that she was his wife, apparently leaving then to deduce on their own that he had again left Angele.[38] Presumably from his aunts, his mother obtained his address.

Archie had last seen his mother, Kittie, at the London General Hospital at Denmark Hill, just after his major operation on his injured right foot.[39] He had so little respect for her that he left England without giving her his address. She wrote to the Canadian government in September 1919.

> Will you kindly inform me if you can of the address of my son A. S. Belaney late Pte. who returned to Canada to obtain his discharge last year.
>
> Also will you tell me if I am entitled to any allowance of any kind from the Canadian Government. My youngest son Hugh Belaney is now an incurable mental case through shell shock & wounds. I am in financial distress

entirely owing to the war. My husband J. Scott Brown who was a prisoner two years civilian is entirely unable to support myself and small son.
I am in receipt of nothing from the English government. An answer will be appreciated.

(Signed K. Scott Brown)[40]

Archie already knew about Hugh, as he had been released from the First East Surrey Regiment of the British Army in May 1917, four months before Archie left England.[41] He had to be institutionalized for the remainder of his life. But what could Archie do? Already he had his own host of problems. Eventually Kittie did reach her son,[42] and they corresponded, she informing him of her husband's death in the mid-1920s. When her son Leonard Scott-Brown decided to join the Hudson's Bay Company, Leonard wrote Archie who, he understood, traded with the HBC. As Kittie later recalled, "A letter came to me in answer to Leonard's. The letter was so poetic that I sent it to *Country Life*. Their reply was that they would like him to write an article. They were so pleased with that they published it. He then sent them *The Men of the Last Frontier*."[43]

Kittie's and Archie's original letters to the English magazine *Country Life* are now lost, but two summaries, one compiled after Grey Owl's death by Lovat Dickson and the second by Grey Owl's friend Betty Somervell, survive.[44] Kittie Scott-Brown began the *Country Life* correspondence in late 1927, or early 1928. Her son replied first from Doucet, Abitibi, on April 5, 1928, as Archie Belaney, and later that year wrote from Cabano, Témiscouata County, in eastern Quebec, on October 3, 1928. At some point between these two dates he reached his decision to renounce the beaver hunt.

Unfortunately, Archie gives no time references in his "autobiography," *Pilgrims of the Wild*. He treats dates so cavalierly that he condenses three entire years in the book (1926 to 1928) into one.[45] He makes only one brief reference to his visit to Lac Simon.[46] He excludes any reference to the summers of 1926 and 1927 spent in a Quebec fire tower. Yet his description of his reluctance in the late 1920s to leave the beaver hunt rings true. He wrote:

> Don't imagine that there was any sudden and complete renunciation such as overcomes the luckless and often temporarily aberrated victim of a highly emotionalized revival meeting; this would have been, at best, but temporary. It was a slow, hard process fraught with many mental upheavals and self-examinations, and numerous back-slidings and reversals to type, and it involved a self-discipline as severe as any that the trail, with all its stern severities, had ever imposed upon me.[47]

Pilgrims of the Wild contains a lengthy section on the one central incident that the author claims led to the adoption of two beaver kits. In the spring beaver hunt, Archie had trapped and killed a mother beaver. Suddenly he heard the crying of two surviving motherless kits. Once he spotted them, he wanted to shoot, but Anahareo begged him to spare them. "Let us save them. It is up to us, after what we've done."[48] Surprisingly Archie agreed to save them, and in so doing made his first important step towards becoming a preserver of the endangered beaver.

During the course of the following winter and the summer of 1929, the two kits won Archie over completely to the cause of working for the animal's survival. After a false start, when they called them "Ivanhoe" and "Hawkeye," he and Anahareo re-named them "McGinnis" and "McGinty," as the kits reminded them of two industrious Irishmen.[49] Movingly Archie wrote of their effect on him:

> Their little sneezes and childish coughs, their little whimpers and small appealing noises of affection, their instant and pathetically eager response to any kindness, their tiny clinging hand-like forepaws, their sometimes impatiently stamping feet, and their little bursts of independence, all seemed to touch a chord of tenderness for the small and helpless that lays dormant in every human heart.[50]

By the end of the summer he had a plan:

> To kill such creatures seemed monstrous. I would do no more of it. Instead of persecuting them further I would study them, see just what there really was to them. I perhaps could start a colony of my own; these animals could not be permitted to pass completely from the face of this wilderness.[51]

For an unknown reason, Archie decided in the fall of 1928 to relocate from Doucet to Cabano in Témiscouata, on the New Brunswick border, and to establish his beaver colony there. It was a foolish decision, as he had hoped to support himself and Anahareo, and his beaver colony, through the continued trapping of fur-bearing animals other than the beaver. But Témiscouata had little fur potential. This forced Archie and Anahareo to live off his army disability pension of $15 a month.[52] To supplement this meagre income, he began to sell articles, the first he did for *Country Life*.

In eastern Quebec, Archie completed his essay for *Country Life*. He did his very best. The article praised the work of the non-Indian trapper. "Side by side with modern Canada lies the last battleground in the long drawn out bitter contest between civilisation and the forces of nature." In striking image, he compared the northern forests to cathedrals. Amidst the "apparently endless black forests of spruce—stately trees, cathedral-like with their tall spires above and their gloomy aisles below," stands "the pathfinder of today," the trapper.[53] Several years later he would improve this image, by eloquently comparing "the solemn, cloistered naves in vast, venerable cathedrals, along whose shadowy aisles silence broods uninterruptedly" to the "age-old forest among whose high transepts the slightest footfall echoes hollowly in seemingly endless, ever lessening reverberations."[54]

Archie's correspondence with his London publisher continued after the publication of his article on March 2, 1929. The piece had impressed this important British magazine. *Country Life* now requested a book. Gradually Archie now transformed himself from a trapper to an Indian. If he wrote as a North American Indian he knew that his public would credit him with an insight into nature denied non-native writers. From Cabano on May 6, 1929, he wrote to *Country Life* of Indians as "them," but claimed to have been adopted by the Ojibwa about twenty years earlier. By November 5, 1929, he reported to his English editor that "for about 15 years he spoke nothing but Indian." On November 12, 1930, he signed himself "Grey Owl" for the first time, after once trying out the name, "White Owl." [55] The choice of his new name came easily. Had he not imitated the hoot of an owl since his boyhood days in Hastings? Like him many owls were active at night.

On February 2, 1931, the new Grey Owl announced to *Country Life* that he had "Indian blood." Five months later he completed his transformation. On July 1, 1931, he declared himself an "Indian writer" who "writes as an Indian." [56]

David White Stone, an Algonquin Indian friend from Ontario in his early fifties, [57] joined Anahareo and Archie at Birch Lake, about sixty kilometres or so northeast of Cabano, where they wintered in 1928–29. Later they moved closer to Cabano, to Lake Touladi where, in the spring of 1929, disaster occurred. They lost McGinnis and McGinty, both nearly a year old, probably to a local hunter. They searched for weeks without success, until Dave finally captured and gave them two new kits. They christened the beaver that lived, "The Boss" or "Jelly Roll." Archie and Anahareo then moved to Hay Lake, only seven or eight kilometres from Cabano, and lived in an empty lumberman's cabin. [58]

Archie's writing at Hay Lake carried a heavy price tag. It cost him the presence of the one human being he wanted with him. Once he started preparing his book, he stopped communicating with her. He retreated once again within himself. He resumed his inner journey. Anahareo could not stand it. As she later told a newspaper reporter: "He needs to be alone when he is writing. If someone is around him it affects his work." [59] Anahareo left for long periods and refused to subordinate her life to his. For once, Archie had met his match. She would not nurse him or take care of him like the other women had.

During Anahareo's absences, Archie's best friends in the small community of Cabano, population 1,500, became the Grahams, one of the town's few English-speaking families. Regularly he went there for meals, and played classical music on their piano. Archie enjoyed the Graham family. "A carefree happy-go-lucky group of people they were, who cared little whether I wore my hat backwards, sideways, or at all, and who made my coming the signal for a gay party of music and singing." [60]

If one accepts alcoholism "as recurring trouble, problems or difficulties associated with drinking,"[61] Archie by 1930 had become an alcoholic. He liked to drink vanilla extract, the heavily alcoholic flavouring. Occasionally he also went with some Cabano men to Rivière-du-Loup and bought beer there, as Cabano had no outlet. Despite his wild nature, the Grahams liked the sober version of their interesting friend. Like others before them, the McCormicks, Angele, the Espaniels, and Ivy, they tried to help him. They gave him warm clothes, fed him, and even lent him money. To pay them back, he gave them deer meat.[62]

Among the French Canadians, Archie believed himself to be living in a "foreign land."[63] He resented the fact that the French Canadians called him a *sauvage*, and not an *Indien*. He replied back, "Je ne suis pas 'sauvage', je suis Indien." When in a restaurant in Rivière-du-Loup once with Bernie Graham, he ordered his meat and vegetables raw. "If they think I'm a *sauvage* I might as well act like one."[64]

In Cabano, Father Jean-Philippe Cyr ran the town. Without using the cleric's name, Archie mentioned him in *Pilgrims of the Wild*. "The priest, a learned gentleman, proficient in languages and a keen student of human nature, took a scholarly and benevolent interest in us and our manner of living, and visited us on more than one occasion."[65] The statement is revealing. It once again hints at the fantasy world in which Archie lived. Did the priest really take "a scholarly and benevolent interest in us and our manner of living"? In fact, Father Cyr only talked once to Archie, when someone had reported to the clergyman that the Indian drank turpentine![66] Others had seen him in a drunken state with his equivalent of a Saint's medal dangling around his neck, an empty vanilla extract bottle.[67]

Turpentine sounds unlikely, but occasionally Archie made moonshine at his camp. He loved to write his articles late at night by the oil lamp, with a case of extract by his side.[68] Alcohol must have stimulated a few of the stories he told his editor at *Country Life*. In March 1930, for instance, he wrote of the time he and some American cowboys attended a Mexican bullfight. "I was with a bunch at a bull-fight in a Mexican village, where some cowboys present were so incensed at the cruelty to the horses, that they shot up the arena, killing the bull, the horses, and one of the fighters. We only got safely out of the ring by a judicious display of hardware."[69]

His drinking, and the fantasies spelt out in his letters to *Country Life*, hint at his chronic loneliness. When Anahareo left for the summer in 1929 he lost his only human bond with the world. He had told her things about himself (without revealing his true identity) that he had never told anyone else. In *Pilgrims* he wrote that after her departure, "I was lonesome for the first time in my life."[70] In reality, he had spent his life in this condition.

We have two independently drawn portraits of Archie in his early forties, the first dates back to the late summer of 1929 and the second probably two months later. Anahareo had returned at the time of both visits. The first sketch of Archie Belaney comes from the pen of Wilfrid Bovey, who met him at Métis, a popular summer resort for English-speaking Montrealers on the St. Lawrence Estuary, east of Rivière-du-Loup. The family of Colonel Wilfrid Bovey, the director of Extra-Mural Relations and Extension at McGill University, and assistant to Sir Arthur Currie, McGill's principal, had summered at Métis for half-a-century.[71] Towards the end of the summer, Archie and Anahareo, with Jelly Roll, had come by train to this fashionable resort in the hopes of raising some money for their proposed beaver colony. Through the kindness of Madeline Peck, a summer resident from Montreal, a lecture was organized at the Seaside Hotel. Mrs. Peck had asked Colonel Bovey to thank the speaker in Indian costume. "Although somewhat reluctant at first," her son, Richard, recalled, the Colonel became Archie's strong supporter "as soon as he was aware of his potential."[72] His fine speaking skills and the quality of his conservationist message impressed Wilfrid Bovey.

One of the best passages in Archie's *Pilgrims of the Wild* relates to his visit to Métis. Before speaking before the crowd of about a hundred at the Seaside Hotel, Archie recalled that he "felt a good deal like a snake that has swallowed an icicle, chilled from one end to the other."[73] Yet, this veteran actor performed very well.

Several months after his Métis visit, Colonel Bovey tried to help Archie by securing him an additional veteran's pension. On November 26, 1929, he wrote to G. A. Harcourt of the Pension Board.

> He told me that finding himself at Cabano without much money, he had come to Metis, not an expensive trip, in hope of making a little. He not only did not make any, but spent all he had and was reduced to exhibiting a tame beaver for ten cents admission. As I frequently visited him at his tent, I know quite well what he had and did not have in the way of food, etc.
>
> At the time that he asked for transportation he had no money. By the time it had arrived, he had made some by doing a little guiding which I arranged for him by giving one or two talks in a hotel. This he did quite well. I cannot at the moment remember how much he made but with some other small gifts, accounting to about fifteen dollars or so, I think the total was about ninety dollars.
>
> . . . As regards his wife, I do not suppose that he is entitled to any additional pension. His wife cannot be more than twenty years of age, if she is that.[74]

Within less than six years this same impoverished woodsman would be renowned as the best-known Canadian author and lecturer of his day. Métis gave him his start.

Early in November 1929 a Quebec City newspaper editor called on Archie at his shack near Cabano. Jean-Charles Harvey, then thirty-two years old, edited the Quebec City daily, *Le Soleil*.[75] He encountered the "beaver man," as he was becoming known in Témiscouata County, and Anahareo on a hunting trip with Jean-Leon Duchêne, his brother-in-law from Rivière-du-Loup.[76]

The Quebec City newspaper editor met Archie and Anahareo on a beautiful late fall afternoon at the abandoned lumber camp where they lived. To his surprise, Harvey discovered an Indian living an Indian's life, but one who was educated, cultivated, and full of poetry.[77] The visitors spent two days[78] with the supposedly part-Apache Indian and his wife and witnessed during their stay their host's amazing ability to call the beaver to him from the lake. Harvey, who loved the forest, once wrote that if he had lived at the beginning of French settlement in the St. Lawrence Valley, he would probably have chosen to be an Iroquois Indian rather than a French settler.[79] With Archie and Anahareo, the sensitive journalist later said, he had spent several of the happiest hours of his life.[80]

Anahareo left with Jean-Charles Harvey and his friends, joining them on their return trip back to Rivière-du-Loup and then on to Quebec City, where she boarded a train for northern Quebec and a winter of prospecting with Dave White Stone. The French Canadian journalist grasped the true nature of her relationship with Archie when he wrote years later that the very beautiful Anahareo was for Archie, "son inspiratrice, sa passion et son tourment"—his source of inspiration, his passion, his anguish.[81]

Again she had left. But what was she to do? Two years later she explained to a newspaper reporter that she needed her independence. "She wants to make her own way in the world, and at the same time she wants to help her husband make a success both of his writing and his chosen work among the beavers."[82]

All that winter of 1929–30, Archie worked fiendishly on his manuscript for *Country Life*, to appear in late 1931 as *The Men of the Last Frontier*. In his words, "I often awoke from sleep to make alterations, made constant notes . . . I erected a table alongside the bunk, so that I could sit there and reach out at any moment and jot down any notions that came along." At the cabin the beaver he called Jelly Roll was his only companion. The pet beaver lived there all winter, Archie sinking a small tank in the floor for his friend, who built a house inside the cabin. As he wrote in *Pilgrims*, "this sociable and home-loving beast, playful, industrious and articulate, fulfilled my yearning for companionship as no other creature save man, of my own kind especially, could ever have done."[83]

The book took infinitely longer than he had planned. When Anahareo returned to Cabano in the summer, he still was writing. Archie continued into the fall of 1930 refining, polishing, adjusting. Finally, Anahareo could not stand it any longer.

> I'd been home five months. It was already November, and I was happy to be there, but living with a person who is writing is worse than being alone. One feels that one must tiptoe at all times and check any spontaneous outburst of conversation, so when Archie told me that the book couldn't possibly be ready before January at the earliest, I had to admit to myself that I couldn't

face another week, let alone two more months, of this morgue-like atmosphere.[84]

She left and obtained a job driving a dog team for the tourists at the Seigneury Club, an exclusive resort in the Ottawa Valley, about half way between Montreal and Ottawa.[85]

The fact that Archie still needed money to supplement his pension cheque forced him to write more magazine articles for sale at the same time as he was writing his book. As Grey Owl, the son of a Scot and an Apache, he wrote a dozen stories in 1930 and 1931 for *Canadian Forest and Outdoors*, published by the Canadian Forestry Association.

Excited by the Indian's articles, Gordon Dallyn, editor of *Canadian Forest and Outdoors*, brought them to the attention of James Harkin, the Parks Branch Commissioner. Contact with Harkin set in motion a chain of developments which would help make Grey Owl a household name in Canada in the 1930s. The energetic and imaginative Commissioner of National Parks shared Grey Owl's concerns about wilderness. Since his appointment in 1911 as the first overseer of Canada's national park system, he had established many new parks and had initiated many measures that contributed to the greater protection of wildlife. Half-a-century before real conservation movements existed in Canada, he fought for both wildlife and wildlands preservation within Canada's national parks.[86] One of his early reports set forth his forward-looking philosophy.

> National Parks are maintained for all the people—for the ill that they may be restored; for the well that they may be fortified and inspired by the sunshine, the fresh air, the beauty, and all the other healing, ennobling agencies of Nature. They exist in order that every citizen of Canada may satisfy his craving for Nature and Nature's Beauty; that he may absorb the poise and restfulness of the forests; that he may fill his soul with the brilliance of the wild flowers and the sublimity of the mountain peaks; that he may develop the buoyancy, the joy, and the activity that he sees in the wild animals; that he may stock his brain and mind with great thoughts, noble ideals; that he may be made better, be healthier, and happier.[87]

James Harkin had already worked to protect the wood buffalo, the muskox, and the caribou.[88] Grey Owl's efforts to conserve the beaver intrigued him. Early in 1930 he sent J. C. Campbell, his office's publicity director, to meet Grey Owl at Cabano. If he agreed, Campbell told Grey Owl, the Parks Board would make a film of him and Jelly Roll and the new recruit, a year-old beaver baptised "Rawhide." The film would "provide a living argument for conservation."[89] Grey Owl agreed to participate.

His fame grew. In mid-November 1930 the Canadian Forestry Association asked Grey Owl to address their annual convention at the Windsor Hotel in Canada's largest city, Montreal,[90] and to show the new beaver film to the delegates. Anahareo left her job at the Seigneury Club to join her husband and to provide moral support.

Archie was extremely nervous. Despite his years of trapping, he still knew relatively little about beavers. Before the age of two, for example, it is extremely difficult to learn a beaver's sex, and he mistakingly believed that Jelly Roll was male—until she bore kits the following spring.[91]

Everything had happened so quickly. The newly acclaimed "beaver man," however, could not be certain that Jelly Roll and Rawhide, now wintering in their own lodge for the first time, would return to him in the spring. It appears that he was so insecure that he decided to announce that they had been killed.

At the very end of his address before the Forestry Association at the Windsor Hotel on January 23, 1931, Grey Owl made an extraordinary announcement. Someone had killed Jelly Roll and Rawhide. "I regret to say that lately, during my absence from camp, our little companions were removed from their lodge and killed."[92] *Canadian Forest and Outdoors* carried the full story in their issue of February 1931.

GREY OWL, VICTIM OF A DASTARDLY ACT

Grey Owl, who is spending his life in an effort to win public appreciation and so protection and conservation of the beaver, has been the victim of a dastardly act that his thousands of readers in Canada and the United States will resent. His beloved "Boss", or King of the Beaver, about whom he has written so appealingly, was just before Christmas brutally killed by a trespasser who, taking advantage of a day's absence on the part of Grey Owl, stole into his beaver home and clubbed the unsuspecting and friendly King of the Beaver to death. Not content with this outrage, the perpetrator did the same for the Boss' mate.[93]

Grey Owl later told the sequel to the tale in an unpublished article he wrote at Riding Mountain National Park in late April or May 1931. To follow his account, he had found an ice hole near the lodge with traces of blood around it and had assumed that a poacher had taken them. "I later ascertained that a passing hunter had cut the hole in the ice that I had found, to take a drink, and a muskrat had evidently used the aperture to climb out into the open some soft evening to be killed by an owl, as the half eaten body exposed by spring thaw revealed. And I had laboured for months under a harrowing but erroneous supposition."[94] In *Pilgrims* he tells a different version of the same story, reducing the period of anxiety to two weeks.[95] It was all fiction. Rawhide and a pregnant Jelly Roll emerged the next spring,[96] and all Archie's fears that they would not return to him were proven groundless.

Despite his fears, Grey Owl's talk went very well.[97] The association's favourable response to the man and the film gave James Harkin a second idea. The realistic Parks Branch commissioner knew only too well about Parliament's reluctance to grant money for parks. Consequently he always stressed their profitability. They brought in badly needed tourist dollars from abroad, and kept Canadians' own tourist dollars in Canada.[98] In Harkin's opinion, Grey Owl was the perfect candidate for a job in one of the national parks. The class of people who read his writings, travelled and, with his presence in one of the parks, would like to visit him.[99] Secondly, the Branch would promote his important conservation work by giving him a job. Years later Harkin described why he gave him a post. "The providing of a position for Grey Owl was entirely to serve our purpose of securing publicity for the National Parks and for wild life conservation by using Grey Owl's beaver and Grey Owl's personality as a spear-head in that connection."[100] Early in 1931 the Parks Branch would make its offer. Jean-Charles Harvey had been the first journalist to interview Archie Belaney, now known as Grey Owl, and, after his talk to the Forestry Association, a Montreal *Star* reporter became the second. The "Indian naturalist and author's" background interested the big city journalist even more than did his plea for the conservation of wild life and details of his home for two beavers in Témiscouata.

> Grey Owl is an Apache. From far Arizona, amid the Gicarilla [Jicarilla] tribe living along the north shores of the Rio Grande, he came to join Buffalo Bill's circus. He earned $60 a month doing war dances twice daily before Americans, and to the delight of pop-eyed London audiences when the circus visited London.
>
> Then Grey Owl came to Ontario to live, and trapped up north for some years. Now he runs a beaver "farm" in Temiscouata, and his founding of the sanctuary was more or less of an accident.
>
> On the floor beside him was an empty beer bottle, and on the bureau was a headache remedy, indicative of the fact he knew the ways of the white man as well as of the redskin. But his outlook was that of an Indian, even though he is fluent in speech. He has a vocabulary that would put many of his paleface brethren to shame.[101]

From the moment of this interview in January 1931 to Grey Owl's death in 1938, he became a favourite of Canada's press. His mission to save Canada's national emblem caught and held the media's attention. Moreover, the beaver man could explain his cause so eloquently, even poetically. And he looked so "Indian."

Anahareo noticed how Archie "liked all the attentions and fuss people lavished on him."[102] He knew exactly what he was doing. Just after the Montreal conference he adopted a new Ojibwa name to reinforce still further his Indian image. *Canadian Forest and Outdoors* spelt his Ojibwa name in their issue of March 1931, "Wa-shee-quon-asier."[103] Later he used the form "Washaquonasin" in *The Men of the Last Frontier* (published in late 1931),[104] and the Canadian edition of *Pilgrims of the Wild* bears "Wa-sha-quon-asin (Grey Owl)" as the author's name.[105]

His choice of this word, *washaquonasie* (it has an "e" not an "n" at the end),[106] offers a fascinating glimpse into his mind. The word refers in Ojibwa to the screech owl (*Otus asio*), many of which are greyish in colour.

In calling himself Grey Owl, he thus identified himself with this very common, small, small owl, and not with the rare, very large Great Grey Owl (*Strix nebulosa*). His self-image was so poor he saw himself as common, small, insignificant.

This one word also reveals more about Archie, his love of free transcriptions and translations of Ojibwa words. At first he translated the name "Washaquonasin, Grey Owl."[107] Yet, as Archie himself knew, *washaquonasie* referred to the screech owl; the Ojibwa do not think of the bird as a "grey owl." Instead their word, *wa-sha-quon-asie*, means "shining beak of the owl" or a "white beak owl."[108] The beak is this owl's important feature. Did Archie forget the proper transcription and translation of his new name when he baptised himself? Or, did he just prefer the sound of his form, "Washaquonasin" over "Washaquonasie"? In any event he later came up with a more original and dramatic translation of "Washaquonasin" than "Grey Owl." He translated it into English as, "He Who Walks By Night."[109] In reality, properly spelt, the word still only meant "white beak owl." Few non-Indians, however, knew Ojibwa and his public never noticed the inaccuracies.

The Canadian Parks Branch were enchanted with him, and they invited Grey Owl in the spring of 1931 to become the "caretaker of park animals" at Riding Mountain National Park in Manitoba. In his articles, books, films, interviews, and lectures, the "beaver man" would publicize the work of the Parks Branch.[110] At the start of the Great Depression, when hundreds of thousands of Canadians were thrown out of work, Archie got a job.

Lloyd Roberts, the son of the famous Canadian writer, Sir Charles G. D. Roberts, and himself a writer, came to know Grey Owl quite well. He first met him at Cabano in the early spring of 1931, at Riding Mountain National Park in October 1931, and several times in Ottawa in the mid-1930s. After he became better acquainted, Lloyd once asked his Apache friend why he presented himself so flamboyantly. He replied, justifying his showmanship: "People expect it. It means a great deal more to them to see me in beads and feathers than if they merely saw a plain woodsman playing with a beaver. This is something they will remember. And, brother, I *want* them to remember. That is part of my job! The more people who remember Grey Owl, the more there will be who will remember Rawhide and Jellyroll, and all small and helpless creatures."[111]

By 1931 Archie Belaney had remade himself into Grey Owl. Through the film and his articles he had proved himself in the eyes of the Parks Branch. And to his surprise, Jelly Roll and Rawhide had returned to him once the ice broke. He never, however, really regained Anahareo. In his autobiography, *Pilgrims of the Wild*, he would immortalize her, but ironically because of it, and his other books, he lost her. He would leave for Western Canada in the spring of 1931. For the next five years, most of the time he would be alone.

One of Archie Belaney's favourite quotes was a statement by the nineteenth-century American writer Ralph Waldo Emerson in his essay

"Friendship." "The essence of friendship is entireness, a total magnanimity and trust."[112] Even with Anahareo, he lacked the personal confidence to apply his cherished philosophy.

Left to right: Ferg Legace, Archie Belaney, and Jack Woodworth making "music" at Biscotasing, around 1920. Archives of Ontario/S13322. Source: Ferg Legace.

Archie Belaney on the extreme right, Gordon Gouett on left. Photo taken around 1925. Gordon Gouett provided the date. Ontario Ministry of National Resources. Source: Rus Duval.

Jim Espaniel on a portage near Biscotasing, with Archie Belaney. The photo was taken by Haddow Keith, a summer forest ranger, 1920. Glenbow Archives, Calgary/PA–3165–1. Source: Haddow Keith.

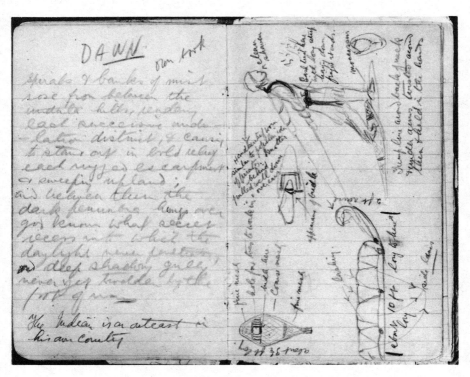

Two pages from one of Grey Owl's notebooks (that for 1929–30). This sketch was included in The Men of the Last Frontier *(1931), Grey Owl's first book.* National Archives of Canada, MG 30 D147, volume 1, Notebook 1929–1930.

Left to right: Slim Massey, Archie Belaney, and Bill Draper in Bisco around 1920. They look as if they are all dressed up to go into Sudbury. Ontario Ministry of Natural Resources. Source: Vince Crichton.

The Espaniel Family, Biscotasing area, circa 1920. Jane Espaniel is shown on the left next to her father. Archives of Ontario/Acc. 23090–5. Source: Jim Espaniel.

"He could enjoy a celebration with the best of them" (Tales, *p. 179). So Grey Owl wrote of Harry Woodworth, the HBC post manager at Bisco. Here Harry is shown holding the pipe of peace at one of Archie Belaney's war dances in Bisco, in the early 1920s. Left to right: Archie, Jim Espaniel, Harry Woodworth, and Bill Miller.* Archives of Ontario/Acc. 23090–3. Source: Jane Espaniel McKee.

Agnes Belaney (Grey Owl's daughter), on the right, with two friends, Lake Temagami, around 1925. Teme-augama Anishnabai, Bear Island, Lake Temagami.

Jonas Papaté, a brother of Chief Nias Papaté, and Anahareo (Gertrude Bernard) at Lac Simon, probably 1926. Archives of Ontario/S14413. Source: Grey Owl and Anahareo Collection lent by Dawn Richardson.

Archie sent this photo to his aunts around 1927 and inscribed on the back: "This is my wife Gertie, an Iroquois chief's daughter. 21 years old. Tall, slim & very strong. A woman of great courage & a true partner. Well-educated, talks perfect English; everybody likes her." Given to Lovat Dickson by the Misses Belaney after Grey Owl's death. A print of the photo is in the park library. Prince Albert National Park, Waskesiu, Saskatchewan.

Archie Belaney and Anahareo (Gertrude Bernard) in Abitibi, Quebec, around 1927. Archives of Ontario/S15547. Source: Bill Cartier.

Grey Owl at Métis, Quebec, late summer 1929. Archives of Ontario/S14232. Source: Peter Davies Co. Ltd.

Left to right: Grey Owl, Yvon Lavoie, Anahareo, Jean-Léon Duchêne (Jean-Charles Harvey's brother-in-law), Jean-Charles Harvey. Photo taken near Cabano, Quebec, November 2, 1929. Yvon Lavoie dated the photo. National Archives of Canada (C–28195).

9 The First Book

The friendship between Grey Owl and Bill Oliver began rather awkwardly one June day in 1931.[1] Bill, then working under contract for the Parks Branch, had just lugged his twenty-five kilograms of camera equipment over the five-kilometre forest trail to Grey Owl's cabin northeast of Clear Lake in Riding Mountain National Park. It had been a long haul for the hearty photographer. Just as he put down his heavy load at Beaver Lodge Lake, Grey Owl greeted him with this remark: "So you're the cameraman. I may as well tell you I have not much use for white men." When Bill asked why, his host replied: "I have never had the pleasure of meeting many who did not want to deface God's earth."[2] Only after Grey Owl's death did Bill Oliver realize the irony of the situation. The Indian making these remarks was born and raised in Hastings, Sussex, just fifty kilometres or so from the village of Ash (near Canterbury), Bill's hometown, in Kent. Their brusque introduction aside, the Calgary film-maker and Grey Owl soon got along very well indeed. Bill's dedication to his work and to the project of making a beaver film, won Grey Owl over.[3]

Commissioner Harkin and the Parks Branch were delighted with the final product and requested W. J. Oliver to complete more Grey Owl films. Schools, church groups, and service clubs across Canada showed them. During the 1930s, audiences throughout Britain and North America would see the Park Branch's films of Grey Owl and the beaver.

Late in 1931, *Country Life* finally published Grey Owl's first book under their own title of *The Men of the Last Frontier*. At the last minute they added as illustrations several of the magnificent stills that Bill Oliver shot at Riding Mountain National Park, as well as photos taken at Waterton, Banff, and Jasper National Parks.[4] The volume attracted great attention on both sides of the Atlantic, although the *Times Literary Supplement* in London protested against the preface. "The publisher offers an apology for 'Grey Owl's' elusive grasp of the English tongue. This takes one a little aback, as it is difficult to recall any record of the great North so brilliantly and lovingly handled."[5]

Probably the very best chapters are those first three, "The Vanguard," "The Land of Shadows," and "The Trail." In these essays Grey Owl describes in wonderful word pictures the life, and the psyche, of the woodsman. Unlike most trappers he had both a keen power of observation and—the second essential ingredient—an unusual talent for writing. His two chapters on the beaver, however, won the greatest public acclaim, as they portrayed in such intimate detail his daily life with them. The remaining five articles recounted various wilderness stories and stressed the need for the preservation of the northern wilderness.

The book earned the praise it received, such as the note in the *Canadian Historical Review* which said it gave "an extraordinarily vivid picture of life and conditions in the Canadian northland."[6] Just to select one important passage from the first chapter, "The Vanguard," Grey Owl's gifts of expression are self-evident. The experienced trapper, he writes, would trade his way-of-life for no other.

> A man who has successfully overcome the difficulties, and endures the privations of the trap-line for a few years, can no more quit it than the confirmed gambler can leave his gaming. Trapping is, after all, a gamble on a large scale, the trapper's life and outfit against the strength of the wilderness and its presiding genii, to win a living; and in the hazard he experiences a rare pleasure.
>
> Nor is his life without its compensations. He may climb a mountain, and look as far as the eye can reach, out over illimitable leagues of forested hill and valley stretching into the dim distance, with a feeling of ownership, and there is none to say him nay. And to all intents and purposes it is his, therein to work his will; surely a vast enough estate to satisfy the most land-hungry, and with no taxes or upkeep attached to it. His sole title to possession is the hard-won supremacy he has attained to by unremitting toil, as potent for him as any letters patent could be. The sense of untrammelled freedom and a wild independence, inculcated by wanderings over an unlimited area, enter his soul, unfitting him for any other walk of life. His is the sport of kings, and he is free as no king ever was.[7]

Now that the truth of his identity is known, one can find passages that reveal his English upbringing and his prejudices.[8] The collie-breeding Aunt Ada, for instance, clearly inspired this passage: "Wolves when hunting exhibit team work similar to that employed by football players, send out scouts, obey the orders of a leader, and will gambol and play on the ice precisely as do pedigreed collies on a lawn."[9] His Victorian writing style—"full of compound-complex sentences of Dickensian proportions"[10]—his love of foreign expressions and Latinized English, all hint at his upper middle-class background.

At the Hastings Grammar School, Headmaster W. H. LaTouche repeatedly told the students: "You learn Latin to help you with your English."

Henry Hopkin, Archie's friend at school, had joked that they "learned English to help their Latin."[11] Archie had actually failed his Latin exam for the Cambridge University junior certificate in 1903, but the value of Latinized English had been impressed upon him at the grammar school. In *The Men of the Last Frontier* many of the rich English words Grey Owl used were derived from Latin. His first chapter, for instance, contains: cognizant, vindictive, taciturnity, and even the Latin phrase *casus belli*, all used in the proper context. In the second chapter he introduced other words of Latin origin, such as: reticent, sinuous, rapacious, predatory, and fastidious.

The influence of his aunts and his early teachers went deeper. One passage in *The Men of the Last Frontier* hints that, in his subconscious at least, Grey Owl retained much of his early Imperial teachings. Of the beaver, Grey Owl wrote: "He is the Imperialist of the animal world. He maintains a home and hearth, and from it he sends out every year a pair of emigrants who search far and wide for new fields to conquer; who explore, discover, occupy, and improve, to the benefit of all concerned."[12]

Archie's early reading—those pleasurable hours spent with Wild West thrillers—also surfaced in his book. This passage, describing the "savages" of the plains, reads as if spoken by William F. Cody, Buffalo Bill himself:

> An old-time buffalo hunt was an inspiring sight. The strings of light-riding savages on their painted ponies, probably the best irregular light mounted infantry the world has ever seen, naked to the waist, vieing with each other in spectacular and hazardous stunts, exhibiting a skill in horsemanship never attained to by trained cavalry; the black sea of rolling humps, and bobbing heads, the billowing clouds of dust through which the fringe of wild, yelling horsemen were intermittently visible; the rumbling of innumerable hoofs, and, in the case of white men, the thudding of the heavy buffalo guns, combined to produce a volume of barbaric uproar, and a spectacle of wild confusion and savagery that had its duplicate in no part of the world.[13]

One of the most imaginative references in his book concerns the story of his own adoption by Ojibwa Indians—by Neganikabo, a Bisco-area Indian who actually existed but whom Grey Owl, in his enthusiasm, elevates to Hiawatha status.[14] As Grey Owl told the tale:

> A blood-brother proved and sworn, by moose-head feast, wordless chant, and ancient ritual was I named before a gaily decorated and attentive concourse, when Ne-ganik-abo, "Man-that-stands-ahead," whom none living remember as a young man, danced the conjurors' dance beneath the spruce trees, before an open fire. . . . The smoke hung in the white pall short of the spreading limbs of the towering trees, and with a hundred pairs of beady eyes upon me I stepped out beneath it when called on. . . . "Hi-Heeh, Hi-Heh, Ho! Hi-Heh, Hi-Heh, Ha! Hi-Heh, Hi-Heh, Ho! Hi-Ho, Hi-Ho, Ha!" and on and on in endless repetition, until the monotony of the sounds had the same effect on the mind that the unvarying and measured markings of a snake have on the eye. The sensation of stepping into the motionless ring

was that of suddenly entering a temple, devoted to the worship of some pagan deity, where the walls were lined with images cast in bronze; and there I proudly received the name they had devised, which the old man now bestowed upon me.[15]

Grey Owl's statement about "the effect on the mind that the unvarying and measured markings of a snake have on the eye" alone rings true. The adoption ceremony, like his alleged Apache childhood, has no factual basis.[16] The Egwunas accepted him (momentarily) in Temagami, and the Espaniels in Bisco warmly befriended him—but his "adoption ceremony" by Neganikabo sprang entirely from his rich imagination. Like the oyster which forms a pearl around a foreign grain of sand within its shell, Archie's imagination once again worked over the realities of his life and came up with an improved, far more exciting, story.

Grey Owl later admitted that he included one major distortion in *The Men of the Last Frontier.* One of his best chapters, "The House of McGinnis," tells the story of the first two beaver that he and Anahareo adopted, McGinnis and McGinty, of their trip from Abitibi to Témiscouata and their adjustment to the new country. It has considerable human interest but, as Archie confessed three years later in *Pilgrims of the Wild,* he implied in the story "that our lost friends still were living."[17] Archie and Anahareo lost them both in the spring of 1929. When writing *The Men of the Last Frontier,* Archie felt that the reader would be disappointed to hear of their disappearance and had altered the story accordingly. More confident three years later, he told the truth about them in *Pilgrims.*

Essentially Grey Owl was a storyteller, an entertainer who appropriated the right to alter his material for the purposes of comic relief or dramatic effect.[18] If he felt that McGinnis and McGinty dramatically best remained alive, he gave them life. A brilliant popularizer, he believed that he must entertain his readers as well as inform them. He would be true to general impressions, if not to minute or exact details.

In *The Men of the Last Frontier* Grey Owl emerged as one of Canada's pioneer conservationists, one of the few Canadians during the 1930s who crusaded for the conservation of Canada's natural resources and wildlife. He was one of the few individuals in Canada in the 1930s who had awakened to the fact that our wildlife, fish, and forests have a limit to them. Like James Harkin, Grey Owl believed in the urgency of preserving something of Canada's unspoilt wilderness.[19] In his first book he wrote from the heart: "Not much longer can the forest hope to stem the tide of progress; change is on every hand. Every year those who follow the receding Border further and further back, see one by one the links with the old days being severed, as the demands of a teeming civilization reach tentacles into the very heart of the Wild Lands."[20] Yet, Grey Owl added, this southern advance brought with it a special responsibility.

> Too many regard the wilderness as only a place of wild animals and wilder men, and cluttered with a growth that must somehow be got rid of. Yet it is, to those who know its ways, a living, breathing reality, and has a soul that may be understood, and it may yet occur to some, that part of the duty of those who destroy it for the general good is to preserve at least a memory of it and its inhabitants, and what they stood for.[21]

In his later books and lectures he would make his conservationist theme ever more emphatic.

No evidence exists that Grey Owl knew of the great American conservationists of the late nineteenth century. The Americans, whose frontier had almost disappeared by the early twentieth century, stood far ahead of Canadians. Grey Owl had read Ralph Waldo Emerson's essays in praise of nature, but he did not know the works of his important New England contemporary, Henry David Thoreau. Surprisingly, for example, he appears not to have been aware of James Harkin's hero,[22] John Muir, the founder of the Sierra Club in the late nineteenth century. Muir had made it his life's mission to educate Americans in the advantages of wild country.[23] Grey Owl's inspiration came from Emerson, Seton and, even more important, from within himself. He could not speak to others about his inner pain and the poison within him from his childhood, but he could articulate, like no other Canadian of the decade, his sense of outrage at Canadians' neglect of their priceless natural heritage.

Both British and North American reviewers liked *The Men of the Last Frontier.* On May 22, 1932, the New York *Times* welcomed it.

> Grey Owl is no stuffed Indian. He is real and honest and he lets his readers behind the scenes of a life comparable for glamour and heroism with that which was lived in the American Rockies during the golden decades of the beaver trade nearly a century ago . . . Grey Owl is a sentimentalist. But his is a worthy sentimentalism about a worthy subject. His book should outlast its season and many another season.[24]

Reader's Digest in the United States and *Chatelaine* magazine and the Toronto *Star Weekly* in Canada all ran excerpts of his beaver stories.[25] Excerpts from *The Men of the Last Frontier* also soon appeared in Canadian school readers.[26] Overall, Edwin L. Sabin provided the best explanation for the book's success in his critique in the American magazine, *Saturday Review.* "The style is smooth, well sustained, and rich in imagery, sympathy with man, animal, and natural aspects of a wilderness country."[27]

The only known negative comment on *The Men of the Last Frontier* came from Western Canada, in a review by Dr. W. T. Allison of the English Department at the University of Manitoba.[28] The Winnipeg *Tribune* ran it on July 16, 1932. This review really hurt because Professor Allison had known Chief Buffalo Child Long Lance, an Indian author whom Grey Owl greatly respected, and to whom he had included a reference as "a splendid savage"²⁹ in *The Men of the Last Frontier.* Only the previous August, Grey Owl had written to *Country Life* about Long Lance:

> I will of course never become a real writer, but I am very anxious to put this frontier stuff over, as I have reason to believe I am the only man who actually belongs to it that has succeeded in getting anything worth while published, with the exception of Buffalo-Child Long-Lance. He is a full-blood Blackfoot and a chief. . . . Being just a [half] breed I had a harder row to hoe than he had to obtain recognition.³⁰

Professor Allison wrote his review just four months after the death of Long Lance. A small group of people had learned Long Lance's true identity. Instead of being a Blackfoot chief, or even a Plains Indian tribesman, he had been born the son of mixed-blood parents and classified as "colored" in his hometown of Winston-Salem, North Carolina.³¹ But that news had not reached Dr. Allison. The university professor accused Grey Owl of having a ghost-writer complete his book.

> Before I had read far in this book I kept asking myself how in the world could a half-breed trapper pick up such an elegant style. Even Longlance, who was a college student, and had long years of experience as a newspaper and magazine writer, would not have produced anything so stylistic as the earlier chapters of this book.
>
> Is not the hand of the editor, a practised literary hand, evident in this sentence in such words as terrain and prototype?—"Conditions have changed, and the terrain has shifted, but the kind of a man who follows the chase for a living remains the same; the desire to penetrate far-away hidden spots, the urge to wander, is there as it was in his prototype of two hundred years ago." In a sentence or two further along, Grey Owl, or his ghost, speaks of the Indian interpreting "the cryptograms in the book that lies open before him, scanning the face of Nature and forestalling her moods to his advantage."³²

The charge that he had a "ghost" made Grey Owl livid. Perceptively, Professor Allison had seen the true Archie Belaney in Grey Owl's writings, and it scared Grey Owl. It also suggested that he had carelessly prepared and executed his masquerade as an Indian author in *The Men of the Last Frontier.* Hastily he scribbled off a note to Hugh Eayrs, his Canadian publisher:

> Thanks very much for the reviews; they are very kind to me, except one that is being circulated in the Western papers by a professor acting as critic who takes about two columns & a half to tell, in a very sarcastic manner, that it is impossible for any mere breed to have written such a book, & that I have a "ghost." He takes my descriptions & phrases that I fought out & wrestled with during whole nights, & proves conclusively that they are the work of the editor. He places doubt on my knowledge of wild life by his slighting references. He steps a little out of his class I think, as I would do

were I to put on cap & gown & try to deliver an oration in Greek. . . . I still hold the original pencilled copy of the first M.S., scrawled over with notes & alterations, written on exercise book paper, with no marks of an editor's pen, but the cuts of the teeth of a beaver who once stole the entire M.S., & took it to make his bed, six feet deep in a tunnell [tunnel] in my winter camp. I got them all after a considerable struggle with the highly indignant robber, but the pages had not yet been numbered, so I had some time.[33]

Professor Allison's review aside, no one else challenged the "beaver man's" amazing literary ability. Surprisingly, looking back from our age of investigative journalism, no one probed into his background. Grey Owl knew only too well that one day someone might. His Parks Branch employers knew him after all by his real name, Archie Belaney.[34]

The thought of an investigation into his past understandably worried Grey Owl. One day someone might link him up with Angele Belaney and his children in Temagami. He did not need that kind of media attention. Nor did he want any inquiring newsmen from the Winnipeg dailies to visit southwestern Manitoba and dig up his cousins, the Belaneys of the Brandon Hills.[35] At Riding Mountain National Park he lived only a hundred kilometres north of the Canadian Belaneys' original farm just south of Brandon. Maggie and George France Belaney, first cousins of Ada and Carrie Belaney, still kept the cherished photo of the Reverend Robert Belaney, the family's nineteenth-century patriarch, on the mantelpiece in the livingroom.[36]

Maggie and George France Belaney (who died in 1933) never forgot their unwelcome relative, their first cousin, George Furmage Belaney, who had tried to steal money from them. They remembered that cousin George had said that his son lived in northern Ontario.[37] When Grey Owl began to achieve national prominence with his book and his films, they knew he was their relative, as Ivy Scott, who married Maggie Belaney's nephew, Peter Scott, discovered.

In the mid-1930s the Scotts lived in Brandon. One day Ivy saw an advertisement in the local newspaper for a film of Grey Owl and the beavers. She decided to take her son. Her husband could not attend the Saturday matinee but commented, out of the blue, that, through relatives in England, he believed Grey Owl was his cousin. This puzzled Ivy until she saw the film and saw Grey Owl with his prominent Belaney nose. Aunt Maggie Belaney confirmed the relationship. "O yes," the elderly Scottish lady said in her broad lowland accent, "he is a cousin."[38] Although no letters have survived, Ada and Carrie must have been in touch with their first cousin, Maggie, in Manitoba.

Another piece of evidence, this time a documentary reference, hints that other members of the family knew Grey Owl's true identity. Archibald Falconer, a second cousin of Grey Owl (he was a grandson of John Belaney, one of Grey Owl's grandfather's brothers), moved just after the First World War from Edinburgh to Duval, Saskatchewan. One suspects that he learned from the Belaneys of Brandon Hills about Grey Owl and wrote back to his two sisters about him. Subsequently the Misses Falconer of Edinburgh apparently contacted their "Indian" cousin, for Grey Owl notes in a letter written probably in the fall of 1933 to Anahareo: "Two old maiden ladies living in some part of Scotland, have written me thru Country Life, & claim to be first cousins or some kind of cousins of my father's side of the family. It seems genuine, although they do not know my uncle (McNeil) but seem to have heard of him. They are called 'Belaneys of Mac—' something or other, & are very old, & are very proud of me." [39] After the death of Archie Falconer and his wife, pictures of Grey Owl were found in their family scrapbook.[40]

Why, one wonders, did the Belaneys of Brandon Hills not come forward and identify their famous cousin? One suspects that Maggie held back for the simple reason of having met his father. After one encounter with George Furmage Belaney she had no desire to become personally acquainted with his son. Or they simply stayed away as they recognized their cousin's job of "being an Indian." In Ada and Carrie's words, "he had adopted Indian costume and Indian ways, so that he could carry on his work among the Red Indians more easily and naturally." [41] Why should they expose him?

Grey Owl's mother, Kittie Scott-Brown, knew of the Belaneys of Brandon Hills. When Betty Somervell interviewed her (shortly after Grey Owl's death in April 1938) she said that "when G[eorge] left her he *went to his cousins in Canada* uncertain when or where." [42] Thus, Grey Owl, too, must have known of the Belaneys of Brandon Hills.

In mid-October 1931 Lloyd Roberts and his father, Sir Charles G. D. Roberts, then regarded as Canada's leading man of letters,[43] visited Grey Owl and Anahareo at Riding Mountain National Park. Anahareo had just rejoined Grey Owl after half-a-year in eastern Canada and had returned to help with their move to Prince Albert National Park. Grey Owl had successfully applied to leave Beaver Lodge Lake, the quiet wooded slough about fifteen kilometres north of the park headquarters at Wasagaming, for Prince Albert National Park which "has a more extensive water range for the expected increase in numbers in the beaver colony." [44] The hot month of August 1931 climaxed a ten-year dry cycle, leaving the water table at Riding Mountain quite low. The level at Beaver Lodge Lake was down to two-thirds of a metre, much too shallow for the beaver to weather through the coming winter. A strong possibility existed that the small lake might even freeze to its bottom.[45] The presence nearby of close Belaney relatives might also have contributed to Grey Owl's decision to move.

Grey Owl's stay at Riding Mountain National Park, while only six months in length, was important. He worked hard and learned a great deal more about the taming of beaver, the symbol of his crusade for the preservation of wildlife in Canada. As W. J. Oliver's film shows, he developed a real confidence with them. Here he awaited the publication of *The Men of the Last Frontier,* which *Country Life* brought out in late 1931.

Without question, in 1931 Grey Owl enjoyed his growing reputation as a voice for wilderness. When Garnet Clay Porter, a Winnipeg *Tribune* columnist, walked into his cabin at Beaver Lodge Lake in the summer, Grey Owl warmly welcomed him. To Garnet's leading question he replied: "Where did I learn the beaver language and their ways? I did not have to learn it. It comes down to an Indian through the ages—instinct. Some Indians have the knowledge more definitely developed than others."[46]

Certainly the presence of Grey Owl in Western Canada livened up the local newspapers. Only a week or so before the visit of Lloyd and Sir Charles G. D. Roberts to Beaver Lodge Lake, Grey Owl travelled to Winnipeg and gave an interview to the *Free Press,* one in which he blasted the administration of the city zoo at Assiniboine Park. He claimed that the treatment of the beaver there was only "a refinement of cruelty" and that they would die within a year.[47]

Grey Owl loved his new role as nature's champion, but he still had some things to learn about the most effective presentation of his arguments. The zoo superintendent, F. T. G. White, benefitted from Grey Owl's impulsiveness. The beaver man had made his remarks before actually visiting the zoo, as Superintendent White told the press:

> The criticism was unfair inasmuch as it was made before Grey Owl had seen our beaver. He admitted to me [after the interview Grey Owl had called at the zoo] he had made the criticism on the word of friends who had visited him in Riding Mountain park last summer. When he visited the beaver here he found conditions quite different from what he had been led to believe.[48]

10 Prince Albert National Park

In the 1930s, Ajawaan became the most publicized and best-known lake in Saskatchewan.[1] Here, 50 kilometres away from Prince Albert National Park's summer headquarters at Waskesiu, and 150 kilometres northwest of Prince Albert, lived Grey Owl, from 1931 to 1938. At Beaver Lodge[2] he wrote three of his four classics: *Pilgrims of the Wild* (1934), *Sajo and her Beaver People* (1935), and *Tales of an Empty Cabin* (1936).

Prince Albert National Park, over 5,000 square kilometres, lies right in the midst of the transitional zone between the prairies and the northern boreal forest. It became a national park in 1927. After winning the Prince Albert riding, Prime Minister W. L. Mackenzie King (who had been defeated in his former Ontario riding of North York and had chosen to run in the safe Liberal seat of Prince Albert) fulfilled his election promise. James A. Wood, the assistant superintendent at Banff National Park, was named the first park superintendent.[3]

The Parks Branch authorities, while conservationists, were not preservationists who believed that parks should be left entirely in a wilderness state. James Harkin, as always, realized that he must sell Parliament on the profitability of parks. Prince Albert National Park would be opened up in summer for tourists who, with the coming of the automobile, could reach it by car.[4] With its large number of white, sandy beaches, Waskesiu, a hundred kilometres north of Prince Albert, became the park's town site. In 1931, Superintendent James Wood placed Grey Owl at Ajawaan knowing that his presence would make the four-year-old park better known. Major Wood had Beaver Lodge built on Lake Ajawaan to meet Grey Owl's specifications.[5]

Beaver Lodge became a popular visiting centre, where Grey Owl warmly welcomed visitors genuinely interested in wildlife. At Beaver Lodge they might see deer, muskrats, and whiskey jacks as well as Charlie, his tame bull moose, and, of course, the beaver.[6] In his words, he wanted to give his guests an "opportunity of studying Canadian Wild Life at close quarters, in their natural state."[7]

One of the best descriptions of Beaver Lodge appears in a letter written in 1932 by Karl Clark, a chemist with the Alberta Research Council in Edmonton. (Clark later developed the hot-water recovery process used today for extracting valuable crude oil from the Alberta tar sands.)[8] Dr. Clark had taken a canoe trip in the park with his two oldest children and had travelled to Ajawaan to visit Grey Owl and his beaver.

> He has a family of them [beaver] living with him. Half the lodge is inside his cabin and the rest outside. We turned up about 2 o'clock and found he had just got up. He makes his day the same as the beaver's day. We sat around for about an hour talking about this and that and finally, about 3.30 the beaver started to put in an appearance. The old lady turned up first. She swam around a bit and then came ashore, looked the visitors over, walked to the cabin door and banged it open and went in. After something to eat she went off on various jobs and we managed to see something of them. They have workings all over the place. They cut down stuff and drag it to the water and swim it to the lodge. Sometimes it goes on the outside part and other times, they land it, drag it through the cabin and put it on the part of the lodge in there. There were five young ones.[9]

In *Tales of an Empty Cabin* Grey Owl described Beaver Lodge's location especially for "those whose souls are longing for the freedom of the open Road, but who are prevented by the invincible decrees of Fate from ever seeing the wonders of the Wilderness save in the pages of a book."[10]

> Thirty miles from the camps, and beyond the distant narrows, accessible only by water, is Ajawaan Lake. . . . Far enough away to gain seclusion, yet within reach of those whose genuine interest prompts them to make the trip, Beaver Lodge extends a welcome to you if your heart is right; for the sight of a canoe approaching from the direction of the portage, or the appearance of some unexpected visitors on the mile-long trail that winds through the forest from larger and more navigable waters, all coming to bid the time of day to Jelly Roll and Rawhide and their band of workers, is to me an event of consuming interest. Save for my animal friends I live here quite alone, and human contacts, when I get them, mean a lot, and are important.[11]

In the mid-1930s a young lawyer from Prince Albert interested in Grey Owl's conservation work visited him with Jim Wood. Years later John Diefenbaker recorded his impressions of Grey Owl and his beaver. Before they left Beaver Lodge, the tall man in buckskins handed the superintendent a thirty- or forty-page manuscript to forward to his publisher. The future prime minister of Canada read the text in the boat on the way back to the park headquarters at Waskesiu. In his memoirs forty years later, John Diefenbaker remembered Grey Owl's prose, "clothed in masterly English and filled with an imagery that only a lover of nature could possibly possess."[12]

Dr. W. G. N. van der Sleen came from Holland in the summer of 1936 after reading about Grey Owl in a German magazine.[13] In his book, *Canada,* he recalled his four days with the beaver man: "We are lucky, Grey Owl is home. . . . A tall, lithe figure, in buckskin pants and a red shirt, his long hair parted into two braids. He greets us in the way of the Redman—his hand held above his brow—and helps us disembark from our canoe. A squirrel climbs up his leg, snatching a peanut from his fingers, while a jay circles around him begging for a piece of bread."[14]

At night by the fireside of Beaver Lodge the Dutch explorer and nature writer listened to his new friend. "He spoke freely, without scruples, intuitively sensing how I as fellow nature lover, stood closer to him than the majority of my race living in the cities."[15] Few of Grey Owl's visitors in the early 1930s met Anahareo at Beaver Lodge.

Anahareo, who joined Archie in October at Riding Mountain National Park after six months in Ontario, was greatly disappointed to hear about the new book. "The picture of Archie writing—always in a haze, no companionship whatsoever—flashed before me. 'Oh, please don't do anything like that—not until I can get out of here.'" But this time Anahareo was caught, for in December she became pregnant. She had to stay at Beaver Lodge while her author-husband continually worked on his manuscript. "All I heard from Archie that winter was the scratch, scratch of his pen, and arguments against taking a bath. Like a kid, he loathed baths." Two weeks before her due date, Anahareo left for Prince Albert where their daughter, Dawn, was born on August 23, 1932.[16]

Grey Owl loved greatly his little daughter,[17] but Dawn did not (to Anahareo's dissatisfaction) weaken his intense commitment to his writing and to the making of his beaver films. Anahareo, in fact, came home to Beaver Lodge with Dawn to find Bill Oliver and a film crew at work. Grey Owl and the men had taken the roof off Beaver Lodge. She saw Bill, perched on top of a bunk, "taking movies of a procession of beaver carrying sticks and armloads of mud across our living-room floor!" Grey Owl was delighted to see them both and excitedly told his wife: "That fellow in there is a government photographer, and those films will be shown in schools and God knows where else, so I figured from the conservation angle, the more people know about beaver, the more they will help to save them."[18]

The old problems of the writer-husband and his excessive devotion to his manuscripts resurfaced. Anahareo and Dawn stayed at the upper cabin that had been built for them just behind Beaver Lodge. It lacked cooking facilities and Anahareo had to prepare meals in Beaver Lodge. This disturbed Grey Owl's sleep because he worked most of the night with the beaver (until freeze-up). Grey Owl's "lack of rest was beginning to tell; he was irritable and unsociable,"[19] Anahareo wrote. Only when the beaver went into their winter quarters did Anahareo and Dawn move down to Beaver Lodge. They stayed there until the ice left in the late spring.

By the spring of 1933 Anahareo had to break free of her confinement. She could not wait to make a prospecting trip to a promising new mining field along the Churchill River. When Dawn was nearly one, Anahareo made arrangements with Mrs. Ettie Winters, a well-respected English woman in Prince Albert, to look after the baby girl in her absence. At first Archie opposed the trip to northern Ontario but became reconciled to it, even later apologizing for his initial responses. "I felt pretty bad having been cross with you, not knowing when I might ever see you again. Try & forget it if you can. My nerves are not as they should be & there has been quite a strain this last year, and a person alone & a wee bit discouraged is inclined to brood over things."[20] He provided the money for her train trip and supplies.

When Anahareo returned to Prince Albert early in the winter, she stayed with Dawn at the Winters' apartment in Prince Albert. Grey Owl wrote her regularly. Before Christmas 1933 he described how the new book, to be published the following year as *Pilgrims of the Wild,* was going. His natural warmth and humour sparkle in this note.

> I am in a great mess. The book is half written, that is the pencil draft, & I can see all the rest of it very clearly. It is quite different to what I expected, as the book has taken me in hand & makes itself the way it wants. I am using only a couple of my original articles, but some of the stuff out of them, & of course all the Frontier tales & a few more. . . . Of course I cant keep you out of it, & I describe vividly how we fought 5 fast rounds to a finish over a tub of moonshine. (Ha! Ha! and again Ha!).[21]

Grey Owl's letters to Anahareo show many of his various moods, from light to serious. He could be so relaxed with her, as this signature to one of his letters indicates: "Archie-bald? (Not yet)."[22] He could also be very serious. When she left in 1934 on her prospecting trip to the Churchill River, he became quite envious. "For a week after I heard you had gone I was all worked up. It stirred the old bush fever up so bad that I could not sleep & hardly was able to eat."[23]

Generously, Grey Owl supplied money and advice for Anahareo's trips. The expert canoeman was worried about Anahareo shooting white water—a sport at which he excelled.

> Don't take any chances in big rapids. Always look at a rapids before going down, keep as much as possible to the side channels [channels], never run too stern heavy, keep a spare paddle always handy, dont fool around in unknown waters, listen to the advice of the people who know the country, & remember it takes strength as well as skill to handle a canoe in heavy water. Never take a chance, especially loaded. *Use the portage* if there is any doubt at all. It is not so glorified, but it is better than a post-mortem, or putting a lot of good fellows to the trouble of hauling you out.[24]

Her absences, though, affected him. In a letter to his American editor at Scribner's, he frankly said that he kept writing so furiously "as a solace to a rather chronic state of loneliness."[25] During the Churchill River trip of 1934 he sent money to Anahareo as well as complaints, later apologizing.

> Look, kid, don't be upset by that fool letter. I should of known better. You up there alone in a strange country, trying hard to make the grade. You know, kid, we quarrelled once in a while, but who doesn't? And what does it amount to? Just words. And they & the few blows etc., are kind of fading in a person's memory. . . . Life is too short, some people say; but I say life is too *big*, to allow any temporary foolishness to cloud the sun and shadow our trail. I think the bond between us all, Jelly (comes first), Rawhide, Dawn, & you & I, is indissoluble. We have seen hard times together & nothing can ever wipe out the memory of it.[26]

Alone, Grey Owl worked away on *Pilgrims*. Powerfully he told the story of his life from 1925, and his departure from Bisco, to his establishment in late 1931 at Prince Albert National Park. In describing the country from Bisco to Temagami, he related how the land had changed dramatically in his lifetime.

> Much of my route lay through a country I had known. It was now almost unrecognizable. A railroad had been built through part of it. There were huge burns, areas of bare rocks and twisted rampikes, miles of staring desolation. Riff-raff bushmen, dirty, unkempt; stolid European peasantry tearing down the forest; settlers on stone farms (two crops a year—one snow and the other rocks) existing, no more. The change was nearly unbelievable. Immured in the fastness of the Mississauga [Mississagi] I had not known what had been going on. . . . Fire, railroads, power projects, the aeroplane, they were tearing the old life apart. The Frontier was rolling back like a receding tide.[27]

The well-polished text, full of excitement, made the book a critical success in Canada, in the United States, and particularly in Britain. The crisis caused by the decline of the beaver population in Ontario and Quebec was real.[28] Harold Innis, the Canadian economic historian at the University of Toronto, summarized and endorsed *Pilgrims*.

> The volume by Grey Owl is a significant book as the autobiography of a famous conservationist. The author describes with many interesting photographs, his life in northern Ontario, his conversion from trapping, the taking of two young beaver to Cabano on the Temiscouata portage, his beginnings as a writer for magazines, the loss of the beaver and the capture of two others, his début as a lecturer, and his appointment and work at Beaver Lodge, Prince Albert National Park in Saskatchewan.[29]

Grey Owl had fought hard for American editions of his books, even to the point of telling Maxwell Perkins at Scribner's that "I am an American myself, & proud of it."[30] He made his loyalty seem so natural. "Although I left the States while yet a boy, I have that attachment to it that any man worthy of the name must have for the land of his birth."[31] At no point did the proud American, however, hide his Indian ancestry, adding in an earlier note: "At eleven years of age I spoke perhaps a hundred words in the English language."[32] In the New York *Times*, Anita Moffett praised the Scribner's edition enthusiastically: "In this book the wilderness, with its values, is made articulate. Told with utter authenticity and fidelity to the truth of the life it describes, it is imbued as well with deeply poetic feeling. 'Pilgrims of the Wild' is a record of a twofold achievement—a victorious struggle against heavy odds in behalf of the wilderness and its inhabitants, and the interpretation of that wilderness to those able to appreciate its significance."[33]

The book's greatest praise, and sales, came in Britain where Grey Owl's new London publisher masterminded the promotional campaign. For changing the title of his first book, "The Vanishing Frontier" to "The Men of the Last Frontier," without even consulting him, Grey Owl had disowned *Country Life*. His interest was in the frontier itself, not in the men who followed it. He angrily told *Country Life* when the book came out:

> That you changed the title shows that you, at least, missed the entire point of the book. You still believe that man as such is pre-eminent, governs the powers of Nature. So he does, to a large extent, in civilization, but not on the Frontier, until that Frontier has been removed. He then moves forward, if you get me. I speak of Nature, not men; they are incidental, used to illustrate a point only.[34]

Grey Owl's new publisher in England was Lovat Dickson, a dynamic thirty-two-year-old Canadian who had just opened up his own publishing firm in London. Hugh Eayrs, Grey Owl's publisher in Canada, had recommended him. Thanks to Lovat Dickson's idea of organizing a lecture tour of Britain for Grey Owl, the book's total sales would eventually reach 50,000 in the United Kingdom.[35]

As soon as it appeared early in 1935 the book received enthusiastic English reviews. Basil de Selincourt of the London *Observer* termed it an "irresistibly charming narrative."[36] The *New Statesman & Nation* wrote: "The rescue of two beaver kittens is described so vivaciously and graphically that we share the author's delight in the companionship of these mischievous, intelligent, tidy, affectionate and talkative animals."[37] But the greatest praise came from the pen of the British novelist Compton Mackenzie, who wrote in the London *Daily Mail*: "Not since when as a child I read 'Black Beauty' have I been so much moved by any story about animals as I have been moved by *Pilgrims of the Wild* by Wa-Sha-Quon-Asin (Grey Owl)."[38]

Elated by these reviews, Grey Owl decided to send a copy to his Supreme Commander in the Great War. He told Mrs. Winters: "I sent King Geordie his book today. Hope he likes it."[39] The secretary to Canada's Governor-General later acknowledged receipt of *Pilgrims of the Wild*. "His Majesty much appreciates Grey Owl's action in sending this book, and is glad to have a copy of it." [40]

Aware of Grey Owl's talent for writing, both Lovat Dickson and Max Perkins asked him for a children's book. [41] He produced the final manuscript early in 1935, and Lovat Dickson published it in Britain just in time for the first British lecture tour that same year. In this book, Grey Owl set his story in the Temagami Forest Reserve. [42] The tale relates the life of two beaver kits who are rescued by an Indian father and given to his mother-less daughter, Sajo. She and her brother, Shapian, fall in love with them and keep them as pets. Hard times later force their father to sell the beaver to a trader who, in turn, sells them to a city zoo. After an exciting series of adventures, the girl and boy retrieve the two kits from the zoo. True conservationists, the two young Indian children return the beaver to their home pond. Grey Owl took special pains to give *Sajo* a happy ending.

The critics lavishly praised the new Grey Owl book. From London, the *Times Literary Supplement* said: "It is not so much a children's book as one of those rare books, which have so catholic an appeal that children and grown-ups read them with equal pleasure—perhaps the secret of every children's classic." [43] The Chicago *Daily Tribune* felt the new book "should take its place alongside 'Pilgrims of the Wild' as one of the outstanding animal books of literature." [44] In the pages of the *University of Toronto Quarterly*, Professor Edmund Broadus of the Department of English at the University of Alberta termed it, "as far as my reading goes, the best work of the creative imagination, in the field of fiction, produced in Canada in 1935." The professor went on to compare *Sajo* with Morley Callaghan's *They Shall Inherit the Earth,* also released that year. "In the quality of his prose, Mr. Morley Callaghan is inferior to 'Grey Owl' . . . his English seems to me to be grasping for something that it cannot quite grasp." [45] Since 1935 *Sajo* has been translated into eighteen languages (including Japanese in 1987) and remains in print in Canada. [46]

Grey Owl had put his very best into both *Pilgrims* and *Sajo,* carefully constructing them in what he felt was the most interesting fashion. Wherever he thought necessary he simplified "his" story in *Pilgrims,* reducing to one year, for instance, the three he spent in Abitibi (1925 to 1928). As it made more sense (in the way he told the tale) for *The Men of the Last Frontier* to appear in the winter of 1930–31, instead of 1931–32, he has it published in late 1930. [47] This allows him to discuss the reviews of the book before he leaves for Riding Mountain National Park and a new chapter in his life. Actually the book was published in late 1931 when he was at Prince Albert National Park.

Even on small points the storyteller reconstructed certain details in *Pilgrims.* He claimed, for instance, that he alone went to obtain Christmas presents in Cabano in late 1928, but Anahareo, in her first book, recalled she had gone as well. [48] Perhaps he simply forgot, or more likely he wanted to convey that he was in charge. When Anahareo returned from her prospecting trip in northern Quebec, 1929–30, Grey Owl wrote: "Anahareo had had her fling and was satisfied."[49] This rings false, as she continued to detest the half-life that a fanatical writer offers a spouse. She made two other major prospecting trips (one in northern Ontario, the other in northern Manitoba along the Churchill River) before the publication of *Pilgrims* in late 1934.

To reinforce his central theme of the decay and degeneration of the life of the woodsman, Grey Owl referred in *Pilgrims* to Andy Luke, an Indian acquaintance from Fort Mattagami. He met Andy again on his journey from Bisco to Temagami in 1925. He found "Andy Luke, who habitually carried 400 lbs. on a portage and who had made big hunts that were a byword in the land, *working in the railroad as a labourer,* his son Sam, lean, wiry Sam with the speed and endurance of a greyhound, a wizard in a canoe, doing odd jobs."[50] Grey Owl is correct in saying that Andy no longer led canoe brigades from Mattagami to Bisco. There were no longer any, as a new transcontinental railway now went directly through the Mattagami district. Yet his statement that Andy had subsequently become a railway labourer goes too far. Sam recalled that his father never worked on the railway.[51]

Constantly in his writings Grey Owl focused on the Indian's difficult adjustment to the white man's society, but Grey Owl exaggerated for effect. He described in *Pilgrims* how Dave White Stone, the Algonquin Indian from the Ottawa Valley who joined him and Anahareo in Quebec, was eventually defeated by modern society. Dave went back to Ontario in 1930 after his mining claim in northern Quebec was jumped. "Dave's last Eldorado was gone; and he was old. Broken and embittered, he had gone out, back to his own land to lay his bones with those of his fathers, beneath the singing pines on the Ottawa."[52] "Old Dave" did not die on his return. He outlived Archie Belaney by thirty years, laying his bones with those of his fathers only in 1969.[53]

Sajo contains some of the same writing for effect as does *Pilgrims*. In order to have an animal villain in *Sajo*, Grey Owl paints the otter in a most ghastly light. "Negik the Otter, the hungry, the cruel and the sly, having broken the dam and so drained the pond, could now get what he had come for—kitten beaver meat!"[54] Otters did eat beaver kittens, but they were not, by any means, the most fearsome predators they faced. Only five years earlier Grey Owl had written of the otter: "He seems to have no quarrel with the beaver, and is a not unwelcome visitor to the lodges, as he removes the muskrats, who, unlike the proprietors, are not cleanly within the house, besides spoiling by their constant nibbling more of the beaver's feed than they eat."[55]

A much greater alteration appears in *Pilgrims*. At no time did Professor Allison, the *Canadian Forest and Outdoors* staff, the Canadian Parks Board, his publishers, or any other individual or organization spot it. After the loss of McGinnis and McGinty, Grey Owl and Anahareo had tamed another beaver they called Jelly Roll. In December 1930 and January 1931, Grey Owl wrote two articles for *Canadian Forest and Outdoors* about Jelly Roll as the "King of the Beaver People."[56] The following spring, however, he discovered that the beaver was really a female. In subsequent references he corrected Jelly Roll's sex. No one spotted this major alteration. In *Pilgrims of the Wild* he even entitled the entire second half of his "autobiography": "Queen of the Beaver People." For *Pilgrims* he lifted entire sentences from his early *Canadian Forest and Outdoors* articles on Jelly Roll and the beaver, written in 1930–31, and merely changed "he" to "she," and "his" to "hers."[57]

The fact that his reading public and the media were so uncritical (content as they were that an Indian who had learned English as a teenager could write so well), did not lead Grey Owl to let his guard down. Consciously the Hastings Grammar School's top student in English in the Cambridge Junior exams of 1903 made sure his prose was not perfect. Within *Pilgrims* he made many grammatical errors and included misspelling and improper punctuation.[58] He did this, of course, to direct any critic away from suspecting his true English background. Then, he insisted that his publishers print his books without making any changes in his texts.[59]

Archie also realized that he must somehow bury his name of Belaney. The Parks Branch, because of his army pension cheques and the name he had used when he joined the parks service, knew him as Archibald Belaney. In Prince Albert National Park he tried to introduce himself as "Archie Grey Owl," using this designation to sign his "Record of Employment" in June 1932.[60] The civil service, however, continued unimaginatively to address him in all correspondence as "A. Bellaney." At least they spelt his name incorrectly, but something more was needed. Archie decided he needed a new family name.

Wally Laird, a special constable with the RCMP, knew Archie reasonably well at the park. On account of his binges in Prince Albert, Archie had met many of the local constables, but Wally he liked. At Waskesiu, the park townsite, Wally had befriended a family of foxes. Grey Owl described the friendship in *Tales of an Empty Cabin*. "In the Winter they make regular visits to the cabin of the interpreter and guide attached to the Mounted Police, one Wally Laird, where they find food and a welcome and above all, a little kindly understanding when they feel the need of it."[61]

On patrol, summer and winter, Wally used to carry Grey Owl's mail and supplies to him at Beaver Lodge. As Wally was a Scot, one day Grey Owl decided to tell him about his own Scottish past. His deceased father was a "McNeil," and two of his father's sisters still lived on the Isle of Barra, the ancestral home of the McNeils.[62] As he prepared to leave on this first British Tour as the Modern Hiawatha, mentally Grey Owl was preparing a new twist to his already wonderfully complex ancestry.[63]

11 The First British Tour

The first British lecture tour was more than half over when Grey Owl reached Kendal in England's Lake District. The famous writer and lecturer stayed in Kendal at the home of Mrs. Betty Somervell.

Mrs. Somervell first heard of Grey Owl from her mother in London. After finishing *Pilgrims of the Wild,* Betty's mother had forwarded a copy to her daughter. The accompanying note added: "You must read this because the beaver are so fascinating, and the man who wrote it is coming to England soon to tell all about them and show films of them."[1] Subsequently, the Kendal branch of the Royal Society for the Prevention of Cruelty against Animals invited Grey Owl to give a public lecture on January 9, 1936, at St. George's Theatre. He accepted, and the organizing committee sold every available seat.[2] Mrs. Somervell welcomed Grey Owl, William Whitaker (his manager), and Laya Rotenberg (his secretary) to stay at her family's home, Plumgarths, during the visit. But the evening before his talk, they received a frantic call, in the middle of a wild storm, from the town of Carlisle on the Scottish border. "This is the lecture tour. Our car's broken down and we're stuck . . . and can't arrive in time for the lecture tomorrow."[3]

Knowing that the organizing committee had sold out the theatre, she had to do something. Without hesitation, Summy, as her friends called her, replied, "I'll come and fetch you," which the next morning she did, reaching them immediately after breakfast in her new Humber car. The drive back to Kendal (a good eighty kilometres over winding, narrow English roads) proved uneventful until Summy noticed a burning smell from the back seat. Was the car aflame? She stopped. To her relief she discovered it was only the pungent odour of Grey Owl's smoke-tanned buckskins, a smell that gained in intensity as the heater warmed up the car.[4]

The Somervells and their "Red Indian" guest got on famously. That evening Grey Owl told countless stories as he elaborated on the theme of his afternoon lecture—that everyone must work for the preservation of wild life. Summy offered to help the cause by driving the trio to Grey Owl's next lecture appointment. She continued as the chauffeur for an entire month, until the end of the tour at Stratford-upon-Avon on February 8.

The new chauffeur soon learned the speed and the popularity of the tour. A crowd of more than two thousand people heard Grey Owl speak at Sheffield, 150 kilometres away, the day after the talk at Kendal, and Summy had to sit on the stairs, as no seats remained. In this industrial city of half-a-million people his talk of clean air and water had a great impact. This city of factory chimneys smelled of sulphur. The shallow river that ran through the town was usually bright yellow, awash with chemicals. Everything was blackened by smoke.[5]

From Sheffield they drove the next day to Helensburgh, just west of Glasgow, 350 kilometres to the north, for a lecture there. The following evening almost 3,000 people heard Grey Owl speak in St. Andrew's Hall in Glasgow.[6] The next evening a huge audience welcomed him to Edinburgh's Usher Hall.[7] In what Grey Owl called Summy's "canoe," the group then left Scotland for a more than 600-kilometre ride to southern England. Grey Owl gave lectures every day—and on occasion up to three a day—in schools, halls, villages, and towns.[8]

Throughout his four-month tour, Grey Owl repeated his central theme: "The difference between civilised man and the savage is just this—civilised people try to impose themselves on their surroundings, to dominate everything. The Indian's part of the background. He lets himself—not just drift—but go with Nature."[9]

He would scribble this message clearly in his notebook, "Remember you belong to Nature, not it to you."[10] He wanted to save the wilderness and had begun his crusade in the heart of the British Empire, in England, where it no longer existed anywhere. Later he would extend the campaign to North America.

He owed much of his success in Britain to his helpers on the tour. Grey Owl, a man without any sense of time or of organization, was indebted to his workers who travelled with him in the exhausting final third of the tour. Thanks to Summy, Peter Bower,[11] and Billy Whitaker, he made his appointments on time. Laya Rotenberg, a twenty-year-old Canadian from Toronto whom he had met on the *Empress of Britain* on her way to study in Paris, also helped. She had volunteered to act as his secretary for the final half of the tour and every day answered the several score letters he received. She also helped form the queues for the lengthy autographing sessions after the talks.[12]

In London, Lovat Dickson, Grey Owl's publisher in Britain, masterminded and supervised the entire tour. The former lecturer in English at the University of Alberta in Edmonton had started his own publishing firm on Bedford Street, Covent Garden, only three years earlier.[13] Of the fifty titles the thirty-two-year-old publisher brought out in 1934, one in particular illustrates his courage and daring: the English edition of Professor Ewald Banse's frightening *Germany Prepares for War.* The militaristic textbook introduced in schools after the Nazi takeover in 1933 showed how Germany could invade England. Against Nazi attempts to prevent publication in England, Dickson pushed ahead, making available to English readers this clear statement that Nazi Germany meant war.[14]

English readers, however, chose not to think of war in 1934, and Lovat Dickson Ltd. lost financially on the venture—in fact, it only sold 7,000 of the 10,000 copies printed.[15] Fortunately, that same year the firm became Grey Owl's publisher in Britain. In 1931, Grey Owl had brought out his first book in England with *Country Life,* which had made a number of unwelcome changes to the author's grammar and syntax. On the advice of his Canadian publisher, Grey Owl had written Lovat Dickson in late 1934:

> Dear Sir:
> Mr. Hugh Eayrs, the head of Canadian Macmillans, writes me that you are a good Canadian and known to be an honest man. I am looking for such a man to be my publisher.[16]

Grey Owl's next book, *Pilgrims of the Wild,* proved an instant success. Within three months of publication, Lovat Dickson Ltd. had sold 35,000 copies of the uplifting story of Grey Owl and his beautiful wife, Anahareo, who worked to transform him from a trapper to a conservationist. The *Illustrated London News* ran lengthy excerpts of *Pilgrims.* Suddenly, after re-reading the book for the third time, a daring idea crossed Lovat Dickson's mind—why not bring Grey Owl to Britain to give a lecture tour?[17] Anxious to spread his message of conservation and respect for wildlife, Grey Owl eagerly accepted.

Although he had never handled a speaking tour before, Lovat Dickson had the impresario's magic touch. Exploiting the human interest angle of a North American Indian coming to lecture in Britain, the enterprising publisher convinced a number of reporters to greet the author at the docks in Southampton. Articles on Grey Owl's arrival appeared in many papers, excellent publicity for the tour. At his home on Moore Street in Chelsea, Rache (as Lovat Dickson's friends knew him) coached his new friend on the techniques of lecturing, in preparation for his first public talks at the London Polytechnic Theatre on Regent Street, to begin ten days later. Dickson had also lined up several other events to ensure that Grey Owl's lectures obtained maximum publicity.

Grey Owl welcomed the idea of a lecture tour of Britain. When Lovat Dickson proposed it in early 1935, he immediately realized its importance in spreading his message. "It will sure be a great medium of getting my ideas before the public & would inevitably lead to a similar campaign in Canada, when we might get direct action on this home wild-life of ours, that so badly needs it." [18] To his publisher in London, and now his tour director, Grey Owl suggested the image his advertising should convey: "I think the truest definition of my status (though I do not of course estimate myself his equal) is that of a modern Hiawatha and perhaps an interpreter of the spirit of the wild." [19] He would become the needed go-between, valued for his ability to interpret the Wilderness to Civilisation. *He would be needed.* Archie Belaney's life had come full circle. He would return to England as Hiawatha, the romantic character who had inspired him as a boy. Like Longfellow's *Hiawatha,* he would make his lectures "very human, very simple, and very real." [20]

While in London, Grey Owl lived with the Dicksons in their cream-and-brown-coloured home in Chelsea. [21] Here Rache and Marguerite Dickson saw at close quarters another side of the modern Hiawatha, a face shielded from the public. With his Bisco enthusiasms, he played the gramophone in the dining room at the loudest level. The man of the wilds splattered the wall of the guest room with ink, the result, he claimed, of frequent arguments with his fountain pen. Sometimes they also awoke to find the level in their liquor decanters alarmingly low. [22] To escape from pressure, he felt he had to drink. Alcohol had become his refuge.

At no point, however, did Grey Owl crack. Over a lifetime he had perfected his role for white audiences so well, so convincingly that even after a number of weeks living in the same household, Lovat Dickson believed his guest to be an Indian. Grey Owl willingly supplied details on his childhood when his publisher asked if he could write his biography. [23]

Naturally Grey Owl told his would-be-biographer nothing about his real father, George Furmage Belaney, who had been born only a few kilometres away from the Dicksons', at number 24 Upper Montagu Street in Marylebone. [24] Instead, Grey Owl told the elaborate story that he believed would impress his publisher. The *Strand Magazine* printed Lovat Dickson's, "Grey Owl, Man of the Wilderness," in May 1936:

> The story has its beginnings in an Indian village in Mexico more than forty years ago. In the house of a white man and an Apache woman a child is born into a world of frontier warfare and Indian fights. It is a world of strife of every kind. Family feuds are waged incessantly and never allowed to die, for the need for vengeance renews them from generation to generation. This is true especially of the Apaches, the most merciless of all Indian tribes.
>
> The white man who has married an Apache is killed in a feud, and in revenging him his eldest son is also killed. The little boy who has been born in the Mexican village is left alone with his Indian mother. Though he is part white, he never remembers this. He grows up an Indian in mentality and physique. The Indians teach him their way of life, and from his earliest youth he is hunting and trapping with the braves.
>
> In this way Grey Owl passed his youth. But in him, strongly welded and

waiting the moment that should reveal them, are the steel of endurance and the idealism given him by his mixed blood.[25]

On October 24 Grey Owl spoke at Foyle's Literary Luncheon, held at Grosvenor House, Park Lane, London. Christina Foyle, the daughter of the owner of the famous bookshop on Charing Cross Road, had begun a series of "literary luncheons," held every two weeks or so, at which the general public could see and hear their favourite authors. Five hundred people attended. Photographers shot pictures of Grey Owl dining with Lord Sempill, a famous British airman who the year previously had flown to Australia and back. Another photograph, in the *Weekly Illustrated,* showed Lady Allenby, the wife of the field marshall, speaking with Lord Lytton, the former British governor of the state of Bengal in India. The caption at the bottom of the photo read: "After the speeches Lady Allenby discusses beaver-trapping with Lord Lytton at Foyle's Literary Luncheon."[26]

As the chairman of the lecture committee of the *Sunday Times* Book Exhibit, Lovat Dickson had a chance to introduce Grey Owl to thousands of book lovers at this popular event. A photographer of the London *Sketch* caught the author of *Pilgrims of the Wild* speaking to Her Royal Highness Princess Marie Louise, the granddaughter of Queen Victoria, after the opening.[27]

The publicity worked. Soon Grey Owl's new book, *Sajo and her Beaver People,* had taken off, and was selling at the rate of 1,000 copies a week.[28] *Pilgrims of the Wild* sold 5,000 copies a month.[29] Mark Kerr, a great-grandson of the Duke of Richmond, a former governor-general of the Canadas, and a grandson of Sir Peregrine Maitland, an early lieutenant-governor of Upper Canada (present-day Ontario) and later Nova Scotia, spoke for many when he came forward and declared that Grey Owl's volumes were "the best books on animals which have been written in any language."[30]

Only two days before Grey Owl's first lecture at the London Polytechnic on October 28, Lovat Dickson scored another coup. The enterprising publisher had arranged with the BBC for a national radio broadcast (Grey Owl's first ever) on Saturday evening's "In Town Tonight" program. One journalist later commented on the rich resonances of the voice that "must be almost an ideal radio one."[31]

Grey Owl's Polytechnic appearances proved so popular that the theatre simply booked him and his films for an additional eleven days at Christmas—from December 17 to 28, for three performances a day, and four a day for five days of the run. On December 28 he accepted the theatre's request to continue with one lecture a day for another full week, hence he had no days off at all during the Christmas holidays. Arthur Leslie, the manager, reported to *Today's Cinema* that the film-lectures "were among the most popular programmes he has ever put on."[32]

The National Parks Branch films that Grey Owl showed also created great interest in his talks. In the pictures Anahareo stepped forward as his leading lady, and their tame beavers at Riding Mountain (and later at Prince Albert) National Park, were the supporting cast. The comments of the Ilfracombe *Chronicle* about his presentation in Torquay, in southwestern England, represent well the British animal-lovers' response: "To watch these most intelligent creatures constructing dams, building their 'lodges' half outside and half inside Grey Owl's own cabin; to see them handling trees and branches; to look at them running upright on their hind feet with loads of river-mud between chin and hands to make their homes: these were joys indeed." [33]

Without the aid of modern equipment such as telephoto and macro lenses,[34] W. J. "Bill" Oliver of Calgary had made these four films. Schools, church groups, and service clubs across North America and Europe—and now Grey Owl himself—showed them.[35] Lovat Dickson used many of Bill Oliver's dramatic stills of Grey Owl, looking so consciously Indian, to illustrate the publicity for the first (and later the second) British tour.

Much of Grey Owl's appeal came as well from the climate of the times: in the winter of 1935–36 the world depression still greatly affected Britain. While unemployment had dropped from its height of nearly three million in January 1933, two million people (out of a total population of nearly fifty million) remained without work.[36] To a society still in a period of continuing economic crisis, the "modern Hiawatha" offered a diversion and an escape. Lovat Dickson very clearly understood the appeal of this gloriously natural man. "He made pure Canada, the Canada outside the concrete urban enclosures come alive. . . . suddenly here was this romantic figure telling them [his audiences] with his deep and thrilling voice that somewhere there was a land where life could begin again, a place which the screams of demented dictators could not reach, where the air was fresh and not stagnant with the fumes of industry." [37]

Grey Owl's championing of the so-called "uncivilised" peoples of the world against the "civilised" was also timely. Only two weeks before Grey Owl reached England, Italian troops invaded the independent African country of Abyssinia (or Ethiopia). Determined to create a new Roman Empire, Mussolini set out to conquer the ancient kingdom, using aircraft and all available modern military equipment against the badly-equipped Abyssinian forces. A strong current of British public opinion favoured the Abyssinians,[38] but both Britain and France (fearing the outbreak of another world war) failed to impose oil sanctions on Italy. The aggressors' mechanized advance toward Addis Ababa continued. (They took the city on May 5, 1936.) Grey Owl supported the Abyssinians, and if served in a restaurant by an Italian waiter, he moved to another table. As he told Betty Somervell "everyone ought to be free, and be left in peace,"[39] and he repeated this constantly in his lectures throughout England and Scotland.

Naturally the greatest credit of all for his success must go to Grey Owl.

He lectured for long periods without rest, and he worked under the fear of possible exposure, perhaps by a boyhood acquaintance from Hastings or by his former wife, Ivy, who then lived in London, or possibly even by his mother who then lived in the south of England. Naturally at times, for comic relief, he overdid it with his exaggerations. To a Glasgow journalist, he confessed: "I love classical music. Wherever you find an Indian camp, you will find a gramophone and a pile of records, most of them of Beethoven."[40] In Edinburgh he told a newsman with the *Weekly Scotsman* this romantic but unlikely tale: "When the old Indians die they go away in the golden rays of the sunset to some other life in which the people very earnestly believe, but the children and the small animals, they go in the silver rays of the moonlight."[41]

Operating as he did under such intense pressures, he performed amazingly well. At Oxford in late January 1936, Geoffrey Turner, a lifelong student of the North American Indian and later to become a consultant on their culture for Oxford's famous Pitt-Rivers Museum (Department of Ethnology and Pre-History, University of Oxford), heard him speak.[42] The young man in his mid-twenties sat that evening in the gallery of the Oxford City Hall and with an ethnologist's eye later recorded what he saw and heard.

> The hall was packed, senior University predominating. Grey Owl himself appeared in fringed tailored buckskin (tanned, unbleached), the shirt & trousers beaded at the cuffs, a geometrically beaded belt, floral-beaded apron & knife sheath, hair thong tied, parted off-centre to the left, & a single eagle plume inclined to the left, knotted with down & having two weasel bands depending from the knot with the plaits. He gave the peace sign & said oratorically, *"How Kola!* I am Grey Owl. I come from *Opeepaesoway* [talking waters]."[43]

This was indeed a bad beginning as Geoffrey, an avid linguist, who would later master Spanish, Portuguese, Swedish, Danish, Norwegian, French, Gaelic, and Welsh, as well as a smattering of a number of North American Indian languages, knew the false ring of Grey Owl's opening. *How Kola* was indeed a term of good will, an expression that could be used in greeting friends,[44] but the Sioux Indians used it, not the Ojibwa, the tribe among whom Grey Owl claimed to have lived, nor the Apache, the tribe to which he said he belonged. Geoffrey continued in his diary, first noting his initial disappointment: "My heart sank. But as he got going the Hiawatha stuff vanished and we got down to the real Grey Owl—a man of acute perception, poetic feeling & whimsical humor, and an ardent faith in his mission of wild life conservation . . . fascinating."[45]

Grey Owl performed at his best when he knew that his audience, or interviewer, knew something about Canada and North American Indians. At the end of his tour, Matthew Halton, a young Canadian reporter working for the Toronto *Star* as their London correspondent, approached him. Halton was born and had grown up in Pincher Creek, in the foothills of southern Alberta, right beside the Peigan Indian Reserve. As a boy he had seen Peigan Indians in the streets of Pincher Creek and had heard them speak their Blackfoot language.[46] The *Star* had instructed him "to go wherever I saw a series of articles in the British Isles or Europe—the newspaperman's dream come true—and though my main preoccupation was the failing peace and the German menace, I wrote on almost every other subject under the sun."[47] He wanted to interview the famous Indian lecturer, and Grey Owl accepted the request of a fellow Canadian. They met in late January in London.[48]

Matt Halton, or perhaps his Toronto *Star* editor, or the typeset composer in the *Star's* printing plant, spelt his name incorrectly as "Gray Owl," but the article itself translates completely the spirit of the man and his message:

> London, January 31.—"In Europe they think of Red Indians as savages," said Wa-Sha-Quon-Asin, that wonderful Canadian half-breed, famous to the world as Gray Owl. "But I fought for three years in the great war, and I know that when it comes to savagery, red men don't know the half of it. In London, they think of red men as unsophisticated children: well, now I have seen London, I am thankful I am not as they!"
>
> So I sat in an artist's studio on a murky London day and as the artist sketched his lean, chiselled aristocratic face, I asked Gray Owl what he thought of England and civilization in general. . . . "When I first saw London," said Gray Owl, "I thought, 'My, this is a jungle!' I knew how an animal feels when he is trapped. There seemed no escape for me from this maelstrom of haggard people and roaring machines; I was caught. Mankind, I thought, has become a stampeding herd. I thought of the wilderness, cold and clean."
>
> Since Gray Owl came to Britain on a lecture tour he has made hundreds of speeches, and the people who have heard him no longer think of Red Indians as savages. He is certainly one of the most civilized men I ever interviewed; and few white Canadians have raised Canada's prestige over here so high as Gray Owl has done. His visit has been a triumphal tour. "But I will soon forget it," he said. "I meet these thousands of people, but they all seem like shadows, in a world that is not for me."

Halton then quickly reviewed the reputed biographical facts about this extraordinary man: Scot father, Apache mother, scout with Buffalo Bill, war service, adoption by the Ojibwa Indians, his marriage to Anahareo, and finally his conversion to conservation:

> "Are you doing all this," I asked, "because you suddenly one day realized animals were living beings with a right to live?" Gray Owl shook his head. "That's only one thing," he said. "My real object is to save as much as possible of the wilds for the nation and for posterity. You know, when people want to know what the past was like, they go to museums or books. I want Canadians of the future generations to be able to get into their cars and drive into wilderness preserves where animals and men live as they lived in earlier times."

Listening to Grey Owl reminded Matthew Halton of the romantic books about Indians he had read as a boy.

> Gray Owl steps right out of the pages of James Fenimore Cooper. He looks too good to be true to life. With his marvellous, sculptured face; his great feather and fringed buckskin costume; his long, lean body and powerful shoulders. He moves with the grace of a cat; or sits motionless as a perched eagle; yet he is absolutely without pose. "For goodness sake," he said, "don't think I am one of these animal sentimentalists! It takes civilization to produce sentimentalists, to fondle animals and torture fellowmen. I am neither a fanatic nor an evangelist. I don't rush up to women wearing furs and tell them how wicked and cruel they are. I merely ask for a dignified approach to the animal world."
>
> "Would you no longer kill a deer or a moose?" "Of course I would if I were hungry. We have to live and only by death can there be life. Only by killing a tree can the beaver live. If we don't kill the caribou, the jaguar will. No, we must eat and be clothed. But what does make me sick is the comic 'sportsman' in his trick outfit who invades the woods, kills the giant moose, hangs his stuffed head in a hall to boast about—and leaves the body rotting in the woods."

In his article Halton described Grey Owl as a "Canadian nobleman," but the lecturer and writer preferred another term:

> "I am a Neolithic man," said Gray Owl. "I am no sophisticate. But I am grateful for that when I sit in a London drawing room and listen to the incredibly futile chatter of smart people. Sometimes I couldn't believe my ears and my eyes. Women would chatter questions at me, and not even listen for the answers. I saw the new Noel Coward play, in which sophisticated people bawd away their lives and say everything but what they mean. There is one whole playlet about some raw colonials who come to London on a holiday and visit some people they met out in the East, somewhere. The whole play is about the hosts trying not to show that they have forgotten their visitors' names. It is, of course, very, very clever and sophisticated; but I didn't understand. I would simply have gone up to my visitors and asked them their names. No one seemed to think of that." [49]

The Toronto *Star* published Matt Halton's article on February 13, 1936, just two days before Grey Owl sailed back to Canada. He returned a public figure, known for his success as a lecturer in Britain, the heart of the Empire. At the very outset of the tour, Canadian newspapers from Halifax to Victoria had run photos of him upon his arrival in England.[50] In a widely reprinted article in Canada, the journalist Gladys Arnold reported on his phenomenal success at the London Polytechnic Theatre: "A new Canadian ambassador is taking London—and all England for that matter—by storm. He is Grey Owl."[51] The organizers of the Golden Jubilee of the City of Vancouver, to be held in the summer of 1936, invited him that February to lecture for one or two weeks during the summer's festivities. "Thousands of people in British Columbia have heard of him and have seen him in pictures. Many more thousands, who will come to British Columbia during the celebration, would also like to see him."[52] Upon his arrival back in Canada, a contract for a North American tour also awaited him.[53]

Grey Owl had given the last lecture of his British tour at Stratford-upon-Avon on Saturday, February 8. What a special joy it was to visit Stratford, as he adored Shakespeare! Originally he had been scheduled to speak here on January 21, 1936, but King George V's death the evening before had made the day one of national mourning. In Stratford he made his pilgrimage with Mrs. Somervell to Shakespeare's birthplace on Henley Street, where she took his picture by the entrance. Grey Owl fully identified with the humanness of Shakespeare, a genius with human failings—"his constant coarse allusions to marriage are not pleasing, and Falstaff's eulogy of sack, as a beverage, would indicate that the immortal bard's acquaintance with the effects of alcohol was not altogether academic." Yet, those same "reprehensible practices" gave him "the deep insight into human nature that his plays reveal" and explained his work's universal appeal.[54]

He concluded his British tour with a final call for peace and understanding. "I often think that if history books were revised it would do a lot of good to drop religious barriers, have less war talk and the waste of so much youth and money, for the sake of conquerors."[55] Then, he returned to London, and that very evening wrote Hugh Eayrs in Toronto about his "epochal" British tour. "From now, things commence and will move swiftly on, carrying us on the crest of a wave that already seems to have swept me into a realm almost of phantasy."[56]

With the completion of the tour, Laya Rotenberg had to return to Paris, but she invited him to stay, while in Toronto, with her parents and family. Who, though, would be able to accompany Grey Owl back to Canada? At the end of the tour he looked so tired and ill. Mrs. Somervell feared the worst. "On the ship he was quite likely to get absent-minded and fall over-board, or give all his money away, which he loved doing."[57] Of all those in his entourage in February 1936, Laya Rotenberg, Billy Whitaker, Lovat Dickson, there was no one free except Betty Somervell who knew this Canadian Indian's ways. She volunteered to escort him back to Ottawa and Toronto. They left London by train for Glasgow and the Canadian Pacific liner, the *Duchess of Bedford,* at neighbouring Greenock.

Fortunately Betty Somervell kept a diary during the three weeks to follow, from February 14 to March 5. Although Grey Owl's British public might well have regarded him "almost as a saint,"[58] Mrs. Somervell already knew, and confirmed on the journey, that the man had several other faces as well. As she later wrote: "Some people thought he was a saint, and others thought he was a wild man of the woods, I think he was some of each, with a few more rolled in, like most people."[59]

Grey Owl had come to England with a knapsack and a small piece of hand luggage. Four months later he left with a trunk and eight large suitcases stuffed with gifts from booksellers and admirers for Anahareo and their daughter Dawn.[60] He brought back for himself a new gramophone and records, as well as a magnificent eagle-feather warbonnet[61] he had just bought in London. Ironically an Iroquois singer from Eastern Canada, Oskenonton (who performed in the annual Hiawatha pageant at the Royal Albert Hall in London), and his English friends, Ted and Curly Blackmore, avid North American Indian hobbyists, had made Grey Owl's new Plains Indian headdress. They completed it in Eastbourne, Sussex, only fifty kilometres or so from Hastings.[62]

Once the train from Glasgow to Greenock started, Grey Owl brought out the warbonnet. As Betty Somervell later wrote, it "proved to be a worse burden than a new born babe—it needed so much airing & personal cherishing."[63] He was afraid that the trunk would crush the bonnet's lovely white down.[64] To protect his classical records, he stuffed his press clippings from the tour around them.[65]

At Princess Pier at Greenock the celebrity had his final words with the newsmen who had gathered by the ship. He told them how impressed he had been "by the hospitality shown me—a savage and pagan—in Britain."[66] How strange, six or so years earlier he had objected when French Canadians in Quebec had called him a *sauvage*, now he freely used the term himself. It attracted attention.

A reporter questioned Grey Owl about how he had been able to speak to thousands of people without hesitation or nervousness. He replied that he was only an interpreter: "When I stood on those platforms I did not need to think. I merely spoke of the life and the animals I have known all my days. I was only the mouth, but nature was speaking."[67] Then the modern Hiawatha departed.

Anxious to ease the pressure of the hectic, stressful last four months, Grey Owl now wanted to drink heavily. From Lovat Dickson and Laya Rotenberg, Summy knew this would happen, and she now tried to take the necessary precautions. As soon as she had taken Grey Owl to his cabin, she brought out his new records and the gramophone. From 8 A.M. to midnight the machine played Greig, Wagner, Tchaikowsky, and other great classical composers.[68] Summy would sit on the cabin floor winding up the gramophone, entertaining him. When she momentarily left for her own cabin, however, Grey Owl acted with lightning speed. He either took out of a suitcase, or purchased on ship, a number of bottles of whisky, which he hid under his bunk. He drank whenever she left the cabin. Just before she returned he chewed a raw onion to banish the whisky smell—Summy thought the onion smell came from an Indian cure he was taking for his sickness. After three days of neither eating nor sleeping, the intoxicated Grey Owl looked like a ghost.

Finally Summy solved the mystery. During the third day at sea the ship lurched, and a bottle gently rolled from under Grey Owl's bunk. Instantly she realized his deception and, in a rage, soundly scolded him. Ashamed for his conduct, Grey Owl promised to stop and did so for the remainder of the voyage. But now another problem arose.

Once he stopped drinking Grey Owl started talking. As Betty wrote in her diary on February 20: "Having remained silent most of his life, G. O. has now found his tongue and nothing will stop him talking—perversely against Doctor's orders." He was very proud of what he had done. One night he read aloud all his favourite passages from *Sajo*.[69] Often he kept her up late at night dictating sections of his new book, *Tales of an Empty Cabin*: "He went at about 60 miles an hour, and I had to scribble away in long-hand, trying to keep up. He used to sit straight up on the edge of a hard chair, and smoke little black cigars and dictate all night."[70] The self-centred Modern Hiawatha never seemed to notice Betty Somervell's strain and exhaustion.

They landed at Halifax on February 21, then boarded the train for Montreal. Through New Brunswick they looked out of the coach windows at snow-covered bush farms. Grey Owl told her "the effort at cultivation by farmers & settlers look like wretched scratches on the earth's surface— ruined houses & spoilt land & massacred forest, burnt & untidy."[71] He had passed through New Brunswick before, over twenty years earlier on his way to enlist at Digby, Nova Scotia, in 1915. On one of his enlistment forms he had indicated that a "John McVane" of Westfield, New Brunswick, was his next of kin.[72]

En route to Ottawa they spent a day in Montreal. To Betty's pleasant surprise, "G. O. turned the tables on me, took charge of me," and invited her on a sleigh ride, covered in buffalo skins, up Mount Royal. "It was bitter cold, sunny & sparkly and we both felt & looked as if we'd had a month's holiday."[73] They later saw Charlie Chaplin's new film *Modern Times*, a satirical skit on civilisation. It promised to be intriguing, particularly as the Nazis had denounced the picture on the grounds that it had "Communistic tendencies and Chaplin is non-Aryan."[74] They enjoyed the film and attended a hockey game that evening, a double bill of fun after the long sea voyage.

The morning of their departure to Ottawa, Grey Owl's demanding side appeared again. As Betty Somervell wrote in her diary: "In G. O.'s room the telephone was broken. At 7:30 a wild figure with flying hair appeared at my door, in despair because no one would wake him up with tea."[75]

The Ottawa visit involved several days of meetings with Parks Branch officials, including James Harkin. Mrs. Somervell prepared Grey Owl's notes for the interviews. Betty also made him see a doctor, who, she noted in her diary, diagnosed his medical problems: "He found G. O. has bronchitis & is in a very bad nervous condition & had undue strain even for a man of his robust type to stand."[76]

The next day, February 25, Grey Owl had to have a cyst removed from under his right eye. He set off alone, only to return to their hotel three times to obtain, Betty noted in her diary: "1. the doctor's name, 2. address, 3. because he had no money for the taxi."[77] How exasperating he could be! Truly, to quote Lovat Dickson's comment in a letter to Hugh Eayrs two months earlier: "I have a very deep affection for him and regard him as a genius but with some of the characteristics of a small child."[78]

Grey Owl's physical appearance two days after the operation would be immortalized by a young Ottawa photographer, a man who later became one of the world's most respected portrait photographers: Yousuf Karsh. This haunting portrait of the famous conservationist shows, if you look closely, the stitches still in place below Grey Owl's right eye (the doctor removed them the next day).[79]

Grey Owl's physical and mental health deteriorated still further in Toronto, the next stop. The comforting glow of his success in Britain had begun to fade. Momentarily his newly acquired fame had, like a tidal wave, covered over many of the old ugly landmarks of his earlier life. In Toronto most of these re-emerged. Here, in the late fall of 1917, he had faced one of the most difficult periods of his life. Upon his return to Canada he had learned of Marie Girard's death. Subsequently he had decided not to invite Ivy to join him in Bisco. Confused and troubled he had momentarily re-united with Angele.

When Laya Rotenberg's parents met Grey Owl and Summy at Toronto's new Union Station[80] that Friday evening, many old memories must have raced through Grey Owl's brain. Many more would surface on Monday, March 2.

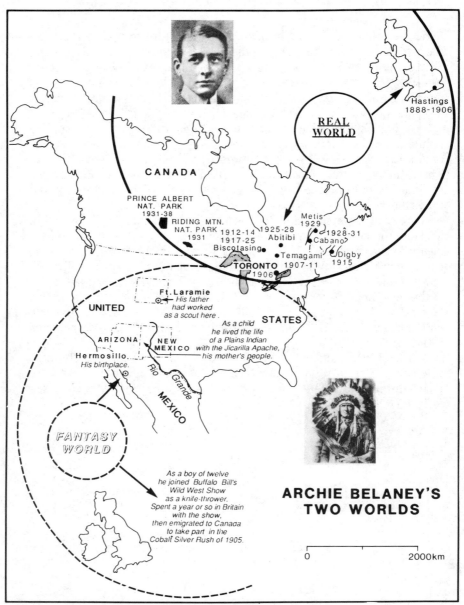

REAL
WORLD

Hastings
1888-1906

CANADA

PRINCE ALBERT
NAT. PARK
1931-38

RIDING MTN.
NAT. PARK
1931

Metis
1929

1912-14
1917-25

1925-28
Abitibi

1928-31
Cabano

Biscotasing

TORONTO
1906

Temagami
1907-11

Digby
1915

UNITED

Ft. Laramie
— His father
had worked
as a scout here.

STATES

As a child
he lived the life
of a Plains Indian
with the Jicarilla Apache,
his mother's people.

ARIZONA

NEW
MEXICO

Hermosillo.
His birthplace.

Rio Grande

MEXICO

FANTASY
WORLD

As a boy of twelve
he joined Buffalo Bill's
Wild West Show
as a knife-thrower.
Spent a year or so in Britain
with the show,
then emigrated to Canada
to take part in the
Cobalt Silver Rush of 1905.

ARCHIE BELANEY'S
TWO WORLDS

0   2000km

Facing page: *The earliest formal portrait of Grey Owl, taken in Montreal in late January 1931 by Batten Limited. It accompanied the important biographical article on Grey Owl in* Canadian Forest and Outdoors, *March 1931, entitled "The Adventurous Career of GREY OWL (wa-shee-quon-asier)." The information Archie gave the magazine is fascinating: "In 1905 or 6 or thereabouts (his age and other early dates being a matter of doubt) he left the band of Jicarilla Apache to which his mother belonged. His father and grand-father before him were free trappers and Indian fighters up and down the West from the Canadas to California. Grey Owl's father served as a Government scout and guide to waggon trains at various military headquarters and frontier posts, including at Fort Laramie, when Colonel Cody (Buffalo Bill) was chief of Scouts at that*

post. *The injustice and unfairness of the wars against Indians eventually drove Grey Owl's father to retire from this work, and he went to England with Buffalo Bill's first show, taking with him an Apache woman (Grey Owl's mother) as his wife. On leaving the band, at the before mentioned date, Grey Owl hired with Buffalo Bill and spent nine months in England with him. Tiring of this, he quit, and influenced by his father's tales of a trapper's life, Grey Owl came to Canada (around 1906 or 1907). He took to the bush in time to participate in the Cobalt Silver Rush. Next he became trapper; was formally and ceremonially adopted by the Ojibway Nation, learned their language and methods of travelling and hunting, being now more of a bush Indian than he ever was a plains Indian."* Archives of Ontario/S14459. Source: Grey Owl and Anahareo Collection lent by Dawn Richardson.

Left to right: Grey Owl, Sir Charles G. D. Roberts, Anahareo, Lloyd Roberts, Riding Mountain National Park, mid-October 1931. Photo by H. U. Green. Whyte Museum of the Canadian Rockies, Banff, Alberta.

Grey Owl at his evening meal, Beaver Lodge, Prince Albert National Park, September 1932. Photo by W. J. Oliver. Glenbow Archives, Calgary/NA-3680-6.

Grey Owl at Beaver Lodge, Prince Albert National Park, 1932 or 1933. Photo by W. J. Oliver. Glenbow Archives, Calgary/NA–3680–7.

Anahareo and Grey Owl at Beaver Lodge, Prince Albert National Park, probably 1932. Canadian Parks Service/W. J. Oliver.

Grey Owl, looking 'a little worse from wear.' Waskesiu, Prince Albert National Park, August 1935. Shown with Billie Ozmun of Kinistino, Saskatchewan, on the right, and a girlfriend of hers from Melfort, Saskatchewan. The two teenaged girls asked Billie's older sister to take a photograph of them with Grey Owl. They had met him, by chance, on the main beach at Waskesiu. Only one month later Grey Owl left for Britain as the Modern Hiawatha. Prince Albert National Park, Waskesiu. Source: Billie Ozmun Rawlinson.

Grey Owl arriving at Southampton on October 17, 1935. He does not have his "Indian face" on for this photo. Notice he is holding one of his precious notebooks. Several of these are now in the National Archives of Canada in Ottawa. Wide World Photos, A. P.

GREY OWL'S TOUR OF BRITAIN 1935-36

From late October 1935 to early February 1936 Grey Owl lectured in each of these British towns and cities

NORTH SEA

ATLANTIC OCEAN

Helensburgh
Glasgow • Edinburgh
• Ayr

Newcastle
• Carlisle

Kendal • Scarborough
Harrogate • York
Leeds • Hull
Wigan • Huddersfield
Liverpool • Manchester
Birkenhead • Sheffield
• Chesterfield

IRELAND

IRISH SEA

Nottingham
Bournville • Leicester
Birmingham • Rugby • Bury St. Edmund's
Leamington Spa •
Henley-in-Arden • Cambridge • Ipswich
Stratford-upon-Avon
Oxford
Watford • **LONDON** • Hayes
Bristol • Maidehead • Maidstone
Bath • Weybridge • Tunbridge • Canterbury
Edenbridge • Wells • Hastings
Bournemouth • Worthing
Exeter • Howe • Eastbourne
Torquay
Crowborough

BELFAST

0   100   200km

Grey Owl and Lovat Dickson, his publisher in England. Taken near Ascot, England, just before Grey Owl began his lectures on his first British lecture tour, October 1935. Archives of Ontario/ Acc. 9291 S14257. Source: Peter Davies Co. Ltd.

Grey Owl liked Lord Sempill, whom he met at Foyle's Literary Luncheon at Grosvenor House in London on October 24, 1935. To the Scottish peer he decided to divulge a new unknown aspect of his romantic ancestry, that his father was a McNeil. Hearing this, Lord Sempill afterwards obtained a silk scarf of the McNeil tartan as a gift for Anahareo. Lady Minto presented Lord Sempill's gift to Grey Owl in Edinburgh on November 29, 1935. (See " 'Grey Owl' in Town. Impressed by Scots Hospitality. Tartan Scarf for his Wife," Edinburgh Evening News, *November 29, 1935.) Photo from the* Weekly Illustrated, *November 2, 1935.*

Grey Owl, portrait by Yousuf Karsh, taken in Ottawa, February 27, 1936. Miller Comstock Inc.

Left: *Inside Beaver Lodge. Bunk at right. "Books on shelf from the authors themselves" (Margaret Winters Charko). War-bonnet on radio over the log. Steamer trunk containing his manuscripts. Summer of 1936.* Archives of Ontario/S14623. Source: Margaret Winters Charko.

Right: *Arthur Lismer, the well-known member of the Group of Seven, sketched the drawing of Grey Owl when he visited the Arts and Letters Club, 14 Elm Street, Toronto, March 3, 1936.* Archives, Arts and Letters Club, Toronto.

Laya Rotenberg (on the left) acted as Grey Owl's secretary during the latter part of the first British tour. Mrs. Betty Somervell (on the right) also assisted with the tour, driving the tour party. Archives of Ontario/S14439. Source: Grey Owl and Anahareo Collection lent by Dawn Richardson.

Grey Owl holding Dawn at the commemoration of Treaty Six at Fort Carlton, Sask., August, 1936. Reproduced from a copy of a print in the Osborne Collection, Toronto Public Library.

Grey Owl throwing knives at Prince Albert National Park, September 1936. Photo taken by Mrs. Betty Somervell. Archives of Ontario/S14256. Source: Betty Somervell.

Sir William Mulock (left), Grey Owl, Sir Charles G. D. Roberts, at the King Edward Hotel, Toronto Book Fair, November 9, 1936. City of Toronto Archives, SC266–41837.

12 Toronto, March 2, 1936

In the early evening of March 2, 1936, Arthur Stevens met Canada's famous writer and lecturer at the home of Grey Owl's friend, Louis Rotenberg, in Toronto.[1] The *Mail and Empire* had announced Grey Owl's return to Canada that morning:

> Grey Owl is resting in Toronto after a strenuous four months in England, where he addressed more than 200 audiences comprising half a million people. Press and people accorded him a reception which, in universal warmth, is only to be compared with the welcomes extended to Artemus Ward and Mark Twain among all foreign literary visitors.[2]

A year or so earlier Stevens had spotted an article with Grey Owl's picture in it. Immediately he had connected him with a young, well-mannered Englishman he had first met nearly three decades earlier. He wrote the postmaster in Prince Albert inquiring what the author's name was. Prince Albert replied: "Archie Belaney."[3] Stevens subsequently wrote his old acquaintance, and received back a fascinating letter, written on February 24, 1935, clearly signed Archie Belaney, with this additional note: "P.S. Please add the name Grey Owl if you should find time to write me again at some future date as I am better known as such, and letters addressed only by my 'civil' name sometimes go astray. Use both names, for safety."[4]

The letter, full of its writer's warmth and personality, struck a responsive chord with Stevens, now seventy years old. Grey Owl began:

> Since I have become a greenhorn writer I have received letters from nearly everywhere in the world. But none of them ever give me the same thrill, the real genuine pleasure that I get when some old friend, that I haven't seen for years, drops me a line and says "Good luck, ol-timer, try again!" Thirty years is a long time. I was a foolish youngster then; I often wonder why I was allowed to live. I have forgotten a great deal of what I knew(?) at that time, & I often feel that it is a wonder, considering some of the

things I said & did, that the boys didn't gang up on me & bury me alive some place. But we grow older and, I hope, wiser.

After nearly half a century in Canada, Stevens still had a strong English accent,[5] but Grey Owl spoke like a northern Canadian woodsman. Stories passed freely between the two men in the Rotenberg's living room, as Mrs. Stevens listened. If Grey Owl seemed a little nervous at first, it was understandable: this man now sitting in front of him was Temagami's Justice of the Peace to whom he had applied for a marriage license to marry Angele Egwuna in the summer of 1910.

Arthur Stevens knew Grey Owl's true identity. Ivy Holmes had contacted him when she learned that Archie was already legally married at the time of their marriage in February 1917. He knew about Archie's birth and upbringing in Hastings, England, from the letters he had received fifteen years earlier from Ivy. He also personally knew Angele and Agnes Belaney, who had both worked for him at his hotel, the Ronnoco, which he had bought in the mid-1920s. But Arthur Stevens would not expose Grey Owl. In weighing in his own mind the balance of the harm and the good that the man had done, this veteran law officer—renowned for his "broad vision and kindliness"[6]—ruled that the positive outweighed the negative.

Archie's new mission as Grey Owl won over Arthur Stevens, who fully sympathized with his conservationist goals. The owner of the Ronnoco Hotel at Temagami, and the Stevens House in Cochrane, Ontario (a town farther up the Temiskaming and Northern Ontario line), knew the need for wilderness. It was important to preserve and to protect the environment. The forests' inhabitants, both human and animal, depended on it. So did Canada's tourist operators. Arthur Stevens realized that the public would spend money, year after year, to see country in its original state. As he himself wrote shortly afterwards: "I had a very delightful talk with Grey Owl last year after his return from the United Kingdom and greatly admire the excellent work he is doing for the preservation of wild animal life. It is a most noble vocation and future generations will greatly benefit by the patience and sagacity displayed by Grey Owl."[7]

No, Arthur would not bring forward the unsavoury details of Grey Owl's youth. After all—appearances aside—he had always liked the personable, if mischievous, Archie. In his diary on March 2, 1936, Arthur made this one entry: "It was 24 years since we met . . . not much change except long black braids."[8]

Stevens had arrived at the end of one of the most exhausting days for Grey Owl. It began with the appearance that Monday morning of three newspaper men on the Rotenbergs' steps. Grey Owl's interview with the *Mail*'s W. A. Deacon, boldly captioned "Christianity Unsuited for Indians of Canada Famous Red Man Thinks," attracted press attention. Just the day before, on Sunday, Grey Owl had given the interview. The *Mail*, in its edition of Monday, March 2, 1936, quoted the famous Indian as having said that his people should not be christianized at the expense of their ancient code of justice and morality:

> I should like to see the aborigine retain his attitude to the world and life. Why should he be asked to accept the youngest religion? The old Indian faith, even sun worship, teaches humanity, honesty, integrity, reverence, love of nature and love of his fellow man as much as Christianity does. Speaking as a pagan, I note that in Biscotasing, those Indians south of the tracks are Catholics, those living north of it are Protestants; but, in spite of this, some practice their ancient rites."
> Are Indians pantheists?
> Yes, but they don't call it that. With the Indian, prayer has never become the servile supplication that it has become with white men. . . . don't let missionaries preach that their native dances are wrong. Their beliefs are not more built on myths than Christianity is, and their conceptions are filled with poetic beauty.

In overwhelmingly Protestant Toronto in the 1930s, religious views were strongly held. Both the churches and the Sunday schools were well-attended. In fact, according to the same W. A. Deacon of the Toronto *Mail* whose interview had opened the discussion: "In Sunday-school attendance Toronto leads the nation, possibly the world." Grey Owl's remarks about the value of Christian missionary work among North American Indians caused an uproar in Toronto, "the City of Churches." [9]

On the morning of March 2, 1936, three newspapermen came in person to 260 Roslin Avenue, North Toronto, a large house overlooking a ravine in the Don River Valley. Others phoned to ask for interviews. That morning, afternoon, and evening, and into the following day, the Rotenbergs' telephone rang constantly. Crank phone callers also joined in, including one "Moose Face" who called up regularly every half hour and whispered.

The *Star* reporter, Robert E. Knowles, personified the press at its worst. He was an ex-minister and a former pastor of the second-largest Presbyterian congregation in Canada and had an aggressive, flamboyant style. Known to the *Star*'s competitor, the *Telegram,* as "the man who interviews himself," the supremely self-confident Knowles usually supplied more of the copy in his articles than did the person he interviewed. Allegedly, the former servant of God bluntly told his subjects: "Just answer my questions, and keep your answers as brief as possible. I find that I generally know more about the subject than the people I talk to." Out his articles came, in the words of Ross Harkness, the historian of the *Star,* "disdainful of geography, historical fact, the accuracy of literary quotations and the exact meaning of words." [10] His readers loved his racy style.

Knowles literally forced his way into the house and walked upstairs into Grey Owl's room without even asking Mrs. Rotenberg. To Grey Owl, he fired off questions such as: "Did you ever know that it was your race that killed Abraham Lincoln's grandfather in the wilds of Kentucky?" [11]

Moreover, the *Star* man thoroughly misquoted Grey Owl and insulted Mrs. Rotenberg, which her Indian guest would not tolerate. They threw him out.[12] Before his important luncheon engagement at the Toronto Writers' Club,[13] an enraged Grey Owl stormed down to the *Star* building on King Street to protest against "the interviewing and misquoting and rudeness of Knowles." Subsequently, the humbled ex-minister phoned Mr. and Mrs. Rotenberg and Grey Owl, and apologized to all three.[14]

That evening the *Star* held back Knowles' interview, running a laundered version the next day—but they did print, in the afternoon of March 2, the local clergy's predictably hostile responses to Grey Owl's remarks in the *Mail* about Indians and Christianity. The Rev. James Endicott, a former moderator of the United Church of Canada and the head of the United Church's Foreign Mission Board, who had served as a missionary for almost twenty years in western China, replied to Grey Owl:[15] "Christianity is the culmination of a great many good things in other religions. . . . I don't make comparisons of religions. Nor do I say that all religions other than Christianity are false," but "Christianity is the light of the world, and Christ is our only hope." Four other Toronto clergymen protested Grey Owl's statements, as did Archdeacon Richard Faries, himself of partial Indian ancestry. The archdeacon, a veteran of nearly half-a-century of Anglican mission work at York Factory on Hudson Bay and the editor of *A Dictionary of the Cree Language*, which would be published in 1938, pointed out: "There is a great deal in what Grey Owl says about caring for animals. In that, I thoroughly agree. But when he says that Christianity is unsuited to Indians, there I think he is wrong. The Indians before Christianity came to them, were a treacherous lot."[16]

The man who, as a schoolboy, had achieved top grades in Religious Knowledge relished the controversy. The clergymen's protests led Grey Owl to elaborate further upon his earlier remarks for the *Mail*. His main criticism of Christianity came from its view that man came first: "In my somewhat meagre researches, I have failed to find in Christianity any emphasis on tolerance to what are known as "lower" forms of life, as in the words of Buddha who said, in effect, that hunting as a pastime was not to be extolled, and that a man should hunt only for necessity. This is a precept which the Indian, till contaminated by the requirements of commercialism, has held to strongly."[17]

How tired he was. After the Knowles interview in the morning, he delivered his protest at the *Star*'s headquarters at noon, attended a luncheon at the Toronto Writers' Club, and then had a second interview with a *Mail* reporter in the early evening about the Christian ministers' protests, followed by the visit of Arthur Stevens who knew his true English background. As soon as Stevens left, Donalda Legace, a daughter of his former landlady at Bisco, appeared with her husband at the Rotenbergs'.[18] While at the Legaces' before the First World War, he had met Marie Girard.

Betty Somervell stayed to hear all the stories. At last Grey Owl had someone who could corroborate many of his Bisco tales. Triumphantly he said to Mrs. Somervell in Donalda's presence: "Now it was *true*, wasn't it, about that time I cut the legs off a house? You see? And it was true when we hog-tied the school teacher? See? And it *was* true when I shot up the dance hall and you brought me a gun and forgot the ammunition. Wasn't it? See! It was all true and I could see you didn't believe a word of it. Now then!"[19]

Donalda, who had helped after school as a waitress at her mother's boardinghouse, knew Grey Owl well in the years 1912 to 1914 when he stayed at the Legaces'. She liked him. Always Archie had playfully enjoyed going beyond the real story for the dramatic effect, but Donalda would not contradict him in front of Mrs. Somervell. The tale, for instance, about chopping the legs of the house in the early 1920s was indeed true, but the future Grey Owl had not done it. When he and his trapping partner Ted Cusson, both drunk, had been refused entrance to a dance at the Legaces' boardinghouse, Archie had excited Ted to begin chopping one of the cedar cornerposts holding up the building (until stopped by the Legaces). The future "modern Hiawatha" had handed over his own ax, but not used it himself. When those inside heard the chopping and burst out, they saw Archie with his arms folded, as if to say, "I didn't do it."[20]

That night at the Rotenbergs' Archie paid for the day's excitement. The evening's talk stirred up many old memories. He became a time traveller going back into his past, to Temagami and then to Bisco. In the Rotenbergs' library, a small room with floor-to-ceiling bookcases filled with books, he stayed up all night, emerging the next morning looking "most dreadfully ill—pale yellow colour, staring eyes."[21]

Without any sleep, Archie faced another taxing day of phone calls, interviews, and a luncheon at the Toronto Arts and Letters Club. At noon Arthur Lismer, a founding member of the Group of Seven and regarded as one of Canada's foremost artists, sketched Grey Owl's portrait in a copy of *Sajo and her Beaver People*.[22] It captures the exhaustion of the tormented man. All night he had faced alone the memories of his past brought to mind by his visit with Arthur Stevens and then Donalda Legace: memories of Angele and Marie had resurfaced again.

*   *   *

Mrs. Somervell (whose diary is the basis of much of this account) stayed for three more days in Toronto, then travelled on to Halifax, where on March 7 she sailed for England. That very day Hitler, in violation of the Treaties of Versailles (1919) and Locarno (1925), sent troops to occupy the supposedly demilitarized Rhineland. These treaties had forbidden Germany to station troops on its western frontier. Now the Nazis did so. Betty noted in her diary: "Rumours of European war sound ominous."[23]

Grey Owl stayed on at the Rotenbergs' until Sunday, March 8. He liked them a great deal, Hugh Eayrs, Grey Owl's Canadian publisher, later noted (in a letter to Lovat Dickson), "because they are Jews: as you know he is not a Christian himself, and he has a special admiration for Jewry as a whole." [24]

On Sunday, March 8, Grey Owl left for Ottawa and appointments with Lord Tweedsmuir, governor-general of Canada, Prime Minister Mackenzie King, and an unexpected meeting with a prominent Canadian Indian political leader. Before he left the man was so out-of-sorts Eayrs recognized something was wrong. At the luncheon meeting of the Toronto Writers' Club, the luncheon at the Arts and Letters Club, and the dinner at the Toronto Chapter of PEN (a writers' organization) he noticed Grey Owl's nervous state.

> Meeting anybody or talking with anybody seems to frighten him until he is assured that he can be himself and speak the thoughts in his mind. Part of this Dora [Eayrs' wife] and I have come to conclude is due to the fact (though he won't come out and say it) that he doesn't like Toronto because it has old associations for him: he is, not to put too fine a point on it, quite scared of meeting people here in Toronto, and he shows it. . . . He gives us the impression of being actually frightened of folk he meets in Toronto, and that has been plain on each occasion. [25]

13 The Mission

The people of Poundmaker and the surrounding Saskatchewan reserves had paid for John Tootoosis's train fare with many small contributions. After several days' travel the young Plains Cree finally arrived, tired and hungry, in mid-March in Ottawa. Getting off onto the platform in the early morning darkness, he had no idea where to find a restaurant and simply chose a street at random. He made out a neon light ahead in the blackness, advertising a small cafe. He entered into a warm room, to the smell of breakfast being prepared by the Chinese owner.[1]

John sat down and placed his order. Then, to his surprise, he saw a hawk-faced man in buckskins who looked familiar. From the press photos, John knew him by sight, although they had never met. Back home in Saskatchewan he had read a great deal about the "beaver man," most recently from newspaper articles about his lecture tour of Britain.

Having noticed the Indian in the restaurant, Grey Owl walked over to introduce himself. A conversation began and John invited Grey Owl to join him. The young Plains Cree leader explained his journey to Ottawa to present the resolutions passed by the meetings of the League of Indians of Western Canada to the Indian Department.

Understandably John was a little nervous in this city of more than 100,000 people. Half-a-century earlier, during the troubles of 1885, a Canadian army officer, Colonel W. D. Otter, had ordered a military attack on his community at Cutknife, about fifty kilometres west of Battleford. The Canadians accused John's great-uncle, Chief Poundmaker, his grandfather Yellow Mud Blanket, and their camp, of supporting Louis Riel and the Métis in rebellion. As a boy of twelve, John's father had witnessed the Battle of Cutknife, in which the Plains Cree and Assiniboine warriors routed the Canadian force.[2]

In mid-March 1936, John Tootoosis had come eastward to meet Canadian government officials. He came with petitions from Indian councils which called for a more humane Indian policy. Since Riel's, and subsequently Poundmaker's, surrender in May 1885, Western Canadian Indians had felt the government's iron hand. The Canadian government tried to force them to live the life of the white man, instead of living their own. On the reserves the Indian agents had dictatorial control over local councils, and the Christian churches had similar controls over Indian schools. Recently naturalized immigrants to Canada had more rights than the original Canadians had.

In the mid-1930s the various Cree bands in central Saskatchewan and Alberta met and passed resolutions calling for a relaxation of the dictatorial rule of the Indian Department. Having studied at a Roman Catholic Indian residential school for four years, John knew English and had acted as the secretary for the Cree bands in central Saskatchewan. The resolutions passed at the councils at Poundmaker and other reserves called for better schools and teachers, and pleaded for religious freedom ("to worship in our own way and according to our past customs the Most High God that created the world and all the beasts thereof").[3]

Upon learning that John had arrived in Ottawa that very morning, Grey Owl invited him to stay in his room at the Plaza Hotel on Sparks Street. They went there by taxi. As he had appointments all day, he welcomed John to treat the room as his own, until he had had a good rest. He told John to look at his books and to help himself to drinks.[4] But in Grey Owl's absence, the exhausted traveller did neither. He simply lay down and slept, right until the moment Grey Owl returned late that afternoon. John thanked his new friend and then obtained a room for himself at the same hotel. For the next couple of days the two men saw a good deal of each other, Grey Owl assisting with introductions at Department of Indian Affairs offices. As he had told him: "If you have any problems or worries let me know and I will help you."[5]

In the evenings the two men had long conversations. The Cree leader grew up at a time when the elders on his reserve still remembered the last war parties and buffalo hunts. John replied as best he could to his new friend's questions but, unlike Grey Owl, he also lived in the present, and he spoke at length of the Crees' contemporary problems.[6]

John recognized a sympathetic friend in Grey Owl. From his years in northern Ontario and Quebec, Grey Owl knew the difficulties Indian bands experienced in dealing with the federal and provincial bureaucracies. The bands at Temagami and Grand Lac Victoria–Lac Simon still had no reserves. Just after the war, in 1920, the Department of Indian Affairs had also refused to grant a reserve to the Indians at Bisco itself.[7] Within Prince Albert National Park the federal government, once it established the park, denied the neighbouring Cree Indians at Montreal Lake the right to hunt and trap. The Crees had hunted and trapped there for decades.[8] Grey Owl felt strongly that the provincial and Canadian governments had treated the Indians despicably, and he had written in *The Men of the Last Frontier* of the attempts to assimilate them: "Under the white man's scheme of existence the Indian is asked to forget his language, his simple conception of the Great Spirit, and his few remaining customs, which if it were demanded of the Hindus, the Boers, the Irish or the French-Canadians, would without doubt cause a rebellion." [9]

Grey Owl fascinated John. When he saw the beaver man up close, he simply could not believe the tall man wearing braids and dressed in buckskin was Indian. Yet, fair skin and blue eyes did not themselves constitute proof, as much racial mixing had already occurred in Canada. Blue-eyed Indians existed, the descendants of unions between fur traders and Indian women. [10] Just south of Prince Albert, for instance, lived a large Cree group almost all of whom were descended from one George Sutherland, an employee of the Hudson's Bay Company. About 1800 he had left the company and went to live on the prairies as a native. He took three Cree wives, who bore him nearly thirty children, the first members of his band. His children married members of other bands, but they returned generally to their own. [11]

John wanted to find out more about Grey Owl's background. He had spotted in his room a little round drum, the same size as those the Plains Cree used. To Grey Owl he said, "I see you people have these little drums too." The Cree suggested that he would sing first, with Grey Owl to begin when he finished. John discovered that his new friend did not put words into his singing. He imitated the sounds but not the words of the Ojibwa language, a tongue closely related to Cree. Now John knew that Grey Owl could not have lived with the Ojibwa for twenty years, as he claimed.

This discovery, however, did not alter the Cree leader's opinion of his new friend, for he respected Grey Owl's fight to conserve the beaver, "and more beavers meant more dams to hold back the water and that in turn meant better conditions for the muskrat and waterfowl population." [12] Forty years later he recalled, "I knew that he was doing good for the country with the wild game, so I never let him know that I didn't believe in him." [13]

Grey Owl, however, imagined that John Tootoosis had accepted him as an Indian. After thirty years of bringing forward his Indian ancestry, he believed that he could fool anyone, even the Indians themselves. His apparent success in this masquerade encouraged him to continue as the voice of wilderness.

Originally Grey Owl had conceived of his mission as one to save the beaver from extinction, just as Michel Pablo had set out to help protect the last of the plains buffalo in the early 1880s. The Mexican-American had saved a small herd in the western United States, which the Canadian government later bought and bred at its Buffalo National Park near Wainwright, Alberta. [14] Writing of the beaver, Grey Owl said in *Pilgrims of the Wild*: "I perhaps could start a colony of my own; these animals could not be permitted to pass completely from the face of this wilderness.

I thought of Michael [Michel] Pablo and the buffalo. His idea had borne fruit: why should not mine?"[15]

Slowly, Grey Owl's original concept grew and broadened from a desire to save the beaver to one to protect the forest and all wildlife as well. In 1936 he wrote in his preface to *Tales of an Empty Cabin*:

> The Wilderness should now no longer be considered as a playground for vandals, or a rich treasure trove to be ruthlessly exploited for the personal gain of the few—to be grabbed off by whoever happens to get there first.
>
> Man should enter the woods, not with any conquistador obsession or mighty hunter complex, neither in a spirit of braggadocio, but rather with the awe, and not a little of the veneration, of one who steps within the portals of some vast and ancient edifice of wondrous architecture. For many a man who considers himself the master of all he surveys would do well, when setting foot in the forest, to take off not only his hat but his shoes too and, in not a few cases, be glad he is allowed to retain an erect position.[16]

In the 1930s, wilderness areas needed a spokesperson, as thousands of people living on impoverished farms in southern Canada sought refuge in northern districts. Families, for example, trekked into the forested area of northern Saskatchewan from drought-stricken prairie farms to begin again. The settlement frontier advanced everywhere in the early 1930s in northern Saskatchewan,[17] without regard to the damage it caused to the forest, the wildlife, and the native peoples. The public perceived the wilderness as infinite. Apart from officials like James Harkin in the Parks Branch, and a few supporters in the general public, Canadians in the 1930s still had a pioneering mentality and believed that an overabundance of wild country and wildlife existed.[18]

Grey Owl became one of the first public figures in Canada to argue for the preservation of wilderness and wildlife. Ingeniously he associated his conservationist message with an animal in which Canadians had the greatest interest: the beaver. In Grey Owl's words, Canada's national symbol was "the animal supreme of all the forest, they were the Wilderness personified."[19] In *Tales of an Empty Cabin* he explained his mission to popularize wildlife and wilderness preservation, using the beaver as the "thin edge of the wedge."

> In order to remove this idea from the realm of pipe-dreams and put it on a basis of reasonable practicability, it was necessary to arouse public interest, to enlist public opinion on my side. To do this I had first, not only to show that I knew what I was talking about, but would have to demonstrate. With this end in view, and greatly because of the company these highly intelligent animals gave to me, I established a colony of beaver, and these docile and friendly creatures, faithful as well-trained dogs, attached themselves to me unconditionally, and are with me yet. Their general behaviour, and the remarkable mental attributes they manifested, convinced

me that the salvation of this useful and valuable animal, representative not only of all North American Wild Life but of the Wilderness itself, was a worthwhile undertaking. And so it has proved; for with my further and more ambitious resolution to broaden my field of activity to include Wild Life in general, I have found that in the beaver, with its almost human, very nearly child-like appeal, I had seized on a powerful weapon. Placed in the vanguard, the beaver constituted the thin end of the wedge.[20]

Grey Owl's mission in Britain had taxed him enormously. On his return to Prince Albert National Park he told Jim Wood, the park superintendent, about the strain of the constant maintaining of "a poise such as would be expected of me."

The work of lecturing itself did not seem so hard, yet the continual facing, *without any let-up*, of all the unfamiliar conditions I found myself in, the maintaining without any training whatsoever, of a poise such as would be expected of me, the constant calls on my very limited abilities, took a lot out of me.[21]

And always he had to wear his stern "Indian face," reflective of the Indian's "harsh, impenetrable exterior."[22]

The constant references during the tour to Anahareo also had taken their toll. They had not really lived together for years, except for at most a few months a year. He had chosen to write books rather than to communicate with her. Before he had left Canada he knew their relationship was over. Yet on tour he promoted his account of their love story, *Pilgrims of the Wild*, and he showed as one of his leading films, "Pilgrims of the Wild," which portrayed her as the heroine of his campaign to save the beaver. During the tour, Lovat Dickson noted, "what people love here is the Beavers and Anahareo, and they like to hear Grey Owl talk about them or read what he has written about them." After the lectures, "all their questions . . . were about her."[23]

Lovat Dickson perceptively saw that Grey Owl had serious problems. In his biographical article on Grey Owl in *Strand Magazine*, he noted, "About the whole man there is a sense of remoteness, almost of loneliness."[24] This same trait appears in his books, as critic R. E. Rashley has observed. "As far as humanity is concerned, Grey Owl is a loner, incapable of human commitments, cold, hard, limited."[25]

Grey Owl, however, did have choices. He did have free will. The very walls of the prison that he had built up around himself he could tear down. He had to communicate with others. But he had convinced himself that he could not.

Grey Owl's thoughts during his Ottawa stay in mid-March 1936 drifted back to the park, and he hesitated to return. Afraid of any close personal contact, he planned to continue to bury himself in work. He knew that he could not meet Anahareo's minimum demand that he reduce his commitments. Back he came with a head full of new book, film, and lecture tour ideas. In May 1936 he confirmed with Lovat Dickson that he would complete *Tales of an Empty Cabin* that summer, and that "I intend to write the children's phantasy 'The Enchanted Forest,' 'Devil in Buckskin' (formerly 'Half-Breed'), and the historical novel later."[26] This would provide Anahareo with no time at all, for as he once told Ellen Elliott, Hugh Eayrs's secretary, "I crucify myself when I write—often 18 hours a day."[27]

While Grey Owl liked Beaver Lodge itself and the work with the beavers, he had few friends there. He had never tried to befriend the wardens who had come to resent the special treatment that Superintendent Wood gave the resident celebrity. Almost anything he asked for he received, and they then had to carry it in to him at Beaver Lodge. Often his English upper-middle-class upbringing surfaced and he treated the other wardens as his servants, making them ever more resentful of him.[28] Grey Owl knew they did not like him and once scribbled down this note: "I can just feel the well of exclusion & hate that rises between those fellows & me when I am alone with two or three of them. No companionship at all, typical farmers of the peasant type, dull, unsociable, & silly about women, hating the bush & everything in it. This is the only country I was ever in where you can walk into a man's place & him not speak to you or stand outside his place & he not ask you in."[29]

How blind he was. Grey Owl did not even realize that if anyone was "silly about women," it was himself. As for his other complaints, Grey Owl had never seriously interested himself in his fellow workers' lives. Grey Owl's inward journey had left him unable to communicate meaningfully, on a personal level, with anyone.

In a notebook he kept in 1936, Grey Owl jotted down all his frustrations about his life at Beaver Lodge in a rough draft of a letter to Parks Commissioner James Harkin. He had descended into self-pity. In his midforties he felt that he must hurry, "I must keep going."

> J. B. Harkin:
>
> Cant go on with this frustrated, dried out, saintly, unfulfilled, static vegetating life. I am an idol in a niche, & getting to be as full of ideas. My mind is empty, my soul shrivelling in that hard, avaricious, narrowminded, (European) farmers West. Jealousy & meanness. Beaver Lodge is truly a refuge but is at times a cell!!
>
> All night work; never spend a day, eyes failing; no inspiration. West is flat, dreary & uninspiring. All right that one spot Ajawaan, but the rest is deadly. Something wanting; like some grave deficiency in diet that undermines the body, so this is undermining my mentality. All my inspiration comes from the wild & rugged Northland, *no trippers, no motor boats, no farmers,* no bathing beauties & dirty politics.
>
> Do you realize that *speed* was my god, 50 miles a day, 2300 miles one Summer, constant rapid, travel. Nothing for the mind; I am supposed

to keep on writing about the bigger issues broad, vast, deep (I speak often in terms of Infinity), yet my life is as circumscribed as that of the beaver themselves; more confined than on a farm, 1 square mile, generally 200 yards of a square for 24 hours a day, & most of it in the dark.

I can see so far ahead. So much depends. I am going to immortalize the Mississauga [Mississagi], the Canadian North, & the North American Indian. I must keep going. I want to tell the world literally. I mean to make success after success. Give me the time & the opportunity to do it.[30]

Grey Owl would work to save the world, but he could not save himself. Instead of hurrying to Beaver Lodge and trying to win Anahareo back, he returned to Ottawa. In mid-March 1936 he came to see the governor-general, Lord Tweedsmuir, and to seek government funding for a film to celebrate his favourite wilderness area, the Mississagi River country.

Again Grey Owl played his role as the Modern Hiawatha, this time for the governor-general and Lady Tweedsmuir at Rideau Hall. His presentation and manner greatly impressed Lady Tweedsmuir who several years later commented that she "thought he was one of the most beautiful and interesting people I have ever met." Their son, John, met him and long remembered his voice, "the most musical speaking voice of any human being to whom I have ever listened."[31] Lord Tweedsmuir himself admired Grey Owl for his remarkable knowledge of wildlife, and for the power of his writing in his books.[32] His Excellency's opinion carried weight on literary matters for he, too, was an author. By the mid-1930s he had fifty titles to his credit. Before his elevation to the peerage in 1935, John Buchan had written highly successful novels such as *Prester John* (1910) and *The Thirty-Nine Steps* (1915), which sold in the hundreds of thousands of copies.[33] As governor-general, Lord Tweedsmuir would institute the Governor-General's Literary Awards in 1937.[34]

After Grey Owl's visit to Rideau Hall, interviews also followed with Tom Crerar, the minister of the interior, and with Mackenzie King, the prime minister.[35] Grey Owl sought support from Crerar and King for his film of the Mississagi River, a country of "ancient trails, untouched forests, Talking Waters, & the traditions of a People, my People." Desperately he wanted to make this picture, one which he hoped would travel "over the U.S.A., & all the British Empire, & me with it."[36]

While in Ottawa, Grey Owl dined with the prime minister at his home, Laurier House, on Friday, March 13.[37] King represented the Prince Albert constituency and as prime minister in 1927 had been very helpful in securing the creation of Prince Albert National Park. Taking a special interest in the film proposal, he had invited Grey Owl and the warden of Hart House at the University of Toronto, Burgon Bickersteth, to learn more about it. As the prime minister told Hugh Eayrs: "I was glad to meet 'Grey Owl' and I was fortunate to secure him for dinner one evening, along with Bickersteth who was in the city at the time. We both much enjoyed our talk with him and I am glad indeed to be able to number him among my friends as well as among my constituents. I do not know whether you know that 'Grey Owl' is one of my supporters in Prince Albert constituency." [38]

Unfortunately King made no mention in his diary of the occasion, but he did note the date, "Friday-13th—for the superstitious two days of ill omen." [39] The dinner itself took place in "a candlelight cavern," as journalist Bruce Hutchinson has described the bachelor prime minister's dining room. It was "darkly paneled, with dim oil portraits of Laurier, Gladstone, the Rebel [King's maternal grandfather, William Lyon Mackenzie], and King's other predecessors staring down from the walls." [40] In these gloomy surroundings Grey Owl did his best to conjure up the magnificent splendours of the Mississagi River. He left believing that King was "in strong accord with the idea." [41]

Apparently the prime minister, however, must have mentioned that the interior department, not he, would make the final decision. An anxious Grey Owl kept up the pressure. While in Ottawa he called daily at the office of the Department of the Interior. [42] Then, finally he broke down and went on a wild binge.

A wonderful opportunity to influence some important government people arose when Yousuf Karsh organized a dinner in Grey Owl's honour. He invited him to his studio, which was close to the Plaza Hotel, also on Sparks Street, the main street of downtown Ottawa. [43] Forty years later Karsh recalled how he had furnished his studio with orange crates upholstered in monk's cloth and had arranged for a catered supper. "Among the guests were Duncan Campbell Scott, former deputy superintendent general of the Department of Indian Affairs, a group of writers and some journalists, and some cabinet ministers. At the appointed hour they all turned up, in high expectation and hearty appetite—all, that is, except Grey Owl." The embarrassed photographer raced over to the Plaza to find him. He did. In Karsh's words, "when I arrived at his hotel he was raising a drunken row in the bar, and I decided to leave him there." [44]

When Grey Owl arrived by train in Toronto he was so drunk that, as Hugh Eayrs wrote of him, "he didn't really know whether he was on his head or his heels." Again the Rotenbergs welcomed him to their home, and kept him in bed for thirty-six hours. Only after he had sobered up did his hosts and Hugh Eayrs break the news that Dawn was terribly ill with pneumonia and had been hospitalized. Immediately Grey Owl came to his senses and sped back to Prince Albert. [45]

Dawn recovered, but Grey Owl's health, already poor, deteriorated further. In his own words, he suffered from "extreme physical weakness (I could hardly walk for a while), derangement of the nerves and a brain that refuses to function." [46] Although he did not admit it, he was emotionally sick as well. The worn-out, sick Hiawatha complicated his breakdown by going on another wild binge in Prince Albert. At the height of the spree he had a terrible row with Anahareo. He claimed that she "tried for about 40 minutes to choke me."[47] After their fight he put the heroine of *Pilgrims of the Wild* on an allowance of $50 a month—quite a generous settlement as the sum constituted nearly half of his monthly pay cheque from the park.[48] Later he informed a shocked Hugh Eayrs and Lovat Dickson about the fight and coldly added: "I am now free to continue my interrupted work." He told Betty Somervell that "the final break has been made," and he did not see Anahareo for nearly half-a-year, until September.[49]

The spectacle of a drunken Parks Branch employee in Ottawa and Prince Albert disgusted his employers. Assistant Deputy Minister Roy A. Gibson, the second-highest-ranking bureaucrat in the ministry of the interior, phoned J. B. Harkin, asking for a full report. The parks commissioner replied on April 25:

Mr. Gibson.

Regarding your telephone inquiry about Grey Owl, I beg to say that Grey Owl for some years has been employed as Caretaker of Park Animals at a salary of $1320. in Prince Albert Park. His duties are primarily to look after the group of beaver which he originally more or less tamed in Quebec and which were subsequently transferred to the West when we provided a position in the Parks Service for Grey Owl.

As you know, the providing of a position for Grey Owl was entirely to serve our purpose of securing publicity for the National Parks and for wild life conservation by using Grey Owl's beaver and Grey Owl's personality as a spear-head in that connection. There is not the slightest doubt that we have secured for our Parks and for general conservation countless thousands of dollars worth of publicity through Grey Owl, his beaver, his books, his magazine articles and the motion pictures which we have secured of him and his beaver. As you know, these films have had a world-wide distribution.

I am sorry to hear that Grey Owl has been indulging too freely in liquor. As a matter of fact, with so much Indian blood in his veins I suppose it is inevitable that from time to time he will break out in this connection. We ourselves are quite annoyed. Sometimes we feel that it would be just as well if we did wash our hands of him, though I do feel there still is quite a field for additional publicity for us in connection with him. With the great success he had on his recent winter lecture tour in England, he has obviously become more difficult to handle and I fear that it will be only a matter of time until we will have to definitely decide upon a break with him.

Harkin's hoary racial stereotype about Indians and alcohol saved Grey Owl his job, as did the commissioner's realization that much of his employee's drinking had been done on his own time.

There is one thing I want to point out in regard to any recent sprees that he may have had that beginning last October he was given leave of absence from the Parks so he could carry on his English lecture work and that that leave was without pay. He reported back for duty officially on the 15th of the present month. Therefore, we must recognize that any spreeing that he has been doing in recent months has been done on his own time.

My own attitude is that we should now write him a formal and emphatic letter, pointing out that we are very much disturbed and disappointed at his outbreaks and that if he resumes them there will be no other course left for us but to dispense with his services.[50]

Anxious to continue his mission, Grey Owl realized his good luck in escaping dismissal. He knew his problem, and in fact only the previous spring had explained it to Mrs. Ettie Winters, who was raising his daughter Dawn in Prince Albert: "I meet up with a group of parasites, take one or two drinks, & I am gone. I am rather a lonely guy, & it eats holes in me, & I go haywire."[51]

Another blow came in mid-May when Grey Owl received word that the government had declined financial assistance for his Mississagi film.[52] In his preliminary review, the controller of the National Parks Branch estimated it would cost $10,000. He suggested to the minister that he reject the proposal, "especially as its main value will be its use on his lecture tours which are carried on under the auspices of his publishers."[53] With that decision Tom Crerar, minister of the interior, concurred. Prime Minister King, who was a personal friend of Hugh Eayrs,[54] reported the verdict to him in mid-April:

I did my utmost to gain favourable consideration by the Department of the Interior with respect to the project in which "Grey Owl" was interested. Mr. Crerar went into the matter very carefully and gave me a report upon it. Reluctant as I was to do so, I felt that I would not be justified, in view of all the existing circumstances, in seeking further to over-ride the Minister's decision, or to press him further unduly in the matter.[55]

The one thing Grey Owl had wanted more than anything else, the Mississagi film, he lost by his own drunken behaviour on Parliament Hill, during what he called "ten days badly needed relaxation in Ottawa."[56] Hugh Eayrs reported to Lovat Dickson.

Mackenzie King precisely and definately wanted the Government to aid, but Grey Owl's present Minister, Tommy Crerar is very much an individualist and goes his own way; confidentially—and I can say this to nobody but you—I really believe from a side wind which has blown this way that the thing would have gone through after Mackenzie King's kindness to Grey Owl but for Grey Owl's unfortunate staying around Ottawa for the next ten days, and shooting up Parliament Hill morning, noon and night.[57]

The letter Grey Owl sent to the Entertainments Department of the White Rock Pavilion in Hastings, England, indicates the depth of his lone-liness and despair. Just after he placed Anahareo on a separation allowance, he wrote asking for the address of "the Misses Belaney (Miss A. and C. Belaney) . . . two maiden ladies, well over middle age, very sweet and kind" who had entertained him during the war and again at the time of his lecture. He had lost Ivy Holmes, Angele and his first family, Marie Girard and their son Johnny, and now he separated himself from Anahareo. His two aunts remained the only individuals in the world with whom this troubled, tormented man felt he could communicate. Grey Owl was crying out for help, a grown man, nearly forty-eight years old, left without anyone to care for him except his two elderly aunts. Norman Gray, the White Rock's entertainments manager, showed Grey Owl's letter to the local newspaper, the *Observer*, which published a summary of it (without mentioning the name Belaney) on June 6, 1936.[58]

All that hectic summer Grey Owl hurriedly scribbled down the last quarter of his fourth book *Tales of an Empty Cabin*, to be published that fall as a collection of short stories.[59] He included a great deal of unpublished material and lengthy excerpts from his previously-published articles in *Canadian Forest and Outdoors*.[60] That summer the Winters' sixteen-year-old son, Stan, helped with the beaver. Margaret Winters, their teenaged daughter, typed the manuscript of *Tales* in the upper cabin located on the ridge behind Beaver Lodge. They also had 700 visitors that summer.[61]

All June and July of 1936, Grey Owl toiled over his *Tales of an Empty Cabin* manuscript.[62] The original *Canadian Forest and Outdoors* material went in almost verbatim, and it reads well. Other essays appear to have been written in one rough draft, very hastily in order to meet his submission deadline of early August. To cite one particularly awkward passage, Grey Owl, in his chapter "Little Pilgrims," recalls his first summer at Beaver Lodge, just after the beaver began building their lodge inside his cabin: "This construction work went on apace, and inside of two weeks there was a beaver house of pretty fair proportions occupying one end of our residence, and at this time I deemed myself justified in recommending to the National Parks Office that the time was propitious to make these activities a matter of photographic record."[63] The well-crafted earlier books, particularly *Pilgrims of the Wild*, contain few such lapses.

Yet, the shortcomings of his pen aside, the book contained more than enough of the author's old magic to make it a critical success. The last third of the book, "Ajawaan," largely devoted to the beaver, won *Time* magazine's praise: "Grey Owl's account makes these kittens sound like something out of a Walt Disney cartoon."[64] Canadian critics praised his conservationist theme in "Ajawaan," as well as *Tales'* first two sections ("Tales of the Canadian Northland" and "Mississauga"). The Winnipeg *Free Press* captioned its review of the book, "Grey Owl Pleads to Save Canada's Forest Heritage."[65] Mary Quayle Innis, Harold Innis' wife, who reviewed the volume for the *Canadian Historical Review*, fully caught the author's intent. "Through the book runs an ardent appeal for the preservation of the northern forest which is one of Canada's most precious resources and of the wild creatures for whom Grey Owl has made himself spokesman."[66]

Grey Owl devoted a great deal of time to "Mississauga," the second section of his book, a four-chapter novelette on the Mississagi River country which he completed in late June. He tried, he wrote, "to make a master-piece."[67] This section, like *Pilgrims*, contains some of his best writing. A wonderful passage, one which conveys his sense of colour and mood, is provided in his description of a long, slow-flowing stretch of his beloved river. "Here the shores are level and in wide spots there are low alluvial islands covered with tall, yellow, waving grasses, with blue irises standing in amongst them, showing brilliantly against the darker, gloomy back-drop of the heavy timber." In his novelette he recreates the river, and he brings back the old-time canoemen of the Mississagi River country, "the happy, careless voyageurs, gay caballeros of the White Water who whooped and laughed and shouted their way down or up unmapped rivers, and thought their day would last for ever. How I loved them for their sharp-barbed, gritty humour, their unparalleled skill in profanity, their easy-going generosity."[68]

While he wrote out his nostalgic tales, one thought sustained him: the Great Plains Indian convention to be held at Fort Carlton, southwest of Prince Albert, in early August 1936. He mentioned it in *Tales of an Empty Cabin*: "And about a week from today I, along with thousands of other interested sightseers, will witness one of the biggest Indian conventions ever held in this part of the country, where bows and arrows, peace pipes, long braided hair, buckskins, beads and feathers and ancient ceremonial will play a very prominent part."[69]

On August 11, 1936, Grey Owl gave his completed manuscript to Herb Winters, Stan's and Margaret's father, to mail from Prince Albert to Macmillan in Toronto.[70] He then travelled with Mrs. Winters, Margaret Winters, and Dawn to the commemoration of the sixtieth anniversary of signing of Treaty Six, at Fort Carlton, eighty kilometres southwest of Prince Albert. They arrived in time for the final activities on August 12, including the Plains Crees' adoption of Lord Tweedsmuir. The Indians gave him the name, "Teller of Tales."[71]

Grey Owl camped in a tent away from the great circle formed by the lodges of the 5,000 visiting Cree, Assiniboine, and Sioux Indians.[72] Stan Cuthand, a grade twelve student at Prince Albert High School, attended and half-a-century later recalled the huge Indian dance organized for Lord Tweedsmuir, in which Grey Owl participated in his own particular style. "It was at this dance that people recognized Grey Owl as not having the genre and ethos of an Indian. He looked awkward and out of place as he danced with the rest."[73]

Grey Owl, the victim now of total self-delusion, apparently believed that his boyhood Hastings dance steps fooled the Plains Indians. When John Tootoosis asked him if he would like to speak at the Indian meeting held after the governor-general's departure, he agreed. The Plains Crees had gathered to talk about the need to become more politically united, to fight for the preservation of their culture, and to defend their treaty rights.

Stan vividly recalled what followed. While John introduced him, Grey Owl stood nearby, wearing a white hat and buckskin leggings. With his white shirt and a slick neckerchief he looked to Stan like an American actor, with braids. Grey Owl took off his hat, stepped forward, and addressed the chiefs. At the Anglican day school he had attended as a boy at the Little Pine Reserve near Battleford, Stan had had many Englishmen as teachers. Although he did not have an English accent, Grey Owl's manner of speaking reminded Stan of his former teachers. John Tootoosis translated what Grey Owl said to those assembled, words that Stan Cuthand still remembered half-a-century later: "If there is anything I can do to help your cause, please let me know, I know a number of their important people in Ottawa and I know they will listen to me, again I thank you all."[74]

If John Tootoosis, and others present at the council, such as Stan Cuthand, suspected that Grey Owl was not exactly what he claimed to be, why did they not expose him? Stan feels that they stayed quiet because they knew that he was on their side. The Indians needed public figures in the dominant society to speak on their behalf. That is what mattered. They agreed with him that the white man was destroying the country and supported his mission to save the environment.[75]

To learn what many whites thought of them, the chiefs needed only to read a summary such as that prepared by anthropologist Marius Barbeau of the National Museum at Ottawa. It appeared in the *Queen's Quarterly* in 1931. "Formerly they idled away their existence in squalor and crass ignorance. Their idiom was a mere growl from the throat. Their tools were of stone and antler, and their artifacts fit only for a bonfire. Their companions were the animals of the forest or the prairies. Their dwellings were huts and movable tents, where they froze in winter and starved between seasons."[76] In contrast, Grey Owl championed their old way of life and their beliefs.

Grey Owl, of course, knew nothing of the Plains Indians' suspicions about him. He returned back to Beaver Lodge, re-charged, with a new confidence in his Indian identity. Proudly he wrote on August 21, 1936, to Superintendent Jim Wood of his new commitment to his life's work:

> At the time of writing I am in the very best of health, mentally and physically. Everything is going one hundred per cent here, the beaver are better and more numerous than they ever were, and that trip to Carlton where I was received and given recognition by my own kind of people, somehow rejuvenated me, rolled back the years of my younger days, gave me

a lift; it was something I wanted for so long; the approval of my own king [kind]. I spoke in council before 43 Chiefs (as computed) and several hundred men, and was cheered and applauded all through. That meant a lot to me, Mr. Wood, I have that to remember and I am wrapped up in my work here. I realize more perhaps than I ever did, that I have a place to maintain in the public eye, a trust to fulfil, not only to the public, *but to my own people who have at last, and in a big way, acknowledged me.*

Every word I write, every lecture I have given, or ever will give, were and are to be for the betterment of the Beaver people, all wild life, the Indians and halfbreeds, and for Canada, in whatever small way I may. After resting a while I am prepared, if permitted, to carry on with my more public work to those ends.[77]

14 Salute a Great Canadian

In late September 1936, Betty Somervell and her husband visited Grey Owl at Beaver Lodge. The leaves of the birches and poplars had just turned to yellow and gold and had begun to fall. During one of their host's very few moments of repose, Betty Somervell snapped a wonderful photo of him, smiling while paddling on Ajawaan.[1] In a canoe he was truly happy.

Mrs. Somervell witnessed the last meeting of Grey Owl and Anahareo[2] and saw first-hand how much Grey Owl's health had deteriorated. As Summy reported to Lovat Dickson in London, who in turn told Hugh Eayrs: "She said that he was so weak that he often fell down when he went to get a drink of water."[3] The intense activity of the past year had taken its toll, and yet Grey Owl still tried to keep going at the same pace. The driven man felt that he could not stop, particularly as he had just, through his British success, captured Canada's attention. Now even the king's representative in Canada wanted to visit Beaver Lodge.

While the Somervells were in the park, the governor-general of Canada flew to Lake Ajawaan, during a visit to Saskatchewan. Lord Tweedsmuir stepped out of the bush plane for his afternoon of sightseeing wearing a tie, tweed jacket, and plus-fours, or knickerbockers, as if all prepared for a walk on the moors.[4] Grey Owl showed him a beaver dam, trees sawn by his animal friends, and the beavers themselves, who came home to feed at 6 P.M., just minutes before His Excellency's plane had to return to Waskesiu.[5]

Determined to secure as much help as he could for the Indians, Grey Owl talked to the governor-general about them. He shared with Lord Tweedsmuir his idea that the Indians should become the guardians of Canada's wildlife and forests. A few days after the viceregal visit, he wrote John Tootoosis at Poundmaker Reserve.

> I went into the matter as fully as time allowed and among other things, brought before him this fact (which he not only agreed to, but had already

seen for himself) that the Indian is not to be an object of pity and charity, but ought to be self-supporting, and has a very real, and very useful place to fulfill in the economic life of Canada.

My suggestion, to which he listened with the greatest attention and sympathy, was that that place lay in work connected with the administering, protection and proper control of our natural resources, particularly in relation to wild life, timber and allied issues; at these the Indian is expert and his technical knowledge, accumulated during thousands of years of study and observation, could be of immense value in helping to save from destruction Canada's wilderness country and its inhabitants, which are, together, Canada's greatest asset, and are suffering great loss from the lack of proper knowledge displayed by many of those who are trying to handle them.[6]

A few months later, Grey Owl would elaborate on the need for Indian stewardship of the forest. "The Indians would be expert game guardians—expert in the preservation of wild life and forests." The idea itself was nearly a century old. As early as the mid-1840s, a recommendation had been made in a government report that they become timber rangers in the Canadas, as Ontario and Quebec were then known.[7] But nothing had been done.

Although tired and in poor health, Grey Owl, a man with a purpose in life, worked to promote the wilderness and its animal and human inhabitants. To do so effectively he felt he needed an ally, a life's companion. Right until late September 1936 this desperately lonely man felt an understanding ally was on her way to him. During his first English lecture tour he met Alexandra Dick, an attractive woman of about thirty. Wherever she went, Alexandra carried her tiny pet marmoset with her, the pet monkey constantly running round her shoulders. A Grey Owl devotee, she followed him from lecture to lecture in England. When Grey Owl, after his final break-up with Anahareo in April, had invited her to come to Canada as his secretary, complete with marmoset, she accepted. Suddenly, in mid-September, she announced that she would not be able to leave England and join him in Saskatchewan.[8]

From the radio to which he listened with fanatical devotion, Grey Owl developed a new romantic interest, Olga Pavlova of Regina, a woman in her mid-twenties. During the day she worked as a clerk at the Simpson's store in Regina, and in the evening she was a professional singer. In Regina she sang on the radio and in concerts in both English and Ukrainian. She lived in the downtown YWCA and was separated from her husband, although still married to him.[9]

Grey Owl and Olga had certainly met by November 4, 1936, as Grey Owl included a reference to her in his will drafted on that day in Regina. His executors (Superintendent James Wood and the Toronto General Trust

Corporation in Saskatoon) must consult "Olga Pavlova of Regina, Saskatchewan, whom I consider a woman of practical experience, ability and artistic
attainment" about his daughter Dawn's future education.[10] In early
November, Grey Owl wanted to marry Olga[11] and to include her in his
next English lecture tour. As an amazed Hugh Eayrs learned from him
and reported to Lovat Dickson: "He still harps on this question of wanting
to settle down and get married to this lady, this Ukrainian who, however,
as I have told you, is still married. That doesn't seem to matter to the
Chief. He also has a wild idea of using her (she is a singer) as a prelude
to his own lecture when he goes on tour."[12]

Olga declined his offer, if indeed he made one. But the two remained
friends. Just before Grey Owl's lecture in Regina in late March 1938, Olga
had Grey Owl to dinner.[13]

Exhausted, yet determined to carry on, Grey Owl reached Toronto
for the book fair at the King Edward Hotel on November 7. He had last
left the city in March 1936 in a most unstable condition. He returned
with a new sense of purpose. Planning ahead, he wrote Yvonne Perrier,
an attractive French-Canadian woman whom he had met briefly on his
last Ottawa visit in mid-March, to say that he would be in the city in mid-
November and that he looked forward to seeing her.[14]

Grey Owl had accepted the invitation of Bill Deacon and his wife to
stay at their home during the Toronto Book Fair. Deacon, the literary
critic of the *Mail*, had interviewed him during his Toronto visit in early
March 1936 and had corresponded with him ever since *Pilgrims of the
Wild* appeared. On April 24, 1935, their friendship had almost been cut
short by a note the book critic sent Grey Owl:

> Dear Grey Owl;
>   Thought you might like to see enclosed review of Pilgrims of the Wild
> from Australia.
>   Met an acquaintaince of your[s] from the woods who says you are all
> Scotch without a drop of Indian blood in you; and suggests you assume
> the Red Brother for artistic effect. Do you want to deny the charge? What
> proofs of origin have you?[15]

To this challenge Grey Owl replied on May 10 from Prince Albert.
After mailing it, he went on a wild, nearly three-week-long, drinking
binge.[16]

> About my friend who suggests I have no Indian blood, but am all
> Scotch. Firstly, the only people who have known me real well since I came
> to Canada 30 years ago, are bush people & Indians of the type who do
> not go to Toronto, nor speak of "artistic effect." No one living in this country
> knows anything of my antecedents except what I have chosen to tell them.

Then he explained what had been one of his favourite conversational topics
since his arrival in Canada: his racial background.

> If I have not analysed my blood-mixture quite as minutely as some
> would wish, let me say here & now that here are the component parts.
> Mother—½ Scotch (American)
>   ½ Indian
> Father— Full White, American
>   *reputed* Scotch descent
> Therefore I am a quarter Indian, a quarter Scotch & the rest reputed
> Scotch, tho unproven.

Of his two heritages, he added, he followed the Indian: "There are
thousands of mixed bloods like myself kicking around the North; some
favour the Indian, some the white; those that favour the white deny their
Indian blood which makes me mad as a wet hen. . . . I feel as an Indian,
think as an Indian, all my ways are Indian, my heart is Indian. They, more
than the whites, are to me, my people."[17]

Bill Deacon accepted all of this, and apologized to Grey Owl on
June 9, 1935. "I'm sorry to have upset you. Never mind. It's nothing. When
a question of fact comes up, I like to go to headquarters to check." He
admitted that he knew little about Indians, although he had seen many
when he worked as a summer fire ranger in Temagami. "I'm not much
of a mixer and the Indian is shy in the white man's presence."[18] He had
made his final amends in the very flattering interview published in the
Mail on March 2, 1936, upon Grey Owl's return to Canada after his first
British lecture tour.[19] As one of the organizers of the book fair, he had
also invited Grey Owl to stay with his family during his Toronto visit in
November of that same year.

Grey Owl's manner and appearance convinced Bill Deacon beyond
any doubt that he was part-Indian. "Not only the texture of his hair, but
the shape of his hands were peculiarly those of an Indian. The blue eyes,
of course, showed the white blood, which he never denied. The colour
of his hair does not matter since, unknown to most people, it was white
during the years of his fame and he kept it dyed."[20] A firm bond grew
between the two men. As Bill later wrote: "Grey Owl was a man you liked
and trusted instinctively. His ready smile, whimsical yet warm and spon-
taneous, was as beautiful an expression as I have seen on a human face."[21]
Possibly—but there would be no reason at the time to record it mentally—
Bill had seen that whimsical smile before, thirty years earlier. For three
summers, from 1907 to 1909, Bill had worked on Lake Temagami[22] at
the very same time that a young exuberant Englishman named Archie
Belaney lived there.

The book fair's organizing committee scheduled Grey Owl to speak
on Monday, November 9. The organizers expected 800 people to hear
Grey Owl at 9 P.M. in the King Edward Hotel's Crystal Ballroom. Instead
1,700 people crowded into the room. The organizers turned 500 more
people away as no space remained in the hall.[23]

No one equalled Grey Owl for crowd appeal at Canada's first book fair, not C. W. Gordon (Ralph Connor), the best-selling Canadian novelist; not E. J. Pratt, the Canadian poet; not the famous American journalist John Gunther; not Carl Van Doren, the well-known American literary critic.[24] The tall, lean man in buckskins and full headdress stole the show with his stirring talk on the "Unknown Canada."[25]

> Canada's greatest asset to-day is her forest lands. In my latest book I have attacked the average Canadian's ignorance of his own country. He is prouder of skyscrapers on Yonge Street and the price of hogs. He can have those any time but we can't replace the natural resources we are destroying as fast as we can. Canada subsists on her natural resources. They make us one of the richest countries in the world; and I call on you to let my people help in preserving these riches for us.[26]

During the afternoons of the book fair, Grey Owl appeared at the Macmillan stall to autograph *Tales of an Empty Cabin*, just released in Canada. Macmillan sold five times as many books as their next competitor, thanks to those appearances. By the end of the year they had sold out all their stock of Grey Owl books.[27]

On November 10, Grey Owl addressed a luncheon meeting of the Canadian Women's Press Club in the Round Room at the Eaton's main store. It must have been a strange sensation to return to the site of his first job in Toronto. Unknowingly, the women journalists missed one of the biggest stories of the decade. With a straight face, Grey Owl told them of his birth in Mexico and explained that by age thirteen he could speak fairly good "pidgin" English. Lucy Maud Montgomery (the author of *Anne of Green Gables*) thanked the guest of honour.[28]

Wednesday evening, November 11, Grey Owl appeared back at the book fair, in a program with Marius Barbeau, the well-known Canadian anthropologist at the National Museum in Ottawa.[29] On two scores Barbeau's presence should have made Grey Owl quite nervous. First, he had visited many Indian groups, from the descendants near Quebec City of the old Huron Confederacy, scattered by the Iroquois nearly three centuries earlier, to the Pacific Coast peoples in British Columbia.[30] He knew Indians. Secondly, he worked for the National Museum from which Grey Owl had borrowed two Sarcee eagle feathers just before his first British lecture tour, which he had still not returned.[31]

On both counts Grey Owl escaped censure, for if Marius Barbeau knew about the missing feathers he made no mention of them. Secondly, the fact that Grey Owl himself looked so European did not arouse the anthropologist's suspicions. As he had written a few years earlier in his essay "Our Indians—Their Disappearance," a number of Eastern Canadian natives looked quite European. "The half-breeds of the eastern provinces are not noticeable when they walk our streets, dressed as they are like others.

Their complexion is not darker than that of most Italians." [32]

Grey Owl made his most important address at noon on Thursday, November 12, to the city's Empire Club, which met appropriately enough in what was then the largest hotel in the British Empire, the Royal York. [33] About a thousand well-fed luncheon guests heard his tales of hunger and near-starvation in the wilderness. [34] He told of the time on one starvation trip he had to eat the frozen intestines of a squirrel which an owl had left behind. [35] For a good many meals to come they would remember his remarks.

Among the club members and their guests sat Sir William Mulock, President Henry John Cody of the University of Toronto (a distant cousin of Grey Owl's great hero, Buffalo Bill Cody), [36] the president of the board of trade, and many other Toronto dignitaries. [37] Years later, John Gray, a future head of Macmillan but in November 1936, Grey Owl's chauffeur for the book fair, recalled his lecture magic. "He had fine commanding gestures and a simple clarity of expression that served every purpose. His listeners sat as though under a spell." [38] Then, at the very end of his Empire Club talk, the beaver man explained his mission:

> I want you gentlemen to remember this one thing. I have often been asked what my work consists of. It begins to be rather ambiguous, I think. It is this: I want to arouse in Canadian people—excuse me speaking off my subject, I do that continually as thoughts come. I won't read a lecture—I want to arouse in the Canadian people a sense of responsibility they have for that north country and its inhabitants, human and animal. [39]

This message of faith in his adopted country thrilled the *Canadian Magazine*. In its next issue the national monthly wrote of him:

SALUTE A GREAT CANADIAN

> At a luncheon of the Empire Club in Toronto recently, Grey Owl, an Apache Indian, stood before hundreds of Canadian business men and challenged them to be all Canadian.
>
> He spoke of the Canada they knew, the Canada of streets and shops and houses, the Canada that runs, a thin strip of land, along four thousand miles of border—well enough in its way, and important in its way, but only a fifth of the picture of Canada as a whole.
>
> He spoke of the great North Country with its limitless miles and its vast resources of timber and game and ore. He spoke of the hundreds of millions of dollars that are spent every year by tourists to Canada, who do not come to see our cities, that indeed differ very little from other similar cities across the line, but to see the great North Country of which most of us Canadians know little if anything.
>
> He spoke of the exploiting of that land, and of the Indians, a once great race, that we have cabined and confined in reservations where they sit in idleness, living in meagreness on government bounty. He spoke of

the beaver and other wild life that is being ruthlessly butchered because no one had thought of them except in terms of profit. And he spoke a challenge to all good Canadians, to remember that their heritage is a heritage of the North and that to forget it is to make ourselves a little people. . . .

In the winter, when the Beaver are secure in their long sleep, he writes and lectures. Last year it was in England; this year in the United States. And wherever he goes he spreads the story of Canada. For while of other birth, Grey Owl is among the greatest Canadians of us all, for he has a vision, sadly enough withheld from many of us, of how great Canada may be.[40]

After the book fair, Grey Owl left for Ottawa. He phoned his friend Lloyd Roberts and got in touch with Yvonne. He shared no confidences with him, but Grey Owl had a warm friendship with Lloyd. When the now-famous writer and lecturer commented, "Down east I was in fact just a lousy breed—nobody knew I existed," Lloyd could immediately fire back, "You sure were lousy. I had to burn my clothes when I got back to Ottawa."[41]

Similarly, Grey Owl responded just as honestly to Lloyd. Once, for instance, Lloyd showed him some of his poetry.[42] Personally caught up in the British Imperialist rhetoric of the day, Lloyd had written an enthusiastic poem, "An English Lad," in honour of King Edward VIII, then the Prince of Wales (and after his abdication in December 1936, to become the Duke of Windsor). The last two verses read:

From Francis Drake to Jellicoe,
From Crecy to Cambrai,
An English lad has met the blow,
Leading us all the way—
And the Prince of Wales is an English lad;
What is there more to say?

For an English lad is an English lad,
Whatever his shield or crest,
Whatever the rank or birth he had
His heart still keeps the quest.
If the Prince of Wales is an English lad,
His blood is the best, the best!

At the end of the poem, Grey Owl simply wrote one word, "Why?," then elsewhere advised his friend: "You have the blessed spirit of Nature and you dig deep into the heart of the Wilderness; it fits you better too, than this 'England is the best' (or any other nation)."[43]

Over a period of five years, from 1931 to 1936, Lloyd had an opportunity to see Grey Owl in a number of situations, at Cabano, Riding Mountain National Park, and Ottawa. He later wrote an insightful sketch of his Indian friend. While admiring Grey Owl's mission, he saw the element of vanity beneath it: "Money to him, largely meant freedom for advancing his cause—better living conditions for Indians, more protection for wild life, eliminating the crueler aspects of trapping. He had sufficient vanity however, and business sense, to buy for himself the best wampum belt, hair ribbons, feathered head-dress, beaded moccasins and sheathknife that money could buy. Many of these things, strange to say, were obtained in London shops."[44]

In Ottawa in March 1936 the two men celebrated Grey Owl's return to Canada from his first British lecture tour. That evening they met Yvonne Perrier out with several girlfriends.[45] The attractive French-Canadian woman worked in Ottawa as a companion and helper for Mrs. Elizabeth Smith Shortt, one of Canada's first female medical doctors.[46] The elderly widow was very pleased with her, describing her as "very practical, very good natured, and a splendid manager of a home."[47] In mid-November Grey Owl called at Mrs. Shortt's, 5 Marlborough Avenue,[48] and asked for Yvonne.

The courtship went extremely well, so well that Grey Owl telegraphed his lawyer, Cy March, in Prince Albert on November 22: "Will you please get me some definition on paper to show my absolution in my illegal marriage. Is marriage performed by U.S. minister in Canada good legal. Wire me Grad's Hotel. Ottawa. Send clearance paper to same address. Am considering marrying. Chief."[49] Then four days later Grey Owl wired again: "Full details can be obtained from Arthur Stevens, 232½ Windermere Avenue, Toronto."[50]

If he married Yvonne, Grey Owl wanted to protect her. But suddenly fearful of something going wrong, he decided just after wiring Cy March on November 22 to ask Yvonne to marry him. She accepted. On November 30, Yvonne resigned her position at Mrs. Shortt's,[51] and one week later she married "Archie McNeil" at St. James United Church on St. Catherine Street in Montreal.[52] He was already married several weeks by the time Arthur Stevens' reply reached Cy March.[53]

Grey Owl had decided that his first marriage to Angele could be regarded as illegal, as it had been performed by an American student minister on Canadian soil. He seems to have overlooked the fact that in 1922 both Canadian and British authorities had judged the first marriage binding, sufficient grounds for Ivy Holmes to obtain a divorce from Archie Belaney for bigamy. To avoid any possible legal problems, he decided to marry Yvonne under this new name, "McNeil." As the Parks Branch knew him (and paid him) as Archie Belaney, he had now to explain the Belaney-McNeil connection to Yvonne. Grey Owl told her this elaborate story, the details of which she recalled for the Regina *Leader-Post* after his death:

> Speaking of the origin of her husband she says his father's name was George McNeil, a third generation Scot in the United States, and an Apache Indian

woman of Arizona was his mother. Shortly before Grey Owl was born the mother and father travelled to Mexico to see an aunt of Grey Owl, a Mrs. Blenay [Belaney], school teacher who lived near the Rio Grande. That is the history of Grey Owl being born in Mexico, otherwise he would have been born in Arizona.

Grey Owl's mother was a near relative of the great Indian, Chief Geronimo, famed in the western border history, and she died in 1921. Grey Owl's father died when Grey Owl was quite young. The only education Grey Owl got was from his aunt, Mrs. Belaney, and that was little.[54]

The newlyweds spent some time in Montreal, then travelled to Toronto, returning to Prince Albert at the end of December and arriving at Beaver Lodge on New Year's Day. Then, two months later, Grey Owl and Yvonne set off to make the winter wilderness picture in Abitibi. This, and the Mississagi or summer picture, were to be the two film highlights of the future British and North American tours. With W. J. Oliver off in Kenya shooting a big African game hunting expedition,[55] Grey Owl employed Bert Bach, an experienced Ontario film maker. Both Lovat Dickson and Hugh Eayrs, for Macmillan, put up $1,000 to help cover the costs of the week to ten days of winter shooting and subsequent editing.[56] It was en route to Abitibi on March 4 that Grey Owl learned that his secret was known by one Canadian newspaper.

The challenge came suddenly and unexpectedly in North Bay, 360 kilometres north of Toronto. Anxious to spread his conservationist message, Grey Owl agreed to meet Mort Fellman at the Empire Hotel on the afternoon of March 4, 1937. The twenty-five-year-old reporter, a seasoned veteran of four years in the North Bay *Nugget*'s newsroom, walked over from the paper's office. The tall, hawk-faced writer and lecturer, moccasined and dressed in buckskins, greeted him in his hotel room. Mort had read a great deal about him. "I was impressed by him. He was one of those men with a mission in life."[57] An eyewitness account of what followed survives, that of Bert Bach, Grey Owl's cameraman, who wrote shortly after the author's death on April 13, 1938: "I remember the interview, during which a young reporter from the local paper in North Bay was talking to Grey Owl and mentioned the name Archie Belaney, associated with the Timagami [Temagami] district. This changed Grey Owl's attitude and brought the interview to a definite close."[58]

Grey Owl's blood froze. Many people in northern Ontario knew him as Archie Belaney, and his government cheques still came to him with that name on them, despite his newly fabricated surname of McNeil. It was the association of the name Archie Belaney and Temagami that scared him. Angele *Belaney* still lived there.

When Mort Fellman reported back to Ed Bunyan, the *Nugget* city editor, Bunyan faced one of the toughest decisions of his career. He already knew Grey Owl's own story of his background, which appeared in a publisher's note in his first book, *The Men of the Last Frontier* (1931). It simply stated: "His father was a Scot, his mother an Apache Indian of New Mexico, and he was born somewhere near the Rio Grande forty odd years ago."[59] Ed Bunyan had a problem with this. He now definitely knew that not a word of Grey Owl's story of his origins was true. Grey Owl's sharp reaction to the two words, "Belaney" and "Temagami," proved it.

Two years earlier, Britt Jessup, an eighteen-year-old reporter on his staff, made a startling discovery. In 1935 the *Nugget*'s city desk received a tip from Jim Graham, the operator of the restaurant at the Temagami railway station. A local Ojibwa woman named Angele Belaney had seen a photo of Grey Owl in a newspaper on the counter of the restaurant. She pointed to the picture and said, "He my husband."[60] Editor Bunyan sent Britt Jessup off to Temagami where Bert Braney, the village police officer, directed him to Mrs. Belaney's small house. While a big vat of rabbit stew simmered on the stove, Angele revealed the true identity of Canada's most famous Indian. He was her legal husband, Archie Belaney, an Englishman, who twenty-five years earlier, in 1912, had left her and their one-year-old daughter.[61]

In March 1937 Ed Bunyan held a story of worldwide interest. Three years earlier he received another sensational scoop from Mort Fellman, his account of the birth of the Dionne quintuplets. City Editor Bunyan sent out the extraordinary news. Yet this solid, dedicated newsman hesitated with this story. He had filed away Britt Jessup's original article in 1935. Two years later Mort Fellman had confirmed the story beyond a doubt. Yet still Ed Bunyan decided against exposing Grey Owl.[62]

The context of the period must be remembered. The Great Depression still held Canada and the world in its grip. At its worst, unemployment in Canada had reached 30 percent.[63] In Europe, Nazi Germany had occupied the Rhineland. Civil war raged on in Spain. In Africa, Italy had attacked and conquered Ethiopia. Japan had seized Manchuria and early in 1937 prepared to conquer all of China. Ed Bunyan dealt with these stories every day. To a world plunged in economic crisis and headed for another world war, Grey Owl presented such a positive, refreshing message, one that called for toleration and kindness, for the protection of the wilderness and its inhabitants. Ed Bunyan would not expose Grey Owl.

No story was forthcoming from the *Nugget* but from that moment on, Grey Owl realized how precarious his assumed identity had become. Now more than ever he buried himself in his mission. Arthur Stevens knew, Angele knew, and now the North Bay *Nugget* knew. He must carry his message as quickly as possible to the widest possible audience.

15 The Summer of 1937

Yvonne proved the perfect helper for Grey Owl. Quickly she learned to snowshoe[1] and although new to winter travelling, loved it, even the camping out in Abitibi in sub-zero temperatures. As Grey Owl wrote to Betty Somervell early in 1937, she also was "true, honest & staunch . . . she neither smokes nor drinks, & is ever beside me. A steadying influence I much needed."[2] After the filming in mid-March in Abitibi, he went on a wild binge in Toronto and greatly needed her steady influence.

Grey Owl and Yvonne stayed in Toronto for two weeks to edit the winter film with Bert Bach. In Hugh Eayrs' absence, Ellen Elliott tried to help Yvonne look after the worn-out prophet whose thirst problem was already well known at the Macmillan office. As Ellen wrote in a note to Lovat Dickson on April 14: "It was much too long for everybody concerned. . . . He has to be taken care of twenty-four hours a day." Yvonne, she added, "couldn't leave him for five minutes, and since his idea of spending time in the city is to sit in his hotel room and pour quarts of beer down his throat, you can imagine what a bright time she had."[3] Each morning he arrived for the film editing at the Macmillan office at 70 Bond Street already having had a few drinks. Only threats by Ellen to cut off all funding for the picture sobered him up.

Intoxicated or not, Grey Owl helped Bert Bach edit the Abitibi footage of winter camping scenes, dog teams, and northern wilderness. Despite all her criticisms of the man, Ellen Elliott enjoyed the completed film.

> It opens with shots of Grey Owl giving an exhibition of snow-shoeing. Close-ups of snow-shoes being put on, and taken off . . . showing quick turns and walking through a narrow space, and so on. It really is fascinating and Grey Owl is a marvellous snow-shoer. (It is a treat to be able to say something nice about him.) Then shots of the dogs pulling a couple of laden toboggans and one sleigh. . . . The whole theme of the picture is the trail—one must be forever moving and the only way to move is on snowshoes and by dog team.[4]

The edited footage revealed, however, what Bert Bach had told her: Grey Owl's health was terrible. Ellen reported to Lovat Dickson that "in one or two shots he looks as though the work entailed was rather too much for him." In contrast, Yvonne, who snowshoed and travelled along with the film crew, did much better than her husband. "By all accounts, Grey Owl was all in at the end of the day, but Yvonne not at all." Moreover, as Bert Bach had mentioned to Ellen, during the shooting in Abitibi, Grey Owl had had "several bad coughing spells which scared him [Bert] to death."[5]

In the second week of April, Grey Owl and Yvonne headed back to Beaver Lodge, but still no real rest awaited him. He had to prepare the captions for the Abitibi film and complete the necessary drawings for the short book Lovat Dickson planned to publish for the second British tour, a re-printing of the chapter entitled, "The Tree," from *Tales of an Empty Cabin*.[6] The story, one of his best, told the history of a tree from the moment, hundreds of years earlier, when a squirrel by mistake dropped an acorn, to the hour when it had to be cut down to make room for a highway.

That May, Grey Owl lost a close friend when Charlie, his tame bull moose, died a kilometre or two away from Beaver Lodge. They found his body, all skin and bone, but could not determine the cause of death.[7] A flood of memories came back, including no doubt a flashback to the night of Grey Owl's big scare. In *Tales of an Empty Cabin* he had recalled, "stepping out from the cabin into the night and almost falling . . . over a beast the size of a horse."[8] He would miss the seven-year-old moose greatly. Next to Jelly Roll and Rawhide, Charlie had become his closest friend. With them he could relax. They did not judge him and did not require any response from him.

Grey Owl had to draw the sketches and write captions quickly because of the necessity of beginning the Mississagi River film in June. Frustrated by the Parks Branch's refusal to help him, and by the inability of Hugh Eayrs and Lovat Dickson (who had paid for the winter film) to finance the summer film as well, Grey Owl had decided to pay for it himself. As he had written a year earlier, he wanted this picture to be "an epochal presentation of the very soul of this Wilderness."[9] He simply had to make it in the summer of 1937. "This picture is the dream of my life, & neither Parks nor financial considerations are to stop me."[10]

In early June 1937, Grey Owl and Yvonne reached Bisco, the jumping-off point for their two-week journey to, and down, the Mississagi River.[11] They arrived in time to catch the high water necessary to run the challenging rapids of Grey Owl's favourite river.[12] A shock awaited Grey Owl. On reaching Bisco he learned that Alex Espaniel, his "adopted father," had died the previous August.[13]

For his canoe crew, Grey Owl hired an Ojibwa Indian from Lake

Nipissing to the east, Antoine Commanda (Jim Espaniel's brother-in-law); his old friend Ed Sawyer of Bisco; and Jim Savard, a rough-tough French Canadian from Abitibi who had also appeared in the winter picture. Bert Bach did the camera work.

Grey Owl came to Bisco with his head full of images of his early days in his hometown. Apart from a brief train stop in 1935 on his way to England,[14] he had not visited there in more than a decade. He had painted a warm sketch of Biscotasing in *Tales of an Empty Cabin*:

> Biscotasing, or Bisco, is a collection of small wooden houses gathered, or scattered rather, around the rocky hillsides that enclose a sheltered bay of Biscotasing lake. In Summer the twinkling camp-fires of the Indians are visible at the edge of the forest that surrounds the clearance on three sides. The fourth side is bordered by the lake, and in all directions from the edge of the clearing the forest stretches as far as the eye can reach.[15]

Once again he saw the characters he had described from memory in *Tales of an Empty Cabin*. Old Zed Chrétien from northern Quebec, earthy and picturesque:

> This huge fellow is Zepherin—misnamed; he is no zephyr, but a kind of human cyclone. He has one of those room-filling personalities, has a fog-horn voice, and a smile that would, if measured, cover about a quarter of an acre. No, I wouldn't shake hands in this case, just bow from the waist; you'll recover quicker. When Zepherin first appeared in the country (from no particular place), he was asked his qualifications, and in reply he boomed, "I'll tell yuh! I'm the best man to curse on the North Shore of Lake Superior"; and when in his cups he was wont to announce, with terrible imprecations, that he was "the best man in the world," and then straightway fall to laughter, in which those present were glad to join.[16]

Grey Owl knew well Harry Woodworth, now retired from the Hudson's Bay Company. The pillar of the community still represented "the law in this neck of the woods." Grey Owl remembered the colour of his eyes, "steel-blue."

> In the event of an arrest being necessary he would swear out the information, and serve the warrant with the utmost consideration, but with an extremely business-like look in his steel-blue eyes. He would go the prisoner's bail, feed him, house him, take a drink with him and generally provide what was probably the most efficient, all-round police service to be found anywhere in North America. The Compleat Police Officer, no less. A parental advisor to those in trouble—he had helped many a repentant transgressor over the lump—a stern disciplinarian of the conspicuously erring, he concealed under a bluff exterior and an habitual expression of suppressed ferocity, a heart as big as a barrel. This last infirmity he kept resolutely hidden, like it was some besetting sin. It was his one big failing, his own particular skeleton in the cupboard. But we all knew about it.

All honour to you, old friend. Very well I knew you, better than perhaps you ever thought. And in the old days, whether we met over a glass of the best, or maybe to discuss some small point of personal conduct concerning which we could not, for the moment, see eye to eye, there was a mutual respect, and an ungrudging appreciation of the other man's qualities. And besides it was all in the Game—the good old, sporting Game that is now so nearly played.[17]

Once again he also saw his very good friend Jim Espaniel. Grey Owl and Yvonne put up their tent on Jim's property, both coming and returning from their two week Mississagi journey. Before he left Bisco, Grey Owl invited Jim to accompany him on his lecture tour, two years in the future, in 1939.[18]

Now I'll introduce you to Jimmy L'Espagnol, wiry, well-knit and hardy, supple as an eel, and having an unconquerable, dogged singleness of purpose that takes him far in a day. He'll get there, or be found dead on the way. Jimmy and I ate often out of the same dish, and we call each other brother— which is as it should be; he is the son of my best friend, Aleck, a veteran guide, full-blooded Indian, quiet, composed and humorous. Once when a cheap witticism, levelled at his dark complexion, was passed by someone, he blew out the light, plunging the room into darkness, and remarked good-humouredly that "we are all the same colour now." Unruffled in the face of any emergency, wise in forest lore, he is a steadying influence in any party. His is the Voice of Experience.[19]

In Bisco, Grey Owl also met Jane, a younger sister of Jim's. Initially she was startled by his appearance. "He was made up like a Plains Indian. His skin was all darkened and long hair dyed black."[20] Years before (when he had stayed with the Espaniels) he and Bill Draper had taught Jane, then a girl of about ten, to read and write. Thanks largely to Bill, Archie, and to her Bisco teachers like Irene Shaughnessy, Jane had completed grade school in three and a half years, gaining her high school entrance certificate in 1926, the year after Archie left Bisco.[21] Grey Owl found Jane as much fun as ever. When Anahareo had planned a prospecting trip in the Chapleau district in 1933, he had told her to contact Jane in Bisco. "She is very intelligent and good company."[22]

In 1935 Grey Owl sent Jane's father a copy of *Pilgrims of the Wild* inscribed "To one whom I am proud to call 'Dad,' and who taught me much of whatever I may know—Alec L'Espagnol. From Grey Owl (Archie Belaney)."[23] Jane read it, cover to cover.

The Espaniels always knew Archie as a white man. They still remembered those long nights when he sat up with Alex, sometimes to 2 A.M., asking about the Indians in the old days. By their oil lamp, the Englishman had scribbled in his notebooks. At the Espaniels he had learned Ojibwa by talking with the family and by reading Anny Espaniel's Roman Catholic Ojibwa prayer book to get the words right.[24]

Some of Grey Owl's statements in *Pilgrims of the Wild* surprised Jane. She liked it, but statements such as "we are Indian, and have perhaps some queer ideas," and his reference to himself as a "representative" of the Ojibwa,[25] seemed quite bizarre coming from an Englishman. His comments about how he had in adult life "studied the English language from dark to sunrise"[26] amused her.

As Jane knew so well, Archie ("We always called him Archie . . . like a member of the family . . . he stayed with us so long")[27] loved to exaggerate. In *Pilgrims* he had written of "the veneration that our people, when savage, had held them [the beaver]."[28] Apart from his self-identification as an Indian and the use of the word "savage" to describe her ancestors, Jane could accept this statement. But Archie could not stop there and added this odd suggestion: "Indian mothers, bereaved of an infant, had suckled baby beavers at their breasts and thus gained some solace."[29] Some solace that would give. At birth the beaver kits already had their full set of teeth.[30]

When Archie met Jane they talked for some time, then he asked: "Have you read any of my books? What do you think about my writing?" Jane liked him too much to lie. She replied that she had read *Pilgrims*, then added: "I can't spin long tales like you do. To me it's just a lot of north wind blowing." To which her author-friend smiled, and said in his gentle, soft-spoken voice: "You're the first one who has ever said that to my face." Then he shook her hand.

They remained excellent friends, Jane even later helping her "brother" (he wanted her to call him that), to dye his hair dark black with notox (the only hair dye available at the time). You had to apply it with a brush and could only do several strands of hair at a time. On his last night in Bisco, Jane and Archie stayed up all night and talked about old times.[31] He needed people like her, and Anahareo, who challenged him and made him relate honestly to them.

Grey Owl previously learned on his brief stopover in Bisco in early October, 1935, that his son and look-alike, John Jero, no longer lived there. This had made it safe to return to Bisco with Yvonne. John spent twelve years at the Chapleau Indian School and then attended grade nine at the Chapleau High School before setting off to "ride the rails" across North America. The tall, handsome young man, a spitting image of his father, had not been seen back in the village since 1933.[32] Now Grey Owl repaid Edith Langevin for looking after his son during his childhood and his school vacations in Bisco, giving her 50 lbs. of flour, 10 lbs. of lard, 25 lbs. of sugar and 2 to 3 lbs. of tea.[33] He had absolutely no idea of the real expense of raising a child and did not want to know.

During the arduous filming that followed on the Mississagi River, one thought sustained Archie. Life on the trail in summer would be immortalized. He wrote of the film:

You see canoes driven at high speed over great lakes whose shores are black with pines; you see dark cavernous forests of huge trees untouched by the hand of man. Men trot over portages under mountainous loads; canoes, inverted on men's shoulders, pass through the wood for all the world like huge running beetles on two legs. You watch while camp is made, discover how we cook and eat in primitive ways. You are made to realize the consummate skill and the unconquerable daring of trained canoemen as they drive their light, frail craft down miles of rapids, each a seething vortex of thundering white water in which canoes reel and plunge and stagger and career, leaping to the rhythmic throbbing of the drum-fire of the rapids.[34]

The two-week canoe trip really tired him out. By its end, he knew very well how fast his physical powers were failing.[35]

Declining physical strength or not, Grey Owl's ego insisted that he put on a war dance his last evening in Bisco. Proudly Grey Owl came to the blazing fire wearing, in the words of the Sudbury *Star,* "a beautiful long, red and fancy beaded Indian costume. On his head he wore long white and brown feathers trimmed with a band of beads."[36] Antoine Commanda, Jim Minnewasqua (one of the leaders of the Bisco Indians), and Jim's brother Dave Buckshot followed. Jim began drumming and singing, then Grey Owl shouted out his old familiar Bisco war song: "Hi-Heeh, Hi-Heh, Ho! Hi-Heh, Hi-Heh, Ha! Hi-Hey, Hi-Hey, Ho! Hi-Ho, Hi-Ho, Ha!",[37] and furiously beat his drum as he jumped around the fire. The Indians present in the large crowd of onlookers were silently amused. Archie's war song contained no surprises. It still lacked rhythm and had no Indian words in it.[38]

From Bisco, Grey Owl and Yvonne left for Toronto and the hard editing job ahead. This time Ellen Elliott wisely placed them away from the Ford Hotel in the downtown area, where he had found it all too easy to obtain liquor, and reserved a room at the Windsor Arms, very close to the University of Toronto campus. The quiet, small hotel did not have a liquor licence.[39]

Grey Owl's growing fame, publicized so effectively in the mid-1930s by the press, led to an important invitation during his first weekend in Toronto. Annually, on the third Saturday in July, the Indian Defense League of America (IDLA), an all-Indian group with some adopted white members, organized a border crossing between Niagara Falls, Ontario, and Niagara Falls, New York. The members of the IDLA, Enos Montour, a Delaware Indian author has written, "were the watch dogs of Indian rights. . . . The IDLA was the nationalist movement of Indian people on the continent, similar to the Gandhi movement of India and the Peoples' Party found in many lands."[40] The border crossing celebrated the right of North American Indians to cross the international boundary between Canada and the United States without restriction.

On this, the tenth year of the event, the defense league invited Grey Owl and Yvonne to join them. They respected him as "a naturalist and champion to the beauty of wild life, notably his beloved beaver." He was "a beacon that others may follow, a man not ashamed of his race and not forgetful of them and their cause in his prosperity."[41]

On the Canadian side of the river, the Niagara Falls *Evening Review* commented that their distinguished western visitor was "known by every Canadian." He arrived at the Niagara Falls city hall to be "besieged by crowding throngs of autograph hunters."[42] Thousands of people also greeted Grey Owl and the 300 Indians as they crossed the Falls View Bridge into Niagara Falls, New York. For the first time in his life, the "part-Apache Indian," who had supposedly been raised in Arizona, stepped on American soil. On the American side, Black Kettle, an Iroquois Indian, adopted Yvonne into the Beaver clan as "Silver Moon."[43]

Having scarcely arrived back in Toronto, Grey Owl and Yvonne sped off to another function on Monday evening, July 20, at the Davidson farm near Brampton, northwest of Toronto.[44] That spring, Jasper Hill, or Big White Owl, had given Toronto's mayor, William D. Robbins, an associate membership in the Indian Association of American (IAA).[45] On Monday evening the Brampton IAA council (it had only white members as Brampton then had no Indian population) invited Mayor Robbins, Grey Owl, and several Iroquois Indians from the Six Nations Reserve at Brantford to join them in inducting four new members into their chapter. The laws and regulations of the Brampton chapter were founded on Ernest Thompson Seton's *The Book of Woodcraft and Indian Lore.* The Brampton *Conservator* reported that: "Chief Grey Owl in his magnificent head dress, led the dance to the beat of the tom-tom, whooping whenever there was a pause in the chant."[46]

Jasper Hill had corresponded with Grey Owl for some time and had first spoken with him in Toronto in March 1936, just after Grey Owl's return from his first British lecture tour. When they met, the Delaware Indian from the reserve at Moraviantown in southwestern Ontario recommended that Grey Owl read Diamond Jenness' *Indians of Canada,* an up-to-date survey of the subject.[47] Grey Owl had impressed Jasper "as an honest and sincere man." But "his one great weakness was the white man's firewater."[48]

No doubt Jasper Hill, or another member of the Toronto Indian Council Club (which like the Brampton Indian Council had recently affiliated with the IAA), had corresponded with their association's headquarters in New York City about Grey Owl. Shortly before Grey Owl departed for Britain in the fall of 1937, Barnabas Shiuhushu, "The Great Sachem and Chief Executive of the Indian Association of America," notified him that the national officers of the Indian Association of America had elected him to "the high honor of National Indian Scout."[49]

A delighted Grey Owl proudly told others of his new title, without checking into the background of Barnabas Shiuhushu and the "Indian Association of America." On his arrival in Britain, for instance, he mentioned to a reporter from the London *Daily Mail* that he was "Chief National Scout of the Indian Confederation of North America." On this occasion it was Grey Owl who had been fooled. As Jasper Hill bitterly discovered only a year or so later, Barnabas Shiuhushu was a fraud. His organization in New York City consisted only of himself and a handful of other questionable characters.[50]

From Toronto, Grey Owl and Yvonne returned to Prince Albert National Park for several days, only to leave for North Battleford, Saskatchewan, in early August to open the annual North Battleford fair. "The internationally famed Indian author and conservationist"[51] performed his official duties and the next evening participated in an Indian war dance on the grandstand stage. While the hundreds of white onlookers might not have noticed anything wrong with his steps, the Indians present certainly did, and several commented to each other on his bizarre style.[52]

Back at Beaver Lodge that August, Grey Owl and Yvonne worked away at his beadwork regalia for the second British tour.[53] He loved beadwork so much that his outfit for his second British tour looked like a beaded suit of armour. A thousand visitors came to Beaver Lodge that summer, including Viscount Clarendon, a British peer, and Major Blacker, an English aviator who had flown over Mount Everest.[54] In Toronto, Hugh Eayrs prepared another tribute to the beaver man, an anthology of his writings, *A Book of Grey Owl*. As he told Lovat Dickson: "My own idea is that there might be two introductions for our edition: one by Grey Owl, and another by Lord Tweedsmuir. I am pretty sure I can get him and I know if I cannot that I can definitely get Mackenzie King—but I am pretty sure of His Ex."[55]

16 The Greatest Triumph

Grey Owl and Yvonne left Beaver Lodge for Britain in early September 1937. At Montreal they boarded the Canadian Pacific liner *Montrose* on September 10. That morning the Montreal *Star* interviewed the "noted Indian beaver authority," providing a fine physical description of the flamboyant lecturer. "Grey Owl is not young, but he is tall and straight yet, and his hair looks so black one might think it was dyed" (actually Yvonne dyed it for him every two to three weeks). The writer continued: "Grey Owl will lecture this winter in the Old Country. He was a picturesque figure in broad-brimmed, round crowned Mexican hat, flaming red shirt, moccasins and other Indian accoutrements."[1]

The North Atlantic passage proved quite rough, but Yvonne made no complaints. As she commented in a note to her former employer, Mrs. Shortt, "This is certainly the time of my life."[2] She stayed close to her tall, buckskin-clad husband at all times. In the ship's lounge one evening they made special friends with Jack Shadbolt, a Vancouver art teacher in his late twenties then on his way to study art in London, and his cousin, Joy Darwin, off to study dance in England. Nearly half-a-century later, Jack, then a well-known Canadian artist, recalled his older friend: "He loved talking and we were a good audience and, as he said to me, I could use words—which he admired and [he] would always parade big words when he could. When he had a few drinks he would often do a tomahawk war-whoop dance around the lobby shouting hilariously. Whether this was for real or a spoof of movie Indians I never knew."[3]

After the ship reached Southampton, the congenial foursome took the train together to London's Waterloo Station, where Jack's uncle and his two boys (whom he had never met before) awaited their cousin from the Canadian wild west. As a signal of recognition for his uncle, Jack's aunt had sent him a green ribbon rosette to wear on his lapel. But on the coach Jack suddenly had an idea. Grey Owl, with his fully developed sense of mischievousness, needed no persuasion to participate in the prank. He wore the green rosette.

> So at Waterloo we all descended and he was immediately surrounded by reporters and I waited around on the fringe to see the results of my stratagem. The platform emptied of people except for a harrassed looking man in thick glasses, cap and tweed plus fours, and two boys, going up and down the empty train peering in carriages. As they came back down the platform all there remained was this knot of reporters with a tall feathered man at the centre and one of the boys, peering through the ring, caught sight of the green rosette and shot off to his father and brother to tell the news. They were dumbfounded and puzzled. But Grey Owl finally called to me. "Sorry, Shad but I've got to go. The queen is waiting," and tossed me the green rosette.

Jack thus broke the surprise to his totally confused relatives. He said good-bye to Grey Owl and then joined his uncle and the wide-eyed boys to rush for the next train out to the suburbs.[4]

As he had in 1935–36, Lovat Dickson built the second tour around London. Grey Owl again lectured for a month at the theatre housed in the London Polytechnic Building on Regent Street in London's West End. He must succeed here, Lovat Dickson explained.

> Now, on this Polytechnic engagement, Chief, everything depends. You see what we have to try to get over is that sense of a crowded house of people striving to get tickets and not being able, the feeling that you *are* a success; and that psychology makes you talked about and from London your name and your success radiate throughout the country, so that there is a rush to get seats at all the country lectures too. It is as though London were the hub of the wheel, and although you can get along with a missing spoke or two you can't get along with a missing hub! So on London we concentrate.[5]

Thanks to an intensive advertising campaign, the new films made for the 1937 tour, the publication of an attractive souvenir program,[6] and most important of all, the strong performance of Grey Owl, enthusiastic audiences filled the Polytechnic Theatre twice daily, and three times on Thursday.[7]

To manage the tour Lovat Dickson hired Ken Conibear, aged thirty, the 1931 Rhodes Scholar from Alberta. Ken had been brought up at Fort Resolution and Fort Smith in the Northwest Territories where his father had worked as the engineer on the Roman Catholic mission's Mackenzie River steamboat, the SS *Sainte-Marie*. Later his parents started a trading post at Fort Smith where Ken met many Chipewyan and Dogrib Indians who came in to trade.[8]

From boyhood Ken often went out on the trapline with his older brothers Jack and Frank (who later became renowned as the inventor of the first and most widely used humane trap, the Conibear, used for trapping small fur-bearing animals).[9] His mother educated him and his sister at home, until she could take them no further. Then the Conibears sent Ken and his sister Mabel off to school in Edmonton. During his summers, Ken returned to Fort Smith and worked on the Mackenzie River steamboats, learning more about the land above the sixtieth parallel, territory thousands of kilometres farther north than Grey Owl ever reached in his lifetime. Ken excelled at high school and at the University of Alberta, earning his Rhodes Scholarship to Oxford University in his final year. From 1931 to 1934 he attended Exeter College at Oxford, where he studied English literature.[10]

Shortly after his graduation from Oxford, through a novelist friend, Ken met Lovat Dickson, a fellow University of Alberta graduate and former instructor at the university. The young publisher expressed great interest in Ken's idea of a novel set in the Fort Smith area and paid him an advance on royalties to allow him to complete it. While writing his first book, *North Land Footprints*, Ken attended one of Grey Owl's London lectures in late October 1935. The Canadian writer enjoyed the talk immensely and after the performance stood in line to shake his hand. When he smelled Grey Owl's smoked tan moosehide, an odour he had not smelled for four years, it transported him right back to Fort Smith.[11]

After Ken's *North Land Footprints* appeared in 1936, Lovat Dickson encouraged him to write a second on the same area, entitled *Northward to Eden*. Again he gave him a small advance on his future royalties, but the writing advanced slowly at best. Soon most of the advance was gone. As Ken put it: Lovat Dickson brought him and Grey Owl together in the fall of 1937 "in order to save me from starving to death, and Grey Owl from drinking himself to death."[12] Ken would act as the tour manager, driving Grey Owl and Yvonne around Britain in the hired Vauxhall car, do the bookkeeping, help with the correspondence and the autographing sessions, and act as a watchdog to keep Grey Owl sober before performances. Fortunately Yvonne, already too familiar with his drinking, also put her foot down. On performance days at least, they generally kept it within bounds.

Right from the very beginning Ken got on superbly with the famous lecturer. After the first week and a half, Lovat Dickson could report to Hugh Eayrs:

> One good thing that has happened this year is that I have got a really first class man to look after Grey Owl: Kenneth Conibear, author of NORTH LAND FOOTPRINTS, a young Canadian, age about 28, whom I taught English to at Alberta and who subsequently got the Rhodes scholarship, did well over here and has been living here ever since. . . . He is husky, good-humoured, intelligent, and he knows as much about wild life as Grey Owl does. They took to each other immediately and now are firm friends, calling each other "Ken" and "Chief."[13]

From September 27 to October 23, Ken assisted Grey Owl at his daily
lectures at the Polytechnic Theatre. Immediately after the British tour of
1937, Ken wrote a short article, "Grey Owl in England," in which he recalled
those fifty performances in London. At the time, like everyone else around
the man, he fully accepted and believed Grey Owl's story of his Indian
ancestry.

> Inside, all is in darkness except the organ, over which a faint light picks
> out the swaying body of the musician. The melody is "Moonlight Sonata,"
> hurled at you, thrilling. No one talks. There is a general air of expectancy.
> The music ceases, the curtain rises, the screen becomes animated with
> a number of figures rushing about in kaleidoscopic confusion. It is a news
> reel. Here is civilisation, as popularly conceived, epitomised. You see bombs
> raining in China, Mussolini banging his desk in Rome, a line of beauty
> queens traipsing down a stairway. . . .
> The curtain drops, the tabs rush together, and in the semi-darkness
> you hear a solemn voice announcing:
> "Two thousand miles and more over the steel trail of a railroad, comes
> Wa-sha-quon-asin, Grey Owl, to revisit the hallowed spot from whence, more
> than a decade ago, he set out on his pilgrimage to interpret the Canadian
> wilderness to civilisation." . . .
> The face is noble. In the hawk-like nose, the high cheekbones, the
> heavy lines, the parted and braided hair, the stern expression, there seems
> typified all you have ever heard of the noble character of the Indian of
> old. . . . His voice is deep, resonant, rhythmic. His diction is a strangely
> pleasing mixture of Canadian colloquialisms, classical idioms, and almost
> Biblical phraseology. . . . The program closes with a short picture of the
> famous and inimitable Rawhide and Jelly Roll at work on a beaver house
> built by them inside Grey Owl's own. You are astounded at the intelligence
> and human qualities of these two animals. You chuckle at Jelly Roll's comic
> turns, are equally amused at Rawhide's solemn dignity. You admire the man
> who has such friends. . . . You get a brief glimpse of him as you shuffle
> by in the queue with a book or a scrap of paper for him to sign. You notice
> that he has blue eyes, that there is a constant twinkle in them, that they
> are tired. . . .
> Outside the fog is settling down, the air is damp, heavy, stinging in
> the nostrils. But you hardly notice these things, for you are still living in
> a world of clean rushing waters and clean driving snow. It was never so
> real to you before—even if you have once lived in it.[14]

Immediately after the final lecture at the Polytechnic Theatre on
October 23, Ken drove Grey Owl and Yvonne (who, if asked, Grey Owl
presented as his secretary in order not to disappoint his British public
by telling them of his break-up with Anahareo) to the lecture halls outside
of London. On his country tour the distances covered were not as great
as in 1935–36, but still their engagements took them throughout most
of England. They travelled to Liverpool on October 27, to Bournville on

the 28th, Leeds on the 29th, Birmingham on the 30th, Roedean School (one of the best and most expensive girls' schools in England) near Brighton on the 31st, to Crowborough and Guildford on November 1, reaching Bath on November 2.[15]

One of the few probing reviews of Grey Owl's performance came in Bath. The reporter from the local *Chronicle and Herald* identified several of the Modern Hiawatha's most obvious contradictions. Critically the journalist wrote:

> Grey Owl is something of a paradox.
>
> "I am not civilised" he told a crowded audience at Bath Pump Room on Tuesday evening, "and I have no intention of being."
>
> Yet he has all the bearing and confidence of one who has lived a lifetime in the midst of civilisation. He has a better command of English than the vast majority of Englishmen or Americans; he visits our country—though he dislikes our climate—and delivers some 60 lectures, lectures in which he is incessant in his speech, though he preaches the virtues of silence.

Yet, the reporter stopped there and failed to ask where and how the lecturer learned to write and speak so well, or even what books he liked to read. Without any further questioning, the journalist accepted him as "Grey Owl, the Indian, who was born in a native village on the borders of Mexico and the U.S.A."[16]

The ultimate test of Grey Owl's Indian identity came in his three months with Ken, who knew Indians and mixed-blood people from his childhood in the Northwest Territories. Day after day the Rhodes scholar ate with him, heard him lecture, drove with him in the same car all over England and Scotland—and like Hugh Eayrs, Lovat Dickson, Superintendent Wood and the Canadian Parks Branch, he believed Grey Owl's story.

Canadians with Indian ancestry in the 1930s simply had no incentive to declare it. In Ken's home, the Northwest Territories, for instance, a number of mixed-blood people looked as if they had little Indian ancestry. The racial climate of the times encouraged those fair-skinned people who left the north to make few, if any, references to their Indian ancestry. By a strange coincidence, Charles Camsell, the federal deputy minister of the Department of Mines and Resources who, in 1937 (among many other responsibilities) oversaw the operations of the Parks Branch (for which Grey Owl worked), belonged in this category. In his autobiography, *Son of the North* (1954), the distinguished civil servant naturally spoke of his birth at Fort Liard, Northwest Territories. He included a lengthy reference to his English father, the fur trader Julian Camsell, but he made no mention at all of his mother's (Sarah Foulds's) racial ancestry.[17] Sarah's mother, hence Charles Camsell's maternal grandmother, was the daughter of a Hudson's Bay Company employee and a native woman.[18]

Instead of hiding from his "racial past," Grey Owl wanted the whole world to know about it. To Ken, Lovat Dickson, Hugh Eayrs, and

Superintendent Wood, Grey Owl's repeated claim to Indian ancestry revealed his deep loyalty to his "true" racial origins. The loyalty was even greater as he told them that he was "just a breed."[19] Lovat Dickson, who had lived for nearly a decade in Alberta in the 1920s, knew how difficult was the life of these people. "Half-breeds" were "looked down upon both by the white man and by the pure-blood Indian."[20]

Thanks to the unceasing efforts of Ken and Yvonne, Grey Owl made his lecture appointments on time. Occasionally he slipped away from Yvonne and Ken, and drank, but even if he began a lecture drunk, he would be sober at the end, in time for the lengthy autographing sessions.[21] After perfecting his Indian story-teller role during a thirty-year period, he performed superbly. The achievement is all the more remarkable when one considers that he made up his performance as he went along. And yet, in Ken Conibear's words, "each was so different from its predecessor that night after night I abandoned what I had planned to do while he talked and simply sat in the wings and listened, rapt." Each talk had the same elements, "the dry humour, the self-belittlement, the exaggerations necessary to give present impact to distant reality, the glorification of Indians and the Canadian North, and the final plea for understanding and compassion."[22]

Daily, Grey Owl popped a regular number of pills, Ken never learning what they were.[23] While at Bexhill in late November, Grey Owl announced that he could not stand the strain of another British lecture tour, "kind as his reception everywhere had been." This would be his last British tour.[24] Yet, despite his fear of exposure, and his own fatigue from lecturing and travelling, he gave his very best to the tour.

A chance to address a large radio audience came on the afternoon of November 14 in Newcastle. A copy of the tape, or rather a minute-and-a-half segment of it, has survived—his other interviews have all been lost.[25] Grey Owl used the broadcast to repeat his deep revulsion against the fox hunt and all blood sports:

> When I look at it, this English scene, and contemplate it in all its tranquil restfulness, I sometimes feel disturbed, as does one when suddenly and unwillingly awakened from a dream, that in this day and age when tolerance and kindness to the weaker are practised so universally, there still exists there, on this English countryside, marring all this peace and restful beauty, in spots, the barbarities of the hunt. To me, an Indian, a savage, this so-called sport seems little more than outmoded mediaeval cruelty, whereby defence-less animals, against all the laws of sportmanship, which proclaim that in killing for sport the animal must have an even break, it is hopelessly outnumbered, and driven to the last extremity of misery and terror by a horde of dogs and mounted men, all bent on his destruction, and, shame-fully, women, and sometimes even children, and the creature standing there exhausted, pitiful, defenceless, and alone, is literally mobbed to death and

that, folks, not for any useful purpose. They make no use of any portion of the fox, but merely for amusement.[26]

No one in England knew Grey Owl's true origins in 1937, apart from three (possibly four) people. Grey Owl was certain after his visit with his aunts in 1935 that they certainly would not reveal his secret. But his mother—her intentions he did not know, nor those of his half-brother, Leonard Scott-Brown, who had written to Grey Owl about the time he joined the HBC in 1928 and who had left the company in 1930. For a number of years he had trapped in the Northwest Territories, but had returned to England by the spring of 1938.[27] However, only if Kittie had spoken a great deal to Leonard about her "Red Indian" son's childhood could he pose a threat, as Leonard himself was born only the year after the future Grey Owl left England for Canada in 1906.

Grey Owl did meet his mother during the 1937 tour, at his hotel in the centre of Oxford. On November 30 an elderly English woman dressed entirely in a subdued black, faded a little by repeated ironing,[28] approached him at the Mitre Hotel on High Street.[29] During the tour, six grandmotherly women had claimed Grey Owl as their own son,[30] but only this tiny Englishwoman was, indeed, the mother of the Modern Hiawatha.

After her son's death, Kittie referred to this extraordinary meeting of several hours as "the happiest I have ever known."[31] Apparently they met at the Mitre between the conclusion of his lecture at the town hall (which began at 3 P.M.) and the second performance at 8 P.M. Ken had left to go for dinner with an old Oxford friend,[32] but Yvonne was initially present. To Mrs. Grey Owl, Kittie explained that she "was closely related to Grey Owl."[33] This strange woman, whom Yvonne had never seen or heard of before, then asked for money to help support her son Hugh, an incurable victim of mental illness as a result of combat in the First World War. No doubt at Grey Owl's urging, Yvonne left at this point.

While alone with Grey Owl, Kittie later recalled that her son told her this: "I have only just begun my life."[34] He had a warm conversation with the woman who he had believed had abandoned him. Kittie later commented: "He really did like me although he pretended not to." Before she left, he gave his mother a ticket for a seat in the second row for his evening performance. She added that at the lecture, "he hardly took his eyes from me."[35]

Kittie's presence in the crowded hall unnerved him. He gave an off-performance that night. We know this from the diary of Geoffrey Turner of Oxford's University Museum who had attended Grey Owl's talk in Oxford in January 1936 and came again to hear him. His diary entry for the evening of November 30 indicates his partial disillusionment: "So to the Town Hall for Grey Owl. Too near to the projector for good hearing. I was less convinced than previously though the beaver stuff was good. Three films: the trail in winter & in summer, & Rawhide & Jelly Roll lodgebuilding. Grey Owl's Indians are pretty well idealized but still interesting." [36]

The next morning, Ken brought around the car to take Grey Owl and Yvonne to their next stop, Southport, 250 kilometres to the northwest. With the mist still, no doubt, floating among the town's towers and spires, the party left for the resort on the Irish Sea. After his lengthy conversation with Kittie, Grey Owl knew that she would not expose him, the son whom she would describe after his death as "a great man with a soul." [37] His spirits had revived. At Southport a relaxed Grey Owl told Mr. C. K. Broadhurst of the bookshop of the same name on Market Street: "They must be very artistic people in Southport to have such a beautiful town. The lights along Lord-Street are magnificent, I have not seen anything that can compare with them—not even the lights of Vancouver." [38] Actually, although invited to the diamond jubilee of the city of Vancouver in the summer of 1936, Grey Owl had not visited the city. His knowledge of Vancouver probably came from Jack Shadbolt. What harm, though, did it do to boost the civic pride of the bookseller? So pleased was Mr. Broadhurst to hear Southport compared to Canada's great Pacific city, that he informed the Southport *Guardian* of "the famous Red Indian's" comment.

The next week raced by quickly with daily lectures throughout England: Liverpool, Sunderland, Middlesboro, Darlington, Scarborough, Harrogate, Bradford, Lincoln, leading to the grandest event of the tour. To Grey Owl had been extended the unusual honour of giving a Royal Command Performance at Buckingham Palace, at 3 o'clock on the afternoon of Friday, December 10. [39]

This was a sad day in the Royal family's memory. Exactly one year earlier, Edward VIII had signed the "instrument of Abdication," renouncing the British throne, the first monarch ever to do so voluntarily. On this unhappy anniversary date, Grey Owl came to entertain the Royal family with a new outlook, a welcome message. "You are tired with years of civilization. I come to offer you—what? A green leaf." [40]

Queen Mary, the widow of the late King George V, greatly admired Grey Owl's books. Grey Owl had mailed the late King *Pilgrims of the Wild*, [41] and Admiral Mark Kerr, an English friend of Grey Owl's, had forwarded to Queen Mary a copy of *Sajo and her Beaver People.* [42] After the performance the Queen recorded her assessment in her diary, "very interesting." [43] Lovat Dickson later wrote to Hugh Eayrs describing what had occurred on the afternoon of December 10:

> As I think probably I told you, Grey Owl was supposed to have met King George V when he was over here last time but the King died in January. This year I reminded [Vincent] Massey of that fact and said I hoped it would

be possible for the present King to receive him. I have mentioned it once or twice since and have got at various people who have connections with the Palace to pull strings. But, of course, that would not have been enough without the King's definite interest and without the lucky fact that Queen Mary highly approves of Grey Owl and had given the Princesses copies of his books. About ten days ago I had notification from the Palace that the King would like to receive him. We got them to accept the only date that Grey Owl had free, December 10th, and last Friday afternoon you might have seen Grey Owl in buckskins, Yvonne in the latest creation, and myself in top hat driving up to the front door of the Palace to make our call. . . . Grey Owl had insisted that Yvonne should appear as his wife. That rather worried me, for I was afraid that Anahareo might have been the heroine of Queen Mary and the consequences might have been disastrous if the second wife had shown up. I therefore went to the Palace a few days before the lecture and saw the King's private secretary and explained the whole situation to him, ran down Anahareo a little but not too much! and puffed up Silver Moon a lot. Grey Owl, by the way, told me some time ago that Yvonne is a half-breed—her appearance certainly gives evidence of that—and that her name amongst the Indians was Silver Moon.

We had the lecture in the Throne Room, which had been specially fitted up with two 35 mm. projectors. The King and Queen were there, the two Princesses, Queen Mary, and the Earl and Countess of Strathmore, the Queen's father and mother, as well as a number of other people attached to the Court. I had instructed Grey Owl how to begin his address, and he started off in grand style with "Your Majesties, Your Royal Highnesses," but when we left the King three hours later—for we were with him that long—Grey Owl said, putting out his hand, "Well, good-bye, Brother, and good luck to you," and the King's face broke into a really genuine smile as he thanked him.

The lecture was an enormous success. Everybody was very interested and when it was over the King and both Queens and the Princesses spoke to Grey Owl for nearly half an hour and finally invited us to have tea at the Palace, which we did. Yvonne was introduced as "Silver Moon" and the Queen talked to her for twenty minutes alone, and we left the place in a blaze of glory and good feeling.[44]

December 10 stood out as one of the highest triumphs in Grey Owl's life. But not perhaps the highest, for another event, one which occurred exactly five days later, eclipsed it: his Command Performance at 24 Wellington Road in Hastings, the residence of the Misses Ada and Carrie Belaney.

Although originally Hastings had been dropped from the 1937 tour itinerary,[45] Grey Owl had asked that it be included, and with some difficulty it was. In order for Grey Owl to speak in Hastings at 8 o'clock on the evening of December 14, Ken had to drive Grey Owl and Yvonne immediately after the afternoon performance at Tunbridge Wells in neighbouring Kent.[46] At the White Rock Pavilion, 1,400 people awaited Grey Owl.[47]

With his customary professionalism Grey Owl gave a magnificent performance. The Hastings *Observer* noted the "deafening applause" he received from the crowded house.[48] Lillian Hazell (later Mrs. Lillian O'Nions), then the Hastings children's librarian, heard him that evening. Fifty years later she still remembered the talk. "Such an enthusiastic audience he had. He really stirred every one with what he said. You went home, cuddled the cat, stroked the dog. He made you feel that way about animals."[49]

Mary McCormick, George's older sister, now Mrs. Mary Champness, still lived in Hastings in 1937. A number of years earlier she had read one of Grey Owl's books and had a strange sensation while doing so. "The way the book was written reminded me of him, and Grey Owl's face in the frontispiece photograph—when you ignored the Indian make-up— was absolutely Archie Belaney's."[50] Out of curiosity she attended his lecture on December 14 at the White Rock Pavilion and confirmed her impression. By chance a few days later she met Bob Overton, her brothers' boyhood friend, who had missed the lecture. She shared her hunch with him. "That's Archie Belaney or I'll eat my hat."[51]

Both Mary and Bob were now convinced that they knew Grey Owl's true identity. In returning to his hometown Grey Owl must have known that something like this might happen. If so, he must have weighed the risks against the joys of seeing his aunts once again, at the very height of his triumphant second British tour. More than anything he wanted them to see him once again at the height of his fame.

The Misses Belaney could not attend the evening performance, as it would finish too late for Carrie, then seventy-eight, and Ada, who was seventy-six. They awaited a call at home the next morning. In the early morning fog, a well-dressed driver, a buckskin-clad Indian, and an attractive woman stepped out of the black tour car at the Misses Belaneys' red brick house, close to Hastings Castle.[52] After being introduced to Grey Owl's "aunties" (he believed this to be a courtesy title as they had put Grey Owl up during the war), Ken left to see the site of the Battle of Hastings about ten kilometres away.[53] Yvonne remained, but she, like Ken, had absolutely no idea that these two elderly ladies were Grey Owl's real aunts. To Yvonne the meeting had no special significance, apart from the renewing of a wartime friendship, and she has no recollection of it.[54]

Grey Owl had introduced Yvonne as his wife, which must have caused some surprise, as the last time he had been in Hastings he had shown a film, "Pilgrims of the Wild," starring Anahareo as his consort. Yet, at this stage, nothing would surprise the two elderly ladies: they already knew of his Ojibwa, his English, his Iroquois, and now apparently his French-Canadian wife. Their memories being sharper on the events of thirty years or so ago than the details of the present, they might well have remembered that Archie as a schoolboy had won a prize for French. Nothing was wasted. Now he could actually use the language.[55]

The two ladies had so much they wanted to say, but they realized that with Yvonne present they could not reminisce about their nephew's English childhood. For Grey Owl, his aunts' parlour brought back memories of his claustrophobic youth, thoughts of Eton suits, shoes, starched collars— and white gloves on Sunday! The room contained the same stiff furniture as at Highbury Villa, and Ada had plants crammed in everywhere.[56] Both of his aunts sat on their favourite chairs, eagerly awaiting every word of their beloved nephew. Archie's dyed black hair, braids, buckskins, and darkened skin (he had taken a sun lamp with him on this trip)[57] may have taken a minute or so to adjust to, as did his Canadian accent, which he must have used in Yvonne's presence so as to avoid raising her suspicions about his relationship with these elderly ladies.[58]

Looking around the room, Grey Owl himself saw the old glass-fronted bookcase, one shelf of it filled with the productions of his grandfather and his great-uncles. Now proudly included were copies of his four books.[59] The sight of the family's old semi-grand piano[60] brought back painful memories, yet the end result had been good: his lifelong love of music. Despite all the trials he had put them through, Grey Owl knew that Ada and Carrie still deeply loved him. His first words in the parlour were simply, "Aunties, you haven't changed a bit."[61]

As a boy Archie had always tried to please his aunts. He had first begun to tell stories to them and now nearly forty years later had fully perfected the art. He wanted to impress them. Knowing so well Aunt Ada's interest in social status and prestige, he would have, without doubt, talked at length of his call at Buckingham Palace five days before. He had bettered the record of his grandfather and namesake, Archibald Belaney. He had received more than a letter—he had actually met the reigning monarchs, the great-grandson of Queen Victoria and his wife. He had given his talk in the very room that contained their thrones and the State Throne of Queen Victoria, upholstered in crimson and gold.[62] To prove to these ladies that he had made something of himself was the greatest triumph of his life.

We do not know what he said directly, but a full transcript of his version of his afternoon with the Royal family exists. About two months later in New York City, Grey Owl shared his memories of the event with Hazel Canning, a reporter.[63] Much of this same information he undoubtedly told his aunts in Hastings on the morning of December 15, 1937.

Grey Owl explained that during the performance he had directed his remarks to the two youngest persons in attendance. The older of the two, Princess Elizabeth, was "the most attentive young lady who ever came to one of my lectures." Little Princess Margaret Rose, he added, "is a very shy, sweet child." In retrospect, the afternoon was "one of the happiest . . . I ever spent. . . . The British royal family are a group of simple, real people. It would be impossible to find a family more natural and friendly and interested; or better listeners." In describing the Royal family, was he not creating a picture of the ideal family he wished to have had, a family full of love and the acceptance that he never had?

Once the lecture (with the accompanying films) had ended, Grey Owl bowed and left the improvised stage, but, as he told his aunts, he had barely reached the dressing room when the Lord Chamberlain knocked on the door. "Wouldn't you like to meet the King and Queen and Queen Mother Mary and the princesses? They said they would like to meet you." A delighted Grey Owl returned to the Throne Room. The King and his mother and the two princesses joined him while Queen Elizabeth spoke separately with Yvonne. Reporter Hazel Canning summarized what Grey Owl told her:

> The King said he was most interested in the need for conservation, not only of woods and waters, all natural resources, but of the animals as well. This need had impressed him gravely, as he listened to the lecture. He asked about the comparative intelligence of beavers and deer and moose and other animals of the Canadian forest. He wanted to know just how Grey Owl spent a typical day in the Prince Albert park, and he said that though Grey Owl had explained that Canadian parks did not pay for themselves, he considered the education in natural history, the preservation of animals, the recreation they furnished to so many people each year made them pay, in one way, over and over again.
>
> "The King impressed me as a keen woodsman and a marvellous listener," said Grey Owl. "It was remarkable the questions he asked, based on small details of my lecture."
>
> Grey Owl came away a warm admirer of Queen Mother Mary. He said she was reserved, at first, but later asked him questions about the details of housekeeping, with two beavers under the same roof. She warmed up, smiled, was most kindly and interested. And while little Princess Margaret Rose stood shyly beside her grandmother, never once speaking a word, Princess Elizabeth was quite the young lady. Her last words to Grey Owl were: "I wish I could go to Canada and see your beavers in their home."

Grey Owl's interlude with the aunts ended with Ken's return. The two elderly ladies' lives had been enormously enriched by his visit, a golden moment to them, a treasured memory for the rest of their lives. They had helped to make this extraordinary man, this creative genius who called on kings and whose public now called him away. Grey Owl must reach the public hall at Ipswich in Norfolk before 3 P.M. that day, his two talks there to be followed by lectures in Cambridge, Norwich, and his final performance on December 18 at London's Phoenix Theatre. In leaving, he asked his aunts to listen to his farewell broadcast on the BBC's Children's Hour at 5 P.M. on December 20, the day before his departure for Canada.

Through the worst of the English winter, Grey Owl kept his final appointments, speaking twice a day. As usual the halls were not always properly warmed and often had very poor acoustics.[64] Yet, he soldiered on, repeating again and again as he did at Norwich: "Civilisation says, 'Nature belongs to man.' The Indian says, 'No, man belongs to nature'."[65] Grey Owl looked forward to addressing the children of Britain on December 20.

Grey Owl worked hard on his text. He made a strong case against the fox hunt but in his attack made one factual error. In his attempt to raise the greatest possible revulsion against the hunt, he cited this story: "I have heard, this last time I am here, of a fox that ran into a house for protection, and was seized by the huntsman as he jumped through a window, bleeding from several cuts he had received from the broken glass; only trying, poor creature, to save his life—the only one he had—and was thrown to the dogs to be torn to pieces—alive—on Christmas Day."[66] While the story could well have been true, the date was not. No packs of hounds in England had hunted on Christmas Day within the lifetime of anyone living in the 1930s.[67] When it served his purpose Grey Owl, as a polemicist, freely used the most colourful material, without properly verifying it.

The BBC required that they examine the text of his farewell speech before he read it on the air. He submitted it a week or so before the broadcast was to take place. Surprisingly the passage about the Christmas hunt went by the reviewer, but another reference did cause problems. At Norwich came the news that the BBC insisted Grey Owl delete the portion of his script in which he spoke against blood sports.[68] A BBC regulation held that there could be no reference to fox-hunting on the air, a subject which would involve the organization in great controversy, unless there was a full debate of its pros and cons. The press reported that the BBC insisted that the following section had to go: "Will you promise me never to take advantage of the weakness of another, human being or animal; never to take the life of a weak and defenceless animal for your own amusement; never to join in the chase where foxes, stags, otters or hares are driven for miles and miles by crowds of dogs and men—and sometimes, I am afraid, by women and children."[69] Grey Owl refused. Lovat Dickson described his confrontation with the BBC in London on December 18.

> I met him, that Saturday morning, at Liverpool Street Station. His face was set and grim, and there was little talk as we drove to Broadcasting House. But there was much talk when we got there, all of it, alas, to no purpose. A nervous young lady whom we interviewed held her ground, and not all Grey Owl's persuasions could remove the heavy hand of authority that backed up everything she said. When we left Broadcasting House he seemed to me suddenly a very tired and dispirited man.[70]

The broadcast would not be made, but Lovat Dickson published the text as a pamphlet. It sold for one penny and went very quickly. In a matter of days, 10,000 copies had been purchased across Britain and by the summer of 1938, 50,000.[71]

Broadcast or not, December 20 had a very happy note to it. Grey Owl served as Ken Conibear's best man at his wedding to Barbara Linke, a Canadian woman from Alberta. Lovat Dickson drove Ken and Grey Owl to the church in the same leased Vauxhall that had been used for the tour. On the way, the modern Hiawatha passed on some advice, strange advice coming from him. In the car, he kept telling Ken to "just treat the little woman right."[72]

Ken and Barbara, and Grey Owl and Yvonne sailed back to North America the next day on the SS *Berengaria*. The ship itself had been taken from the Germans by the British after the First World War as part of their war reparations. Its built-in ashtrays still bore the labels "Zigaretten." The passage proved very rough with the Christmas trees held in large planters sliding back and forth, side to side, in the ship's dining room on Christmas Day. With much sadness Ken and Barbara parted with Grey Owl and Yvonne in New York City on New Year's Day, 1938.[73]

For three more months in the United States and Canada, the prophet maintained his gruelling pace. He gave twenty-eight lectures in the United States from Boston to Springfield, Illinois,[74] and visited nine cities in Canada from Quebec City to Regina. Together he and Yvonne travelled nearly ten thousand kilometres in overheated trains, between widely separated destinations.

The intense activity exacted its toll, as Grey Owl's health steadily deteriorated. But in many ways, he loved his never-ending crusade. He was doing what he wanted to do, preaching the need for conservation. He was lost in work that took up every moment of his day. His life had meaning and purpose. He was needed. He finally belonged to the human society around him.

A photo taken during the shooting of the Winter film, Abitibi, March 1937. Grey Owl appears in the centre and Yvonne at the far right. Photo by B. J. (Bert) Bach, the cameraman for the film. Ontario Ministry of National Resources.

Grey Owl (in front) and Antoine Commanda (in rear) during the shooting of the Summer film on the Mississagi River, early summer 1937. Photo by B. J. (Bert) Bach, the cameraman for the film. Ontario Ministry of Natural Resources.

Pilgrims of the Wild

by

WA-SHA-QUON-ASIN

(GREY OWL)

To one whom I am proud to call "Dad," & who taught me much of whatever I may know — Alec L'Espagnol

From:

grey Owl

(Archie Belaney)

TORONTO:

THE MACMILLAN COMPANY
OF CANADA LIMITED

The inscription in the copy of Pilgrims of the Wild *that Grey Owl sent Alex Espaniel. Jane Espaniel read this copy.* Archives of Ontario. Source: Rene Espaniel.

Left to right, on the Biscotasing station platform: Susan Espaniel (Jim's wife), Grey Owl, Anny Espaniel (Alex's wife), Florence Friday, Jane Espaniel, others unidentified. Early summer 1937. Archives of Ontario/S14473. Source: Dawn Richardson.

Grey Owl at the border crossing celebrations, Niagara Falls, July 17, 1937. Archives of Ontario/S14482. Source: Grey Owl and Anahareo Collection lent by Dawn Richardson.

Grey Owl at the Central Hall, Liverpool, during the second British lecture tour, October 27, 1937. Yvonne, standing on the right in this photo, handed the book to be autographed to Grey Owl, who then signed it with a fountain pen. Ken Conibear, standing beside Grey Owl, would apply a blotter to the signature and return the autographed book to its owner. The photo appeared in the Liverpool Post *on October 28, 1937.* ©*Daily Post,* Liverpool, 1937.

Grey Owl with students at the John Campbell School in Windsor, Ontario. He talked with thousands of school children in Windsor, in mid-February 1938. Courtesy of The Windsor *Star* Library.

Left to right: Jack Miner, Yvonne, Grey Owl, Annie McIntyre (director of special activities for Windsor's public schools). In mid-February 1938, Grey Owl visited Jack Miner at Kingsville, Ontario. Source: Manly Miner, Kingsville, Ontario.

Grey Owl opening some of his fan mail at the offices of his publishers, Macmillan of Canada, 70 Bond Street, Toronto, early 1938. From *Canadian Forest and Outdoors,* April 1938, p. 110.

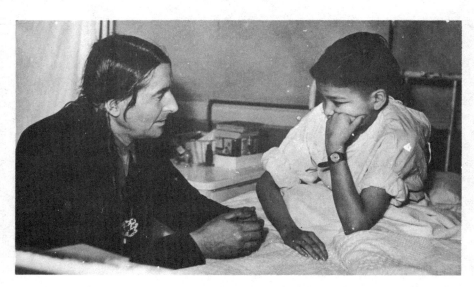

Grey Owl with Gerald Johnston, an Ojibwa boy, at the Nicholls Hospital, Peterborough, Ontario, on March 11, 1938. Grey Owl visited him as soon as he learned of the boy's serious operation. They had never met before. Archives of Ontario/S13338. Source: Gerald Johnston.

This is the last known photograph of Grey Owl, taken on March 12, 1938, in Toronto. On that occasion he was made a member of the Toronto Indian Council Club. To the left of Grey Owl stands Jasper Hill, a Delaware Indian. Jasper's father, Daniel C. Hill, is standing at the extreme left. All the other club members were non-native. The man to the right of Grey Owl was Albert Middleton, or "Fighting Wolf," a white man who had read a great deal about Indian customs. At the extreme right is George H. Carson, who farmed in Islington, now a completely urbanized part of Metropolitan Toronto. Dr. John Sussmuth, a German-American engineer, hosted the meeting at his home at 177 Lakeshore Road, near the mouth of the Humber River. Yvonne is seated directly in front of Grey Owl. Jasper Hill supplied the identifications of the club members on June 10, 1988. City of Toronto Archives, SC 266–50108.

WITH US AGAIN WITH WONDERFUL FILMS!

After a brilliant and overwhelmingly successful tour

of

The British Isles and the United States

and

A Command Performance at Buckingham Palace

GREY OWL

WILL SHOW HIS PICTURES AND TALK ON

"BACK TO MY BEAVER PEOPLE"

— AT —

MASSEY HALL, SATURDAY, MARCH 26th

Commencing 8 p.m. sharp.   Doors open 7.30.

RESERVE YOUR SEATS EARLY AND BRING YOUR FRIENDS!

Tickets: $1.00 and 50c.

Remember! If you want your seats in blocks book early!
Tickets may be secured by telephoning Mr. Eric Gaskell, RA. 2867, or Mrs. King, HU. 1441.

THE STUDENT'S IMPRESSION OF GREY OWL!

The Toronto Branch of The Canadian Authors' Association offers two prizes for the best essays by any high or secondary school student on the theme of Grey Owl's appearance and remarks while on the Massey Hall platform on the evening of March 26th.

FIRST PRIZE!
ANY TWO OF GREY OWL'S BOOKS (AUTOGRAPHED)

"Tales of an Empty Cabin"   "Sajo and Her Beaver People"   "Pilgrims of the Wild"
"Men of the Last Frontier"   "The Tree"

SECOND PRIZE!
ANY ONE OF THE FIVE

Preferred length 300 words.   Limit 500 words.   Entries to reach Mr. Eric Gaskell, 40 Nanton Ave., Toronto, by April 9th.   Presentations will be made at the Canadian Authors' Association Annual Dinner May 14th.

UNDER THE AUSPICES OF THE TORONTO BRANCH
OF THE CANADIAN AUTHOR'S ASSOCIATION

Circular advertising Grey Owl's lecture on March 26, 1938, at Massey Hall, Toronto. Archives of Ontario/Acc. 9291 S14255. Source: The Macmillan Company of Canada.

Beaver Lodge, Prince Albert National Park, mid-1930s. Grey Owl is buried on a knoll immediately behind the cabin. Archives of Ontario/Acc. 9291 S14234. Source: Peter Davies Co. Ltd.

Left to right: Agnes, Angele, and Flora Belaney around 1938. Ontario Ministry of Natural Resources. Source: Agnes Belaney Lalonde. *As a result of a court ruling in late November 1939—even though she was not mentioned in Grey Owl's will—Angele obtained a one-third share of his estate. See "In re Belaney ('Grey Owl') Estate,"* Western Weekly Reports, *3(1939): 591–601. Yvonne and Grey Owl's daughter, Dawn, both of whom were mentioned in Grey Owl's will, were the other beneficiaries, sharing equally the remainder of the estate.*

Mrs. Winters holding Dawn at Grey Owl's funeral in Prince Albert, April 15, 1938. Archives of Ontario/S14250. Source: Peter Davies Co. Ltd.

Johnny Jero, raised from early boyhood by Edith Langevin. Photo taken in Biscotasing at the station, around 1940. Johnny had recently returned from five years of "riding the rails" in Canada and the United States. Archives of Ontario/S14488. Source: Dave Langevin.

17 The Exposé

Following his talk at Pittsburgh's Carnegie Music Hall on March 10, 1938,[1] Grey Owl left for Peterborough, Ontario. Although relatively small (population 25,000),[2] Grey Owl knew the city's name, thanks to its Peterborough Canoe Campany, which made a popular canvas-covered canoe used by many northern woodsmen.[3] For six months, non-stop, the famous writer and lecturer had spoken throughout Britain, Canada, and the United States. By March, 1938, he had given nearly 200 lectures.[4] Jack Peterson of the Peterborough *Examiner* stood that afternoon among those welcoming him and his wife, Silver Moon, to the city located about 120 kilometres northeast of Toronto.

While interviewing Grey Owl at the train station, Jack Peterson mentioned that Gerald Johnston, an eleven-year-old Ojibwa (Mississauga) boy, lay in a cot at the Nicholls Hospital. His leg had been amputated two weeks earlier. Before the operation, he had been hospitalized for nearly a year. Grey Owl was scheduled to lecture in the auditorium of Peterborough's Trinity United Church in less than three hours, but he made a visit to the Nicholls Hospital his top priority. The photo Jack Peterson took of Grey Owl at the young Indian's bedside shows the weariness and the strain he felt after six months of constant lecturing, travelling, and the ever-present threat of exposure.

During the half-hour visit, the young Mississauga asked: "Tell me what you told the King about our people." The *Examiner* the next day summarized Grey Owl's reply, of how he "told the story of Canada's heritage; told how this land of ours holds unknown and undreamed of wealth; told his opinion that Indians should be the fire rangers, the forest rangers, the game wardens; told of the beaver and the mink and the deer and the moose."[5] As he left he gave Gerald a five-dollar bill.[6]

The paper in that same issue of March 12, 1938, carried a depressing front-page story, "Hitler Vienna-Bound to Proclaim 'Conquest.' German Troops Pour Into Austria By Land and Air." The Wehrmacht had occupied

Austria. In contrast, the *Examiner's* account of Grey Owl's lecture at Trinity United was headlined, "Holds Audience Spellbound As He Lovingly Told Of His Friends The Animals."

To his audience closely packed into the crowded hall, Grey Owl called for a kindlier view of Canada's forests and wildlife. He had earlier told Jack Peterson as they drove to the Nicholls Hospital that he had two aims in life: "one was to help his fellow Indian reach a position of respect and a means of livelihood in Canada; the other was to teach protection of this country's diminishing wild life." That evening he elaborated on that second vital point.[7] He had delivered a similar message in all his Canadian talks.

Grey Owl's message blended both conservation, or the wise use of natural resources, and preservation, or the total protection of wildlands and wildlife. He wrote in *Tales of an Empty Cabin* in 1936 of the need to keep "some of this great Northern heritage . . . *in its original, unspoiled state*."[8] Later in the same book he elaborated on this theme. "The function of the forest is *not* exclusively that of providing lumber, though judicious and *properly controlled* garnering of a reasonable forest crop is essential to industry."[9] In an earlier letter he provided one of the best summaries of his own philosophy of wilderness, a philosophy of conservation and preservation that he now shared with hundreds of thousands of people.

> I do not think hunting should by any means be abolished, but that more consideration should be shown in the treatment of animals destined for slaughter (on fur farms) & that the methods used in trapping should be less cruel, & that Wild Life should not be made a burnt offering on the altar of the God of Mammon. No one could accept my views in their entirety, being as they are a purely personal point of view, but they might learn to think, & to remember that an animal is as capable of both physical, & to some degree mental suffering as are some humans. Also that the forest is not a place to turn into a shambles, just on account of the greed of people who care nothing for the Wilderness or its inhabitants, human or animal.[10]

The strategy of Hugh Eayrs and Lovat Dickson was working. "The plan was that Grey Owl should tour in England and if successful should tour in the States, and finally have his last triumphant tour in his country."[11] Grey Owl agreed that to awaken Canadians' concern about their diminishing natural resources he must first succeed overseas, for only then would Canadians take notice.

The American tour had begun in early January in New York City, unhappily, too. The American agency handling Grey Owl lacked Lovat Dickson's flair and his commitment to the speaker. Nor were North American Indian lecturers as much of a novelty in New York City as in London.[12] Somehow the urgency of Grey Owl's message became lost amidst the towering skyscrapers of New York City. John Gray, a Macmillan's employee, met him and Yvonne shortly after their arrival: "He hated New York, where he felt trapped and a figure of fun. Our conversation in his dreary little hotel room lightened a little when he produced a small skin drum and thumped out a rhythm that cheered him a good deal. He was sick of walking the streets of New York in Indian regalia and having playful people ask him what cigar store he was working for." [13]

Even Grey Owl's entry to New York had not gone smoothly. When the ship landed, the customs authorities had carefully examined his declaration form. True to his fantasy, he gave his name as "Archie Grey Owl," and stated that he was a "North American Indian" who was born at Hermosillo, Mexico. From shortly after his birth to 1905 (when he had left the United States), he had lived in Arizona. [14] The U.S. customs people questioned the blue-eyed Indian further about his extraordinary background and only accepted his story after detaining him for some time. Later a furious Grey Owl thundered, "And I was the only real American on that ship!" [15] After three decades he probably believed (away from his mother and his aunts) that he was an Indian.

By chance, the Bisco fur buyer, Jack Leve, was in New York City at the time. He visited Archie—or rather Grey Owl as he now respectfully called him—at his hotel. Jack always considered him "the finest person you could find when sober." Unfortunately, this time he was in the opposite condition. [16]

Everything had seemed to go wrong. He and Yvonne had only arrived when *Time* magazine, based in New York, ran an article on January 3 stating that he was "married twice legally, five times according to Indian custom." [17] To counter the story, Grey Owl would point dramatically at Yvonne, "There are my seven wives." [18]

Another disappointment followed. For years Grey Owl had developed a warm correspondence with Max Perkins, his editor at Scribner's. Just the previous year Grey Owl had told him about his forthcoming visit to New York City. "I will make a special point of visiting you & so increasing the mutual goodfellowship that exists between us two Americans." [19] Yet, Perkins, perhaps having read the story in *Time,* had not even bothered to see him when he called at the Scribner's office in early January. He did not attend Grey Owl's first New York lecture. [20]

The American tour did eventually turn around. Grey Owl spoke on January 11 to an influential group of Brooklyn businessmen and was invited to address New York's exclusive Harvard Club. He also lectured to an important dental fraternity, Delta Sigma Delta, at the Biltmore Hotel. [21] Inevitably the dentists must have looked at his teeth. If so, they must have observed that the Modern Hiawatha had false teeth. [22]

Grey Owl obtained an excellent response in Canada from the moment of his first lecture in Montreal to his last in Regina. The organizers of his talks in Montreal had to add a third performance to meet the public demand.[23] His diction amazed Montrealers. When questioned by a reporter about how he learned English, he declared himself entirely self-educated: "I learned English from Shakespeare, Dickens, Emerson and the Bible."[24] Once again he saw Jean-Charles Harvey,[25] to whom he had given his first newspaper interview at Cabano, and Haddow Keith, one of his fire rangers on the Mississagi River right after the war. Now a pediatric neurologist, Dr. Keith worked with Wilder Penfield at the Montreal Neurological Institute.[26] Mrs. Madeline Peck, who had organized the first Métis lecture in 1929, attended one of the lectures as well.[27]

From Montreal, Grey Owl and Yvonne travelled to speak in Boston.[28] Under normal circumstances he might have visited Henry Wadsworth Longfellow's home in neighbouring Cambridge, where the poet composed Grey Owl's beloved "Hiawatha"—or perhaps visited nearby Concord, where his favourite American essayist Ralph Waldo Emerson had lived. But there was no time. Back he came to Canada. In late January he lectured to 1,000 people at Hamilton's Royal Connaught Hotel. Several hundred others were turned away for lack of chairs.[29] He spoke next at Port Hope,[30] on his way back to the United States. He returned to Canada in mid-February.

Grey Owl's enthusiastic reception in Windsor, Ontario, hints at the response he might have received on a full Canadian tour. He arrived in mid-February after speaking in Detroit. Even before he spoke to a teacher's convention at Windsor's Prince Edward Hotel, several hundred teachers surrounded him to ask for his autograph.[31] Windsor loved him, and over the course of the next two days he spoke to several thousand children at twenty Windsor schools. As Yvonne wrote in a note to Ellen Elliott, Hugh Eayrs' secretary at Macmillan, "He now begins to realize what a power for good he is."[32] Children had become Grey Owl's target audience for his message. In *Tales of an Empty Cabin* he wrote that he wanted "to implant in fertile minds, anxious for knowledge, seeds that perhaps will blossom into deeds after the planter has been long forgotten."[33]

The distances to be covered on this tour were immense. Back to the United States after his talks in Windsor, Grey Owl visited Kenosha, Wisconsin;[34] Milwaukee, Wisconsin;[35] and Springfield, Illinois.[36] In early March he returned to Canada for an important lecture at the Château Frontenac in Quebec City. The lieutenant-governor of the province attended. But the city's small English-language paper, the *Chronicle-Telegraph*, was furious. At the lecture, the speaker suggested that Canada reject two reminders of its colonial past, the Union Jack and "God Save the King," and adopt its own national flag—and "O, Canada" as its anthem.[37]

From Quebec City, Grey Owl and Yvonne took the train to Ottawa for several important meetings. Grey Owl secured an appointment with Tom Crerar, the powerful federal minister of mines and resources, who also served as superintendent-general of Indian affairs.[38] The two men had last met to discuss Grey Owl's unsuccessful proposal to make a film of the Mississagi River with the federal government's backing. That approach had failed. This time Grey Owl spoke to the minister about the Canadian Indian and his welfare. With conservation, the welfare of the Canadian Indian had become Grey Owl's great concern.

Crerar confirmed that Canadian Indians could no longer be described as a vanishing people. Only six or seven years earlier, experts like Marius Barbeau and Diamond Jenness predicted that they would eventually become extinct, on account of population loss and intermarriage with non-Indians.[39] Now, Crerar reported that Canada's Indian population was growing at the rate of about one-and-one-half percent annually. He credited better medical care and better hospitalization. Grey Owl encouraged him with his plans to set aside large tracts of land where the 40 percent of Canada's Indians who still supported themselves through hunting and fishing would alone have access.[40]

While in Ottawa, Grey Owl also called on new boss, the replacement of J. C. Campbell as the park's publicity officer, Robert Stead.[41] Unfortunately no notes have survived which describe their meeting. A quarter of a century before, Stead had written a poem, "The Mixer," published in his collection, *The Empire Builders and Other Poems*. He had described how Canada turned immigrants into Canadians "all but the yellow and brown."

On the evening of March 8, Grey Owl gave an important talk at Ottawa's Chalmers United Church. He had been drinking heavily before the presentation, a fact which had not escaped his embarrassed host, Rev. Dr. John Woodside.[42] The talk itself, however, gave no indication of his intoxication. He was magnificent. Marilyn Legge, an Ottawa high school student, attended and never forgot his address. Thirty years later she wrote:

> He was a most impressive figure dressed in white fringed buckskins and wearing a single feathered headband. His talk made an indelible impression on me and, although I had always cared for animals, it was certainly Grey Owl's influence that made me realize how important conservation was. . . . He struck me as a very sincere, dedicated man passionately trying to get his message of conservation across and I have felt his influence to this day.[43]

(Marilyn Legge became an active member of the conservation movement in the Ottawa area and later started the newsletter for the Ottawa Humane Society).

More travelling came after the Ottawa talk: Toronto, then Pittsburgh, then Peterborough. From Peterborough, Grey Owl left for more speaking appearances in the northeastern United States, followed by his final lecture in eastern Canada at Toronto's Massey Hall on March 26. The pace was frantic. While in Peterborough the exhausted lecturer told Jack Peterson that "another month of this sort of thing will kill me." When he described Jim Espaniel in *Tales of an Empty Cabin,* in effect, he had described himself. Jim, he wrote, had "an unconquerable, dogged singleness of purpose that takes him far in a day. He'll get there, or be found dead on the way." [44]

One of the most taxing days of the North American tour was that of March 26. To give his major Toronto lecture, Grey Owl arrived at Union Station from Buffalo minutes before 6 P.M. en route from Providence, Rhode Island. He and Yvonne had been on the train for seventeen hours. He had just two hours to spare before his appearance at a packed Massey Hall, the largest concert hall in Canada. In Hugh Eayrs' words "for two hours [he] enchanted everybody. He really was superb." [45] On that evening, nearly three thousand Canadians gave him the greatest ovation of his life. [46] How far he had come from his lonely days in this city in 1906, 1911, and 1917. Just seconds after the enthusiastic, unrestrained applause died down, the organizers of the lecture rushed Grey Owl back to Union Station. He and Yvonne boarded the Canadian Pacific transcontinental at 10:50 P.M. to arrive in Regina the evening before his final lecture there on March 29. [47]

Meanwhile in Ottawa, an important decision was made. Some doubts had been raised about the value of retaining his services on account of behaviour in Prince Albert and his frequent absences from the park on his tours. Major Wood had defended him, and he had won. Jim Wood had pointed out that, while his work with the beaver could be done by "almost anyone" as efficiently as Grey Owl did it, the man had a celebrity status. The publicity, he wrote, "which we obtain for this Park and for the Parks Branch as a whole, from the fact that Grey Owl is located in one of the Parks during the summer months, and is recognized as a Park employee, is of much greater value than what is actually spent in employing him." [48] On March 31, Charles Camsell, deputy minister of mines and resources, confirmed Grey Owl's reappointment for six months beginning April 1.

The North American tour, unfortunately, had not had a Lovat Dickson to co-ordinate the lectures, nor did it have a Ken Conibear to act as tour manager. Yvonne had to do everything, and it ruined her health. Just after they reached Prince Albert in early April, the overworked, totally exhausted woman had to be hospitalized. [49]

Grey Owl, too, had given his very best to the crusade. He returned totally exhausted and run-down. During the last weeks of the tour he ate only two raw eggs a day, that was his only meal. [50] Desperately Grey Owl wanted to return to Beaver Lodge to rest. Major Wood arranged to have him taken by car over the ice on the lakes to within a kilometre or so of his cabin. Grey Owl reached his cabin on Thursday, April 7, but only three days later he reported by telephone from his cabin that he was quite sick. Major Wood immediately instructed the ranger at Waskesiu and the supervising warden to bring him to Prince Albert immediately. In Jim Wood's words:

> They arrived about 11 o'clock Sunday night, and Grey Owl seemed to be quite bright and cheery, but I put him in the Hospital immediately. On Monday I visited him twice, and he was very bright, not eating very much but sitting up in bed reading. On Tuesday, I could not visit him, but his Doctor advised me by phone about 3 o'clock in the afternoon, that he was in wonderful shape and that there was nothing to worry about. At 8 o'clock that evening he developed a temperature. At 10 o'clock he became delirious and at 12 o'clock sank into a coma. I received a call from the Hospital about 3 o'clock in the morning from his Doctor, saying that he was very low and that there was little hope for his recovery. I immediately arranged for a consultation, and when I arrived at the Hospital this had been completed; two other Doctors having been called in, and they advised me that he would not live throughout the day. At 8.25 in the morning, he died very quietly, and pictures taken show that the congestion in his lungs [pneumonia] was very slight, which all goes to prove that he had absolutely no resistance whatever.[51]

Another important glimpse of Grey Owl, early on his last evening of his life, comes from Bill Houghton, a telephone operator for the park staff.[52] He came over to visit Grey Owl at the Holy Family Hospital. From the door he heard, and saw, one of the Sisters at the Roman Catholic hospital having a very serious conversation with Grey Owl. The nun had asked him a question concerning his religion. "He told her," Bill later recalled, "the only religion he had, was the great outdoors, the trees and wildlife of the forests."[53]

                    *   *   *

Once the North Bay *Nugget* received the wire story from Prince Albert on April 13, it ran Britt Jessup's three-year-old article. The story, published that same afternoon, began with a quote from Mrs. Angele Belaney: "No matter what they say, Grey Owl was my husband and the father of my daughter, Agnes." The article continued, "Grey Owl, Mrs. Belaney claims, is not an Indian but a full-blooded white man, probably of English descent, who settled in Temagami in the early days of the district." Ed Bunyan, the humanitarian and fair-minded city editor had protected the famous conservationist to the moment of his death. Now he needed protection no longer. Newspapers across the English-speaking world picked up the *Nugget's* story and published its surprising revelations, at the same moment that Grey Owl was buried on the ridge immediately behind Beaver Lodge.

The Toronto *Star* gave considerable attention to the story, assigning Gregory Clark, Claud Pascoe, and Matt Halton, their European correspondent in London.[54] Taken completely by surprise, Lovat Dickson,

Betty Somervell, and Major Wood denied these preposterous charges. But more and more details of the Canadian side of Archie Belaney's double life gradually surfaced. With Parliament on vacation, and relative quiet on the European diplomatic front,[55] the London papers gave considerable play to the contradictory theories about the twentieth-century Hiawatha, repeating all the Canadian stories, as well as their own speculations. Still, no one had any hard evidence of his English origins.

The breakthrough came on April 19, from Hastings. Harry Cawkell, a sub-editor on the Hastings edition of the Brighton *Evening Argus* suddenly remembered Grey Owl's letter to Norman Gray, the White Rock Pavilion's director of entertainments, written several years earlier. Harry had forgotten the name of the two ladies that Grey Owl had wanted to contact, but Norman Gray found the information in his files. Fifty years later, Harry recalled how the Misses Belaney had received him at 24 Wellington Road. He had walked over to their home during his lunch break:

> Ada, the younger of the two sisters, opened the front door a few inches and Carrie stood behind her in the hallway. I introduced myself, said I knew Grey Owl had asked to meet them when he visited Hastings, and could they tell me something about him: how, for example, had they first met?
>
> Miss Ada said they knew nothing about Grey Owl, and when I pressed her Miss Carrie urged her to "shut the door." Just as she was about to do so I said on chance: "Can you just tell me what relation you were to Grey Owl?" Without thinking she replied: "He was our nephew." I said that now she had told me that, surely she ought to explain things a little. I was then invited in and the two sisters gave me a few reluctant details about their nephew; his early life and his obsession with Red Indians.
>
> There was no question of their truthfulness, but as a further check I went to see the registrar of births and deaths, explained the position, and within a few minutes he found the registration of Grey Owl's birth and gave me a copy of the certificate. There had been suggestions in the Press that Grey Owl may have had an English wife, so I asked the registrar, Mr. Stephen Bumstead, if he could possibly trace whether Grey Owl had been married in the area sometime during the War. He must have had a good filing system for those pre-computer days, for within ten minutes he produced a copy of the wedding certificate. The marriage was at Hollington Church-in-the-Wood, St. Leonards.[56]

Harry returned to his office with a world scoop, the true identity of Grey Owl. That afternoon the *Argus* carried the story under the banner "Extra Special":

"GREY OWL" WAS NOT A RED INDIAN—HE WAS A SUSSEX MAN!

With the publication of this bulletin, the London dailies descended on the Misses Belaney. To divert some of the press attention, they told the newsmen about Ivy Holmes, who had since remarried and lived in Twickenham in London. Ivy reported Grey Owl's missing toe, amputated during the war. This led the search to Prince Albert, Saskatchewan, where Hamilton's Funeral Home confirmed that Grey Owl's right foot indeed had one of the middle toes on the right foot missing.[57] As the London *Daily Express* affirmed on April 21: "Lost toe proves masquerade." The day before, they had interviewed two of Grey Owl's schoolmates at the Hastings Grammar School, Henry Hopkin and Con Foster.[58] With all the fuss about him, the London *Times* declared in an editorial on April 22: "His death has done as much for the renown of Hastings as ever did the death of HAROLD."

18 Grey Owl's Legacy

Grey Owl knew he would not live much longer. When in Ottawa in early March 1938, he and Yvonne visited Elizabeth Shortt, his wife's former employer. He told Dr. Shortt, "I have a presentiment. I am not going to live long. I have a feeling here" (and then he rapped his chest).[1] It was an anxious time for him. He realized that the North Bay *Nugget* knew his secret, and that *Time* magazine had obtained some inside information about his several wives (five, not seven as the magazine claimed).[2]

Unknown to him, the Department of Indian Affairs that February had begun an investigation into his past. Grey Owl had started a fight on Fifth Avenue with a New Yorker who had called him a "faker".[3] The department now wanted to know more about him and had already contacted Tom Saville, who had acted as his best man at his wedding in 1910 to Angele.[4] Moreover, once Angele and Agnes heard of his talk at Massey Hall, they vowed to attend the next address in Toronto and confront him.[5] Grey Owl's days as the Modern Hiawatha were numbered in the early spring of 1938.

After he died on April 13, 1938, a battle waged on both sides of the Atlantic about his origins. Archie Belaney had been so convincing as Grey Owl. After the initial disclosures about his Canadian and English past, neither Major Wood, nor Betty Somervell, [6] nor Lovat Dickson believed the allegations. Lovat Dickson led the fight in Britain, and Major Wood in Canada, to gain acceptance of Grey Owl's own story about his past and to put his valuable work in perspective.

In the summer of 1938, Lovat Dickson published a tribute to Grey Owl, *The Green Leaf. A Memorial to Grey Owl.* The small book did much to restore Grey Owl's name as a great writer and conservationist. *The Green Leaf* contained press commentary on Grey Owl, excerpts from his writings and pictures, as well as testimonies about him by Lovat Dickson and Superintendent Wood. Within its pages, Major Wood eloquently summarized the man's work, regardless of his origins.

I care not whether he was an Englishman, Irishman, Scotsman or Negro. He was a great man with a great mind, and with great objectives which he ever kept before him. He will be remembered for his efforts to educate the people to the disastrous effect of forest fires. His vivid comparison of a burnt-over area with an area covered with waving trees is one that no thinking person could ever forget. He will be remembered for his efforts to eliminate cruel practices in the capturing of fur-bearing animals. Not for one moment was he an opponent of the fur trade, but he readily felt that no fur-bearing animal should suffer a long and lingering death. He will be remembered for his courageous stand in regard to blood sports, whether it was the running down of a fox by riders and hounds, or whether it was the destruction of a moose or elk by some fat millionaire, enjoying every comfort that money can buy, purely for the purpose of hanging the head in a hunting lodge, and leaving the rest of the animal in the bush; and finally, he will be remembered for his efforts to rehabilitate the Indian, to a point where he would again possess some of his old-time dignity and independence.[7]

In Canada the press reported the story of Grey Owl's masquerade in a surprising manner. Of the eight major dailies, from Ottawa to Calgary, that commented editorially on his exposure, not one condemned him.[8] One of the best columns appeared in the Winnipeg *Tribune* on April 20, 1938:

FUN TO BE FOOLED

BARNUM maintained that the public not only can be fooled but likes to be fooled. A great chuckle has gone right across Canada at the suggestion that the national leg has been well and truly pulled.

The chances are that Archie Belaney could not have done nearly such effective work for conservation of wild life under his own name. It is an odd commentary, but true enough, that many people will not listen to simple truths except when uttered by exotic personalities.

Another strong editorial appeared in the Ottawa *Citizen* on April 23, 1938. Perceptively, the paper identified the man's genius.

Few stories in recent years have contained more of the elements of human interest, literary romance and legendary adventure than that being written about the life of Archie Belaney or Grey Owl. Of course, the value of his work is not jeopardized. His attainments as a writer and naturalist will survive and when in later years our children's children are told of the strange masquerade—if it was a masquerade—their wonder and their appreciation will grow. He is assured a place in the annals of his adopted country.

The revelation about Grey Owl's true identity confused Anahareo. She had never doubted what he had said about his past, "Scotch and Indian, born in Mexico."[9] Lovat Dickson and Betty Somervell invited her to England in the late summer of 1938 to meet Grey Owl's mother, Kittie

Scott-Brown, in the hope that Anahareo would detect in her a drop of Indian blood.[10] Anahareo detected none, and this troubled her: "When, finally, I was convinced that Archie was English, I had the awful feeling for all those years I had been married to a ghost, that the man who now lay buried at Ajawaan was someone I had never known, and that Archie had never really existed."[11] Her comment reveals Archie Belaney's tragic personal dilemma, one that he never resolved.

Abandoned by his parents, young Archie desperately wanted love and affection. His two aunts did their best, but these ladies, both entering middle age, could not understand or help him in any meaningful way. He sought refuge in a warm, friendly fantasy world. Influenced greatly by the books he had read about the old American West, he conjured up an imaginary Scots-American guide as his father and chose an Apache woman as his mother.

Over the years Grey Owl continued his retreat from reality. He perfected his imaginary identity, making it plausible. The fact that he was born in an Indian encampment in Mexico helped to explain why he could produce no birth certificate. He coloured his skin and dyed his hair. To his writing he added oddities of punctuation, capitalization and sentence structure[12] to give the impression that he had learned to write with difficulty. He liked to use split infinitives and sentences ending in prepositions, to look more authentic.[13]

In his life in Canada he had at least two opportunities to escape from himself, from his self-pity, his shame, his insecurity. The first opportunity was with Angele, and the second with Anahareo. For probably the first time in his life, when he met Anahareo he opened up and began to communicate freely and honestly with another human being. But then he panicked, and stopped. His insecurities proved too strong.

On the boat back to Canada after his triumphant first British tour, Grey Owl told Betty Somervell what he considered the purpose of his life. He had been talking with her about how his campaign to help save the beaver had grown to embrace all animals, as well as the Indians and finally all humanity. "Down the avenue of trees," he said, "I see a spot of sunlight. And I am trying so hard to get there."[14] This statement reveals the essential tragedy of Grey Owl. He already stood in a clearing and could not identify the light from the darkness. Angele loved him for what he genuinely was, as did Anahareo. But he could not recognize this and could not truly communicate with either of them. As a middle-aged man he still could not reach out and help his children, who needed a father as much as he had as a boy in Hastings.

One of Grey Owl's favourite essays by Ralph Waldo Emerson was "Compensation," the message of which Grey Owl interpreted to mean, "that the effect blooms in the cause, that no sustained effort, good or bad, but had its inevitable complement of reward or punishment." A dark cloud lurked behind every silver lining, and a silver lining behind every dark cloud.[15] In his case the silver lining behind his tormented, unhappy childhood was the time he spent with animals. He broke away completely from those in the mainstream and gained insights denied to most. Through his books, articles, films, and lectures, he opened the eyes of many Canadians to something that they were previously unable to see, or to appreciate. He helped to create an atmosphere and climate of concern that the Canadian environmental movement, which emerged thirty years later, could build on. With a vision denied to the four-year politicians of his day, and to the public commentators of the decade, he called on Canadians to conserve their natural resources, which he knew were very limited. The timely nature of his message has kept him in the Canadian consciousness.

Grey Owl's masquerade, and particularly his Royal Command Performance, also kept his story alive after his death. Trent Frayne's "Grey Owl, the Magnificent Fraud," in *Maclean's* on August 1, 1951, reviewed his life story for a large Canadian readership. The Ontario government officially recognized his contribution to that province with the erection of an historic plaque in his honour in a Temagami provincial park in July 1959.[16] The text neatly summarizes his life: "Alarmed at the rapid despoliation of the wilderness, the wanton slaughter of wildlife, and the threat to Indian cultural survival, he became an ardent conservationist." Four years later a mass-circulation American magazine really turned public attention back to Grey Owl's conservationist message. On April 8, 1963, *Sports Illustrated* published R. Cantwell's "Grey Owl: Mysterious Genius of Nature Lore."

All this time, Grey Owl's daughter Dawn, his child by Anahareo, kept up her campaign to regain public attention for her father's conservationist message. She almost succeeded, with John Diefenbaker's support, in having a small display on her father at the Indian Pavilion at Montreal's World's Fair, Expo 67.[17] With Dawn's encouragement, Anahareo published her memories in her book *Devil in Deerskins. My Life with Grey Owl*, which appeared in 1972.

A new generation of readers discovered his books when conservation became a popular concern in the 1960s and 1970s. Macmillan reprinted all of his books in paperback in the early 1970s. The Montreal *Gazette* commented on April 8, 1972: "Ecology Fad returns Grey Owl to Fashion." Two decades later, all the books remain in print, quite a compliment to the memory of an author who died over half a century ago.

Bill Oliver's still photos and his magnificent films of Grey Owl and the beaver still had great popular appeal in the 1970s, as had Yousuf Karsh's stunning portrait taken in Ottawa in late February 1936. Vera Fidler's well-illustrated article in the *Canadian Geographical Journal*, with the title "Grey Owl: A Man Ahead of his Time," summarized the new appreciation of the man, in a polluted, contaminated universe. The essay appeared in the issue for May 1972. Using stills and documentary film footage, as well as interviews with those who had known Grey Owl, Nancy Ryley of CBC Television produced a moving portrait of the man, released in early December 1972. This film, with lengthy interviews with Lovat Dickson who had returned to live in Canada in the mid-1960s, Anahareo, and several of Grey Owl's friends in Biscotasing, probably did more than anything else to date to stimulate a new wave of interest in the man. Lovat Dickson's publication the following year of *Wilderness Man* provided readers with the first full biography of Grey Owl.

The fact that Grey Owl's cabins at both Riding Mountain and Prince Albert national parks were restored in the 1970s adds greatly to his continuing reputation today. At first the parks had been reluctant to remember him, after Superintendent James Wood left and took up his new post as superintendent at Jasper National Park in late 1938. The new administration at Prince Albert National Park and the Parks Branch did little to keep alive Grey Owl's memory. Grey Owl's friend Dr. van der Sleen of the Netherlands, who had visited him in 1936, returned in 1939. The neglect of Beaver Lodge after Superintendent Wood's departure surprised the internationally-known natural history lecturer and writer. He wrote a senior official in Ottawa about his concerns and urged that Beaver Lodge be kept up.[18] Nothing was done. The Canadian writer Kathleen Strange visited Beaver Lodge in the late 1940s to find it "falling into a sad state of decay and disrepair." "The cabin, in which Grey Owl lived and wrote his famous stories and books, was dirty and neglected; his snowshoes, propped against an outside wall, were rotting away; and his canoe, in which he spent so many happy hours, was lying on the ground broken in half."[19]

But with the rebirth of interest in Grey Owl in the early 1970s, the Canadian Parks Service finally acted, making the area around Beaver Lodge a wilderness sanctuary and restoring the cabin itself. Edwin and Margery Wilder, a concerned American couple, became so influenced by Grey Owl's conservationist philosophy that in August 1988 they gave $750,000 to ensure the preservation of the wilderness canoe routes in the nature sanctuary, as well as to take care of Beaver Lodge. As Margery Wilder explained: "There is something so unique about this area that it just has to be preserved."[20]

Thanks to Prince Albert National Park's protection of Beaver Lodge and Lake Ajawaan, which can only be approached by a forest path, the magic story of the English boy who became Grey Owl, a Canadian folk hero, will live on as long as the park itself. One of the most moving passages in *Pilgrims of the Wild*[21] eloquently speaks to everyone willing to make the water and overland journey to Grey Owl's wilderness home:

On all sides from the cabin where I write extends an uninterrupted wilderness, flowing onward in a dark, billowing flood Northward to the Arctic Sea. No railroad passes through it to burn and destroy, no settler lays waste with fire and axe. Here from any eminence a man may gaze on unnumbered leagues of forest that will never feed the hungry maw of commerce.

This is a different place, a different day.

Nowhere does the sight of stumps and slashed tops of noble trees offend the eye or depress the soul, and the strange, wild, unimaginable beauty of these Northern sunsets is not defaced by jagged rows of stark and ghastly rampikes. . . .

Every wish has been fulfilled, and more. Gone is the haunting fear of a vandal hand. Wild life in all its rich variety, creatures deemed furtive and elusive, now pass almost within our reach, and sometimes stand beside the camp and watch. And birds, and little beasts and big ones, and things both great and small have gathered round the place, and frequent it, and come and go their courses as they will, and fly or swim or walk or run according to their kind.

Death falls, as at times it must, and Life springs in its place. Nature lives and journeys on and passes all about in well balanced, orderly array.

The scars of ancient fires are slowly healing over; big trees are growing larger. The beaver towns are filling up again.

The cycle goes on.

The Pilgrimage is over.

Acknowledgements

       I re-discovered Grey Owl in the winter of 1968–69 while preparing my M.A. thesis in Canadian history at Université Laval in Quebec City. In my thesis I examined the way in which French Canadian historians presented North American Indians in their works. By chance one particular afternoon I strayed into the literature section of the library and came across numerous copies of books in French, written by a man named Grey Owl. This was extraordinary, as I thought I had fully researched all works in French on Indians. Then, it came back to me. I must have been about ten or eleven when a friend of mine in public school gave a talk on Grey Owl in our oral composition class. This same mysterious Grey Owl, who had captured my imagination in the mid-1950s, had re-surfaced.

       The following fall I began my Ph.D. in Canadian history at the University of Toronto, preparing my thesis on the Mississauga, or Ojibwa (Chippewa), Indians who lived on the north shore of Lake Ontario. My doctoral studies complemented my growing fascination with Grey Owl, who had lived in Ojibwa country in northern Ontario for nearly twenty years, from 1906 to 1925. To my surprise I discovered that only one biography of Grey Owl had been written, *Half-Breed* (1939) by Lovat Dickson, his Canadian publisher in England. The character of this talented man, who fought to protect what remained of Canada's wilderness, intrigued me. I wanted to know more about him. Fortunately, in the winter of 1969–1970 I met Lovat Dickson, who had moved back to Canada from England. Over a sixteen-year period we met many times at his home in Toronto and I came to know him and his wife, Marguerite Dickson, as personal friends. I assisted him by showing him some of my early research notes when he prepared his second biography of Grey Owl, *Wilderness Man*, which appeared in 1973.

       While I lived in Toronto from 1969 to 1974, I made more than a dozen trips to northern Ontario and Quebec to tape the reminiscences of Grey Owl's Indian and Métis friends and of the white trappers, guides, and old forest rangers still living in the north who had known him half-a-century earlier. I met wonderful people, the Cussons, the Espaniels, the Kohls, the Langevins, the Legaces, the Phillips, the Sawyers, the Woodworths, and many others, all of whom helped me. Grey Owl's daughter, Agnes Lalonde in North Bay, Ontario, became a close friend, and in late 1974 I met Grey Owl's son, John Jero, in Thunder Bay, Ontario. I became involved in the early 1970s with helping the Ojibwa Indians of Lake Temagami with the historical research for an outstanding land claim they had in the Temagami area, where Archie Belaney lived from 1907 to 1911. Thanks to this involvement, I learned much about the history of the area.

In 1971, I also visited Western Canada where Grey Owl lived in the 1930s. I myself moved in 1974 to teach Canadian history at the University of Calgary. I frequently visited Grey Owl's wife Anahareo and Grey Owl and Anahareo's daughter, Dawn, in Kamloops, B.C. I met Ken Conibear, Grey Owl's tour manager in Britain in 1937, on many occasions at his home in Vancouver.

I went to Britain four times (1971, 1972, 1975, and 1976) to locate and to interview Grey Owl's childhood friends: George McCormick, Henry Hopkin, and Percy Overton. I also found and interviewed Ivy Holmes, Grey Owl's English wife. Mrs. Betty Somervell assisted me greatly with her reminiscences of Grey Owl, as did Laya Rotenburg Kurtz, whom I visited at her home in Paris in 1972.

During the past two decades I have attempted to document each important factual statement about Grey Owl, to explain how this gifted young Englishman became one of the greatest forces for the protection of the Canadian wilderness in this century.

I must thank my employers, the University of Calgary, for generously awarding me a special Killam Resident Fellowship in the fall of 1987 and a Sabbatical Leave in the fall of 1988 to complete this manuscript. I also warmly thank Jane McHughen of Western Producer Prairie Books, and her colleagues, Nora Russell and Ricki Lane, for their constant support. My editor, Bob Beal, read all four drafts and copy-edited the final text. I have incorporated in the book many of his helpful comments and suggestions. My readers, Phil Chester, Ken Conibear, and Bill Waiser, also read my manuscript at various stages and assisted greatly in improving it. After reading my second draft, Phil Chester made several penetrating comments on Grey Owl's character which helped me to understand him much more fully.

Marta Styk of the Department of Geography, University of Calgary, completed the maps and my sister Barbara Nair prepared the index. I thank Doris Pullen for her research on Grey Owl's second British lecture tour in 1937 and for locating H. A. L. Foster, the son of Con Foster, a schoolmate of Archie's at the Hastings Grammar School. I thank the University of Calgary Inter-Library Loan Office for their assistance in ordering books, articles, and newspapers on microfilm. Joyce Woods and Laureen Quapp have assisted enormously with the typing of the several drafts of the text.

Over a twenty-year period I have incurred many debts to those who inspired me and helped me, and who kept alive my dream of one day writing this biography. The accompanying list acknowledges special debts. If I have overlooked anyone who assisted, I hope they will accept my apology.

For general research information and assistance I thank the following individuals: John Adams, Charles Armour, Arthur Andrews, Walter Bauer, R. E. Bennett, Carl Berger, Jim Black, Betty Brehaut, Urban Burke, Father Romuald Boucher, Lloyd Bowen, Mike Buss, Susan Saunders Bellingham, Renu Barrett, Kristin Bonney, Donna Bowler, Dick Bunyan, Phebe Chartrand, C. H. D. Clark, Communications Media of the University of Calgary, Frank Conibear, Lloyd Cook, Jocelyn Currie, Maureen Dolyniuk, Patrick Duffy, James Eayrs, Yorke Edwards, Ray Fadden, Vera Fast, Jerry Fielder, Julia Finn, Caroline Forcier, Mrs. Albert Rotenberg Gallander, Ian Getty, Graham Gillan, Blanche Gooch, Anne Goddard, Jean Goodwill, Peter Greig, André Guindon, Gillian Hawes, Susan Haigh, Judy Hall, Ethelyn Harlow, Alex Huculak, Jack Heyink, Dorothy Kealey, Helen Kirk-Greene, Leo La Clare, Sharon Larade, Redfern Louttit, Heather Lysons, Bennett McCardle, Craig Macdonald, Frank MacDougall, Jean McNiven, Ken Macpherson, Caroline MacWhannell, Michelle Miles, Jim Miller, Sarah Montgomery, Toby Morantz, Jim Morrison, Peter Murphy, Joan Murray, Blair Neatby, Peter Newman, Milan Novak, Edo Nyland, Dave Ohasi, Kathleen Owens, Marie-France Paquet, Theresa Peters, Raymond Peringer, Don Pugh, Brion Purdey, Murray Randall, Thomas Raddall, R. E. Rashley, Ed Rea, Dawn and Bob Richardson, Lady Joan Roberts, Judy (Mrs. Lloyd) Roberts, J. R. G. Robillard, Ed Rogers, Jan Rollins, Nancy Ryley, Barney Sandwell, C. A. Santoro, Ivan Saunders, Evelyn Scrivens, Phyllis Senese, Mary Sheppard, D. H. Simpson, Norma Sluman, Shirlee Anne Smith, Marion Somers, Jonathan Somervell, Stephen Speisman, Sheila Staats, Graham Storms, Viola Summers, Audrey Swaffield, Karen Teeple, Monica Turner, N. P. van der Sleen, Margaret Van Every, John Wadland, Bill Waiser, Lloyd Walton, Lynette Walton, Joan Waldegrave, Kenneth Wallace, Leon Warmski, Maude Watt, Roger Wheate, Bruce Whiteman, Rex Williams, Sheila Woolner, Doug Wyatt, Kensei Yoshida, Morris Zaslow, and Mary Zdunich.

I am indebted to the following people for details about Archie Belaney's youth in Hastings, the Misses Belaney, and Hastings at the turn of the century: J. Manwaring Baines, H. R. Beck, Bessie Cole, Bill Dyer, John Fletcher, H. A. L. Foster, Berryl Friend, Pamela Haines, Kathleen Harman, Daresbury Hatton, George and Dolly Head, G. H. Henshall, Ivy Holmes, Henry Hopkin, Geoffrey McCormick, George McCormick, Leslie McCormick, Roger Mitchell, Percy (Bob) Overton, Mrs. Sargent, Leonard Scott-Brown, Colin and Betty Taylor, John Taylor, Helen McCormick Watkins, and Christopher Whittick.

222   ACKNOWLEDGEMENTS

For background on Archie Belaney in the Temagami area from 1907 to 1911 and for the history of the region I am indebted to: Brian Back, Jamie Benidickson, Caroline Brown, Gilles Cantin, Carol Cochrane, Dewey Derosier, J. C. Elliott, Ted and Molly Guppy, John Hart, Bruce Hodgins, Charlie Labarge, Agnes Belaney Lalonde, George Le Duc, Isobel (Billie) Le Duc, Mrs. Arnold Leishman, Donald McKenzie, Joy Stevens MacMillan, Charlotte McLean Morrison, Millard Newcomb, Rita Moore O'Sullivan, Charlie Potts, Gary Potts, Tom Potts, Lisa Neveu Saville, Tom Saville, Jr., Jack Stewart, Madeline Katt Theriault, Jim Turner, and Selina and Gerry Twain. For information on his journey through Algonquin Park in 1909 I thank Ottelyn Robinson Addison.

A great many individuals helped me to understand Archie Belaney's years in, and near, Biscotasing, 1912–1914, 1917–1925: Keith Acheson, Tom Bain, Célina Legace Barnes, Hector Bléau, Art Boice, Joe and Mary Cameron, Antoine Commanda, Mildred Cowper, Vince Crichton, Ted Cusson, Rus Duval, Carrington Eddy, Adam Espaniel, Jim and Susan Espaniel, Rene Espaniel, Shirley Espaniel, Yvette Espaniel, Ken Gibbs, Gordon Gouett, R. T. Gibson, Carolyn Hryhorchuk, John Jero, Haddow Keith, Maurice Kingsford, Harry and Katie Kohls, Mary Kohls, Bill Langevin, Dave Langevin, Gordon and Hilda Kohls Langevin, Omer Lavallée, Robert Laurence, Ferg Legace, Frank Legace, Jack Leve, Tom Linklater, Sam Luke, Stuart MacDougall, Madeline Woodworth McLeod, Jane Espaniel McKee, Robert McWatch, A. E. O'Neill, Bill Orange, Jr., Bert Phillips, Colin Phillips, Rueben Phillips, Elizabeth Miller Robinson, Ed and Charlotte Sawyer, Libby Sawyer, Irene Shaughnessy, Sudbury Public Library, Charlie and Grace Sykes, Robert Wilson, and Jack Woodworth.

Background on Archie Belaney's years in the Canadian Army was provided by: Albert Chandler, Bert Crookes, W. A. B. Douglas, Wayne McCorrister, Mrs. W. E. Macfarlane, John Paveling, D. F. Rennie, Gordon Weedmark, and Glenn Wright. C. Bruce Ferguson assisted with information on Nova Scotia in 1915, at the time of Archie Belaney's enlistment.

I thank those who helped with my research on Grey Owl's years in Quebec, from 1925 to 1931: Anahareo, Joseph Bérubé, John Bovey, Bill Cartier, Lorenzo Charest, Roland Chamberland, Gertrude Côté, Thérèse Côté, Msgr. Jean-Philippe Cyr, Gordon Dallyn, Emma Dufond, Marcel-Aimé Gagnon, Bernie Graham, Eleanor Kalil, Yvon Lavoie, Adélard Leblanc, Richard Peck, Mario Pelletier, Peter Pichette, Frank and Alice Richardson, and Walter Strong.

The following individuals assisted with my understanding of Grey Owl's films: James Bach, Doreen Huffman, Sheilagh Jameson, Bill Kirst, A. J. Langford, Marjorie Oliver, Charlie Quick, and Gordon Sparling.

Many people kindly provided me with details on Grey Owl's years in Western Canada, from 1931 to 1938: Kenneth Aitken, Margaret Winters Charko, Don Cameron, Harry Charmbury, Ron Davies, John Diefenbaker,

Hubert Green, Wally Laird, Candace Loewen, Fergus Lothian, Kathleen Munro, John Nicol, Billie Ozman Rawlinson, George Rochester, Jim Sceviour, Hazel Sorenson Schmitz, Georgean Short, Merv Syroteuk, Clarence Tillenius, John Tootoosis, Bill Waiser, Ettie Winters, and Stan Winters.

I learned of Grey Owl's first cousins in Western Canada from: Ann Brownlow, Wilmott McComb, Nan Morse, Ivy Scott, Doreen Stanford, and Catherine Tweed.

Assistance with information on Grey Owl's two British tours came from the following: Ted Blackmore, John Burton, Isla Burnett, Ken Conibear, Elizabeth Cuthbert, Lovat Dickson, David Hayes, Eunice Hirst, Margaret Horsfield, Rosemary Kerr, Laya Rotenberg Kurtz, Ray Morley, Lillian O'Nions, Stephen Patterson, Oxfordshire County Council Libraries' Service, Doris Pullen, Jack Shadbolt, Betty Somervell, Ian West, Michael Wilson, and Bridget Wright.

My thanks to those who assisted with information on Grey Owl's North American lectures and Canadian appearances in the years 1935 to 1938: Radha Rotenberg Ahuja, Major Benton, Yvonne Perrier Clare, Adam Cuthand, Stan Cuthand, Wilhelmine Davidson, Marilyn Legge Godfrey, John Gray, Maurice Hackman, Hollee Haswell, Fernand Harvey, Clara Heggie, Karen Hicks, Harry Hodges, Jasper Hill, Charlie Huffman, Gerald Johnston, Mary Joselin, Yousuf Karsh, Ken Kidd, Edna McLean, Manly Miner, Mrs. D. Pendlebury, Shirley Rowe, Isabel Syme, Paula Torihey, and Louise Wright.

Concerning the investigation into Grey Owl's background I received information from: Orville Brunelle, H. A. R. Cawkell, Gregory Clark, Mort Fellman, Jim Graham, Britt Jessup, and George Wallace.

Over the years I benefited enormously from the encouragement of my late father, John Caulfield Smith, and my mother, Jean Boyd Smith. I reserve my greatest thank-you for my wife, Dove, who sacrificed enormously to allow me to complete this obsession of more than twenty years.

Notes

Throughout these notes, a number of abbreviations are used to indicate collections and repositories:

ARMY. Army service files, Personnel Records Centre, National Archives of Canada, Tunney's Pasture, Ottawa.

DEACON. William Arthur Deacon Papers, Thomas Fisher Rare Book Library, University of Toronto.

DICKSON. Lovat Dickson Papers, MG 30, D 237, National Archives of Canada.

FRASER, H. J. Fraser Papers, Saskatchewan Archives Board, Saskatoon, Saskatchewan.

GREY OWL. Grey Owl Collection, MG 30, D 147, National Archives of Canada.

McMASTER. Macmillan Archive, The William Ready Division of Archives and Research Collections, McMaster University Library, Hamilton, Ontario.

NAC. National Archives of Canada.

PANP. Prince Albert National Park, Waskesiu Lake, Saskatchewan, Beaver File, PA 61.

PERSONNEL FILE. Civil service personnel file of "A. Bellaney," RG 32, vol. 18, National Archives of Canada.

SCOTT-BROWN. Copies of Kittie Scott-Brown letters, in Donald B. Smith, Grey Owl Collection, Glenbow Archives, Calgary.

SCRIBNER'S. Grey Owl's Correspondence with Charles Scribner's Sons, Rare Books and Special Collections, Princeton University Library, Princeton, New Jersey.

SHORT. Georgean Short, "Report on Investigations 'The Grey Owl Project,'" in Prince Albert National Park Library, Waskesiu, Saskatchewan.

SMITH. Donald B. Smith, Grey Owl Collection, Glenbow Archives, Calgary.

SOMERVELL. Copies of materials collected and written by Betty Somervell, in Donald B. Smith, Grey Owl Collection, Glenbow Archives, Calgary.

VETERANS AFFAIRS. Notes on the file on Archibald Belaney once held by the Department of Veterans Affairs (the file itself is currently misplaced), in Donald B. Smith, Grey Owl Collection, Glenbow Archives, Calgary.

Chapter 1. The Modern Hiawatha

1. There are two very good newspaper reviews of the talk: "Famous Indian Author at Hastings. Big Audience Welcomes Grey Owl," *Evening Argus* (Hastings edition), December 3, 1935; "Grey Owl's Thrilling Travelogue," Hastings *Observer,* December 7, 1935. John Burton, Norman Gray's assistant in the 1930s, remembered the occasion well, as at first the lighting staff had missed finding Grey Owl on the stage with the pin light, the tiny light that

would pick up his head, then the aperture would open to show his entire body. Grey Owl had returned backstage furious about the mistake. In order not to miss him again the staff set the light in a corner and, successfully this second time, Grey Owl walked out with it. Telephone conversation with John Burton, Hastings, September 21, 1988.

2. "Grey Owl and the Lesser People," London *Times*, November 2, 1935; "Mr. Grey Owl Speaks," Manchester *Guardian*, October 25, 1935; C. A. Lyon, "Strange Tales of Grey Owl's Life in Britain," *Sunday Express*, April 24, 1938.

3. Grey Owl, quoted in "Famous Indian Author at Hastings," *Evening Argus*, December 3, 1935. See also Lovat Dickson's comments on his opening remarks, in *The Green Leaf. A Tribute to Grey Owl*, edited and arranged by Lovat Dickson (London: Lovat Dickson Limited, 1938), p. 14.

4. Grey Owl, "Author's Special Preface to his English Readers, October, 1935," *Pilgrims of the Wild* (London: Lovat Dickson & Thompson Ltd., 1935), p. v.

5. "Log Cabin to Hotel," Manchester *Evening News*, November 19, 1935.

6. F. G. H. Salusbury, " 'Grey Owl', in his Deerskin, is here as Envoy of the Wild," *Daily Express*, October 18, 1935; the story also ran, with several minor alterations, in the *Scottish Daily Express*, October 19, 1935.

7. "The Third 'Sunday Times' Book Exhibition," *Sunday Times*, November 10, 1935; V. G. G., "Books Made and in the Making," *The Observer*, November 10, 1935; Charles Graves, "Between Ourselves," *Sunday Graphic & Sunday News*, November 10, 1935.

8. Enclosure of an excerpt from a letter from Mrs. L. Day of Isleworth-Middlends, England, to Professor and Mrs. T. D. A. Cockerell, dated London, November 7, 1935. It is in a letter from Professor and Mrs. T. D. A. Cockerell to Major James Wood, Park Superintendent, Prince Albert National Park, dated Boulder, Colorado, November 22, 1935, PANP.

9. A. R. G. M., "Grey Owl—His life among the Beavers," *Cambridge Review*, November 15, 1935.

10. Sir Sydney Cockerell to T. D. A. Cockerell, dated Cambridge, November 11, 1935, T. D. A. Cockerell Collection, Box 6, folders 6–13, Sydney Cockerell, Western Historical Collections, University of Colorado at Boulder, Colorado. The comparison of Grey Owl to Lawrence of Arabia appears in a letter Sir Sydney wrote on January 12, 1936, to his brother T. D. A. Cockerell. This letter is also in the T. D. A. Cockerell Collection. Sir J. J. Thomson was the winner of the Nobel Prize for physics in 1906 and master of Trinity College, Cambridge. David Vaisey, *T. E. Lawrence. The Legend and the Man* (Oxford: Bodleian Library, 1988), pp. 31, 96.

11. Sir Sydney Cockerell to T. D. A. Cockerell, dated Cambridge, September 30, 1935, T. D. A. Cockerell Collection, Box 6, folders 6–13, Sydney Cockerell, Western Historical Collections, University of Colorado at Boulder, Colorado. On Sir Sydney's friendship with Kipling, see Wilfrid Blunt, *Cockerell* (London: Hamish Hamilton, 1964), pp. 96–98.

12. The phrase is that of Mrs. Trevelyan's husband, G. M. Trevelyan, in his *History of England*, quoted in D. D. Calvin, "Despoiling a Continent," *Queen's Quarterly*, 42 (1935): 356.

13. Grey Owl, quoted in "Grey Owl, Impressions of Scotland. Ambassador of the Wild," *The Scotsman*, November 30, 1935.

14. Photo, " 'Grey Owl' Comes to Edinburgh," Edinburgh *Evening News*, November 30, 1935.

15. The wife of Governor-General Minto, Lady Minto, claimed to be a descendant of Pocahontas in an address to the Blood Indians in present-day southern Alberta. R. Burton Deane, *Mounted Police Life in Canada. A Record of Thirty-One Years' Service* (London: Cassell and Company, 1916), p. 89; Edmund Montague Morris, *The Diaries of Edmund Montague Morris, Western Journeys 1907–1910,* transcribed by Mary Fitz-Gibbon (Toronto: Royal Ontario Museum, 1985), p. 118.

16. Donald B. Smith, *Long Lance. The True Story of an Impostor* (Toronto: Macmillan, 1982), pp. 123–24.

17. C. E. G. H. "Wintering in England," *The Field*, November 30, 1935. Grey Owl's cold is mentioned in "Famous Indian Author at Hastings," *Evening Argus*, December 3, 1935. "He appeared against doctor's orders, having caught a cold in Scotland a few days ago."

18. Grey Owl to Norman Gray, quoted in " 'Grey Owl's' Quest," Hastings *Observer*, June 6, 1936.

19. T. D. A. Cockerell, "A Visit with Grey Owl," *Natural History*, 37 (1936): 225. Just before leaving for Britain in early October 1935, Grey Owl completed the editing and captioning of "Pilgrims of the Wild." See Grey Owl to Rache [Lovat Dickson] and Marguerite [Dickson, his wife], dated May 4, 1936, McMASTER.

20. "Famous Indian Author at Hastings," *Evening Argus*, December 3, 1935. For his methods of lecturing on his first British tour, see also the reviews of his talks in the Bath *Chronical and Herald*, December 11, 1935; the Ayrshire *Post*, January 17, 1936. Grey Owl showed four films in his performances. See, "Grey Owl and his Films," *Manchester Guardian*, December 13, 1935.

21. David Thornton, *Hastings: A Living History* (Hastings: Hastings Publishing Company, 1987), p. 29.

22. Grey Owl to Lovat Dickson and Hugh Eayrs, dated Beaver Lodge, July 2, 1935, in *The Green Leaf*, ed. Dickson, p. 68.

23. J. C. and J. A. Belaney, "Letter to the Editor," Hastings *Observer*, April 30, 1938.

24. Grey Owl to Maxwell Perkins, dated Beaver Lodge, April 1937, SCRIBNER'S. "After each performance from one to three hundred books were sold, autographed by me at a table provided on the stage (I wear full native costume by the way)." See also Betty Somervell, Letters to her daughter, Kristin, 1953, p. 5, copy in SMITH. "After lectures Grey Owl used to sit at a table and sign books for people, there was always a long queue waiting to come to shake hands & talk to him and to get autographs."

25. J. C. and J. A. Belaney, "Letter to the Editor," Hastings *Observer*, April 30, 1938. The Queen's Hotel was Hastings' most prestigious in the 1920s and 1930s. After officially opening the White Rock Pavilion in April 1927, Edward, Prince of Wales, lunched there. Thornton, *Hastings*, p. 133.

26. The full letter is given in the Hastings *Observer's* exposé of Grey Owl's true identity on April 23, 1938. Excerpts from the letter (without the name of the

Misses Belaney being given) were printed in a short article in the *Observer* on June 6, 1936, entitled " 'Grey Owl's' Quest." This article begins: " 'Grey Owl', the Red Indian lecturer on Canadian wild life who appeared at the White Rock Pavilion last winter, has sent to the Entertainments Department a delightful letter, in which he seeks to get in touch with former friends in Hastings." In my transcription of the letter I follow the 1938 version in all instances, except with the fifth paragraph. The 1936 version alone contains the description of the Misses Belaney as "well over middle age"—I've included this. When he inserted the Misses Belaney's names in the 1938 article, the editor of the Hastings *Observer* diplomatically dropped this reference.

27. Professor Alex Lucas termed Grey Owl Canada's most famous writer and lecturer both at home and abroad in the 1930s in "Nature Writers and the Animal Story," in Carl F. Kinck, ed., *Literary History of Canada* (Toronto: University of Toronto Press, 1965), p. 376.

28. Betty Somervell, "Diary of my First Visit to Canada," entry for February 15, 1936, copy in SMITH.

29. Grey Owl, *Pilgrims of the Wild* (Toronto: Macmillan, 1934), p. 70.

30. Kittie Scott-Brown mentions Ada's arthritis in her letter to Lovat Dickson, dated Boscombe, Bournemouth, June 11, 1938, DICKSON. It was a joyful meeting for Ada, and I have made the assumption that her pain, for a few minutes at least, ceased to concern her.

31. Dedication in Grey Owl, *The Men of the Last Frontier* (London: Country Life, 1931).

32. Ada Belaney, quoted in the Hastings *Observer,* April 30, 1938.

33. Grey Owl, *Pilgrims*, p. xvi. The misspelling of "gunnell" for "gunnel" appears in the original passage.

Chapter Two. The Belaneys

1. Grey Owl to Mrs. Bertha Weston Price, cited in "Grey Owl Subject of Talk to I.O.D.E.," Montreal *Gazette*, June 7, 1938.

2. For full details on the Belaney family, see Donald B. Smith, "The Belaneys of Brandon Hills," *The Beaver,* Outfit 306:3 (Winter 1975): 46–50; and Donald B. Smith, "Grey Owl's Origins," Letter to the Editor, Toronto *Globe and Mail*, October 20, 1975. Details on the Belaney family have been obtained at the Scottish, Irish and English Register Offices. All of my genealogical notes on the Belaney family are with my Grey Owl papers at the Archives of Ontario. The descendants of John Belaney (1771–1851) of Berwickshire, Scotland, are the only individuals in England in the late-nineteenth and twentieth centuries to bear the name "Belaney." This facilitated the research. The family name must be one of the rarest in England and, to the best of my knowledge, became extinct in England with the deaths of the Misses Belaney in the late 1940s.

3. "The Rev. Robert Belaney, M.A.," *The Tablet*, September 2, 1899, pp. 363–364; "Robert Belaney," in J. A. Venn, comp., *Alumni Cantabrigienses* (Cambridge: University Press, 1940), Part II, Volume 1, p. 217; Rev. William S. Donegan, *Lucania Topographical, Biographical, Historical* (Dublin: Browne and Nolen, 1902), p. 37.

4. Robert Belaney, *Vivisection viewed under the light of the Divine Revelation* (2nd ed., London: William Ridgway, 1877), p. 2.

5. Biographical Sketch of Archibald Belaney (1822–1865), DICKSON; Betty Somervell, "Interview with Misses Belaney, May 11, 1938," DICKSON.

6. The best source of information on James Cockburn Belaney is the eighty-four page booklet: *A Full Report of the Evidence Taken at the Thames Police Court, and the Coroner's Inquest, before Mr. Baker, and a Respectable Jury, at Stepney, on the 10th of June, 1844; on the Alleged Poisoning Case, also, the Trial of J. C. Belaney, for the Murder of his Wife, at the Central Criminal Court, on August the 21st and 22nd, 1844; with all the Letters and Opinions of the Public Press* (Alnwick: Printed and Published by G. Pike, 1844).

7. James Cockburn Belaney, *A Treatise Upon Falconry in Two Parts* (Berwick-Upon-Tweed: Printed for the Author, 1841), p. 94.

8. William Weaver Tomlinson, *Comprehensive Guide to Northumberland* (London: Walter Scott, 1888), p. 448. See the reference at the beginning of the description, "Bamburgh to Dunstanburgh." My thanks to Arthur Andrews of Seaton Delaval, Tyne and Wear, England, for verifying this reference. Probate of Will of Rachel Belaney, formerly Skelly, March 25, 1847, Probate 6/223, Public Records Office, London.

9. Grey Owl, *Pilgrims of the Wild* (Toronto: Macmillan, 1934), p. 123. Rachel Belaney actually died of "the effects of prussic acid," rather than opium. See "Mysterious Case—Charge of Murder against J. C. Belaney of North Sundeerland" in *A Full Report of the Evidence*, p. 3. Archie could have forgotten this—the reference in the *Comprehensive Guide to Northumberland* (1888) simply stated he had been "committed to trial on suspicion of poisoning his young and lovely wife, and her mother, Mrs. Skelly."

10. A description of Archibald Belaney's profession appears in the marriage certificate of George Furmage Belaney and Rose Ethel Hines, April 13, 1881, where George describes his father as a "deceased Merchant and Ship Broker." General Register Office, London.

11. Gordon Mackenzie, *Marylebone, Great City North of Oxford Street* (London: Macmillan, 1972), p. 138.

12. Beryl Friend, *Named After My Ancestors. A Family History* (Uckfield, East Sussex, England, n.p., 1984), pp. 31–36; Andrew J. Murray, *Home From the Hill. A Biography of Frederick Huth* (London: Hamish Hamilton, 1970), p. 158.

13. Interview with Ivy Holmes, Waverley Abbey House, Farnham, Surrey, England, September 29, 1971.

14. The Misses Belaneys gave their copy of the epic poem to their neighbours George and Dolly Head at 26 Wellington Road, who in turn gave it to me in 1971. The volume is now in the Archives of Ontario, as is a photocopy of the letter of acknowledgement of its reception from Queen Victoria's secretary.

15. The letters written by Grey Owl's mother, Kittie Scott-Brown, in May and June 1938 to Lovat Dickson and to Mrs. Betty Somervell—who assisted Lovat Dickson with the preparation of the biography, *Half-Breed. The Story of Grey Owl* (London: Peter Davies, 1939)—are the best sources of information on George Belaney, and Kittie's life with him. Photocopies are included in

SCOTT-BROWN. The physical description of George Belaney appears in Kittie Scott-Brown's letter to Lovat Dickson, dated Boscombe, May 17, 1938. SCOTT-BROWN and DICKSON.

16. Ivy Homes, Grey Owl's childhood girlfriend, who married him in 1917, told me Ada and Carrie's opinion of their brother in an interview at Waverley Abbey House, Farnham, Surrey, on December 13, 1972. The "Aunts loathed him . . . an absolute ne'er do well."

17. Kittie Scott-Brown to Lovat Dickson, dated Boscombe, May 31, 1938, SCOTT-BROWN. Frances Caroline Marshall was Julia's second cousin.

18. Biographical Sketch of George F. Belaney, DICKSON.

19. Kittie Scott-Brown to Lovat Dickson, dated Boscombe, May 31, 1938, SCOTT-BROWN.

20. A family servant apparently led George Belaney to Rose Ethel Hines. The 1871 Census lists Emma Bennett, a seventeen-year-old unmarried domestic servant, as living at the home of Julia Belaney, The Crescent, Croyden. Her place of birth is listed as Mellis, Suffolk. The Bennett and the Hines families appear in the 1871 Census for Mellis, Suffolk, Public Record Office, London. In 1871 Rose Hines is listed as a child of four. Her age on the marriage certificate is given as 15, on April 13, 1881. Rose Ethel Belaney died May 29, 1883, Certificate of Death, General Register Office, London. For a few more details on their marriage, see the biographical sketch of Rose Ethel Hines, DICKSON.

21. Kittie Scott-Brown to Lovat Dickson, dated Boscombe, May 31, 1938, SCOTT-BROWN; Margaret B. Anderson to H. P. Osborne, dated Palatka, Florida, June 6, 1938, DICKSON.

22. The Marriage License of George F. Bellaney [sic] and Kitty Cox dated November 27, 1886, State of Florida, Putnam County. I am grateful to Audrey Swaffield of Ottawa, Ontario, for securing a copy of this document for me.

23. Margaret Anderson to Lovat Dickson, dated Palatka, Florida, July 28, 1938, DICKSON.

24. Kittie Scott-Brown to Lovat Dickson, dated Boscombe, May 31, 1938, SCOTT-BROWN.

25. Julia and her daughters lived at 52 St. Helen's Road from 1888 to 1895. See the Hastings directories for the period.

26. Kittie Scott-Brown to Lovat Dickson, dated Boscombe, May 17, 1938. SCOTT-BROWN.

27. Margaret A. Banks, "Marriage with a Deceased Wife's Sister—Law and Practice in Upper Canada, with a summary of Post-Confederation Changes," *Western Ontario Historical Notes*, 25,2 (1970): 1–6. The article reviews the state of the law in Canada and Britain—in England it was only permitted in 1907.

28. Betty Somervell, Interview with the Misses Belaney, May 11, 1938, DICKSON. I am very grateful to Ken Conibear for pointing out that possibly Rose Hines, George's first wife, was still alive. If so, George's and Kittie's marital status was even more complicated. It meant that George's marriage to Elizabeth (if it had indeed taken place), and his recent marriage to Kittie, were both illegal.

29. Kittie Scott-Brown to Lovat Dickson, dated Boscombe, May 17, 1938, SCOTT-BROWN.

30. Baptismal entry for Archibald Stansfeld Belaney, 139 Queen's Road (already he and his parents had moved), Hastings, November 27, 1888, Christ Church, Blacklands, Hastings.

31. Kittie Scott-Brown to Lovat Dickson, dated Boscombe, May 17, 1938, SCOTT-BROWN.

32. Kittie Scott-Brown to Lovat Dickson, dated Boscombe, May 17, 1938, and May 31, 1938, SCOTT-BROWN. Hugh Cockburn Belaney's birth certificate states that he was born on November 30, 1890, 23 Blenheim Road, Deal. His father's occupation is given as that of "typewriter." General Register Office, London. Archie was living with his grandmother and aunts at 52 St. Helen's Road, Hastings, by April 5, 1891, as he is listed at that address in the 1891 Census, General Register Office, London.

33. Kittie Scott-Brown to Lovat Dickson, dated Boscombe, May 31, 1938, SCOTT-BROWN.

34. In a "Workbook Chronology" that Lovat Dickson kept in 1938, he includes this fascinating note: "When 9 or 10 they (George, Kitty, Archie & Hugh) often had holidays at a farm Worsfolds, Copthorne, nr. Crawley, Sussex. George was a very good shot & taught Archie to shoot well. Many happy family memories there" (p. 1). In his finished book, *Half Breed* (1939), Lovat Dickson makes no reference to this information and I assume he discovered the information to be too questionable to include. In any event he dates the final parting of George and Kitty as 1897. "George left her & went to his cousins in Canada" (p. 6), DICKSON. When she visited the Misses Belaney in May 1938, Betty Somervell saw one of Archie's childhood books with this inscription, "To dearest Archie from his Father and Mother on his 8th birthday—Sept 18th 1896." Betty Somervell, Interview with the Misses Belaney, May 11, 1938, DICKSON. Did his aunts give him this book with the inscription? Or did his mother? Or did George himself actually give the present with Kittie and write the inscription?

35. Interview with Ivy Holmes, Waverley Abbey House, Farnham, Surrey, England, September 29, 1971.

36. Interview with Wilmot McComb, Brandon, Manitoba, August 10, 1974. This visit was also confirmed by Catherine Tweed, Brandon, Manitoba, August 12, 1974. Wilmot McComb was the stepson of Jessie Belaney McComb, George Belaney's first cousin (Jessie was a daughter of Charles Belaney). Catherine Scott Tweed was a daughter of Eliza Belaney Scott, hence also a first cousin of George Belaney (Eliza was a daughter of Charles Belaney).

37. Interview with Ivy Scott, Surrey, B.C., March 14, 1975. Mrs. Scott's husband, Peter Scott, was a second cousin of Archie Belaney. In Mrs. Scott's possession is Maggie Belaney's birthday book, in which family members have written their names beside their birthdates. When he visited, George Furmage Belaney signed in his very elegant hand beside his birthday, June 14. (This signature in his first cousin's birthday book is the only surviving example of his writing.) His birth certificate in the General Register Office, London, confirms his birthdate as June 14, 1857.

38. Lovat Dickson to Major J. A. Wood, dated April 28, 1938, McMASTER. Kittie estimated that he died about ten years after their final separation.

39. The Belaneys lived at 36 St. Mary's Terrace from 1895 to 1899. See the Hastings' Directories. Archie's age at the time of his photo portrait, three years, is listed in the caption to the shot, reproduced in the *News Chronicle* (London, England), April 20, 1938, and the Toronto *Star Weekly*, May 21, 1938.

40. Interview with Ivy Holmes, Waverley Abbey House, Farnham, Surrey, England, September 29, 1971.

41. Grey Owl quoted in Anahareo, *Devil in Deerskins. My Life with Grey Owl* (Toronto: New Press, 1972), p. 31.

42. Grey Owl to Gertrude [Anahareo] dated Prince Albert National Park, May 16, 1934, GREY OWL.

43. For a description of Ada's child-rearing methods, see: Betty Somervell, Interview with the Misses Belaney, May 11, 1938, DICKSON; Kittie Scott-Brown to Lovat Dickson, dated Boscombe, May 17, 1938, SCOTT-BROWN. Kittie's quotation is taken from this letter.

44. Anahareo, *Deerskins*, p. 29. As Phil Chester has pointed out, while Archie switched to writing with his right hand, he threw knives with his left (see illustration, p. 142), and also filleted fish with his left hand (his Summer film has a filleting scene).

45. Grey Owl, *Tales of an Empty Cabin* (London: Lovat Dickson, 1936), p. viii.

46. Ibid., p. 162.

47. Grey Owl, "Preface to the Special Tour Edition," *The Men of the Last Frontier*, Tour Edition 1937 (London: Country Life, 1937), p. xiii.

48. Interview with Ivy Holmes, Waverley Abbey House, Farnham, Surrey, England, September 29, 1971.

49. Details on the menagerie appear in the letter from Kittie Scott-Brown to Lovat Dickson, dated Boscombe, May 17, 1938, SCOTT-BROWN. Ada was quoted in "Parentage of Grey Owl," London *Times*, April 21, 1938.

50. Interviews with Ivy Holmes, Waverley Abbey House, Farnham, Surrey, England, September 29, 1971, and December 13, 1972.

51. Betty Somervell, interview with Misses Belaney, May 11, 1938, DICKSON; Kittie Scott-Brown to Lovat Dickson, dated Boscombe, May 17, 1938, SCOTT-BROWN; interview with Ivy Holmes, Waverley Abbey House, Farnham, Surrey, England, September 29, 1971, and December 13, 1972.

52. Anahareo, *Deerskins*, pp. 180–81.

53. Grey Owl to Lloyd Roberts, dated June 5, 1932. With certainty one can say that Archie Belaney only spent the "better part of three years" with his father as an infant, before his aunts took him into their household.

54. Kittie Scott-Brown to Lovat Dickson, dated Boscombe, May 17, 1938, SCOTT-BROWN.

55. L. R. Conisbee in J. Manwaring Baines et al., *The History of Hastings Grammar School* (Hastings: Hastings Grammar School Foundation, 1967), p. 55.

56. Ojibwa Indians quoted by the fur trader George Nelson, cited in Jennifer S. H. Brown and Robert Brightman, eds., *"The Orders of the Dreamed," George Nelson on Cree and Northern Ojibwa Religion and Myth, 1823* (Winnipeg: University of Manitoba Press, 1988), p. 22.

57. Grey Owl, *Tales*, p. 172.

58. Conisbee in Baines, et al., *School*, p. 77; "Hastings Grammar School: Cambridge Local Examinations," Hastings *Observer*, December 26, 1903.

I am extremely grateful to Roger Mitchell, headmaster of the William Parker School (the successor school to the Hastings Grammar School), for putting me in touch with H. R. Beck of the University of Cambridge Local Examinations Syndicate, Cambridge, England, who kindly forwarded me the results of Archie Belaney's examinations for the University of Cambridge preliminary and junior certificates, taken respectively in 1902 and 1903.

Chapter Three. Young Archie

1. Interview with Henry Hopkin, May 21, 1975.
2. Interview with W. H. Dyer, Hastings, December 12, 1972. See also, Conisbee in Baines, et al., *School*, p. 72.
3. H. L. Hopkin to the Public Relations Officer, Hastings, dated Cowes, Isle of Wight, England, May 14, 1975. Thanks to this letter I was able to reach Henry Hopkin. In my interview with Henry Hopkin on May 21, 1975, he described the Misses Belaney as "prim and proper," very much the old English "tea and cake type of people."
4. Conrad Arthur N. Foster (1890–1977) attended Hastings Grammar School from February 1901 to July 31, 1907. An excellent student, he won the school's Dietz Scholarship in 1907, an award tenable at any English university. See Baines, et al., *School*, pp. 83, 215. The London *Daily Express* published his recollections of Archie Belaney in their exposé of Grey Owl's true origins on April 20, 1938. Doris Pullen, a private researcher in London, England, diligently located his descendants for me in July 1989, and we were able to corroborate the *Daily Express* account. As well, his son, H. A. L. Foster, located the 600-word text, written a week after Grey Owl's death on April 13, 1938, in which his father recalled Archie Belaney at the Hastings Grammar School. H. A. L. Foster to Donald B. Smith, dated Combe Martin, Devon, England, August 26, 1989.
5. Ada Belaney, quoted in "Parentage of Grey Owl," London *Times*, April 21, 1938.
6. Frank Sparkes, quoted in Hastings *Observer*, April 23, 1938.
7. "He was always drawing pictures of Indians, and some of the drawings which appear in one of his recent books are very similar in type to the sort of thing he drew as a boy." Ada Belaney, quoted in "Parentage of Grey Owl," London *Times*, April 21, 1938. When Betty Somervell visited the Misses Belaney on May 11, 1938, they allowed her to look at his childhood books. She wrote in her notes on the visit: "One old school book with scribbled pictures of Indians fighting, and sailing ships fighting—one very good ink sketch of an Indian in fringed buckskins, with one feather—very like Grey Owl became later."
8. Grey Owl, *Tales*, pp. 79–90.
9. Henry Wadsworth Longfellow, *Hiawatha*, quoted in Grey Owl, *Tales*, p. 82.
10. Henry Hopkin, quoted in Sean Fielding, "Grey Owl's Quest for Two Sisters. Was he their Vanished Nephew?" London *Daily Mail*, April 20, 1938.
11. The best source book on Seton is John Wadland's *Ernest Thompson Seton. Man in Nature and the Progressive Era 1880–1915* (New York: Arno Press, 1978). Two popularly-written treatments are Betty Keller's *Black Wolf. The Life of Ernest Thompson Seton* (Vancouver: Douglas and McIntyre, 1984), and the short—but enjoyable—article by Fred Bodsworth, "The Backwoods

Genius with the Magic Pen," *Maclean's Magazine*, June 6, 1959, pp. 22, 32, 34, 38–40.

12. Ernest Thompson Seton, *Wild Animals I Have Known* (Toronto: McClelland and Stewart, 1977), pp. 11–12. For references to Seton's views on nature, see Wadland, *Seton, passim*. See, for instance, p. 167. For Seton's opinions on and knowledge about North American Indians, consult Wadland, *Seton*, pp. 318–33.

13. The reference by Grey Owl to Seton is in Grey Owl, *Tales*, p. 228.

14. J. G., "Review of *Sajo and her Beaver People* by Grey Owl," *New Republic*, May 22, 1935, cited in *The Book Review Digest, 1935–36*, ed. Mertice M. James and Dorothy Brown (New York: H. W. Wilson Company, 1936), p. 408.

15. On May 11, 1938, Betty Somervell was able to visit the Misses Belaney in Hastings, very briefly. Ada and Carrie showed her their nephew's books in their library. One of the notes Mrs. Somervell hurriedly wrote down was "The Little Savage," with the inscription, "To Archie with love from Hugh." I suspect that the title of the book was really "Two Little Savages." Mrs. Somervell had so little time to record the titles that it is possible that the book Hugh Belaney gave his brother was Seton's classic. [Betty Somervell] Interview with Misses Belaney, May 11, 1938, DICKSON, copy in SMITH. For a reference to Mrs. Somervell's visit, see Lovat Dickson to J. A. Wood, May 13, 1938, McMASTER.

16. Ernest Thompson Seton, *Two Little Savages. Being the Adventures of Two Boys Who Lived as Indians and What They Learned* (New York: Doubleday Page & Company, 1903; New York: Dover Publications, 1962), p. 1. In the book the boys build a teepee in the woods, prepare their own food, learn how to build a fire without matches, construct a beaver dam, study how to find their way when lost, learn how to identify the respective animal tracks, make Indian drums and war bonnets.

17. "The 'Wild West' Visit. Col. Cody's Show at Hastings." Hastings *Observer*, August 22, 1903.

18. He enrolled in the grammar school in September 1899 and left on July 28, 1904. Percy Walker, Clerk to the Board of Governors to the Hastings Grammar School, to Dawn Bruce, dated Hastings, February 11, 1965.

19. I am extremely grateful to H. R. Beck of the University of Cambridge Local Examinations Syndicate, Cambridge, England, for looking up Archie Belaney's grades in his examinations for both the preliminary (1902) and junior (1903) Cambridge University Certificate exams. Mr. Beck also located the exam questions for me. The junior certificate exams were tough. Henry Hopkin, for instance, also missed his mathematics and experimental science exams— and even Conrad Foster, the future Hastings Grammar School scholarship student, failed experimental science. I suspect that as the Hastings Grammar School had just started its science program it was not very strong in this area. Archie Belaney's prize in French (awarded in 1903) is mentioned in the article, "Hastings Grammar School. Annual Prize Distribution. An Encouraging Report. Commendation by the Mayor," Hastings *Observer*, Saturday, December 26, 1903. In view of Archie's subsequent career, the name of Hastings' Mayor at the time is quite amusing—Archie was given his prize by a tree. The Mayor's name was Ben Henry Went Tree!

20. See footnote 4 of this chapter. The quotation is taken from Con Foster's 600-word text written a week after Grey Owl's death.

21. Grey Owl, Notebook, 1932–1936, GREY OWL. The quotation is found about twenty-five pages before the end of the unpaginated book.

22. My information on Grey Owl's friendship with the McCormick family is taken from interviews with George McCormick in Maidstone, Kent, England, December 2, 1972; December 11, 1972; December 18, 1972; May 24, 1975. Mary McCormick's (Mrs. Mary McCormick Champness') recollections are reported in the "Baffling Riddle of Grey Owl's Identity. Woman Says 'He's Belaney or I'll Eat My Hat'," Hastings *Observer,* April 23, 1938. Margaret McCormick recorded her memories of Archie Belaney in her article, "Grey Owl. Recollections of his Boyhood," *West Australian,* April 30, 1938. Leslie McCormick assisted me in a letter mailed on July 17, 1972, from his home at Lesmurdie, West Australia. His sister, Mrs. Helen McCormick Watkins, kindly wrote me from Perth, West Australia, on August 6, 1972. The tapes of my interviews with George McCormick are all in the Moving Image and Sound Archives, NAC. My notes of all interviews and my correspondence with members of the McCormick family are in SMITH.

23. Margaret McCormick, "Grey Owl. Recollections of his Boyhood," *West Australian,* April 30, 1938.

24. Interview with George McCormick, Maidstone, Kent, England, December 2, 1972.

25. Helen Watkins to Donald B. Smith, dated Perth, West Australia, August 6, 1972.

26. Margaret McCormick, "Grey Owl. Recollections of his Boyhood," *West Australian,* April 30, 1938.

27. Ibid.

28. Interviews with George McCormick, December 2, 11, 18, 1972; and May 24, 1975. Unless otherwise specified, all the subsequent details about George's and Archie's friendship are taken from these interviews.

29. The physical description of the adders is taken from the pamphlet, "Hastings Country Park. Warren Glen Nature Trail." Fairlight Glen is now included in the Hastings Country Park established in 1971.

30. Interview with George McCormick, December 18, 1972.

31. Grey Owl, "My Mission to My Country," *Canadian Forest and Outdoors,* February 1938, p. 52.

32. Anthony Belt, ed., *Hastings. A Survey of Times Past and Present* (Hastings: Kenneth Saville, 1937), p. 230; Frank Partridge, *T. A. B. A Memoir of Thomas Allnutt Second Earl Brassey* (London: John Murray, 1921), p. 80; "Sussex (East)," *Baily's Hunting Directory 1950–51,* pp. 194–95. My thanks to Brion Purdey of Hastings for this reference on the East Sussex Hunt.

33. Grey Owl, *Farewell to the Children of the British Isles* (London: Lovat Dickson Ltd., 1937). The pamphlet has no page numbers.

34. Interviews with George McCormick, December 2 and December 11, 1972. See, for example, James Fenimore Cooper, *The Last of the Mohicans* (New York: New American Library, 1962), pp. 304, 336–38; and Seton, *Two Little Savages,* pp. 88–94.

35. Interview with George McCormick, December 2, 1972.

36. Mrs. Mary McCormick Champness, quoted in the Hastings *Observer,* April 23, 1938.

37. Interviews with George McCormick, December 2 and 11, 1972. I am very grateful to Christopher Whittick, assistant archivist, East Sussex County Record Office, for the information he supplied on September 28, 1989, to my enquiry about Police Constable Stone.

38. Interviews with George McCormick, December 2 and 11, 1972; Helen McCormick Watkins to Donald B. Smith, dated Perth, Western Australia, August 6, 1972.

39. Interview with Percy (Bob) Overton, Hastings, October 6, 1971.

40. Interviews with Ivy Holmes, Waverley Abbey House, Farnham, Surrey, September 29, 1971, and December 13, 1972.

41. Betty Somervell, interview with the Misses Belaney, May 11, 1938, DICKSON. A wonderful passage in *The Men of the Last Frontier,* p. 155, compares the beaver and the elephant. "It would seem that by evolution or some other process, these creatures have developed a degree of mental ability superior to that of any other living animal, with the possible exception of the elephant."

42. Interview with George McCormick, December 11, 1972.

43. Interviews with George McCormick, December 2 and 11, 1972.

44. Interview with George McCormick, December 2, 1972.

45. Anahareo, *Deerskins,* pp. 30–31.

46. Fred Gray, et al., *Hastings Voices, Hastings Modern History Workshop* (Hastings: Hastings Modern History Workshop, 1982), pp. 8–9.

47. Margaret McCormick, "Grey Owl. Recollections of his Boyhood," *West Australian,* April 30, 1938; Interview with George McCormick, December 2, 1972.

48. Interview with Ivy Holmes, September 29, 1971. Betty Somervell, interview with the Misses Belaney, May 11, 1938, DICKSON. 641 of the passengers on the ship travelled steerage, 386 second cabin, and 40 saloon (first class), NAC, RG 76 (Immigration) series C1(a), Records of Entry: Halifax, reel T-500, *Dominion,* 6/6/1906. Lovat Dickson, *Half-Breed* (London: Peter Davies, 1939), p. 69.

49. A. L. Hatton, "Grey Owl Drove Panic from the Wilds," London *Daily Herald,* December 18, 1935.

50. Lovat Dickson, who interviewed Ada and Carrie Belaney for two hours on April 27, 1938 (Hastings *Observer,* April 30, 1938), mentioned Archie's story-telling in *Half-Breed,* p. 45. Unfortunately Lovat Dickson's original notes from this interview have not survived.

51. Georges Vanier to J. C. Campbell, dated London, November 4, 1935, RG 25, A-5, vol. 382 (Grey Owl), NAC.

Chapter Four. Lake Temagami and Angele

1. This passage from the original torn exercise book appears as an illustration in Howard French's article, "Grey Owl—City Shop Assistant or Red Indian?", *Sunday Dispatch* (London, England), April 24, 1938.

2. Bill Guppy, quoted in Hal Pink, *Bill Guppy. King of the Woods* (London: Hutchinson, 1940), pp. 108, 103. Hal Pink was a mystery writer and the author

of novels with titles such as, *The Black Sombrero Mystery, The Rodeo Murder Mystery, The Green Triangle Mystery*. Hal Pink met Bill Guppy in the fall of 1938 and then returned to Temagami in the late spring of 1939 to write his life-story. See Pink, *Guppy*, preface. Pink writes of the style of his biography (p. 16): "He would talk, I was to do the rest. I decided that his story, after careful weeding for ambiguities and repetitions, should go to the public, as nearly as possible, the way it came from his lips to me." Ted Guppy, Bill's youngest brother, in an interview with me at Temagami, August 3, 1970, recalled Hal Pink's visit to the lake to write the book.

3. Archie Belaney, upon reaching Halifax, gave his destination as "Toronto." A railway order, number 16546, was issued. Ship's Passenger Manifest for the *Dominion*, RG 76 (Immigration) series C1(a), Records of Entry: Halifax, reel T–500, *Dominion*, 6/6/1906, NAC. My thanks to Bennett McCardle for this reference. Donald Mackenzie, a member of the Teme-augama Anishnabai band, who was born in 1884, remembered Archie Belaney as the "Englishman who came from Toronto." Interview with Donald Mackenzie, Bear Island, Lake Temagami, August 13, 1971. Archie Belaney's Ojibwa friend Michel Mathias was Donald Mckenzie's half-brother.

4. For details on Toronto in 1906 see Karl Baedeker, *The Dominion of Canada with Newfoundland and an Excursion to Alaska. Handbook for Travellers* (Leipzig: Karl Baedeker Publisher, 1907), pp. 190–97.

5. See Donald B. Smith, *Sacred Feathers. The Reverend Peter Jones (Kahkewaquonaby) and the Mississauga Indians* (Toronto: University of Toronto Press, 1987), for a review of the history of the Mississaugas of the Credit River.

6. Another clue exists. In Toronto, in early March 1936, Grey Owl visited the Eaton's department store with Betty Somervell. At the store he amazed Betty with some insiders' knowledge. He identified the company's plainclothes detectives walking around the shopping aisles. "That's a house dick." Interviews with Betty Somervell, Toronto, October 12, 1971, and Kendal, England, June 1, 1975.

7. The summary of the manuscript appears in Howard French, "Grey Owl—City Shop Assistant or Red Indian?", *Sunday Dispatch* (London, England), April 24, 1938. Excerpts appear in a text prepared for radio broadcast on the BBC, but never delivered, by Lovat Dickson, around 1963. Thomas Raddall Papers, Dalhousie University Archives, Halifax, Nova Scotia. A few excerpts also appear in Lovat Dickson, *Half-Breed* (London: Peter Davies, 1939). Thomas Raddall wrote in a letter to the author on September 26, 1970, that the manuscript's dialogue "was clearly an imitation of O. Henry." In his biographical article, "Grey Owl," in *Footsteps on Old Floors* (Garden City, N. J.: Doubleday, 1968), pp. 101–3, Thomas Raddall suggests that Archie travelled first in the Maritimes before heading to northern Ontario. To my satisfaction, his own manuscript establishes that he did indeed travel on to Toronto. See also footnote 3 of this chapter.

8. Bill Guppy quoted in Pink, *Guppy*, pp. 109–10.

9. Ibid., pp. 110–11.

10. Ibid., pp. 111–12, 114.

11. Ibid., pp. 112–13, 116.
12. For the general historical background to the Temagami area, see Bruce W. Hodgins and Jamie Benidickson, *The Temagami Experience: Recreation, Resources, Aboriginal Rights in the Northern Ontario Wilderness* (Toronto: University of Toronto Press, 1989). Two good contemporary surveys of Lake Temagami at the turn of the century are Alfred Ernest Barlow, *Report on the Geology and Natural Resources of the Area Included by the Nipissing and Temiskaming Map-Sheets* (Ottawa: King's Printer, 1899); and Karl Baedeker, *The Dominion of Canada with Newfoundland and an Excursion to Alaska* (Leipzig: Karl Baedeker, 1907), pp. 237–38.
13. The ice on Lake Temiskaming generally left about the end of the first week of May, and on Lake Temagami usually by about May 24, Barlow, *Report*, p. 32. The Guppys departed before the arrival of the mosquitoes, see Pink, *Guppy*, p. 124. The route, following lakes Temiskaming to Temagami, is outlined in Pink, *Guppy*, pp. 123–26, as well as in Brian Back, *The Keewaydin Way. A Portrait: 1893–1983* (Temagami: Keewaydin Camp, Ltd., 1983), p. 42. Back describes a similar trip taken in 1903 over the same route by the founder of Keewaydin Camp, A. S. Gregg Clarke. Grey Owl's quotation is taken from *Men*, p. 66.
14. Pink, *Guppy*, pp. 123–26; Back, *Keewaydin*, p. 42.
15. George P. Cockburn, Indian Agent, "Temagami Band," *Annual Report of the Department of Indian Affairs, 1907–08*, pp. 37–38.
16. Aleck Paul, quoted in Malcolm Read Lowell, "Penn Professor's Discovery Confounds Indian 'History'," Philadelphia *Public Ledger*, November 23, 1913.
17. Petition to Geo. Cockburn, Indian Agent, dated Temagami Lake, February 23, 1907, RG 10, vol. 7757, file 27043–9, part 1, NAC. the Teme-augama Anishnabai had not participated in the Robinson-Huron Treaty of 1850 south of their hunting grounds, nor had they taken part in Treaty Nine, north of Lake Temagami. In 1989 they still had not obtained their reserve. For an overview of the unresolved issue see James Morrison, "Temagami Indians' historic land claim," Toronto *Star*, July 5, 1988, p. A13. The best summary of the claim is Chief Gary Potts and James Morrison, "The Temagami Ojibwa, Frank Speck and Family Hunting Territories," paper presented to the American Society for Ethnohistory Conference, Williamsburg, Virginia, November 11, 1988.
18. Pink, *Guppy*, pp. 127–28. The Annual Report for the Department of Indian Affairs 1907–1908, p. 38, states of the Temagami Indians: "The principal occupations of these Indians are hunting and fishing and acting as guides to tourists, who frequent Temagami in large numbers each summer. They cannot supply the demand, which necessitates bringing in outside guides from the other reserves."
19. The phrase is Grey Owl's. He wrote on May 10, 1935, to W. A. Deacon, of "the smoky, balsam scented tents of the Ojibway Indians," DEACON.
20. Interviews with Charlotte McLean Morrison, Temagami, August 3, 1970, and August 3, 1975.
21. "Recalls Change in Belaney," Winnipeg *Free Press*, April 23, 1938. Although not mentioned by name, the Ojibwa-speaking man identified as "a former

storekeeper, who was in business at Timagami when Archie made his first appearance . . . who now lives in Winnipeg" was undoubtedly Harry Woods, who retired in 1931 from a posting in northwestern Ontario. See *The Beaver,* September 1931, p. 316.

22. "Recalls Change in Belaney," Winnipeg *Free Press,* April 23, 1938.

23. Grey Owl, Notebook, 1927–31, GREY OWL.

24. Interview with George McCormick, Maidstone, Kent, England, December 2, 1972. Archie had returned to Lake Temagami by mid-September 1908. The Sudbury *Journal* on September 24, 1908, p. 5, carried this story entitled "Temagami Tragedy": "Frank C. Ellor, a negro who has been working at odd jobs around Temagami this summer was shot early Tuesday morning by a prospector named 'Dutchy' Eaton. The men had been drinking together and quarrelled." Archie apparently knew all about the crime as he jotted down this line in one of his notebooks in a list of events that had occurred during his early years in Canada: "the shooting of the nigger at Temagami." See Grey Owl, Notebook, 1927–31, GREY OWL. The word he uses to describe the murdered Black is curious, in view of his own preaching of racial tolerance and understanding in the late 1930s. Margaret McCormick, "Grey Owl. Recollections of his Boyhood," *West Australian,* April 30, 1938. Interview with Henry L. Hopkin, Cowes, Isle of Wight, England, May 21, 1975.

25. Kittie mentioned George Belaney's death date to Lovat Dickson in late April 1938. See Lovat Dickson to Major J. A. Wood, dated London, April 28, 1938, McMASTER. For an account of George Belaney's visit to his Canadian cousins in Manitoba, see Donald B. Smith, "The Belaneys of Brandon Hills," *The Beaver,* Outfit 306:3 (Winter 1975): 46–50.

26. See the biographical sketch of Kathleen Verina Cox, DICKSON.

27. Angele Belaney, quoted in Examination for Discovery, Court House, North Bay, June 12, 1939, p. 3, FRASER.

28. Tom Saville to T. J. Godfrey, dated Shining Tree, Ontario, March 4, 1938, RG 10, vols. 7995, 1/1–15–2–4, NAC; "Say Letters Show England His Birthplace," North Bay *Nugget,* April 18, 1938, p. 2.

29. "Say Letters Show England His Birthplace," North Bay *Nugget,* April 18, 1938, p. 2; Angele Belaney quoted in Examination for Discovery, June 12, 1939, p. 3, FRASER.

30. I am very grateful to James Morrison for this genealogical information, based in the Roman Catholic Church registries at St.-Marc de Figuery, in Amos, Quebec. Although the church records clearly state that Ned White Bear was her grandfather (on her mother's side), Agnes Belaney Lalonde believes that he was her mother's uncle, hence her great-uncle.

31. Unpublished manuscript (written about 1917) cited in Howard French, "Grey Owl—City Shop Assistant or Red Indian?", *Sunday Dispatch,* April 24, 1938. The paper incorrectly transcribed Temagami Ned's Ojibwa name as "Both-ends-of-the-Way." It should read "Both-ends-of-the-day." See Grey Owl, *Men,* p. 222. I have corrected the name here from "Both-ends-of-the-Way" to "Both-ends-of-the-day."

32. Dewey Derosier, "In the Good Old Days," *Temagami Centennial Booklet,* ed. J. C. Elliott (Temagami: Temagami Centennial Committee, 1967), p. 50.

33. Grey Owl, *Men*, p. 222.
34. Grey Owl, *The Adventures of Sajo and her Beaver People* (London: Lovat Dickson & Thompson Ltd., 1935), pp. xiii–xiv. It was still on display in the Ethnology section of the Royal Ontario Museum in Toronto in the early 1970s and is now in storage there. The caption reads: "Birch Bark Canoe, Lake Temiscaming Ontario. Made by an Indian named QUILL (Ojibwa) at White Bear Lake." December 15, 1901, was the date of acquisition.
35. Unpublished manuscript, cited in Lovat Dickson's radio script, Thomas Raddall Papers, Dalhousie University Archives, Halifax, Nova Scotia. For references to Misabi, see Pink, *Guppy*, p. 142; Back, *Keewaydin*, p. 57; Madeline Theriault, *Moose to Moccasins* (North Bay, Ontario: Printed by the author, 1985), mimeographed, p. 6; and Frank G. Speck, *Family Hunting Territories and Social Life of Various Algonkian Bands of the Ottawa Valley* (Ottawa: Government Printing Bureau, 1915), p. 14.
36. For a very good description of Ojibwa religious beliefs among Misabi's people, the Ojibwa of the Georgian Bay, see Diamond Jenness, "Chapter 3, Man and Nature," in *The Ojibwa Indians of Parry Island, Their Social and Religious Life* (Ottawa: King's Printer, 1935), pp. 60–68.
37. Smith, *Sacred Feathers*, p. 11.
38. Henry Wadsworth Longfellow, *The Song of Hiawatha* (New York: Bounty Books, 1968), pp. 230–33.
39. On the differences between English and Ojibwa, see Smith, *Sacred Feathers*, pp. 41–42.
40. J. S. Wood, Saskatoon Librarian, quoted in "Grey Owl Studied Dictionary While on his Traplines," Saskatoon *Star-Phoenix*, April 16, 1938.
41. Interview with Agnes Lalonde, North Bay, Ontario, April 29, 1973.
42. Interview with Agnes Lalonde, North Bay, Ontario, January 1973, taped interview, Acc. 1974–57, Moving Image and Sound Archives, NAC.
43. Ibid.; interview with Michael Paul [son of Aleck Paul], Corbeil, Ontario, August 4, 1975.
44. Excerpts from park ranger Mark Robinson's diary for March 15–22, 1909, in Ottelyn Addison, *Early Days in Algonquin Park* (Toronto: McGraw-Hill Ryerson, 1974), pp. 53–54; "Grey Owl No Half-Breed Says Man Who Nursed Him," Toronto *Star*, April 18, 1938.
45. M. H. Halton, "Grey Owl Sought," Toronto *Star*, April 19, 1938.
46. "Early Friend of Grey Owl Tells of Experiences with Noted Naturalist," Chapleau *Post*, April 22, 1938.
47. Madeline Theriault, "Recalls when Archie Belaney became the famed Grey Owl," North Bay *Nugget*, February 13, 1973; interview with Agnes Belaney Lalonde, Calgary, July 2, 1988.
48. Grey Owl to *Country Life*, May 6, 1929, quoted in "A Bookman's Diary," *John O'London's Weekly*, April 29, 1938.
49. Interview with Agnes Belaney Lalonde, North Bay, Ontario, April 29, 1973. Samuel Hearne provides the classic description of taming beavers (which he himself did in 1771), in his *A Journey to the Northern Ocean. A Journey from Prince of Wales's Fort in Hudson's Bay to the Northern Ocean in the Years 1769, 1770, 1771, 1772*, ed. Richard Glover (Toronto: Macmillan, 1958),

pp. 156–57. See also D. W. Moodie and Barry Kaye, "Taming and Domesticating the Native Animals of Rupert's Land," *The Beaver*, Outfit 307:3 (Winter 1976): 16. For an Indian's comment on taming beaver, consult George Copway, *The Life, History, and Travels of Kah-Ge-Ga-Gah-Bowh* (Albany: Weed and Parsons, 1847), p. 32.

50. Aleck Paul, quoted in an unpublished manuscript by Frank Speck, an American anthropologist, in the F. G. Speck Collection, American Philosophical Society Library, Philadelphia, Pennsylvania. See also, Speck, *Hunting Territories*, p. 5. My thanks to Jim Morrison for the description of John Egwuna's hunting territory. Jim Morrison to Donald B. Smith, February 20, 1989.

51. Grey Owl, *Sajo*, pp. 5–6.

52. I am indebted to Brian Back, Keewaydin's historian, for this information. He wrote me on March 24, 1979. "There are only two single references to Archie Belaney: two handcrafted wooden plaques hanging in the Lodge, listing staff and campers for the years 1910 to 1911. Under the 'guide' category on the 1910 plaque is the name 'Archie Belaney,' and in the same category for 1911 is the name 'A. Belaney.' These plaques were carved each year by the director's wife, so there is little likelihood of error."

53. Back, *Keewaydin*, p. 55.

54. "The Woodcraft Indians," *The Keewaydin Kicker*, 1911, p. 47.

55. This physical description of Archie around 1910 is taken from several sources: Pink, *Guppy*, pp. 109, 128; Angele Belaney quoted in Claud Pascoe, "Witnesses Describe Grey Owl's Wedding to Temagami Woman," Toronto *Star*, April 16, 1938; "Bisco People Identify Grey Owl as A. Belaney with Wife at Temagami," North Bay *Nugget*, April 18, 1938.

56. Eva-Lis Wuorio, "Grey Owl's Widow Gives Happy Hilarity to Camp," Toronto *Globe and Mail*, July 24, 1947.

57. Angele Belaney quoted in Examination for Discovery, June 12, 1939, p. 6, FRASER; Claud Pascoe, "Witnesses Describe Grey Owl's Wedding to Temagami Woman," Toronto *Star*, April 16, 1938; "Beaucage Man Knew Grey Owl as Belaney," North Bay *Nugget*, April 18, 1938, p. 2.

58. Angele Egwuna, quoted in Eva-Lis Wuorio, "Grey Owl's Widow Gives Happy Hilarity to Camp," Toronto *Globe and Mail*, July 24, 1947.

59. Ibid.

60. Registres Baptêmes, St-Marc de Figuery, numéro 15, Amos, Quebec. My thanks to Jim Morrison for this reference. Archie again worked as a guide at Keewaydin Camp in the summer of 1911. Apparently he was on a canoe trip northwest of Temagami at the time of Agnes's baptism. He later claimed to have witnessed from thirty-five kilometres away the Porcupine forest fire of July 11, 1911, which possibly killed as many as 200 people in the town of South Porcupine and the surrounding region. After the fire, he later claimed, "I assisted in the work of recovering some of the bodies scattered through the charred forest, prospectors caught far from water by the sudden rush of fire; they were mostly in crouching positions, with the hands held over the face, sights terrible to see." Grey Owl, *Men*, p. 166. For a description of the fire see S. A. Pain, *The Way North* (Toronto: Ryerson, 1970), pp. 158–61.

61. Angele Belaney, quoted at the Court Case, October 10, 1939, pp. 6–7, 25–26, FRASER.

62. Grey Owl to Miss E. Elliott Boothe [Ellen Elliott], dated July 20, 1934, McMASTER.

63. Archie Belaney, "An Old Hastonian amongst the Indians," *The Hastonian*, number 10 (July 1914), pp. 5–7. The quotation appears on p. 5. How *The Hastonian* obtained the letter is unknown. They printed it with this statement, "we have not been able to secure his permission to print this, but here goes!"

64. Interview with John Stewart, Victoria, B.C., August 26, 1982.

65. Thomas F. Gossett, *Race: The History of an Idea in America* (Dallas: Southern Methodist University Press, 1964), pp. 144, 253. The best example of Archie's own acceptance of race theory appears in *Men*, pp. 174–78, where he attacks (p. 175) the entry into Canada of "the South-eastern European [who] will work for less wages than the 'white' races."

66. Robert J. C. Stead, *The Empire Builders and Other Poems* (Fourth Edition, Toronto: William Briggs, 1910), p. 20.

67. The following quotations are all taken from "An Old Hastonian amongst the Indians," *The Hastonian*, number 10 (July 1914), pp. 5–7.

68. Angele Belaney, quoted at the Court Case, October 10, 1939, p. 7, FRASER; "Say Letters Show England His Birthplace," North Bay *Nugget*, April 18, 1938, p. 2.

69. Grey Owl, *Sajo*, pp. xiii–xiv.

70. My thanks to Michelle Miles for her comment on the similarity of the drawing and the enclosure at the Riverdale Zoo. The drawing appears opposite p. 172.

71. The large city in *Sajo* must be modelled on Toronto. For a reference to the Toronto police uniform in the early twentieth century, see J. M. S. Careless, *Toronto to 1918. An Illustrated History* (Toronto: James Lorimer, 1984), p. 192. The train took the two beavers directly from Temagami to Toronto, as is indicated in the book, pp. 148, 152, 168–71. The page references are made to the original edition of *The Adventures of Sajo and her Beaver People* (London: Lovat Dickson & Thompson Ltd., 1935).

72. Will of Juliana Mary Henrietta Belaney, probated June 28, 1912. Effects £252 11s 8d. English Register Office, London.

73. Ferg Legace, "Memoirs," p. 29 (Grey Owl section).

74. "Say Letters Show England His Birthplace," North Bay *Nugget*, April 18, 1938, p. 2; Angele quoted at the Examination for Discovery, June 12, 1939, p. 5, FRASER.

Chapter Five. Biscotasing

1. Interview with Madeline Woodworth Macleod, Biscotasing, November 1, 1972.

2. Mattawagaminque Post Journals, 1815–1818, entry from April 1, 1815, MS 209 (reel 2), Archives of Ontario. My thanks to Jim Morrison for this reference.

3. Anon. *A Canadian Tour: A Reprint of Letters from the Special Correspondent of the Times* (London: Times Office, 1886), p. 14. The news item was dated August 30, 1886.

4. Vincent Crichton, "Biscotasing," in *Pioneering in Northern Ontario. History of the Chapleau District* (Belleville, Ontario: Mika Publishing Co., 1975), pp. 230–34.

5. Lady Aberdeen, cited in John T. Saywell, ed., *The Canadian Journal of Lady Aberdeen, 1893-1898* (Toronto: The Champlain Society, 1960), p. 154.

6. In 1899 it was estimated that about 200 Indians were attached to the Bisco HBC Post. See HBC Archives, Commissioner's report on fur trade for Outfit 1898-99, dated 9 February 1900. Cited in the unpublished report, "Biscotasing," p. 4, Ontario Ministry of Natural Resources, Toronto.

7. Crichton, "John Sanders," *Pioneering*, pp. 91-94.

8. Charles Camsell, *Son of the North* (Toronto: Ryerson, 1954), p. 140.

9. It still did not have any sidewalks, roads, or electricity when I visited in the early 1970s.

10. "Mississaga Reserve," Ontario, Legislative Assembly, Sessional Papers, 37, part 1 (1905), pp. 12-17.

11. Archie Belaney's name appears under the entries: "Mississaga Reserve 1911-12," Appendix No. 6, Ontario Legislative Assembly, Sessional Papers, 45, part 2 (1913), p. 27; "Mississaga Reserve 1912-13," Appendix No. 6, Ontario Legislative Assembly, Sessional Papers, 46, part 2 (1914), p. 26; "Mississaga Reserve, 1913-14," Appendix No. 6, Ontario Legislative Assembly, Sessional Papers, 47, part 2 (1915), p. 29. For details on fire-fighting in this period, consult *A History of Chapleau Forest District* (Toronto: Department of Lands and Forests, 1964), pp. 3-6. Under the pseudonym of "Charlie Dougal," Grey Owl mentions Charlie Duval in *Tales*, p. 176.

12. Ferg Legace, "Memoirs," pp. 28-29 (Grey Owl section).

13. Ferg Legace, "Memoirs," p. 30 (Grey Owl section); interview with Célina Legace Barnes, Thunder Bay, Ontario, July 14, 1971.

14. Interviews with Ferg Legace, Owen Sound, June 12, 1971, and Petawawa, August 5, 1972; Ferg Legace, "Memoirs," pp. 66-67 (Grey Owl section).

15. Donald Phillips, quoted in William C. Taylor, *Donald "Curly" Phillips, Guide and Outfitter* (Jasper, Alberta: Jasper-Yellowhead Historical Society, 1984), p. 20.

16. Interviews with Colin Phillips, Biscotasing, Ontario, September 29, 1970, and February 5, 1971.

17. Interview with Harry Woodworth, by Vince Crichton, Biscotasing, November 20, 1939. Vince Crichton, manuscript on Grey Owl, copy in SMITH. Vince Crichton's manuscript also contains other negative comments on Archie's abilities as a trapper. See the interviews with Jim Espaniel, July 6, 1947, and Bill Orange, August 7, 1948.

18. J. W. Cowper, "Grey Owl in Ontario," Letter to the Editor, Toronto *Globe and Mail*, April 28, 1938. Interview with Mrs. J. W. Cowper, Baltimore, Ontario, February 20, 1972. Contrary to Cowper's testimony, other early Canadian acquaintances of Archie's recall that he liked to wear a hat. See chapter 7, footnote 10.

19. Frank Coryell to Thomas H. Raddall, dated July 7, 1940, Thomas Raddall Collection, Dalhousie University Archives, Halifax. In 1914, Frank Coryell was the manager of Bedell's Furnishing Co. Ltd. See the Toronto Directory for that year. (My thanks to Ethelyn Harlow of the Archives of Ontario for this reference.)

20. Ibid.

21. My knowledge of George McCormick's meeting with Archie in Montreal in 1913 comes from two interviews with Mr. McCormick in Maidstone, Kent, England, December 2, 1972, and July 31, 1976. The information in this section, unless otherwise specified, comes from these interviews.
22. If they had known, they would never have permitted him in 1917 to marry Ivy Holmes, the daughter of their good friend Florence Holmes. They were furious when they learned of his previous marriage. Interview with Ivy Holmes, Waverley Abbey House, Farnham, England, December 13, 1972.
23. Ferg Legace recalls Marie Girard (Gerrard or Jero) in his "Memoirs," pp. 5–6, 38–39, 44 (Grey Owl Section).
24. This section on Bob Wilson is based on an interview in Windsor, Ontario, July 10, 1973; and the article, "R. H. Wilson knew Grey Owl in 1914. Tells of Spending Two Months in Cabin with Archie Belaney. Mysterious Outstanding Personality," Windsor *Star*, April 21, 1938, pp. 3, 20. For a sketch of Bob Wilson's life, see "Prominent lawyer R. H. Wilson Dies," Windsor *Star*, July 25, 1977.
25. Interview with Ted Cusson, Monetville, January 16, 1972.
26. Information on Bill Draper can be obtained from his army service file, ARMY. His service number is 2500892. He joined the army at Sudbury, Ontario on June 6, 1918. [Vincent Crichton]. *A History of Chapleau Forest Reserve* (Toronto: Department of Lands and Forests, 1964), p. 13. Bill Draper recalled his memories of Grey Owl in "Early Friend of Grey Owl Tells of Experiences with Noted Naturalist," Chapleau *Post*, April 22, 1938. Jane Espaniel McKee told me many stories about Bill Draper. Interviews in Toronto, June 2, July 29, September 30, 1973. Libby Sawyer in an interview in Sudbury, Ontario, March 17, 1972, recalled for me the amusing story about Bill's three or four annual birthdays.
27. Interview of Bill Draper by Vince Crichton, July 17, 1938, Vince Crichton manuscript, copy in SMITH.
28. Harry Woodworth, cited in "Bisco People Identify Grey Owl as A. Belaney with Wife at Temagami," North Bay *Nugget*, April 18, 1938.
29. "Early Friend," Chapleau *Post*, April 22, 1938. Ralph Bice also makes reference to this story in "Along the Trail, Grey Owl," *Almaguin News* (Burk's Falls, Ontario), December 20, 1972, p. 21. He states the man's name was "Barney McGraw." Bill Draper also gives his name as "McGraw."
30. Ibid.
31. Interview of Bill Draper by Vince Crichton, Chapleau, Ontario, July 17, 1938. Vince Crichton, manuscript on Grey Owl, copy in SMITH. "Early Friend," Chapleau *Post*, April 22, 1938.
32. Interview with Madeline Woodworth Macleod [daughter of Harry Woodworth], Biscotasing, November 1, 1972.
33. Interview with Ferg Legace, Owen Sound, Ontario, June 12, 1971; interview with Célina Legace Barnes (Ferg's oldest sister), Thunder Bay, Ontario, July 14, 1971.
34. Ferg Legace, "Memoirs," pp 5–6, 38–39, 44 (Grey Owl section). Célina Legace Barnes remembered his departure date as she got married at approximately the same time. See the account of their marriage on November 17, 1914, "Barnes-Legace," Sudbury *Journal*, November 19, 1914, p. 1.

35. Frank Coryell to Thomas H. Raddall, July 7, 1940, Thomas Raddall Collection, Dalhousie University Archives, Halifax.

36. Archie Belaney, Attestation Paper, ARMY.

37. Caroly Hryhorchuk, Chapleau High School, to Donald B. Smith, dated May 9, 1988.

38. Lovat Dickson learned of this letter (written to Bill Draper) when he began his research for *Half-Breed* in 1938. Someone in Biscotasing apparently sent a letter written by Bill Draper about Archie Belaney to Lovat Dickson. Workbook Chronology, vol. 24, p. 10, DICKSON. Draper himself mentions the letter but does not discuss its contents, in "Early Friend of Grey Owl Tells of Experiences with Noted Naturalist," Chapleau *Post*, April 22, 1938. Both old-time Bisco residents Ed and Lottie Sawyer (interview, Biscotasing, July 16, 1971) and Ferg Legace (interview, Petawawa, August 5, 1972) believe that Archie did not know that Marie was pregnant before he left.

39. Interview with Gordon Langevin [son of Edith Langevin], Biscotasing, Ontario, December 7, 1974.

40. Interview with Herb Winters by Ron Dutcher of Prince Albert National Park, March 25, 1970. A copy of the taped interview is available at the Park Interpretative Office, Waskesiu, Saskatchewan. Perhaps Archie had indeed signed up previously—and deserted? In his application for naturalization, dated April 5, 1934, he stated that he "joined Canadian Army Nov 1914." How could he make such a mistake, when he had really signed up in May 1915? A copy of the document was sent to the author by the Dept. of the Secretary of State, June 16, 1971.

41. Angele quoted at the Court Case, June 12, 1939, p. 3, FRASER. "I claim that Belaney wrote to a Mr. Woods who used to be a Hudson Bay factor up there. He wrote to Mr. Woods telling him to inform me that he was leaving for over-seas. That is how I got to know."

42. Archie Belaney, Attestation Paper, ARMY.

43. He sailed aboard the transport *Caledonia* from Halifax on June 15, 1915. See his military service papers, ARMY.

44. This quotation by Walt Whitman appears as the preface to Book Two of *Pilgrims of the Wild*, p. 165.

45. I have adopted this last line from the opening lines of the poem by Charles C. Finn in "Please Hear What I'm Not Saying" in Charles L. Whitefield, *Healing the Child Within. Discovery and Recovery for Adult Children of Dysfunctional Families* (Deerfield Beach, Florida: Health Communications, Inc., 1987), p. 13. My thanks to Phil Chester for his thoughts on Archie's flight from reality. Phil Chester to Donald B. Smith, November 13, 1989.

Chapter Six. Archie and the Great War

1. Interview of James E. McKinnon, Smith's Cove, Nova Scotia, by Thomas Raddall, May 23, 1963. Testimony reprinted in Thomas Raddall, "Grey Owl," in *Footsteps on Old Floors* (Garden City, N. J.: Doubleday, 1968), p. 108. McKinnon's service number was 415594. He was born in 1890.

2. "Digby's Soldiers Left Yesterday. Big Demonstration at the Court House and at the Train," Digby *Weekly Courier*, May 14, 1915.

3. Service Record of Archibald Belaney, service number 415259, ARMY. He became a lance corporal on July 15, 1915 but, due to an absence, was reduced to ranks on August 26, 1915. An excellent review of life in the Canadian army in Britain appears in Desmond Morton and J. L Granatstein, *Marching to Armageddon, Canadians and the Great War 1914–1919* (Toronto: Lester & Orpen Dennys, 1989), pp. 48–52.

4. Archie Belaney, as Grey Owl, claimed that he had refused to wear the regulation army boots in England and that he had appeared on the parade ground in moccasins. "Noted Indian Interpreter of Beaver to Public Here," Prince Albert *Herald,* October 27, 1931.

5. Grey Owl to William A. Deacon, dated January 30, 1935, DEACON. My thanks to Karen Teeple of the City of Toronto Archives for identifying the Palmer House for me. It was located in the early twentieth century at the northwest corner of King and York Streets.

6. Interview with Ivy Holmes, Waverley Abbey House, Farnham, Surrey, England, December 13, 1972; Bessie Cole to Donald B. Smith, dated 11 Upper Glen Road, Hollington, St. Leonards-on-Sea, October 2, 1971, and November 17, 1971. In her letter of November 17, Miss Cole writes: "The Aunts had a Poultry Farm here & ran the chickens over the garden, so we had quite a lot to do when we came." The Coles bought the house in 1920 from the family that rented it to the Misses Belaney. Ada and Carrie were so angry that they had to leave that they made the Coles "pay for the apple crop before there were apples" (Miss Cole's letter of October 2, 1971). "H. Wilson" is listed as the "Manager of the Hollington Poultry Farm" in the Hastings Directories from 1915 to 1918. Harry Wilson, a well-educated gentleman and long-time family friend, ran the farm and stayed with the Misses Belaney.

7. David William Thornton, *Hastings: A Living History* (Hastings, Sussex, England: The Hastings Publishing Company, 1987), pp. 28–29.

8. Thornton, *Hastings,* pp. 28–31; Leslie McCormick to Donald B. Smith, dated Lesmurdie, West Australia, July 17, 1972; Church of St. Clement, Hastings (Old Town), Roll of Honour, 1914–1918.

9. Henry Ewart Banks, "Grey Owl in Kilty Outfit. War Veteran Tells How He Met Belaney in Folkstone. Mexican Blood," Windsor *Star,* April 25, 1938. The statements made in the article about Banks' service can be confirmed by examining his service file, ARMY. Banks' obituary appeared in the Wallaceburg (Ontario) *News* on August 17, 1939. A sketch of Colonel F. C. Bowen appears in V. E. Morrill and Erastus G. Pierce, *Men of Today in the Eastern Townships* (Sherbrooke: Sherbrooke Record Company, 1917), p. 113.

10. Henry Ewart Banks, "Grey Owl in Kilty Outfit," Windsor *Star,* April 25, 1938.

11. Ibid.

12. R. C. Fetherstonhaugh, ed. and comp., *The 13th Battalion Royal Highlanders of Canada, 1914–1919* (Montreal: Royal Highlanders of Canada, 1925), p. 72.

13. 13th Battalion War Diary, RG 9, III, vol. 4921, NAC.

14. Fetherstonhaugh, ed., *13th Battalion,* pp. 73, 82.

15. Elmer Weedmark and Archie McWade, quoted in "Ottawa War Comrades Say Grey Owl Indian," Ottawa *Citizen,* April 22, 1938. Elmer Weedmark's service number was 408237, and that of Archie McWade, 412410, ARMY.

16. Raddall, "Grey Owl," pp. 111–12; Interview with Albert Chandler, Melfort, Saskatchewan, September 21, 1974. Albert Chandler's service number was 23252, ARMY.

17. W. E. Macfarlane to Thomas H. Raddall, dated October 1, 1963. Thomas Raddall Papers, Dalhousie University Archives, Halifax, Nova Scotia. Walter Elliott Macfarlane's record of service gives his date of birth as 1893. He won the Military Cross in the First World War, ARMY.

18. Fetherstonhaugh, ed., *13th Battalion*, pp. 75, 77.

19. W. E. Macfarlane to Thomas H. Raddall, dated September 4, 1963, Thomas Raddall Papers, Dalhousie University Archives, Halifax, Nova Scotia.

20. W. E. Macfarlane quoted in Raddall, "Grey Owl," p. 111; also W. E. Macfarlane to Thomas H. Raddall, dated September 4, 1963, Thomas Raddall Papers, Dalhousie University Archives, Halifax, Nova Scotia.

21. See the medical information cards and the "Casualty Form—Active Service" in his service file, ARMY. Jim Espaniel recalled that Archie had a bullet scar on his right wrist. Interview with Vince Crichton, July 6, 1947; Vince Crichton manuscript on Grey Owl, a copy in SMITH.

22. Anon. *A Short History of the Royal Sussex Regiment. (35th Foot—107th Foot), 1701–1926* (Aldershot: Gale and Polden, Ltd., 1927), p. ii.

23. Fetherstonhaugh, ed., *13th Battalion*, p. 82.

24. Interview with George McCormick, Maidstone, Kent, England, December 11, 1972.

25. Lovat Dickson provides the best description of Grey Owl's loping stride in *Half-Breed*, p. 106—he stilled walked in the same manner, thirty years after his short service in the Royal Sussex Regiment.

26. From March 11 to April 8, 1916, he attended sniper's school, then rejoined his unit. Archibald Belaney's service file, ARMY.

27. Fetherstonhaugh, ed., *13th Battalion*, p. 83; Morton and Granatstein, *Armageddon*, p. 54.

28. Ibid.

29. 13th Battalion War Diary, entry for April 17, 1916, RG 9, III, vol. 4921, NAC.

30. Fetherstonhaugh, ed., *13th Battalion*, p. 89; W. E. Macfarlane to Thomas H. Raddall, dated October 1, 1963, Thomas Raddall Papers, Dalhousie University Archives, Halifax, Nova Scotia.

31. Fetherstonhaugh, ed., *13th Battalion*, p. 90.

32. 13th Battalion War Diary, entry for April 24, 1916, RG 9, III, vol. 4921, NAC.

33. Archie Belaney, quoted in *The Hastonian*, no. 14 (June 1916), p. 2.

34. Leslie Meacher, service number 408152, later reported in the London *Times*, April 22, 1938, that (as a fellow sniper) he had known "Archie Delaney" in the 13th Battalion. Meacher's testimony included this statement as well: "The last I heard of Delaney was that he got to England, where he became an Army Instructor." The testimony is weakened by the fact that Archie never served as an army instructor after his foot injury, but, in Meacher's defence, he had only "heard" this report, and claimed no more. One might add, however, that Archie's story rings truer than Meacher's, as his injury is reported on April 24, 1916, and not on April 23, 1916, in the 13th Battalion War Diary, RG 9, III, vol. 4921, NAC. Anything is possible—in the absence of proper documentation.

35. Thomas Raddall, in his research on Archie's foot injury, contacted W. E. Macfarlane in 1963. Major (his rank at the end of the war) Macfarlane then lived in Montreal. In reply to Thomas Raddall's suggestion that perhaps Archie had shot himself in the foot to get himself out of the war, Major Macfarlane ruled out the idea: first, because discipline in the battalion was strict and the commanding officer of the battalion would have thoroughly investigated any self-inflicted wound; secondly, "Belaney was too intelligent to stick at a scratch—he would have made a better job of a self-inflicted wound." W. E. Macfarlane to Thomas H. Raddall, dated Montreal, October 1, 1963, Thomas Raddall Papers, Dalhousie University Library, Halifax, Nova Scotia. Major Macfarlane's rank, and award, are mentioned in Fetherstonhaugh, ed., *13th Battalion*, p. 339.

36. The fullest description of the injury itself appears in the document "Table 11. Only for admissions to Hospital," service file of Archibald Belaney, ARMY.

37. Grey Owl to Anahareo, dated June 24, 1934, GREY OWL.

38. "Mrs. C. R. Parsons, a nurse of Henley-in-Arden, Warwickshire, believes she nursed Grey Owl at a convalescent home for soldiers at Stanmore"—so reported the *People's Journal* (Dundee, Scotland) on April 23, 1938, in a story entitled, "Mystery of Grey Owl's Parentage." I assume that "Stanmore" is a typographical error for the "Stamford" Street Hospital. The existence of a Mrs. Parsons is confirmed in a reference in a letter Grey Owl sent Ellen Elliott, Hugh Eayrs's secretary on August 16, 1934, McMASTER: "Mrs. Parsons, England (a former nurse in a military hospital under whose care I spent some months)." Archie Belaney's hospitalization record in his military service file, ARMY, reveals that in 1916 he apparently only spent "some months" at one hospital—the King George Hospital on Stamford Street in London, April 30, 1916, to August 24, 1916. The other convalescent hospitals in which he was a patient are mentioned in his service file.

39. Interview with Jane Espaniel McKee, Toronto, June 18, 1973. I am assuming that this occurred at Messines, rather than at the second location to the north, closer to Ypres—the weather presumably being warmer in the late summer in Flanders, than in the mid-spring. Archie was at Messines in the late summer and fall of 1915, and closer to Ypres in spring 1916.

40. W. E. Macfarlane to Thomas H. Raddall, dated September 4, 1963, Thomas Raddall Papers, Dalhousie University Archives, Halifax, Nova Scotia.

41. Grey Owl, *Pilgrims*, p. 15.

42. My notes on Ivy Holmes are based on several interviews with her at Waverley Abbey House, Farnham, Surrey, England, September 29, 1971; December 13 and 20, 1972; and June 8, 1975. Unless otherwise stated the information that follows is taken from these interviews. Only direct quotations are cited.

43. Grey Owl, *Tales*, p. 163. Usually Grey Owl wrote the river's name as "Mississauga," but the spelling, "Mississagi" is that followed today. This is closer to the word's actual pronunciation, which Grey Owl explains is indeed *Miss-iss-awg-y*.

44. Interview with Ivy Holmes, Waverley Abbey House, Farnham, Surrey, England, December 13, 1972.

45. Archie Belaney quoted in Dickson, *Half-Breed*, pp. 98–99. I am very grateful

to Phil Chester for his comments on this passage, in a letter dated January 2, 1989. After Archie had gone back to Canada in September 1917, Ivy gave these manuscripts to Helen Ryan, a typist friend of hers. The typist prepared clean copies of all of the texts, and returned them to Ivy with the originals, with the exception of one exercise book full of hastily pencilled writing, 136 pages long. In this text Archie wrote about his first year or so in Canada, 1906–07. The typist kept this, as "it was so beautifully-written," and only came forward with it after Grey Owl's death in April 1938. For more details on this manuscript see Howard French, "Grey Owl . . . Long-Hidden Manuscript," *Sunday Dispatch* (London), April 24, 1938. Of all his early manuscripts only excerpts of this one survive. Fortunately Lovat Dickson obtained and published one lengthy section of it in *Half-Breed*, his first biography of Grey Owl, published in 1939. See also chapter 4, footnote 7, for more information about this early manuscript.

46. Marriage certificate for Archibald Stansfeld Belaney and Florence Ivy Mary Holmes, Hollington, Sussex, England, February 10, 1917, General Register Office, London.

47. The date (March 24, 1917) and place of his operation appears in his "Medical History," p. 4, army service file of Archibald Belaney, ARMY; interview with Ivy Holmes, Waverley Abbey House, Farnham, Surrey, England, September 29, 1971.

48. Army service file of Archibald Belaney, ARMY.

Chapter Seven. Back to Bisco

1. Medical Report, May 10, 1918, file on Archibald S. Belaney, Department of Veterans Affairs, Ottawa, Ontario. I saw this file in the summer of 1971 in the reference section of the Records Management Branch, Tunney's Pasture, Ottawa. It has since been lost. Fortunately I made notes on the file's contents, VETERANS AFFAIRS.

2. Medical History of an Invalid, Archibald Belaney, Oct. 26, 1917, army service file of Archibald Belaney (415259), ARMY.

3. Ibid.

4. Interview with Ferg Legace, Petawawa, Ontario, August 5, 1972. Archie wrote to Mrs. Legace for moccasins while in hospital in Toronto. He did not know about Johnny until he came back from the war. Interviews with Ed and Lottie Sawyer, Bisco, July 16, 1971; and Ferg Legace, Petawawa, Ontario, August 5, 1972.

5. Angele recalled her short meetings with Archie at Lindsay and Bancroft at the Grey Owl Estate Trial, October 10, 1939, Court Case, pp. 8–10, 14–16, 28–29, FRASER.

6. In the Bear Island Ojibwas' calendar, November was the "whitefish month." The whitefish are spawning at this time. Madeline Theriault, *Moose to Moccasins*, p. 8.

7. Angele cited in Court Case, pp. 10, 14, FRASER.

8. Archibald Belaney, army service file, ARMY. Another clue as to the date of his return to Bisco appears in his article (as Grey Owl), "The Vanishing Life of the Wild," *Canadian Forest and Outdoors*, June 1930, p. 322: "Returning from Europe in 1917, I found the open beaver season in full swing."

9. The letter appears in Grey Owl, *Tales,* pp. 91–95. Lovat Dickson mentioned that Grey Owl had himself written the letter in a comment to his preface to *A Book of Grey Owl. Pages from the Writings of Wa-Sha-Quon-Asin* (London: Peter Davies, 1938), p. xi. If Matthew Halton is correct, Lovat Dickson also once met Mrs. Parsons during the first British lecture tour. See Matthew Halton, "Grey Owl Sought Friends in Belaney's Native Town," Toronto *Star,* April 19, 1938. Lovat Dickson is quoted as saying: "He was in hospital here for four months in 1918 [1916–17] after two war wounds. I know his nurse, who knew him very well." J. S. Wood recalled seeing the letter in the article, "Grey Owl Studied Dictionary While on His Traplines," Saskatoon *Star-Phoenix,* April 16, 1938. "Mr. Wood revealed that he had been privileged to see a copy of the first letter Grey Owl had written in English. It had been written to a nurse who took an interest in the young man while he was in hospital in England, recovering from a wound in the foot suffered while Grey Owl was a sniper in France." See chapter 6, footnote 38, for a previous reference to Mrs. Parsons. Mrs. C. R. Parsons worked as a nurse in Henley-in-Arden, Warwickshire, in the spring of 1938 (so reported the *People's Journal* of Dundee, Scotland, April 23, 1938, in the article "Mystery of Grey Owl's Parentage"). Grey Owl lectured at Henley-in-Arden on December 14, 1935 (this is mentioned on the itinerary of the 1935–36 British lecture tour). Perhaps he met her again at that time, and it was on this occasion that she returned his original letter to him (which he included the next year in *Tales of an Empty Cabin*). The letter was later re-printed from *Tales* by *Reader's Digest* in their section, "Letters Perfect," published in their issue of November, 1939, page 50. The magazine prefaced the abridged letter, "A North American Indian, ex-sniper in the Canadian Expeditionary Force, to a nurse in the English hospital where he had recovered from wounds." In 1918 Archie would never have believed that his "Indian" letter would have such international circulation.
10. Betty Somervell, "Letters," p. 1, copy in SMITH; "They Didn't Forget Archie," Sault *Star,* April 22, 1938.
11. Peter Jones, *History of the Ojebway Indians* (London: A. W. Bennett, 1861), p. 135. For details on the timing of the maple sugar run in northeastern Ontario, see John J. Rowlands, *Cache Lake Country, Life in the North Woods* (New York: W. W. Norton & Co., 1959; first published 1947), p. 111.
12. Interview with Jim Espaniel, March 29, 1973, Levack, Ontario. After I read out the complete letter to Jim I asked, "Is that true?" I still treasure his reply: "Well, not as a rule."
13. For my criticism of his introduction of "singing bird" in his letter, I am indebted to Frank Conibear (interviewed in Victoria, B.C., August 26, 1982) and Tim Myres (phone interview, Calgary, December 30, 1988) for their comments.
14. Only a hundred kilometres to the northeast of Bisco, in the Shining Tree district, songbirds only returned in number in May. Rowlands, *Cache Lake,* pp. 68–69.
15. Grey Owl, *Tales,* p. 94.
16. My sketch of Edith Langevin is based on the following interviews at Bisco: Gordon Langevin (her eldest son), December 15, 1971; Bill Langevin (her youngest son) December 16, 1971; Bella Langevin Soulière (her eldest

daughter, interviewed at Missinabie, Ontario) June 6, 1973; Mary Kohls, March 20, 1972; Libby Sawyer, April 22, 1973. Mrs. Langevin's age appears in the entry recording her death on February 7, 1939, St. John's Church Parish Registry, Biscotasing.

17. Interview with John Jero, Thunder Bay, Ontario, December 6, 1974; interview with Gordon Langevin, Biscotasing, September 29, 1970.

18. Anahareo, *Deerskins*, p. 54.

19. Interview with Gordon Langevin, Biscotasing, February 4, 1971.

20. Arthur Stevens, J. P., to A. C. March, K. C., dated December 26, 1936, typewritten copy in the North Bay *Nugget's* news morgue. In a slightly abridged form, the Toronto *Star* reprinted the letter on April 16, 1938. The typewritten draft of the letter reads: "During the Great War I received some letters from a Lady in England concerning Archie Belaney, requesting information as to his marriage ceremony with Angele Aguena [Egwuna]. I gave the information I had and learned afterwards that the London, England newspapers contained considerable comment concerning the two parties but I did not myself see the account."

21. J. J. O'Connor is quoted in the Sudbury *Star*, April 20, 1938, on the servicing of the divorce papers. The divorce became final on August 9, 1922. See "Decree Absolute for Nullity of Marriage," High Court of Justice, Divorce Registry, London.

22. Interview with Ivy Holmes, Waverley Abbey House, Farnham, Surrey, England, December 13, 1972. "The aunts were horrified by Archie's duplicity. Once Archie made his name though, they forgave him."

23. Interview with Lottie Phillips Sawyer, Biscotasing, Ontario, CBC documentary transcript, mid-August 1971.

24. Interview with Agnes Lalonde, Calgary, August 2, 1988.

25. The Misses Belaney, Letter to the Editor, Hastings *Observer*, May 14, 1938. "Our nephew was never lost, and we corresponded at long intervals." Ada did save a photo of Anahareo that Archie sent her in 1927, but she destroyed his letters. See Hastings *Observer*, April 30, 1938.

26. On Archie's foot, see Anahareo, *Deerskins*, pp. 108, 109, 111; Anahareo, *Life*, p. 221. Ted Cusson gave me a full physical description of his trapping partner's foot, in an interview, Monetville, Ontario, January 11, 1971. War Service Gratuity, army service file of Archibald Belaney, ARMY.

27. Stuart L. MacDougall, "More about Grey Owl," unpublished five-page manuscript, copy obtained from the author, December 10, 1974. For further details on the survey, see the "Report and Field Notes of the Survey of the Township Outlines. District of Algoma, 1919. Townships of Frances, Flanders, Foch, Hiawatha, Nagagami, Lessard," Ontario Ministry of Natural Resources, Toronto.

28. MacDougall, "More about Grey Owl."

29. Ferg Legace, "Memoirs" (Grey Owl section), p. 66; Harry Woodworth interviewed by Vince Crichton, November 20, 1939, Vince Crichton, "Archie Belaney (Chief Grey Owl)," unpublished manuscript, p. 19, copy in SMITH.

30. Interview with Ferg Legace, Owen Sound, Ontario, June 12, 1971; Ferg Legace, "Memoirs" (Grey Owl section), pp. 59–60.

31. Interview with Jim Espaniel, Levack, Ontario, March 29, 1973. In northern Quebec, Archie would move up in terms of what he drank. There he could obtain straight alcohol from the French islands of St. Pierre and Miquelon (off Newfoundland) which he and his friend Ted Cusson mixed with port wine and water to make what they called "moosemilk." Interview with Anahareo, Kamloops, B.C., July 6, 1971.
32. Interviews with Gordon Langevin, Biscotasing, Ontario, December 16 and 17, 1971.
33. Interview with Lottie and Libby Sawyer, Sudbury, Ontario, March 22, 1972.
34. Interview with Bill and David Langevin, Biscotasing, Ontario, July 7, 1971.
35. Interview with Gordon Langevin, Biscotasing, Ontario, December 7, 1974.
36. Interview with Jack Leve, Toronto, Ontario, February 28, 1972.
37. Interview with Ferg Legace, Owen Sound, Ontario, June 12, 1971.
38. Interview with Ed and Lottie Sawyer, Sudbury, Ontario, November 18, 1972.
39. Interview with Jack Woodworth, Cartier, Ontario, December 14, 1971.
40. Interview with Ferg Legace, Owen Sound, Ontario, June 12, 1971.
41. Interview with Ted Cusson, Monetville, Ontario, December 6, 1970; January 16 and 17, 1972.
42. Interview with Jim Espaniel, CBC documentary, Biscotasing, mid-August 1971. Archie's name appears for both years in the *Public Accounts of the Province of Ontario for 1920* (Toronto: King's Printer, 1921), p. 572; and *Public Accounts of the Province of Ontario for 1921* (Toronto: King's Printer, 1922), p. E71.
43. Ken McCracken, "Just Flying World War I Planes was an Adventure, Veteran Recalls," Rochester (Minnesota) *Post-Bulletin*, November 11, 1981; Haddow Keith to Donald B. Smith, dated Rochester, Minnesota, April 7, 1976; interview with Haddow Keith, Rochester, Minnesota, May 24, 1976.
44. Interview with Haddow Keith, Rochester, Minnesota, May 24, 1976.
45. Interview with Ed and Lottie Phillips Sawyer, Biscotasing, July 16, 1971 (they told me of his signs); interview with Kate Phillips Kohls (Lottie's sister), Biscotasing, November 2, 1972.
46. Interview with Lottie Phillips Sawyer, Biscotasing, November 18, 1972.
47. Interviews with Libby Sawyer, Biscotasing, August 21, 1971; March 17, 1972; March 22, 1972.
48. Interview with Libby Sawyer, Biscotasing, March 22, 1972.
49. Grey Owl to Lovat Dickson, dated May 4, 1936, McMASTER.
50. "Spanish River, March 27, 1885," Toronto *Globe*, April 4, 1885. When Louis Espaniel married in 1863, the Roman Catholic priests recorded that his grandfather (the original "Espagnol") had been made a prisoner. Regardless of how he arrived, the original Espaniel married an Indian woman and became chief of the Ojibwa around the HBC post of La Cloche on the north shore of Lake Huron. "Louis Sakwegijig, al. Espagnol. Son gd père fut fait prisonnier et donné à une seur[?]," Ontario Archives, Indian Genealogical Records, Acc. 11936, volume 2, p. 16. On June 3, 1863, he married Angélique Beaudry. My thanks to Jim Morrison for this reference. The British made the original "Espagnol" a chief of the La Cloche band for his loyalty during the War of 1812 against the Americans. T. G. Anderson

to Samuel Jarvis, dated Manitowaning, August 6, 1837, RG 10, volume 2289, file 5761, microfilm reel C–11,196, NAC. My thanks to Jim Morrison for this reference. In 1843, the original Espagnol (or his son) led a band of 131 Indians. T. G. Anderson, Total Number of Indians who received Presents at the Manitoulin Island in the year 1843, Jarvis Papers, S125 B59, p. 141, Metropolitan Toronto Library.

51. Interviews with Jane Espaniel McKee (one of Alex and Anny Espaniel's daughters), Toronto, June 2, 1973; July 29, 1973; December 31, 1979; September 29, 1987.

52. Interview with Jane Espaniel McKee, Toronto, June 18, 1973; interview with Jane Espaniel McKee, Toronto, by Cindy Baskin, July 28, 1980, tape held at the Spadina Road Public Library, Toronto.

53. Interview with Jim Espaniel, Estaire, Ontario, September 27, 1970. Jim Espaniel cited in "Bisco People Identify Grey Owl as A. Belaney with Wife at Temagami," North Bay *Nugget*, April 18, 1938, p. 5.

54. Grey Owl, Notebook, 1932–1936, GREY OWL.

55. Interview with Jim Espaniel, Biscotasing, August 22, 1971.

56. Interview with Jane Espaniel McKee, Toronto, July 29, 1973. A good contemporary description of the Ojibwas' hunting territories system in northeastern Ontario and northwestern Quebec appears in C. C. Farr's article, "Unscientific Facts about the Animals that Live in the Bush—The Beaver," *Rod and Gun in Canada*, 1 (1899–1900), p. 97.

57. Interviews with Jane Espaniel McKee, Toronto, June 18, 1973; December 31, 1979; September 9, 1982. A photo of the inscription appears in both the North Bay *Nugget*, April 18, 1938, and the Sudbury *Star*, April 18, 1938. The Espaniel family kindly allowed me to photograph the inscription in their treasured copy of *Pilgrims of the Wild*.

58. Nettie Magder, "The Grey Owl Legend," Toronto *Star Weekly*, May 21, 1938; Anny Espaniel quoted in "Bisco People Identify Grey Owl as A. Belaney with Wife at Temagami," North Bay *Nugget*, April 18, 1938, p. 5. This story also appeared in the Sudbury *Star*, April 18, 1938, "Evidence Proves that 'Grey Owl' was Sudbury District's 'Archie Belaney'." The *Nugget* published a slightly longer version.

59. Jim Espaniel quoted in "Evidence Proves," Sudbury *Star*, April 18, 1938.

60. Interview with Ted Cusson, Toronto, January 16, 1972.

61. Interview with Gordon Langevin, Biscotasing, December 16, 1971.

62. Interview with Ferg Legace, Owen Sound, June 12, 1971.

63. Interview with Ted Cusson, Monetville, Ontario, December 18, 1971.

64. Grey Owl, *Men*, pp. 62–63.

65. Ibid., p. 14.

66. Ibid., p. 95.

67. Interview with Bill Draper by Vince Crichton, July 17, 1938, Vince Crichton, "Grey Owl," p. 6, copy in SMITH.

68. Interview with Gordon Langevin, Biscotasing, December 15, 1971.

69. Harry Woodworth quoted in "Evidence Proves," Sudbury *Star*, April 18, 1938.

70. Interview with Jack Leve, Toronto, October 28, 1971.

71. Con Foster, "Grey Owl-Belaney," a 600-word manuscript prepared in April 1938, after Grey Owl's death, copy in SMITH.
72. Interviews with Jim Espaniel, Estaire, Ontario, September 27, 1970; March 25, 1972; CBC documentary interview, mid-August 1972; March 29, 1973.
73. Interview with Gordon Langevin, Biscotasing, February 4, 1971.
74. Interview with Robert McWatch, Chapleau, Ontario, February 6, 1971.
75. For a review of the use of the word *nottaway*, or *nahdoway* to use Peter Jones's transcription (Jones, *History*, pp. 32, 111), see Donald Chaput, "The Semantics of Nadowa," *Names*, 15,3 (1967): 228–234. J. A. Cuoq, the famous Algonquian linguist, translates the word *natowe* in his *Lexique de la Langue algonquine* (Montréal: J. Chapleau, 1886), p. 263, as "a kind of big serpent" ("espèce de gros serpent"). Interviews with Gordon Langevin, Biscotasing, July 16, 1971, and August 8, 1974.
76. Bill Draper, interviewed by Vince Crichton, July 17, 1938, Vince Crichton, "Grey Owl," p. 6; Ferg Legace, "Memoirs" (Grey Owl section), p. 28.
77. Interview with Jane Espaniel McKee, Toronto, September 29, 1987; Also notes prepared on the war dance by Jane Espaniel, February 1989, SMITH.
78. Grey Owl, *Men*, p. 226.
79. CBC documentary, interview with Jim Espaniel, Biscotasing, mid-August 1972.
80. Interview with Ed Sawyer, Biscotasing, July 16, 1971.
81. Interview with Irene Shaughnessy, Toronto, August 20, 1972.
82. Interview with Irene Shaughnessy, Toronto, November 8, 1972.
83. Harry Woodworth saved the warrant, which was reproduced on the front page of the Sudbury *Star* on April 18, 1938.
84. Frank Porter, who lived on Pansy Island at the north end of Biscotasi Lake, recorded in his diary on July 1, 1925, "Raining all day cleared toward evening, repaired roof. Archie Belaney here in evening." Frank Porter Diaries, copies in SMITH.
85. Harry Woodworth quoted in "Evidence Proves," Sudbury *Star,* April 18, 1938.
86. Testimony of Angele Egwuna, October 10, 1939, Court Case, p. 12, FRASER.
87. Ibid., p. 14.
88. Interview with Agnes Belaney Lalonde, North Bay, Ontario, January 1973.
89. Testimony of Angele Egwuna, October 10, 1939, Court Case, p. 15, FRASER.

Chapter Eight. Anahareo

1. Anahareo, *Deerskins*, pp. 1–2.
2. Grey Owl, *Pilgrims*, p. 14.
3. Interview with Anahareo, Kamloops, B.C., July 5, 1971. Interview with Joanna Bernard Murphy, North Bay, Ontario, January 30, 1971 (Anahareo's older sister); interview with Ed Bernard, Mattawa, Ontario, February 12, 1973 (Anahareo's younger brother); Anahareo, *Deerskins*, pp. 33–36.
4. Anahareo, *Deerskins*, pp. 36–40.
5. Grey Owl, *Pilgrims*, p. 15. Pony had only completed Grade Four, interview with Anahareo, Kamloops, B.C., July 8, 1971.
6. Anahareo, *Deerskins*, pp. 10–11, 5, 14. The quote appears on p. 14.
7. *My Life with Grey Owl* (London: Peter Davies, 1940), and *Devil in Deerskins* (Toronto: New Press, 1972).

8. Grey Owl, *Pilgrims*, p. 14.
9. Anahareo, *My Life with Grey Owl* (London: Peter Davies, 1940), pp. 13–14.
10. Isobel LeDuc to Hugh Eayrs, dated April 28, 1938, McMASTER.
11. Anahareo, *Deerskins*, p. 12.
12. Anahareo, *Life*, p. 33.
13. William Cartier to Jack Leve, dated Doucet, P.Q., February 24, 1926, copy in SMITH; interview with Bill Cartier, Monetville, March 25, 1972.
14. Interview with Ted Cusson, Monetville, December 6, 1970.
15. Interview with Ted Cusson, Toronto, January 17, 1972. (Ted had also previously helped Archie with his train fare from Temagami to Abitibi, interview at Monetville, December 18, 1971.)
16. Anahareo, *Deerskins*, pp. 15–17.
17. Anahareo, quoted in "Grey Owl's Wife Leaves Alone on Search for Gold," Calgary *Herald*, September 12, 1933.
18. The Misses Belaney gave the photo with its inscription to Lovat Dickson in 1938. The photo is reproduced in Dickson, *Wilderness Man*, opposite p. 145, and the inscription is included as a caption. It is also reproduced in this book.
19. Grey Owl to Hugh Eayrs, dated January 29, 1937, McMASTER.
20. "White Trappers are Hard Hit by New Regulation. Over 1200 Affected by Beaver-Otter Ban," Sudbury *Star*, June 13, 1925. A provincial order-in-council dated June 25, 1925, made it illegal for anyone except "resident Indians" to take beaver or otter, Ontario *Gazette*, volume 58 (July–December 1925), pp. 861–62. I am very grateful to Malcolm Davidson of Toronto for his help in explaining Ontario's twentieth-century trapping regulations.
21. Interviews with Ted Cusson, Monetville, December 6, 1970; and Toronto, January 16, 1972.
22. D. Sutherland Davidson, "The Family Hunting Territories of the Grand Lake Victoria Indians," *Atti del XXII Congresso Internazionale degli Americanisti Roma—Settembre 1926*, Volume 2, pp. 69–95, see particularly pp. 72, 88. Today there is still no reserve at Grand Lac Victoria, although an Indian community lives there. A small reserve of 272 hectares was granted at Lac Simon in 1962. Larry Villeneuve and Daniel Francis, *The Historical Background of Indian Reserves and Settlements in the Province of Quebec* (Ottawa: Department of Indian and Northern Affairs, 1984), pp. 20, 24.
23. Chief Tcabewisi Papaté, dated Simon Lake, October 4, 1927 (translation) in RG 10, file 420–10A, NAC. "Tcabewisi" was Nias Papaté's nickname. See Davidson, "Territories," p. 90.
24. "As children's books are invariably read aloud to the younger ones by their elders," Grey Owl to Hugh Eayrs, dated March 17, 1935, McMASTER.
25. Anahareo, *Life*, p. 77; interview with Anahareo, Kamloops, B.C., July 5, 1971; interview with Ted Cusson, Monetville, December 18, 1971.
26. Anahareo, *Life*, pp. 71–72.
27. Anahareo, *Deerskins*, 28–31, 45–54. For some unknown reason, Anahareo refers to Archie's son as "Stanley," not as "John."
28. Grey Owl, Notebook, 1932–36, GREY OWL. The quotation appears about three-quarters of the way through the unpaginated notebook.

29. Anahareo, *Deerskins*, pp. 33–35. A Mohawk chief named "Anahario" existed, a Sachem named Saghsanawano Anahario is mentioned at a council in 1763, "A Meeting with Canajoharies, Canajoharie, March 10, 1763," *The Papers of Sir William Johnson*, ed. James Sullivan et al. (14 vols.: Albany, New York, 1921–65), 4: 50, 54. A similar name also appears in a census taken in 1850 at Oka, Recensement des Iroquois du Lac des Deux Montagnes, 1850, ASSM, T. 41, no. 74, Archives du Séminaire de Saint-Sulpice, Montréal. Three people are listed as members of the "Ane8ariio" or "Anewariio" (the missionaries used the "8" symbol for a sound close to "W") family.

30. Grey Owl's letters to Anahareo, GREY OWL.

31. Anahareo, *Life*, p. 67.

32. Ibid., p. 163.

33. Anahareo, *Life*, pp. 163–64. Grey Owl to Mrs. Ettie Winters, dated sometime in 1935, GREY OWL (he told her the story about the spoon).

34. Anahareo, *Deerskins*, pp. 65–66. Dr. J. J. Wall, in "Report of Medical Service to Indians located along the line of the Canadian National Railways from Cochrane, Ont. to La Tuque, Que. June to October 1929," mentioned: "The promiscuous use of strychnine as employed by the white trappers is to be condemned. The Indians complained bitterly of this unfair practice. May I quote a personal experience; Two years ago Indians of Simon Lake Band burned a shack tenanted by an American trapper north of Amos. This individual has infringed on every right of the owner of a hunting ground which had come down to him through generations. The Indians were only driven to such a drastic step by sheer desperation." RG 10, volume 6750, file 420–10A, NAC. A trial was held. One wonders if this trial was perhaps the same one that Archie Belaney spoke at—but Dr. Wall says it took place in 1927 ("two years ago"). It is also possible that Dr. Wall was mistaken, and the trial was three years earlier, in 1926. See footnote 35 of this chapter.

35. Whether this visit occurred in June 1926 or June 1927 cannot be definitely determined. In *Deerskins* (pp. 66–74), Anahareo gives 1926 as the date, but in her earlier *Life* she suggests that it was 1927 (pp. 120–49). The anthropologist Sutherland Davidson, however, mentions that Chief Papaté's son, Miranda, had lost his wife in 1926. See Davidson, "Grand Lake Victoria Indians," p. 76. As Anahareo notes that she and Archie witnessed the funeral (*Deerskins*, p. 70; *Life*, pp. 124–25), I favour the 1926 date.

36. Grey Owl, *Pilgrims*, p. 23.

37. Ibid., p. 48.

38. The photo and inscription appear opposite p. 145 in Dickson, *Wilderness Man*.

39. Kittie stated that she met Archie at the London General Hospital at Denmark Hill in 1917. See the biographical sketch of "Kathleen Verina Cox," DICKSON. "1917. Mrs. Scott-Brown states she visited Archibald when he was in hospital at Denmark Hill."

40. K. Scott-Brown, 5 Parkfield, Topsham, S. Devon, to "Sir," September 2, 1919, VETERANS AFFAIRS.

41. L. W. Burnett, Army Records Centre, Bourne Avenue, Hayes, Middlesex, England, to Donald B. Smith, dated April 25, 1973.

42. In one of his early notebooks Archie has this friendly note: *"Write Mrs. Brown* for Recipe of Xmas Plum Pudding. Ask for walnut juice. Tell about bear etc." Grey Owl, Notebook, 1927–31, GREY OWL. On the first page of the book appears this note, "mail change address pension. Write Mrs. Scott-Brown." He would have written this in the late 1920s.

43. Kittie Scott-Brown to Lovat Dickson, dated Boscombe, England, May 17, 1938, copy in SCOTT-BROWN.

44. *"Country Life* Correspondence," three pages typed. Lovat Dickson kindly gave me a copy of these summaries, copy in SMITH. See also Mrs. Betty Somervell's summary of the letters, SOMERVELL. Several references also appeared in "A Bookman's Diary," *John O'London's Weekly,* April 29, 1938.

45. Grey Owl only makes one time reference in the Abitibi section of his book. On p. 57 of *Pilgrims* he writes, "It had been raining steadily in that part of Quebec for three straight summers, and living in a tent we were always damp and none too comfortable." The year is not specified, nor is it mentioned whether or not he and Anahareo themselves were in Quebec for three summers.

46. Grey Owl, *Pilgrims,* p. 48.

47. Ibid., p. 22.

48. Ibid., p. 29. Interestingly, in his first description of his leaving the beaver hunt, Archie made no reference at all to this incident and instead mentioned three other events which convinced him to stop trapping beaver. See Grey Owl, "The Vanishing Life of the Wild," *Canadian Forest and Outdoors,* June 1930, p. 323.

49. Grey Owl, *Pilgrims,* pp. 119–20.

50. Ibid., pp. 36–37.

51. Ibid., p. 53.

52. Anahareo, *Life,* p. 207; Grey Owl to Mrs. Ettie Winters, dated August 21, 1933, GREY OWL.

53. H. Scott-Brown [Archie Belaney], "The Passing of the Last Frontier," *Country Life,* March 2, 1929, p. 302. By mistake, *Country Life* published the article in his mother's name, as it was the only name written on the manuscript. They ran her correction identifying the author as her son, Archibald Stansfeld Belaney, in their "Correspondence" column, on March 9, 1929, p. 342.

54. Grey Owl, "Preface to Special Tour Edition," *The Men of the Last Frontier* (London: Country Life, 1937), p. ix.

55. The first letter written in April 1928 is signed "White Owl." "A Bookman's Diary," *John O'London's Weekly,* April 29, 1938.

56. The references appear in SOMERVELL.

57. In *Pilgrims* Grey Owl mentions that Dave White Stone was born around 1863 (p. 180). His daughter believed that the correct date was 1877; interview with Emma Dufond, Kippewa, Quebec, May 18, 1973. I accept the daughter's figure.

58. Anahareo, *Life,* p. 224. The lake is near Round Lake, just east of the northern end of Lake Témiscouata. Interview with Walter Strong, Montreal, April 6, 1972. Lloyd Roberts, who visited the lake in early 1931, used the term "Mud Lake." See Lloyd Roberts, "Grey Owl: Beaver Man," 13 radio scripts for the

CBC, prepared around 1950, script 9. Mrs. Lloyd Roberts showed me this manuscript in January 1971. Grey Owl referred to the lake as "Hay Lake." See the caption of the picture showing a beaver dam—"Beaver house at Hay Lake—several years old"—in Grey Owl, "Who Will Repay?", *Canadian Forest and Outdoors*, March 1931, p. 120. "Hay Lake" appears just north of "Lac Rond" or "Round Lake" on the topographical map, Edmundston 2IN Edition 1, Department of Mines and Technical Surveys, Ottawa.

59. Anahareo quoted in "Mrs. Grey Owl's Amazing Life Story," Vancouver *Sun*, October 6, 1936.
60. Grey Owl, *Pilgrims*, p. 217.
61. Charles L. Whitfield, *Healing the Child Within* (Deerfield Beach, Florida: Health Communications Inc., 1987), p. 25.
62. My sketch of Archie Belaney at Cabano is based on these three sources: Frank Richardson to Donald B. Smith, dated Campbellton, New Brunswick, June 28, 1971; interview with Bernie Graham, Campbellton, New Brunswick, April 4, 1972; interview with Frank and Alice Graham Richardson, Campbellton, New Brunswick, April 2, 1972.
63. Grey Owl refers to Témiscouata and eastern Quebec as a "foreign land" in *Pilgrims*, p. 231.
64. Grey Owl, "Little Brethren of the Wilderness. Part One," *Canadian Forest and Outdoors*, September 1930, p. 501; interview with Bernie Graham, Campbellton, N.B., April 4, 1972.
65. Grey Owl, *Pilgrims*, p. 171.
66. Interview with Mgr. Cyr, Cabano, Quebec, April 14, 1971.
67. Interview with Yvon Lavoie, Ottawa, December 31, 1972.
68. Interview with Bernie Graham, Campbellton, N.B., April 4, 1972.
69. Grey Owl to *Country Life* dated March 1930. The excerpt appears in Lovat Dickson's summary of the *Country Life* letters, copy in SMITH.
70. Grey Owl, *Pilgrims*, p. 183.
71. Interview with John Bovey [son of Wilfrid Bovey], Canmore, Alberta, August 26, 1988.
72. Richard Peck to Donald B. Smith, Ste-Agathe-des-Monts, Quebec, October 19, 1988.
73. Grey Owl, *Pilgrims*, p. 175.
74. Wilfrid Bovey to G. A. Harcourt, dated November 26, 1929, VETERANS AFFAIRS.
75. A short biographical sketch of Jean-Charles Harvey appears in the introduction to his *Fear's Folly (Les Demi-civilisés)*, translated by John Glassco, edited and introduced by John O'Connor (Ottawa: Carleton University Press, 1982), pp. 2–24.
76. Interview with Yvon Lavoie, Ottawa, December 31, 1972. Yvon Lavoie, a seventeen-year-old, travelled with them and dated the visit as having taken place at the beginning of November, 1929. He vividly remembers the date as being at the time of "Toussaint," All Saint's Day, November 1. He recalls this because it was the first time he had ever missed mass. When he told Grey Owl that he wanted to go to mass, Grey Owl replied that it should not bother him. The best place to thank God for his blessings was in full nature.

For Grey Owl's comments on his friend, Jean-Léon Duchêne, see *Pilgrims*,
p. 231.
77. Jean-Charles Harvey, "Un Apache au pays des Hurons," *Le Jour* (Montréal),
22 janvier 1938.
78. Jean-Charles Harvey, *Des Bois, Des Champs, Des Bêtes* (Montréal: Les
Editions de l'Homme, 1965), p. 85.
79. Harvey, *Des Bois*, p. 84.
80. Jean-Charles Harvey, "Un Apache au pays des Hurons," *Le Jour* (Montréal),
22 janvier 1938.
81. Jean-Charles Harvey, "Grey Owl est Mort," *Le Jour* (Montréal), 23 avril 1938;
Anahareo, *Deerskins*, pp. 121–22; Harvey, *Des Bois*, p. 77.
82. "Quest for Gold to Buy Airplane Takes Mohawk Girl Prospecting Alone,"
Manitoba *Free Press*, October 10, 1931.
83. Grey Owl, *Pilgrims*, pp. 207–8, 198.
84. Anahareo, *Deerskins*, p. 135.
85. Ibid., pp. 135–36.
86. Janet Foster provides an excellent sketch of Harkin in *Working for Wildlife.
The Beginning of Preservation in Canada* (Toronto: University of Toronto,
1978), pp. 77–82, 220–23.
87. James Harkin quoted in M. B. Williams, *The Banff-Jasper Highway*
(Saskatoon: H. R. Larson Publishing Co., 1963), pp. 13–14.
88. Foster, *Wildlife*, pp. 116–19.
89. Grey Owl, *Pilgrims*, p. 242; G. M. Dallyn to Donald B. Smith, dated Ottawa,
April 14, 1971.
90. Grey Owl addressed nearly 500 people at the convention on January 23,
1931. See "The Grey Owl Controversy," *Canadian Forest and Outdoors*,
May 1938, p. 152.
91. On the difficulties of determining a beaver's gender, see Lars Wilsson, *My
Beaver Colony*. Translated from the Swedish by Joan Bulman (Garden City,
N.Y.: Doubleday & Co., 1968), pp. 7, 55, 81.
92. *Canadian Forest and Outdoors*, January 1931, p. 122.
93. *Canadian Forest and Outdoors*, February 1931, p. 12.
94. Grey Owl, "The Great Adventure," p. 5. A copy is in the Park Library, Prince
Albert National Park, Waskesiu, Saskatchewan.
95. Grey Owl, *Pilgrims*, p. 247. My thanks to Mike Buss, Fish and Wildlife
Specialist, Frost Centre, Dorset, Ontario, for his assessment of this incident.
96. Anahareo, *Deerskins*, p. 144.
97. Ibid., p. 137; Grey Owl, *Pilgrims*, p. 259; "Importation of Soviet Lumber
is Protested Here," *The Gazette* (Montreal), January 24, 1931; interview with
Gordon Dallyn, Ottawa, May 10, 1971.
98. Foster, *Wildlife*, pp. 78–79.
99. J. B. Harkin to J. M. Wardle, September 18, 1935, PERSONNEL FILE.
100. J. B. Harkin to R. A. Gibson, April 25, 1936, PERSONNEL FILE.
101. "Grey Owl Devotes Life to Protection of Beaver," *Montreal Star*, January 24,
1931. Other papers apparently picked up the story and later ran an abridged
version, see for instance, "Indian Devotes Life to Beaver," Brandon (Manitoba)
Sun, February 12, 1931 (clipping in RG 10, volume 168, file R.M. 272,
interim #8, NAC).

102. Anahareo, quoted in "Wife of Grey Owl Declares He was English, Not an Indian," Toronto *Star,* July 27, 1938.
103. The photo illustrates the article, "The Adventurous Career of GREY OWL (wa-shee-quon-asier)," *Canadian Forest and Outdoors,* March 1931, p. 118.
104. Grey Owl, *Men,* p. 243. This must have been one of his last additions to the book before publication in London, England, in late 1931.
105. See the frontispiece, *Pilgrims of the Wild* by Wa-Sha-Quon-Asin (Grey Owl), (Toronto: Macmillan, 1934).
106. Interviews with Jim Espaniel, Estaire, Ontario, March 30, 1973, and the interview for the CBC documentary, Biscotasing, mid-August 1971. Perhaps Archie had first chosen the name "White Owl" as he was aware that the actual Ojibwa word *washaquonasie* referred to a "white beak owl," not to a "grey owl."
107. Grey Owl, *Men,* p. 243.
108. Interview with Jane Espaniel McKee, Toronto, September 29, 1987; interviews with Jim Espaniel, Estaire, Ontario, March 30, 1973, and the interview for the CBC documentary, Biscotasing, mid-August 1971. Grey Owl was aware of the Ojibwa's name for screech owls as he wrote in *Tales* (p. 302) of "the weird and ghoulish cachinnation of the grey owls, they of the Shining Beak." He then added in a footnote "so called by the Indians on account of his white shiny beak. This bird laughs hideously in certain seasons." At least once he used the proper "-asie" ending in writing his "Indian name." See the inscription on the photo he gave Lloyd Roberts at Riding Mountain National Park in October 1931. A copy of this photo is in the Archives of Ontario, archival number S12935.
109. Grey Owl, *Tales,* p. 18. Betty Somervell, Letters to her daughter, 1953, p. 1, copy in SMITH. Mrs. Somervell also reported that his name meant, "He Who Travels By Night."
110. Grant Dexter, "Sidelights and Silhouettes. Introducing Grey Owl," *The Canadian Magazine,* August 1931, p. 20. Apparently there was some hesitation about making the appointment, until early 1931. See Lloyd Roberts, "The Causerie," Winnipeg *Free Press,* July 2, 1948; W. F. Lothian to Donald B. Smith, dated Ottawa, February 10, 1971. To this point only one film had been made with Grey Owl and his beavers.
111. Lloyd Roberts, "Brother to the Beaver," unpublished manuscript, prepared about 1951, pp. 109–10. Shown to me by Mrs. Lloyd Roberts, Scarborough, Ontario, in January 1971.
112. In Ottawa in February 1936, Grey Owl gave Betty Somervell a copy of *Emerson's Essays and Representative Men* (London & Glasgow: Collins' Clear-Type Press, n.d.). He marked in ink a number of passages, this being one of them (p. 131). Betty Somervell showed me the book at her home in Kendal, England, June 1, 1975. Grey Owl wrote the following inscription in the book: "In times of stress, when trouble hangs like a cloud of darkness, when you fumble weakly in this darkness for light, this book will prove for you, as it has done for me, a sure refuge."

Chapter Nine. The First Book

1. Grey Owl to *Country Life,* dated Riding Mountain National Park, July 1, 1931, SOMERVELL.

2. W. J. Oliver, "Memoirs," p. 37. My thanks to Mrs. A. J. Langford, daughter of Bill Oliver, for forwarding this reference.
3. Ibid.
4. The shots include Bertha Lake, Waterton Lakes National Park (opposite p. 21), Indian Falls, Snake Indian River, Jasper National Park (opposite p. 32), The Giant Steps, north fork of Paradise Creek, Paradise Valley, Banff National Park (opposite p. 215). My thanks to the Whyte Museum of the Canadian Rockies, Banff, for the identifications.
5. *Times Literary Supplement*, March 10, 1932.
6. "Review of *The Men of the Last Frontier* by Grey Owl," in "Recent Publications," *Canadian Historical Review*, 13,4 (December 1932): 465.
7. Grey Owl, *Men*, p. 20.
8. Grey Owl himself recognized this. "Writing is a curious business. A person writes into his work, if he is sincere, a most revealing resumé of his own character, all unknown to himself." Grey Owl to Kathleen Garland, dated December 13, 1934, GREY OWL.
9. Grey Owl, *Men*, p. 40.
10. I am indebted to Phil Chester for this description, in his comments on my second draft of this manuscript, August 1989.
11. Interview with Henry Hopkin, London, July 29, 1976. For the words cited of Latin origin in the first two chapters of *Men*, see pp. 5, 10, 19, 20, 29, 31, 41, 42. Some of these expressions, I suspect, came naturally, others from his thesaurus. Yvonne Perrier Grey Owl, whom he married in 1936, mentions his *Thesaurus* in a letter to Lovat Dickson, dated May 31, 1938, McMASTER.
12. Grey Owl, *Men*, p. 154.
13. Ibid., p. 86.
14. He seems to have based his story on Neganikabo's father, at least in respect to his age. Neganikabo's father died at "over a hundred years old," in 1913. Interview with Lottie Phillips Sawyer, Sudbury, July 16, 1971. Neganikabo trapped on the east branch of the Spanish River, near Archie's grounds on Lake Mozhabong. Interview with Jim Espaniel, Estaire, Ontario, March 25, 1972. Neganikabo and his family were related to the Espaniels. Interview with Jane Espaniel McKee, Toronto, August 29, 1973. Grey Owl mentions Neganikabo's father in a note in one of his notebooks (Notebook, 1932–36, GREY OWL): "Old Neganikabo, his attitude when walking; hauling toboggan had made its mark on him." Perhaps on hearing from the son about his father he mentally elevated the father to "the patriarchial ruler of the vanished people, a reincarnation of the fabled Hiawatha" (*Men*, p. 245).

Archie was not adopted by the Bisco Indians (see footnote 16). Every fall, before returning to their trapping grounds, the Indians had a Wabeno, or thanksgiving festival with dancing and feasting all night, which special non-Indians (Archie being one) could attend. Adoptions did not occur at the Wabeno and non-Indians were not invited to the council and pow-wow at Woman River to the west. Interview with Jim Espaniel, Estaire, Ontario, March 29, 1973. I asked Jim in this interview if Archie could attend the Woman River Council. Jim replied, "No, they'd shoot him if he did. No white men allowed."

15. Grey Owl, *Men*, p. 225–6.
16. In Bisco I met a number of people in the early 1970s who remembered Neganikabo (that is, the son of the old Neganikabo), but none (Indian or non-Indian) who recalled Archie Belaney being adopted by the Bisco Indians. See also footnote 14.
17. Grey Owl, *Pilgrims*, p. 202.
18. I am grateful to Phil Chester for his comments on this section.
19. Grey Owl, *Men*, p. 218.
20. Ibid., p. 45.
21. Grey Owl, *Men*, p. 171.
22. Foster, *Wildlife*, pp. 34, 80.
23. For background on the American conservation movement, see Roderick Nash, *Wilderness and the American Mind* (New Haven, Conn.: Yale University Press, 1967), particularly the chapter on "John Muir: Publicizer," pp. 122–40.
24. R. L. Duffus in the New York *Times*, May 22, 1932, p. 4, cited in *The Book Review Digest, 1932–33*, ed. Marion A. Knight et al. (New York: H. W. Wilson Company, 1933), p. 402.
25. Excerpts from *The Men of the Last Frontier* appeared as "My Busy Buddy, the Beaver," in *Reader's Digest*, September 1933. The Toronto *Star* ran the same condensation on August 29, 1933. The Canadian women's magazine, *Chatelaine*, ran an excerpt on Grey Owl's beavers in its issue of October 1933. See Napier Moore to Grey Owl, dated August 21, 1934, McMASTER.
26. Ellen Elliott to Lovat Dickson, dated Toronto, August 1, 1934, McMASTER. "Several excerpts from his first book have already been used in school readers."
27. Edwin L. Sabin, "Review of *The Men of the Last Frontier* by Grey Owl," *Saturday Review*, June 29, 1935, p. 5.
28. A short sketch of William Talbot Allison (1874–1941), appears in W. Stewart Wallace, *The Macmillan Dictionary of Canadian Biography* (3rd ed., Toronto: Macmillan, 1963), p. 10.
29. Grey Owl, *Men*, p. 210.
30. Grey Owl to *Country Life*, dated August 1931, quoted in "A Bookman's Diary," *John O'London's Weekly*, April 29, 1938.
31. For his full story see Donald B. Smith, *Long Lance, The True Story of an Imposter* (Toronto: Macmillan, 1982).
32. Professor W. T. Allison, "'Beaver Man'—Reveals Secrets of Mother-Nature," Winnipeg *Tribune*, July 16, 1932. See also Grey Owl, *Men*, p. 8.
33. Grey Owl to Hugh Eayrs, dated July 31, 1932, McMASTER.
34. Although he signed his name as Archie Grey Owl, he was also known as Archie Belaney, or rather as "Archie Bellaney," as a clerk made a mistake with the transcription of his name and the error was repeated from that point on. His parks personnel file is actually under the name "A. Bellaney," PERSONNEL FILE.
35. Donald B. Smith, "The Belaneys of Brandon Hills," *The Beaver*, Outfit 306:3 (Winter 1975): 46–50.
36. Interview with Catherine Tweed, Brandon, Manitoba, August 12, 1974;

interview with Wilmot McComb, Brandon, Manitoba, August 10, 1974. Charles Belaney died in 1890. See his gravestone in the Brandon Hills United Church cemetery. George France Belaney's tombstone is also there. He died in 1933.

37. Interview with Ivy Scott, Surrey, B.C., March 15, 1975.

38. Ibid. Wilmot McComb described Maggie's accent in our interview, Brandon, Manitoba, August 10, 1974.

39. Grey Owl to Anahareo, n.d., probably written in late 1933 (or late 1934), GREY OWL. In the letter fragment Grey Owl mentions that he has "written one book," hence the letter was written before *Pilgrims of the Wild* appeared in December 1934. He asked Anahareo about their daughter, Dawn, who was born August 23, 1932. He also adds, "this is a wonderful fall."

40. Gerald Gwillim (a cousin of Lena Gwillim Falconer, Archibald Falconer's wife) to Donald B. Smith, dated October 22, 1988.

41. Ada Belaney quoted in the Hastings *Observer,* April 30, 1938.

42. Betty Somervell, Notebook containing notes on her first interview with Kittie Scott-Brown (late April 1938), copy in SMITH.

43. W. J. Keith, "Sir Charles George Douglas Roberts," *The Canadian Encyclopedia* (2nd ed.: Edmonton: Hurtig, 1988), p. 1878. Almost concurrently with Ernest Thompson Seton (in the 1890s), Roberts developed the realistic animal story. Roberts, however, never rivaled Seton's commercial success. See John Coldwell Adams, *Sir Charles God Damn. The Life of Sir Charles G. D. Roberts* (Toronto: University of Toronto Press, 1986), pp. 82–84. Grey Owl disliked Sir Charles's animal stories. He felt that they were not always credible. Interview with Ken Conibear, Vancouver, July 8, 1971.

44. Grey Owl, "The Beaver Family Migrates," *Canadian Forest and Outdoors,* September 1933, p. 229.

45. A short summary of his stay at Riding Mountain appears in Wayne Boyce, "Grey Owl. Riding Mountain the turning point of his life?", Brandon *Sun,* June 2, 1973; and in D. T. Tabulenas, "A Narrative Human History of Riding Mountain National Park and Area: Prehistory to 1980," Parks Canada Microfiche Report Series 102 (1983), pp. 229–34.

46. G. C. Porter's article appeared on August 1, 1931. I am very grateful to the library of the Winnipeg *Free Press,* for forwarding a copy.

47. Frank H. Williams, "Archie Grey Owl Issues Warning That Housing of Beaver Must be Changed," Manitoba *Free Press,* October 5, 1931.

48. "Objects to Criticism by Friends of Beaver. Parks Superintendent Declares None Have Died as Result of Bad Conditions," Manitoba *Free Press,* October 8, 1931.

Chapter Ten. Prince Albert National Park

1. Edward McCourt, *Saskatchewan* (Toronto: Macmillan, 1968), p. 178.

2. James Short provides a full description of Beaver Lodge in "A Structural and Furnishings History of the Grey Owl Cabin Site, Ajawaan Lake, Prince Albert National Park," Parks Canada, Manuscript Report Number 264 (1978). For the site itself, see pp. 8–9.

3. This sketch of Prince Albert National Park relies heavily on Bill Waiser's *Saskatchewan's Playground. A History of Prince Albert National Park* (Saskatoon: Fifth House Publishers, 1989), particularly pp. 26–27, 35.

4. Waiser, *Park*, p. 37.

5. Ibid., p. 77.

6. Grey Owl to Isa Whiteford, dated October 17, 1934, Saskatchewan Archives Board, Regina, Saskatchewan. "I sincerely hope that I will see some of your group, beside others, up here next Summer. Such visits give me a great deal of pleasure, especially when my guests show a real interest, such as you people did, in what I have to show them."

7. Grey Owl to Lloyd Acheson, dated August 1, 1934. The original letter was shown to me by Lloyd's son, Keith Acheson, copy in SMITH.

8. On his life, see Mary Clark Sheppard, ed., *Oil Sands Scientist. The Letters of Karl A. Clark 1920–1949* (Edmonton: University of Alberta Press, 1989). A short one page sketch of his life appeared in *Horizon Canada*, number 91 (1987).

9. Karl Clark to Sid [S. M. Blair], dated Edmonton, November 16, 1932, S. M. Blair Papers, University of Alberta Archives, 85–31: 46/2/211/3. Three other excellent accounts of visits to Beaver Lodge can also be cited. Ken Doolittle's "A Day with Grey Owl," *The Fish and Game Sportsman*, 8, 4 (Winter Edition 1976): 31–36, which describes a visit in 1933; Anne Garland's [Kathleen Garland], "My Visit to Grey Owl," *Canadian Forest and Outdoors*, March 1935, pp. 790–91, on a trip in 1934; and T. D. A. Cockerell's account of a journey in 1935, "A Visit with Grey Owl," *Natural History*, 37 (1936): 223–30.

10. Grey Owl, *Tales*, the Dedication.

11. Ibid., p. 274.

12. John Diefenbaker, *One Canada. Memoirs of the Right Honourable John G. Diefenbaker. The Crusading Years 1895–1956* (Toronto: Macmillan, 1975), p. 118.

13. Dr. W. G. N. van der Sleen's visit is mentioned in "Weather Prophecies Doubted," Regina *Leader-Post*, November 2, 1936. A sketch of Dr. van der Sleen appears in *Who's Who in the Netherlands 1962–63*, ed. Stephen S. Taylor and Marinus Spruytenburg (Amsterdam: De Mutator N.V., 1963), p. 654.

14. W. G. N. van der Sleen, *Canada. Met Vier En Twintig Fotopagina's* (2nd revised edition, Tilburg: Nederland's Boekhuis, 1947), pp. 162–63. My thanks to Laurie Meijer-Dreis for the translation.

15. Ibid., p. 167.

16. Anahareo, *Deerskins*, pp. 148, 151.

17. See his very affectionate references to her in his correspondence with Mrs. Ettie Winters, 1933–1936, GREY OWL.

18. Anahareo, *Deerskins*, pp. 153–54. The film would be released as "Strange Doings in Beaverland." See the letter, J. C. Campbell to E. Elliott Booth [Ellen Elliott], dated March 1, 1935, McMASTER.

19. Ibid, p. 156.

20. Grey Owl to Anahareo, dated August 21, 1933, GREY OWL.

21. Undated fragment of a letter from Grey Owl to Anahareo written in late 1933, GREY OWL.
22. Grey Owl to Anahareo, dated November 17, 1934, GREY OWL.
23. Grey Owl to Anahareo, dated July 11, 1934, GREY OWL.
24. Ibid.
25. Grey Owl to the editor, Charles Scribner's Sons, dated Beaver Lodge, July 13, 1934, SCRIBNER'S.
26. Grey Owl to Anahareo, dated September 27, 1934, GREY OWL.
27. Grey Owl, *Pilgrims*, pp. 10, 12.
28. Milan Novak, "The registered trapline system in Ontario," *Ontario Fish and Wildlife Review*, 18, 1 (Spring 1979): 4; J. W. Anderson, *Fur Trader's Story* (Toronto: Ryerson, 1961), pp. 183–90.
29. Harold Innis, "Review of *Pilgrims of the Wild* by Wa-Sha-Quon-Asin (Grey Owl)," *Canadian Historical Review*, 16 (June 1935): 199.
30. Grey Owl to Maxwell Perkins, dated May 5, 1935, SCRIBNER'S.
31. Grey Owl to the editor, Charles Scribner's Sons, dated June 3, 1934, SCRIBNER'S.
32. Grey Owl to Charles Scribner's Sons, dated December 5, 1933, SCRIBNER'S.
33. Anita Moffett in the New York *Times*, April 7, 1935, p. 19; cited in *The Book Review Digest 1935–36*, ed. Mertice M. James and Dorothy Brown (New York: H. W. Wilson Company, 1936), p. 409. She uses the form "in behalf of the wilderness" rather than "on behalf of the wilderness."
34. Grey Owl to *Country Life*, dated January 14, 1931 [1932], Lovat Dickson's summary of the *Country Life* letters, copy in SMITH. See also Grey Owl to Hugh Eayrs, dated Prince Albert National Park, January 23, 1932, McMASTER. In this letter Grey Owl lists his other exasperations with *Country Life*, namely their editorial attempts to alter his text and their final presentation of the book.
35. Dickson, *Half-Breed*, p. 301.
36. Basil de Selincourt, "Grey Owl and Anahareo, Champions of the Beaver," London *Observer*, January 13, 1935.
37. *New Statesman & Nation*, 9:84 (January 19, 1935), quoted in *The Book Review Digest, 1935–36*, ed. Mertice M. James and Dorothy Brown (New York: H. W. Wilson Company, 1936), p. 408.
38. Compton Mackenzie, "A Beautiful Fairy Tale that is All True . . . How a Scots-Redskin became Protector of the Wild," London *Daily Mail*, February 12, 1935. My thanks to Helen Kirk-Greene for this reference. Later in the year he reviewed *Sajo* and pronounced it to be, "the best tale of this kind since *Black Beauty*," thereby putting *Pilgrims* in the third slot, not the second, after *Black Beauty*. See Compton Mackenzie, "Compton Mackenzie Chooses . . . Gift Books Children Will Love," London *Daily Mail*, November 21, 1935.
39. Grey Owl to Mrs. Winters, n.d. [probably May or June 1935], GREY OWL.
40. A. F. Lascelles, Secretary to the governor-general, to the deputy superintendent-general of Indian Affairs, Department of Indian Affairs, July 13, 1935. The message was conveyed on to Grey Owl. A. F. Mackenzie to J. A. Wood, Superintendent, Prince Albert National Park, July 17, 1935, RG 10, vol. 7995, 1/1–15–2–4, NAC. The fact that Grey Owl had "been specially

honoured by the King putting a copy of 'Pilgrims of the Wild' on his book-shelf," greatly impressed James Harkin. See his letter to J. M. Wardle, September 18, 1935, PERSONNEL FILE.

41. Grey Owl to Hugh Eayrs, dated December 11, 1934, McMASTER.

42. Grey Owl, *Sajo*, p. xiii; Grey Owl to Lovat Dickson, dated Beaver Lodge, March 17, 1935, in Lovat Dickson, ed., *The Green Leaf, A Tribute to Grey Owl* (London: Lovat Dickson, 1938), p. 59.

43. *Times Literary Supplement*, September 19, 1935, p. 577, cited in *The Book Review Digest, 1936–37*, ed. Mertice M. James and Dorothy Brown (New York: H. W. Wilson Company, 1937), p. 414.

44. Chicago *Daily Tribune*, October 17, 1936, p. 16, cited in *The Book Review Digest*, 1936–37, ed. Mertice M. James and Dorothy Brown (New York: H. W. Wilson Company, 1937), p. 414.

45. E. K. Broadus, "Letters in Canada: 1935. II. Fiction," *University of Toronto Quarterly*, 5 (1935–36): 368. Professor Broadus had been one of Lovat Dickson's teachers at the University of Alberta. See Lovat Dickson, *The Ante-Room* (Toronto: Macmillan, 1959): 230–31.

46. The languages include: Czech, Danish, Dutch/Flemish, Estonian, Finnish, French, Georgian, German, Hungarian, Moldavian, Norwegian, Polish, Russian, Serbo-Croat, Swedish, Ukrainian, and (since 1987) Japanese. Joan Waldegrave, Peter Davies Ltd. Publishers, London, to Donald B. Smith, August 28, 1970. The existence of a Russian translation is mentioned in Alexander Vaschenko, "Some Russian Responses to North American Indian Cultures," in *Indians and Europe: An Interdisciplinary Collection of Essays*, ed. Christian F. Feest (Aachen: Ed. Herodot, Roder-Verl., 1987), p. 307. My thanks to Colin Taylor for this reference. In 1981, Yevgeni Pozdnyakov, a USSR embassy counsellor in Ottawa, reported that Grey Owl was the second best-selling Canadian author in the Soviet Union (after Ernest Thompson-Seton). See "You Asked Us," *Today Magazine*, December 12, 1981. Andrei Stulov, Second Secretary, Press Information, Press Office of the USSR Embassy in Canada, supplied me on February 9, 1989, with the titles of Grey Owl's books translated into various languages in the Soviet Union. I learned of the Japanese translation of *Sajo* from the translator, Kensei Yoshida of Tokyo, Japan. (My thanks to Doug Cass for putting me in touch with him). Macmillan has kept the book in print in Canada since 1935. The edition of *Sajo* brought out in 1961 mentions that it is the nineteenth printing. The latest paperback edition appeared in 1987.

Grey Owl's books have enjoyed great popularity around the world. The reviewer of *Sajo* in the *Times of India* (January 24, 1936) stated that the book "has stirred me more profoundly than any story I have read about animals." In France, his books were recommended for use in French schools in the 1930s. See "French Children Learn of Canada by Written Word," Canadian Press story reprinted in the Peterborough *Examiner*, April 21, 1938. In Sweden as late as the 1970s he was still read. Mary Orvig, a Swedish specialist in the theory and history of children's books, stated in 1972 that Canadian books translated into Swedish have left the impression that Canadians "worship nature. We have everything Grey Owl had written." Jo

Carson, "Canadian Image as Nature-Worshippers, Thanks to Grey Owl. Children's Books are Country's Ambassadors for Young, Swedish Woman Says," Toronto *Globe and Mail*, May 4, 1972, p. W6. Recently, Soviet Alexander Vaschenko noted: "The call raised by Grey Owl in Canada for the preservation, not destruction, of the kingdom of the wilds was promptly heard by prominent Soviet writers. Some of them, moved by the personality of Grey Owl, thought that his works deserved greater attention." Alexander Vaschenko, "Some Russian Responses to North American Indian Cultures" in Feest, ed., *Indians and Europe*, p. 313.

47. Grey Owl, *Pilgrims*, p. 253.
48. Grey Owl, *Pilgrims*, p. 142; Anahareo, *Life*, p. 216.
49. Grey Owl, *Pilgrims*, p. 252.
50. Ibid., p. 11.
51. Interview with Sam Luke [son of Andy Luke], Timmins, Ontario, May 5, 1973.
52. Grey Owl, *Pilgrims*, p. 206.
53. Interview with Emma Dufond [daughter of Dave White Stone or Pelon], Kippewa, Quebec, May 18, 1973. Grey Owl gives Dave's age as 67 around 1930, see *Pilgrims*, p. 180, which would mean he was born about 1863. His daughter, though, told me that he was born in 1877, and lived until 1969, when he died at the age of 92.
54. Grey Owl, *Sajo*, pp. 39–40.
55. Grey Owl, "Little Brethren of the Wilderness," *Canadian Forest and Outdoors*, September 1930, p. 500.
56. "The Boss" and "Jelly Roll" and "King of the Beaver People" are all names for the same beaver; see "The King of the Beaver People," *Canadian Forest and Outdoors*, December 1930, p. 684.
57. For instance, compare the text of *Pilgrims of the Wild*, on p. 219, and at the top of the second column, on p. 686, of Grey Owl, "The King of the Beaver People," *Canadian Forest and Outdoors*, December 1930.
58. Ken Conibear kindly compiled a list for me of Grey Owl's misuse of English in *Pilgrims of the Wild*, Ken Conibear to Donald Smith, September 22, 1984, SMITH. The list includes examples of errors in: grammar (a confusion between intransitive "lie" and transitive "lay," the wrong case in pronouns, the wrong sequence of tenses, subject and verb disagreement), diction, spelling, and punctuation. Of Grey Owl's punctuation, Ken Conibear writes: "His punctuation is old-fashioned, interruptive, illogical, confusing. He seems to have no knowledge of the distinction between essential and non-essential modifiers and frequently omits the second in a pair of commas. Examples are too numerous to detail."
59. Grey Owl to Ellen Elliott, July 20, 1934 and August 10, 1934, McMASTER; Grey Owl to the editor, Charles Scribner's, June 3, 1934, SCRIBNER'S; Grey Owl to Lovat Dickson, July 4, 1935, in *The Green Leaf*, ed. Dickson, pp. 72, 74–75; Hugh Eayrs to Donald Klopfer, Random House, August 25, 1936, McMASTER.
60. Civil service personnel file, "A. Bellaney," PERSONNEL FILE.
61. Grey Owl, *Tales*, pp. 278–79.
62. Interview with Wally Laird, Calgary, August 30, 1988.

63. In 1937 Archie renewed his passport under the name of McNeil, his "real name." Belaney, he explained to the passport authorities, was "only the name of his next of kin who had brought him up and educated him." This statement is cited in a memorandum prepared by the under-secretary of state on September 8, 1937, addressed "To Whom It May Concern," naturalization file, number 8154, 1934, for Grey Owl (Archie Belaney). A xerox copy of the file was supplied to me by W. R. Martin, Registrar, Department of the Secretary of State, Ottawa, June 16, 1971 (file 2900–03). The first reference I could find in print of a mention by Grey Owl to his McNeil heritage appears in the article, "'Grey Owl' in Town. Impressed by Scots Hospitality. Tartan Scarf for Wife," Edinburgh *Evening News*, November 29, 1935. "His father was descended from Scots people—his name was M'Neil." See footnote 39, chapter 9, for his first reference in a letter to his McNeil connection. In this note to Anahareo (written in late 1933) he claimed he had an uncle by the name of McNeil.

Chapter Eleven. The First British Tour

1. Betty Somervell, "Letters to my Daughter," 1953, p. 1, copy in SMITH.
2. "Famous Indian Lecturer. Grey Owl's Plea to Large Kendal Audience," Westmorland *Gazette*, January 11, 1936.
3. A photo of Grey Owl at Carlisle appeared in the Cumberland *Evening News*, January 9, 1936; Somervell, "Letters," p. 2, copy in SMITH.
4. Somervell, "Letters," pp. 2–3, copy in SMITH.
5. Ibid., p. 4; "Knife from Sheffield Indian Tribe's Heirloom," Sheffield *Daily Independent*, January 11, 1936. The description of Sheffield in 1936 is taken from George Orwell, *The Road to Wigan Pier* (London: Victor Gollancz, 1937), p. 138.
6. "Grey Owl in Glasgow Again. Enthusiastic Audience," Glasgow *Evening Citizen*, January 13, 1936; "Grey Owl Lectures in Glasgow. St. Andrew's Hall Crowded for Second Visit," Glasgow *Herald*, January 14, 1936.
7. "'The Beaver People.' Grey Owl's Return Visit to Edinburgh," Edinburgh *Evening News*, January 15, 1936.
8. Somervell, "Letters," pp. 2, 5, copy in SMITH. The itinerary was published and included in the promotional booklet for the tour: "Grey Owl. The Man and His Story."
9. "'Grey Owl' in London. Protector of Wild Life," *The Observer* (London), October 20, 1935.
10. Grey Owl, Notebook 'A' 1936, GREY OWL.
11. Peter Bower, another employee of Lovat Dickson, also assisted. See Lovat Dickson, *The House of Words* (London: Macmillan, 1963), p. 169.
12. Somervell, "Letters," p. 5, copy in SMITH. Lovat Dickson mentions in a letter to Hugh Eayrs, dated London, January 29, 1936, McMASTER, that Grey Owl received "several score" letters daily. Laya Rotenberg Kurtz to Donald B. Smith, dated Paris, April 5, 1971; Memorandum of Agreement, December 13, 1935, with Laya Rotenberg, Peter Davies Papers, Heinemann Group, London, England; interview with Laya Rotenberg Kurtz, Paris, December 9, 1972.

13. The best sources of background information on Lovat Dickson are his two autobiographical volumes: *The Ante-Room* (Toronto: Macmillan, 1959); and *The House of Words* (Toronto: Macmillan, 1963). For a short sketch of his life see his obituary in the London *Times*, January 8, 1987.
14. Dickson, *House of Words*, pp. 132–49.
15. Ibid., pp. 146–47.
16. Grey Owl to Lovat Dickson, quoted in Dickson, *House of Words*, p. 161.
17. Dickson, *House of Words*, p. 164. *The Illustrated London News* ran the excerpts from *Pilgrims* in their issues of August 25, September 1, 8, 15, 22, 1934, pp. 282–83, 310, 318–19, 354–55, 398–99, 426–27.
18. Grey Owl to Ellen Elliott, dated March 24, 1935, McMASTER.
19. Grey Owl to Lovat Dickson and Hugh Eayrs, dated July 2, 1935, in *The Green Leaf*, ed. Dickson, p. 68.
20. Grey Owl, *Tales*, p. 83.
21. The house is described in "A Canadian Woman's Diary, Last Week in London," *Canada's Weekly*, December 20, 1935. The street address appears in Lovat Dickson's letter to Hugh Eayrs, dated February 15, 1937, McMASTER.
22. Dickson, *House of Words*, p. 187.
23. Lovat Dickson to Hugh Eayrs, dated May 20, 1938, McMASTER.
24. Birth Certificate, George Furmage Belaney, June 14, 1857, English Register Office, London.
25. Lovat Dickson, "Grey Owl, Man of Wilderness," *Strand Magazine*, May 1936, p. 64.
26. "Thereby Hangs a Tale," *Sunday Mail* (Glasgow), November 3, 1935; "Grey Owl for Lunch," *Weekly Illustrated*, November 2, 1935; details on the life of Lord Sempill appear in the *Dictionary of National Biography, 1961–1970*, pp. 377–79. On the subject of Foyle's Literary Luncheons, see Louise Morgan, "Literary Luncheon. Key Women. Christina Foyle," *News Chronicle*, February 27, 1936.
27. Photo, *Daily Sketch*, November 5, 1935.
28. Dickson, *Half-Breed*, p. 303.
29. Dickson, *Wilderness Man*, p. 242.
30. Trefoil, "Girl Guide Activities," Liverpool *Evening Express*, November 8, 1935. Mark Kerr's mother, Emily Sophia Maitland, was born August 22, 1827, at Stamford Cottage, near Niagara Falls, in present-day Ontario. At the time her father, Sir Peregrine Maitland, served as the lieutenant-governor of Upper Canada. Sir Peregine's wife, Lady Sarah Lennox, was the second daughter of the Duke of Richmond. Rosemary Kerr [daughter of Mark Kerr] to Donald B. Smith, dated London, March 12, 1982.
31. The talk was printed in the BBC magazine, *The Listener*, on November 6, 1935. The comment on his voice appeared in the article, "Interesting New Talk Series by S. P. B. Mais," Worthing *Herald*, November 2, 1935.
32. Lovat Dickson's agreement with the Polytechnic Theatre, November 11, 1935. Peter Davies Papers, Heinemann Group, London; Lovat Dickson to Hugh Eayrs, dated London, December 31, 1935, McMASTER; *To-Day's Cinema*, January 20, 1936.
33. "Grey Owl. Life in the Wild," Ilfracombe *Chronicle*, January 24, 1936.

34. On the impact of the new technology on nature films, see Thomas R. Dunlap, *Saving America's Wildlife* (Princeton, New Jersey: Princeton University Press, 1988), pp. 102–3.
35. For more details on Bill Oliver's career, consult Sheilagh S. Jameson, *W. J. Oliver: Life Through a Master's Lens* (Calgary: Glenbow Museum, 1984). The films used by Grey Owl in Britain, 1935–36, included: "Hunting Without a Gun," "Home of the Buffalo" (both Oliver nature films), as well as the films on Grey Owl—"Beaver People," "Beaver Family," "Strange Doings in Beaverland," "Grey Owl's Neighbours," and "Pilgrims of the Wild" (with the exception of "Beaver People" these were all Oliver films). Grey Owl also had with him two other short silent films: "Sanctuary" (by W. J. Oliver) and "Stalking Big Game." W. Whitaker to Office of the High Commissioner, Canada House, January 3, 1936, RG 25 A–5, vol. 382 (Grey Owl), NAC. In the same file also see the letter Canadian High Commission, London, to J. C. Campbell, dated July 9, 1936.
36. David Thomson, *England in the Twentieth Century* (Harmondsworth, England: Penguin, 1965), pp. 144, 19.
37. Lovat Dickson, *Wilderness Man* (Toronto: Macmillan, 1973), pp. 239–40.
38. Robert Graves and Alan Hodge, *The Long Week-end. A Social History of Great Britain 1918–1939* (Harmondsworth, Middlesex: Penguin Books, 1971; first published in 1940), p. 322.
39. Somervell, "Letters," p. 6, copy in SMITH.
40. "Grey Owl in Glasgow," Glasgow *Evening Citizen*, November 28, 1935.
41. Cynthia, "Through the Looking-Glass. Grey Owl's Visit. Films of his Beaver Friends," *Weekly Scotsman*, December 7, 1935. See also Richard Haestier, "His Mission is to Save Wild Animals," London *Star*, December 14, 1935. Grey Owl also made this assertion in a slightly different fashion in his first book, *The Men of the Last Frontier* (1931), p. 217: "The band of white thrown across a lake at night by the moonbeams, is, to the red man, the path that little children and small animals take when they die; the Silver Trail to the Land of Spirits. All others take the Sunset Trail." The anthropologist Frank Speck did discover in 1913, though, that the Temagami and Lake Temiskaming Indians believed that the spirits of the dead journeyed along the Milky Way, which they termed the "Spirit path." Frank Speck, *Myths and Folk-lore of the Timiskaming Algonquin and Timagami Ojibwa* (Ottawa: Government Printing Bureau, 1915), p. 23.
42. Biographical details on Geoffrey Turner (1910–1984) are taken from his obituary prepared by Colin Taylor in 1984 for the English Westerners' Society, and from information supplied in an interview with his widow, Monica Turner, at Oxford, September 16, 1988.
43. Geoffrey Turner's Diary, entry for January 24, 1936. The excerpt was kindly provided to me by his widow, Monica Turner.
44. Royal B. Hassrick, *The Sioux, Life and Customs of a Warrior Society* (Norman: University of Oklahoma Press, 1964), p. 111.
45. Geoffrey Turner's Diary, entry for January 24, 1936. The excerpt was kindly provided to me by his widow, Monica Turner.
46. The history of the Halton family in Pincher Creek is presented in *Prairie*

Grass to Mountain Pass, History of the Pioneers of Pincher Creek and District (Pincher Creek, Alberta: Pincher Creek Historical Society, 1974), pp. 49–55. Interview with Ernie Halton, a nephew of Matt Halton, Calgary, December 19, 1987. David Halton, political correspondent for the CBC (1989), is the son of Matthew Halton.

47. Matthew Halton, *Ten Years to Alamein* (Toronto: S. J. Reginald Saunders, 1944), p. 41.
48. To be precise, Matt Halton and Grey Owl met between January 28 and 31. Within the story, Grey Owl mentions having seen a Noel Coward play. In Betty Somervell's notes on a copy of the itinerary of the 1935–36 British tour: "January, Mon. 27th [London] Go to Noel Coward." Halton datelined his article January 31, but does not state the precise date that the interview occurred.
49. M. H. Halton, "Grey Owl Seeing London has Trapped Animal Feeling," Toronto *Star,* February 13, 1936.
50. See, for example, the following Canadian papers: "Grey Owl in England," Windsor *Star,* October 26, 1935; "Grey Owl on Lecture Tour," Halifax *Chronicle,* October 30, 1935; Regina *Star,* October 31, 1935; Ottawa *Journal,* October 31, 1935; Calgary *Herald,* November 2, 1935; Victoria *Daily Colonist,* November 5, 1935.
51. Gladys A. Arnold, "Grey Owl and his Beavers, London Sensation," Regina *Leader-Post,* November 27, 1935. The story also appeared in the following newspapers (and probably in many others as well): the Saskatoon *Star-Phoenix,* November 28, 1935; the Winnipeg *Tribune,* November 29, 1935; the Medicine Hat *News,* December 2, 1935.
52. I. A. Matheson, Managing Director, Vancouver Golden Jubilee Committee to Harold W. McGill, Deputy Superintendent General of Indian Affairs, dated Vancouver, February 11, 1936, RG 10, volume 7995, 1/1–15–2–4, NAC. Grey Owl was not able to attend the Vancouver Golden Jubilee. In Saskatchewan, as well, there was also great interest in Grey Owl. Canadian Clubs in Prince Albert, Saskatoon, and Biggar all approached Superintendent Wood of Prince Albert National Park, in February and March 1936, requesting that Grey Owl address them. See PANP.
53. Hugh Eayrs to Colston Leigh, Colston Leigh Inc., dated Toronto, January 30, 1936, McMASTER.
54. "Grey Owl Speaks. Voice of the Western Prairies: 'Modern Hiawatha' at Stratford," Evesham *Journal,* February 15, 1936; Grey Owl, *Tales,* p. 85.
55. Grey Owl, quoted in "Grey Owl Speaks. Voice of the Western Prairies: 'Modern Hiawatha' at Stratford," Evesham *Journal,* February 15, 1936.
56. Grey Owl to Hugh Eayrs, dated London, February 8, 1936, McMASTER.
57. Somervell, "Letters," p. 7, copy in SMITH.
58. Dickson, *Half-Breed,* p. 142.
59. Somervell, "Letters," p. 25, copy in SMITH.
60. "Grey Owl Goes Back," *The Bookseller,* February 19, 1936, p. 169.
61. Somervell, "Letters," p. 7, copy in SMITH.
62. Interview with Ted Blackmore, Eastbourne, Sussex, England, May 19, 1975. Edward H. Blackmore, "Our late dear Friend and brother Chief Os-Ke-Non-Ton

(Running Deer)," *The English Westerners' Tally Sheet,* 23, 1 (October 1976): 5–15.

63. Betty Somervell, Diary, entry for February 15, 1936, copy in SMITH.
64. Betty Somervell, "Letters," p. 7, copy in SMITH.
65. Betty Somervell, Diary, entry for February 14, 1936, copy in SMITH.
66. Grey Owl quoted by "Megaphone," "Ships that Pass. Grey Owl Goes Home," Glasgow *News,* February 17, 1936.
67. Grey Owl quoted by Ross Kennedy, "'Savage' Red Indian Ends Lecture Tour," *Daily Express* (Scottish Edition), February 17, 1936.
68. The story of Grey Owl's drinking on ship is told in: Betty Somervell, Diary, entry for February 15, 1936, copy in SMITH; Somervell, "Letters," p. 8, copy in SMITH.
69. Betty Somervell, Diary, entry for February 20, 1936, copy in SMITH.
70. Betty Somervell, "Letters," p. 9, copy in SMITH.
71. Betty Somervell, Diary, entry for February 21, 1936, copy in SMITH.
72. Archie Belaney, Attestation Paper, ARMY. I was unable to locate any information about anyone by the name of "McVane" at Westfield, New Brunswick, in 1915.
73. Betty Somervell, Diary, entry for February 22, 1936, copy in SMITH.
74. *Canadian Pacific Gazette,* February 19, 1936. Betty Somervell showed me this at her home, Plumgarths, Kendal, England, December 17, 1972.
75. Betty Somervell, Diary, entry for February 23, 1936, copy in SMITH.
76. Dr. John Alford was the doctor. Betty Somervell, Diary, entry for February 24, 1936, copy in SMITH. Grey Owl met James Harkin on February 26. He later sent him a copy of one of his books with this inscription: "To J. B. Harkin. In remembrance of the happy occasion of my first meeting with him." McMASTER. The book was probably *Sajo and her Beaver People.*
77. Betty Somervell, Diary, entry for February 25, 1936, copy in SMITH.
78. Lovat Dickson to Hugh Eayrs, dated London, January 29, 1936, McMASTER.
79. Betty Somervell, Diary, entries for February 25 and 27, 1936, copy in SMITH.
80. Ibid., entry for February 28, 1936, copy in SMITH.

Chapter Twelve. Toronto, March 2, 1936

1. "Mrs. A. Stevens Says Grey Owl is Belaney," North Bay *Nugget,* April 20, 1938, p. 14.
2. William Arthur Deacon, "Christianity Unsuitable for Indians of Canada. Famous Red Man Thinks," Toronto *Mail and Empire,* March 2, 1936.
3. Arthur Stevens, J.P. to A. C. March, K.C., dated December 26, 1936, typewritten copy in the North Bay *Nugget's* news morgue. See also the transcript of the letter in the Toronto *Star,* April 16, 1938, in the article on Grey Owl by Claud Pascoe.
4. Grey Owl to Arthur Stevens, dated Beaver Lodge, Prince Albert National Park, February 24, 1935. Phil Chester obtained the photostats of the original letter from the owner of a used book store in Stouffville, Ontario. The photostats bear the annotation: "No. 4 Belaney vs. Perrier et al. This Exhibit the Property of Plaintiff is produced by the Plaintiff Solicitor this 10th day of Oct. 1939. A. B. Girard, Examiner." The letter was brought forward at

the Grey Owl Estate Trial. A slightly altered transcription of the letter appeared in the Toronto *Star,* April 16, 1938.

5. Interview with Agnes Belaney Lalonde, North Bay, April 29, 1973.
6. Editorial "Severe Loss to the North," Cochrane *Northland Post,* December 23, 1937.
7. Arthur Stevens, J.P. to A. C. March, K.C., dated December 26, 1936, typewritten copy in the North Bay *Nugget's* news morgue.
8. Arthur Steven's diary entry for March 2, 1936, cited in "Mrs. A. Stevens Says Grey Owl is Belaney," North Bay *Nugget,* April 20, 1938, p. 14.
9. James Lemon, *Toronto Since 1918, An Illustrated History* (Toronto: James Lorimer, 1985), pp. 56–57; W. A. Deacon, "Toronto," *Canadian Geographical Journal,* 2 (1931): 340.
10. On R. E. Knowles, see Ross Harkness, *J. E. Atkinson of the Star* (Toronto: University of Toronto Press, 1963), pp. 166–68; and the sketch by Jock Carroll in *The Life and Times of Greg Clark* (Toronto: Doubleday Canada, 1981), pp. 174–75.
11. R. E. Knowles, "White Man's Religion Boon to Indian, Says Grey Owl," Toronto *Star,* March 3, 1936.
12. Betty Somervell, Diary, entry for March 2, 1936, copy in SMITH.
13. The club's membership included E. J. Pratt, poet; C. W. Jeffreys, artist; Sir Charles G. D. Roberts, writer; Gordon Sinclair, journalist. Clara Thomas and John Lennox, *William Arthur Deacon. A Canadian Literary Life* (Toronto: University of Toronto Press, 1982), p. 135.
14. Hugh Eayrs to Lovat Dickson, dated Toronto, March 9, 1936 (dictated March 8, 1936), McMASTER.
15. A short sketch of the Rev. James Endicott's life appears in *The Canadian Encyclopedia* (4 vols., Edmonton: Hurtig, 1988), vol. 2, p. 697.
16. Richard Faries quoted in, "Dr. J. Endicott Says Time Not Religion's Test," Toronto *Star,* March 2, 1936. For a sketch of Archdeacon Richard Faries' life see his "Autobiography" in the *Journal of the Canadian Church Historical Society,* 15, 1 (March 1973): 14-23. Richard Faries, ed., *A Dictionary of the Cree Language as spoken by the Indians in the Provinces of Quebec, Ontario, Manitoba, Saskatchewan and Alberta* (Toronto: The General Synod of the Church of England in Canada, 1938).
17. "Grey Owl Answers Christian Protests," Toronto *Mail,* March 3, 1936.
18. The visit is recorded in Mrs. Somervell's diary, "Mr. and Mrs. Stevens of Temagami, appeared, who had known him 25 years ago, and were as friendly and affectionate as if he'd been their son. Then Donalda Legace, daughter of his old friend Mrs. Legace, who was so good to him and is dead; a delightful woman entirely with a nice husband." Entry for March 2, 1936. My description of all events at the Rotenberg's on March 3, 1936, is also taken from Betty Somervell's diary, copy in SMITH. Donalda Legace died in the 1950s. I learned a great deal about the family's friendship with Archie Belaney from her brother, Ferg, and her older sister, Célina. Interviews with Ferg Legace, Owen Sound, June 12, 1971; and Petawawa, Ontario, August 5, 1972; and with Célina Legace Barnes, Thunder Bay, Ontario, July 14, 1971. Ferg also allowed me to see a manuscript he had written in 1971-72 about his early days,

referred to in subsequent footnotes as his "Memoirs." Pension file, Department of Veterans Affairs, cited in Thomas Raddall, "Grey Owl" in *Footsteps on Old Floors* (Garden City, N.J.: Doubleday, 1968), p. 118.

19. Betty Somervell, "Letters to my Daughter," 1953, p. 12, copy in SMITH.
20. Typescript of CBC "Man at the Centre," interview with Ted Cusson, mid-January 1972, SMITH. This story actually occurred in the early 1920s, after the war.
21. Betty Somervell, Diary, entry for March 3, 1936, copy in SMITH.
22. The Archives of the Arts and Letters Club in Toronto, 14 Elm Street, has the copy of *Sajo* containing Lismer's sketch.
23. Betty Somervell, Diary, entries for March 5, 6, 7, et. seq., copy in SMITH.
24. Hugh Eayrs to Lovat Dickson, dated Toronto, April 7, 1936, McMASTER.
25. Hugh Eayrs to Lovat Dickson, dated Toronto, March 9, 1936 (dictated March 8, 1936), McMASTER.

Chapter Thirteen. The Mission

1. Interview with John Tootoosis, Poundmaker Reserve, Saskatchewan, October 20, 1974; Norma Sluman and Jean Goodwill, *John Tootoosis. A biography of a Cree Leader* (Ottawa: Golden Dog Press, 1982), pp. 168–69. The description of their first meeting in Ottawa is based on these two sources.
2. John Tootoosis, quoted in Blair Stonechild, *Saskatchewan Indians and the Resistance of 1885. Two Case Studies* (Regina: Saskatchewan Education, 1986), p. 49.
3. For a study of the League of Indians of Western Canada, the Indian organization to which John Tootoosis belonged, see Stan Cuthand, "The Native Peoples of the Prairie Provinces in the 1920s and 1930s," in *One Century Later. Western Canadian Reserve Indians since Treaty 7*, ed. by Ian A. L. Getty and Donald B. Smith (Vancouver: University of British Columbia Press, 1978), pp. 31–35. For copies of the resolutions prepared in 1933, see the enclosures within John Tootoosis' letter to the Department of Indian Affairs, Ottawa, dated December 22, 1933, RG 10, vol. 3211, file 527,787, NAC. The resolutions of the convention of the League of Indians of Canada, held at Poundmaker Reserve, are dated July 10–12, 1933.
4. Norma Sluman to Donald Smith, dated Mississauga, Ontario, September 26, 1978. We know that Grey Owl stayed at the Plaza Hotel from a note of a telephone message taken by "HRLH," for Prime Minister King. See HRLH's memo, dated March 11, 1936, Mackenzie King Papers, MG 26 J1, vol. 217, file 1936—GRAV, p. 186260, NAC. According to the *Ottawa City Directory* for 1936, the Plaza Hotel was located at 219–233 Sparks (p. 455).
5. Sluman and Goodwill, *Tootoosis*, p 169.
6. David G. Mandelbaum, *Anthropology and People: The World of the Plains Cree*, University of Saskatchewan University Lectures, no. 12 (1967), p. 10. Dr. Mandelbaum did field work among the Plains Cree in the mid-1930s.
7. J. D. McLean to Jim Menahwestguan et al., October 2, 1920, c/o T. J. Godfrey, Indian Agent, Chapleau, RG 10, vol. 3180, file 412065. See also other letters in this file. Over half-a-century later, the Temagami case still remains unresolved.

8. Waiser, *Park*, pp. 40–41, 55. Grey Owl visited the Montreal Lake band once, or at least met Edward Ross, Chief Senior Councillor of the band. There are notes on an interview with him in Grey Owl's Notebook, n.d., #1, GREY OWL.

9. Grey Owl, *Men*, p. 212.

10. Selwyn Dewdney mentions blue-eyed Ojibwa Indians in northern Ontario who spoke no English in "The World of Norval Morriseau," in *Legends of My People. The Great Ojibway* by Norval Morriseau (Toronto: Ryerson, 1965), p. xvii.

11. David G. Mandelbaum, *The Plains Cree* (Regina: Canadian Plains Research Centre, 1979; first published in 1940), p. 10.

12. John Tootoosis quoted in Sluman and Goodwill, *Tootoosis*, p. 169.

13. Interview with John Tootoosis, Poundmaker Reserve, Saskatchewan, October 20, 1974.

14. Buffalo National Park was later closed and the buffalo there transferred to Wood Buffalo National Park in northeastern Alberta, established in 1922.

15. Grey Owl, *Pilgrims*, p. 53.

16. Grey Owl, *Tales*, pp. vii–viii.

17. T. J. D. Powell, "Northern Settlement, 1929–1935," *Saskatchewan History*, 30, 3 (Autumn 1977): 81–88, reprinted in Michiel Horn, ed., *The Depression in Canada. Responses to Economic Crisis* (Toronto: Copp Clark Pitman Ltd., 1988), pp. 51–73; see particularly p. 70. Between 1930 and 1936, 35,000 to 45,000 people moved into northern Saskatchewan (p. 72).

18. Roderick Nash, "Wilderness Man in North America," *The Canadian National Parks. Today and Tomorrow*, volume 1, ed. J. G. Nelson and R. C. Scace (Calgary: University of Calgary, 1968), pp. 1–31.

19. Grey Owl, *Pilgrims*, p. 203.

20. Grey Owl, *Tales*, pp. viii–ix.

21. Grey Owl to James Wood, dated August 21, 1936, Beaver File, PANP.

22. Grey Owl to Bill Somervell, dated May 6, 1936, GREY OWL.

23. Lovat Dickson to Hugh Eayrs, dated April 27, 1937, McMASTER.

24. Lovat Dickson, "Grey Owl, Man of the Wilderness," *Strand Magazine*, May 1936, p. 64.

25. R. E. Rashley, "Grey Owl and the Authentic Frontier," *The English Quarterly*, 4, 3 (Fall 1971): 63.

26. Grey Owl to Lovat Dickson, May 4, 1936, McMASTER. He intended to write his historical novel on "the old Indian and French wars around 1750–60–70 in Canada." See his letter to Lovat Dickson, dated March 17, 1935, in *The Green Leaf*, ed. Dickson, p. 60. Grey Owl's lecture tour and film ideas are outlined in a letter from Lovat Dickson to Hugh Eayrs, dated January 29, 1936, McMASTER.

27. Grey Owl to Ellen Elliott, dated May 1936, McMASTER.

28. On Grey Owl's relations with the other Wardens consult: Interview of Francis Mildred Martin by Jackie Keesey, completed 1986, Prince Albert National Park Library, Waskesiu, Saskatchewan; Emmet Millard, interviewed by Georgean Short, May 15, 1971, in SHORT; B. I. M. Strong, interviewed by Georgean Short, May 26, 1971, in SHORT; interview with Wally Laird, Calgary, August 30, 1988; Bill Waiser, *Saskatchewan's Playground. A History of Prince Albert National Park* (Saskatoon: Fifth House Publishers, 1989), p. 82.

29. Grey Owl to Anahareo, undated letter fragment, written in late 1934, Grey Owl Collection, NAC.

30. Grey Owl, Notebook 'A', 1936, GREY OWL.

31. "Received at Rideau Hall," Ottawa *Journal*, March 10, 1936. Lord Tweedsmuir received Grey Owl, the mayor of Ottawa, and the president of the Press Gallery on March 9, 1936. For Lady Tweedsmuir's comments see "Oxfordshire Women's Institutes," *The Oxford Times*, July 1, 1938, p. 12, c. 5. Her son's remarks appear in his book, John Buchan, *Always a Countryman* (London: Robert Hale Ltd., 1953), p. 237.

32. Janet Adam Smith, *John Buchan. A Biography* (London: Rupert Hart-Davis, 1965), p. 392; Janet Adam Smith, *John Buchan and his World* (New York: Scribner's, 1979), p. 105.

33. Guy Clarence Vanderhaeghe, "John Buchan: Conservatism, Imperialism and Social Reconstruction." M.A. thesis (History), University of Saskatchewan (1975), p. 7.

34. The same Guy Clarence Vanderhaeghe would win one of these awards in 1982, the fiction award in English for his novel *Man Descending*. See *The Canadian Encyclopedia* (4 vols., Edmonton: Hurtig, 1988), vol. 1, p. 291; vol. 2, p. 920.

35. F. H. H. Williamson, Controller, National Parks Board, to J. M. Wardle, Deputy Minister of the Interior, dated March 20, 1936, Mackenzie King Papers, MG 25, J, 4, vol. 170, file 1579, p. C–121314, NAC.

36. Grey Owl to Bill Somervell, dated May 6, 1936, GREY OWL.

37. Thanks to a daily journal kept by Burgon Bickersteth, the warden of Hart House at the University of Toronto, the dinner can be dated, as well as its location. Burgeon Bickersteth Journal for 1936, entry for Friday, March 13, 1936, Hart House Records (A73–0050/151), University of Toronto Archives, Toronto. My thanks to Sharon Larade, reference archivist, for this item. I subsequently learned that Grey Owl signed the guest book at Laurier House on this date, giving his address as "Prince Albert National Park." Paul M. Couture to Donald B. Smith, August 28, 1989.

38. W. L. Mackenzie King to H. S. Eayrs, dated April 13, 1936, King Papers, MG 26, J 1, v. 216, p. 186267, NAC.

39. Mackenzie King Diary, typescript on microfiche, fiche 102, entry for Friday, March 13, 1936, NAC.

40. Bruce Hutchinson, *The Incredible Canadian. A candid portrait of Mackenzie King: his works, his times, and his nation* (Don Mills, Ontario: Longmans Canada, 1970; first published in 1952), p. 80. Hutchinson was a frequent visitor at Laurier House in the 1940s. My thanks to Pat Brennan for this information.

41. Grey Owl to Hugh Eayrs and Lovat Dickson, May 9, 1936, McMASTER.

42. Hugh Eayrs to Lovat Dickson, dated April 21, 1936, McMASTER.

43. According to the *Ottawa City Directory*, 1936, Karsh's studio was on 130 Sparks (p. 282), and the Plaza Hotel at 219–223 Sparks (p. 455).

44. Yousuf Karsh, *Karsh Canadians* (Toronto: University of Toronto Press, 1978), pp. 68–69. Mr. Karsh's dinner must have been held in mid-March 1936. Grey Owl was once again in Ottawa, alone, in late November 1936, but on that occasion he mostly stayed at J. C. Campbell's cottage in the Gatineau Hills, not at a hotel. Hugh Eayrs to Lovat Dickson, dated December 4, 1936,

McMASTER. Initially he had taken a room at the Grads Hotel, 687–691 Somerset St. W., but this hotel was far from Karsh's studio on Sparks St.—it is unlikely that the photographer could leave his guests and quickly run over to the Grads Hotel, as he could to the Plaza, which was almost next door. The *Ottawa City Directory*, 1936, contains the address of the Grads Hotel (p. 225). Grey Owl mentioned that he planned to stay there in a note dated November 22, 1936, to his lawyer in Prince Albert, Cy March, FRASER.

45. Hugh Eayrs to Lovat Dickson, dated April 7, 1936, McMASTER.

46. Grey Owl to Hugh Eayrs, dated April 23, 1936, McMASTER.

47. Grey Owl to Hugh Eayrs and Lovat Dickson, dated May 9, 1936. Macmillan Archives, McMASTER.

48. Ellen Elliott, Hugh Eayrs' secretary, mentions the amount of the allowance in a letter to Lovat Dickson, dated April 14, 1937 (p. 12), McMASTER. Grey Owl's salary was $1320 per annum. See "Notification to Department" form, dated March 28, 1934, PERSONNEL FILE. The Parks knew him as Archibald Belaney, and they issued his cheques to him in this name.

49. References to Grey Owl's separation from Anahareo: Grey Owl to Hugh Eayrs and Lovat Dickson, dated May 9, 1936, McMASTER; Grey Owl to Betty Somervell, dated April 24, 1936, GREY OWL; Anahareo, *Deerskins*, p. 175; Ellen Elliott to Lovat Dickson, dated April 14, 1937 (p. 12), McMASTER.

50. J. B. Harkin, Commissioner, National Parks of Canada, to R. A. Gibson, Assistant Deputy Minister of the Interior, dated April 25, 1936, PERSONNEL FILE.

51. Grey Owl to Ettie Winters, probably written in May or June 1935, GREY OWL.

52. Grey Owl's telegram to Hugh Eayrs, dated May 18, 1936, McMASTER, indicates he has just received the news of the government's refusal.

53. F. H. H. Williamson, Controller, National Parks Board, to J. M. Wardle, Deputy Minister of the Interior, dated March 20, 1936, Mackenzie King Papers, MG 25, J, 4, vol. 170, file 1579, p. C–121314, NAC.

54. Hugh Eayrs to Mackenzie King, dated March 5, 1936, King Papers, MG 26, J, 1, vol. 216, p. 186259, NAC.

55. W. L. Mackenzie King to H. S. Eayrs, dated April 13, 1936, King Papers, MG 26, J, 1, vol. 216, pp. 186266–68, NAC.

56. Grey Owl to Hugh Eayrs and Lovat Dickson, dated May 9, 1936, McMASTER.

57. Hugh Eayrs to Lovat Dickson, dated April 21, 1936, McMASTER.

58. "'Grey Owl's' Quest," Hastings *Observer*, June 6, 1936. See also chapter one, footnote 26.

59. Lovat Dickson to Hugh Eayrs, dated January 29, 1936, McMASTER.

60. At least one story from *Canadian Forest and Outdoors* appears almost verbatim in *Tales*. Chapter five even has the same title as the earlier article in *Canadian Forest and Outdoors*, April 1931 (pp. 177–80), "A Day in a Hidden Town."

61. The figure of 700 guests is mentioned in the interview with Stan Winters by Georgean Short, July 2, 1971, SHORT. See also "Grey Owl to be Guest Speaker at Book Fair," Prince Albert *Herald*, November 3, 1936. The *Herald* wrote that "close to a thousand visitors from Canada, Great Britain, and the United States" came in 1936 to visit Grey Owl at Beaver Lodge.

62. See Grey Owl's correspondence with his Canadian publishers, Macmillans, throughout the summer of 1936, McMASTER.
63. Grey Owl, *Tales*, pp. 255–56.
64. "Beaver Man," *Time*, 28 (December 21, 1936), p. 63.
65. L. R. H. "Grey Owl Pleads to Save Canada's Forest Heritage," Winnipeg *Free Press*, March 20, 1937; see also B. G. R., "A New Grey Owl," Toronto *Globe and Mail*, December 5, 1936; and W. R. C., "The Outdoors from an Arm Chair," Montreal *Gazette*, December 26, 1936.
66. M. Q. Innis, "Review: *Tales of an Empty Cabin* by Grey Owl," *Canadian Historical Review*, 18 (1937), p. 97.
67. Grey Owl to Hugh Eayrs, dated July 2, 1936, McMASTER.
68. Grey Owl, *Tales*, p. 214 (his description of a long, smooth-flowing stretch of the Mississagi), pp. 171–72 (on the canoemen).
69. Ibid., pp. 143–44.
70. H. S. Winters to Hugh Eayrs, dated August 12, 1936, McMASTER.
71. "Crees Lose Great Friend, Great Chief," Saskatoon *Star-Phoenix*, February 19, 1940.
72. "Indian Seek Better Status," Regina *Leader-Post*, August 14, 1936, p. 11.
73. Stan Cuthand to Donald B. Smith, dated Saskatoon, Saskatchewan, and mailed in early August 1988. This four-page letter fully describes Grey Owl's participation at the Fort Carlton council, copy in SMITH.
74. Grey Owl's words recalled in a letter from Stan Cuthand to Donald B. Smith, dated early August 1988.
75. Interview with Stan Cuthand, at Brandon, Manitoba, November 5, 1981, and a telephone interview with him in Saskatoon, August 9, 1988.
76. Marius Barbeau, "Our Indians—Their Disappearance," *Queen's Quarterly*, 38 (1931): 705. On the deep-rooted prejudice against Indians in Canada in the period between 1920 and 1930, see Diamond Jenness, "Canada's Indians Yesterday. What of Today?", *Canadian Journal of Economics and Political Sciences*, 20, 1 (February 1954): 95–100.
77. Grey Owl to J. A. Wood, dated August 21, 1936, PANP.

Chapter Fourteen. Salute a Great Canadian

1. Somervell, "Letters," p. 23, copy in SMITH. The photo referred to appears on the back of this book. Mrs. Somervell shot it on her Kodak 620 camera. Interview with Kristin Bonney, Calgary, May 29, 1989.
2. By early October, Anahareo had reached Vancouver, on her way to California. See "Mrs. Grey Owl's Amazing Life Story," Vancouver *Sun*, October 6, 1936.
3. Lovat Dickson to Hugh Eayrs, dated November 13, 1936, McMASTER.
4. See the photo of Lord Tweedsmuir at Beaver Lodge reproduced in Janet Smith, *John Buchan and his world* (New York: Charles Scribner's Sons, 1975), p. 105.
5. Janet Smith, *John Buchan* (London: Rupert Hart-Davis, 1965), p. 392; "Viceregal Holiday Ends," Montreal *Gazette*, September 29, 1936.
6. Grey Owl to John Tootoosis, dated September 30, 1936, FRASER.
7. Grey Owl is quoted in "Grey Owl asks wildlife to be put in Indians' care," Toronto *Star*, November 9, 1936. The Bagot Commission of 1842 to 1844

made this recommendation. See James Douglas Leighton, "The Development of Federal Indian Policy in Canada, 1840–1890," Ph.D. thesis (History), University of Western Ontario, 1975, p. 111.

8. C. Alexandra Dick to Lovat Dickson, dated August 18, 1936, McMASTER; Lovat Dickson to Hugh Eayrs, dated August 20, 1936, McMASTER; Grey Owl to Herb Winters, dated September 1, 1936, GREY OWL; Grey Owl to Ellen Elliott, dated September 5, 1936, McMASTER; Lovat Dickson to Hugh Eayrs, dated September 11, 1936, McMASTER.

9. Photo, Olga Pavlova, Regina *Leader-Post*, December 6, 1938; *Henderson's Greater Regina Directory*, 1936, p. 459; *Directory*, 1937, p. 456; *Directory*, 1938, p. 459; Henry Scheer to Donald B. Smith, dated Regina, July 24, 1988 (Mr. Scheer knew Olga Pavlova, and I am very grateful for his help in completing this sketch of her).

10. Will of Archie McNeil, "familiarly known as Grey Owl," November 4, 1936, FRASER.

11. Hugh Eayrs to Lovat Dickson, dated November 20, 1936, McMASTER. "Grey Owl wants to settle down and get married! He tells me of a lady in Regina, a Ukrainian: musical, gifted and artistic, in whom he is extremely interested, and rather indicates that that should be the lady. Unfortunately, she, herself, is married at present!"

12. Hugh Eayrs to Lovat Dickson, dated December 4, 1936, McMASTER.

13. "Wilderness Life Cleverly Depicted by Grey Owl in Films and Lecture," Regina *Leader-Post*, March 30, 1938, p. 6.

14. Interview with Yvonne Perrier, Ottawa, May 10, 1971.

15. W. A. Deacon to Grey Owl, dated April 24, 1935, DEACON; in a letter to Grey Owl dated June 9, 1935, the book critic identifies Sandy MacDonald, a northern Ontario bushpilot, as his source of information, DEACON.

16. James Wood to J. C. Campbell, dated June 18, 1935, J. A. Wood Confidential File, Prince Albert National Park Library, Waskesiu, Saskatchewan. Grey Owl "went to town on the 9th of May to have his picture taken for the cover of his new book [*Sajo*] and, although a number of searches were made, we did not locate him until around the end of the month."

17. Grey Owl to W. A. Deacon, dated May 10, 1935, DEACON. Almost all of Grey Owl's letter is reprinted in Clara Thomas and John Lennox, *William Arthur Deacon. A Canadian Literary Life* (Toronto: University of Toronto Press, 1982), pp. 153–56. It is fascinating to follow how the racial background of Grey Owl's "Indian" mother was altered by its creator. In 1931 he told *Canadian Forest and Outdoors* (March 1931, p. 118) that she was a member of the Jicarilla Apache band. He said to Sir Charles G. D. Roberts, whom he met at Riding Mountain National Park in October 1931 and later in Toronto in November 1936, that his mother was a "half-breed Apache Indian." See the entry for "Grey Owl (Wa-sha-quon-asin)," in *The Canadian Who's Who*, ed. Sir Charles G. D. Roberts and Arthur Leonard Tunnell, vol. 2, 1936–37, p. 447. To Marion Gridley, the compiler of *Indians of Today* (Chicago: Indian Council Fire, 1936), he reported he was "Apache-three-eights" (p. 60), which would have made his mother three-quarters Indian! His father is always presented as white.

18. W. A. Deacon to Grey Owl, dated June 9, 1935, DEACON.
19. William Arthur Deacon, "Christianity Unsuitable for Indians of Canada Famous Red Man Thinks. Grey Owl, as Author, was lionized at 200 Meetings Overseas," Toronto *Mail and Empire*, March 2, 1936.
20. William Arthur Deacon, "Friends Sure of Half-Breed in Grey Owl," Toronto *Globe and Mail*, April 16, 1938.
21. William Arthur Deacon, "To the Portals of the Sunset," a four-page handout prepared by Macmillan after Grey Owl's death on April 13, 1938, copy in SMITH.
22. W. A. Deacon's name appears in the lists of forest rangers in the summers of 1907, 1908, and 1909, see the Ontario Legislative Assembly, Sessional Papers, 40, pt. 1 (1908), p. 33; 41, pt. 1 (1909), p. 32; 42, pt. 2 (1910), p. 34.
23. Hugh Eayrs to Harry Burton, dated December 1, 1936, Box 20, folder 5, Book Fair 1936, McMASTER; Hugh Eayrs to Lovat Dickson, dated December 4, 1936, McMASTER.
24. See the book fair's program for the list of speakers and activities, Box 20, folder 5, Book Fair 1936, McMASTER. Hugh Eayrs, the chairman of the book fair, believed that the largest crowd was at the opening, when Grey Owl spoke. See Hugh Eayrs to Harry Burton, dated December 1, 1935, Box 20, folder 5, Book Fair 1936, McMASTER. In a letter to Lovat Dickson on November 20, 1936, Hugh Eayrs wrote: "As to Grey Owl he, of course, stole the Fair. He was absolutely magnificent," McMASTER. The Toronto bookseller, Dora Hood, also recalled that "the biggest drawing card of the first Fair was Grey Owl." See *The Side Door: Twenty-Six Years in My Book Room* (Toronto: Ryerson, 1958), p. 229.
25. Grey Owl mentioned the title of his talk in a press interview the day before. William Arthur Deacon, "Famed Canvases Found in Cabin," Toronto *Mail and Empire*, November 9, 1936.
26. Grey Owl, quoted in "Book Fair Opening Gathers 2,000. Grey Owl Given Ovation as He Appears on Platform," Toronto *Mail and Empire*, November 10, 1936.
27. Hugh Eayrs to Lovat Dickson, dated November 20, 1936, McMASTER; Hugh Eayrs to Colston Leigh, dated December 30, 1936, McMASTER.
28. "Says West not Wild until Whites Came," Toronto *Star*, November 11, 1936; "Famous Grey Owl Luncheon Guest of Press Club," Toronto *Globe and Mail*, November 11, 1936. Lucy Maud Montgomery's comments on the luncheon appear in a letter to Ephraim Weber, June 18, 1937, Ephraim Weber Papers, MG 30 D 36, NAC. My thanks to Virginia Careless for the reference.
29. William Arthur Deacon, "Canadian Unity Book Fair Theme," Toronto *Mail and Empire*, November 12, 1936.
30. On Marius Barbeau's life, see Nansi Swayze, *Canadian Portraits, Jenness, Barbeau, Wintemberg. The Man Hunters* (Toronto: Clarke, Irwin & Co., 1960), pp. 101–40.
31. The two eagle feathers were loaned to J. C. Campbell of the National Parks Branch at the request of Grey Owl on October 4, 1935. Edward Sapir of the museum had obtained them on the Sarcee Reserve near Calgary in 1922. According to Sapir's notes, eagle plumes were worn attached to the hair to show the number of enemies killed by the wearer in war. "In earlier days

no one would wear an eagle plume unless he had killed an enemy." The National Museum of Canada still (1988) has the original loan card, catalogue number V–D–169. Sapir's notes are on the card. On April 28, 1936 (PANP), J. C. Campbell of the Parks Branch wrote Superintendent Wood: "Just prior to Grey Owl's departure for England last Fall, this office borrowed for him from the Museum here, a set of Eagle's feathers to be used by him as part of his Indian attire for his public appearances. These feathers have been definitely catalogued in the Museum and are, of course, considered by them as quite valuable, so you will realize the difficulty we are in, in not being able to return them, since Grey Owl, unfortunately, neglected to hand them back to us . . . if they are still in his possession, secure them and return to this office with as little delay as possible." According to museum records (1988), the feathers were never returned.

32. Marius Barbeau, "Our Indians—Their Disappearance," *Queen's Quarterly*, 38 (1931): 692.

33. The luncheon's location is mentioned in a review of the talk, "Gives Beaver killing as Drought's Cause," Toronto *Star*, November 12, 1936. William A. Deacon states the Royal York was the largest hotel in the British Empire in his article, "Toronto," *Canadian Geographical Journal*, 2 (1931): 341.

34. For an estimate of the number attending the luncheon, see Hugh Eayrs to Colston Leigh, dated December 2, 1936, McMASTER.

35. Grey Owl, "A Plea for the Canadian Northland," in *Empire Club of Canada. Addresses Delivered to the Members during the Year 1936–37* (Toronto: Printers Guild Limited, 1937), p. 95.

36. "Canon Cody believes he is kin of the famous 'Buffalo Bill'," Toronto *Star*, November 23, 1931. They were indeed distant cousins; see Luther Morrill Cody and Ernest William Cody, *The Cody Family Directory, 1936. Descendants of Philip and Martha LeCody at Beverly, Massachusetts, 1695* (n.p., n.d.), pp. 14–15, 27.

37. Hugh Eayrs to Lovat Dickson, dated December 4, 1936, McMASTER.

38. John Morgan Gray, *Fun Tomorrow* (Toronto: Macmillan, 1978), p. 216.

39. Grey Owl, "A Plea for the Canadian Northland," in *Empire Club of Canada. Addresses Delivered to the Members during the Year 1936–37* (Toronto: Printers Guild Limited, 1937), p. 102.

40. "Salute a Great Canadian," *Canadian Magazine*, December 1936, p. 1.

41. Lloyd Roberts, "Grey Owl: Beaver Man," script 4, p. 5. Mrs. Lloyd Roberts showed me this manuscript in January 1971—it was prepared in 1950.

42. Lloyd Roberts, *Along the Ottawa. A Book of Lyrics* (Toronto: J. M. Dent and Sons Ltd., 1927). The inscription reads, "To my friends the 'Grey Owls' and to the 'Little People' asleep under the snow. How Kola! Lloyd Roberts. Rawhide Lake, March 10, 1931." Grey Owl's daughter Dawn showed me this book of her father's.

43. Ibid., pp. 39, 27.

44. Lloyd Roberts, "Grey Owl: Beaver Man," script 13. Mrs. Lloyd Roberts showed me this manuscript in January 1971—it was prepared in 1950.

45. Lloyd Roberts recorded his memories of the meeting in his manuscript, "Brother to the Beaver," prepared in 1950, and shown to me by Mrs. Lloyd

Roberts in January 1971 (pp. 153–54); and in "The Causerie," Winnipeg *Free Press,* July 2, 1948.

46. For a short review of Elizabeth Smith Shortt's life, see the introduction by Veronica Strong-Boag to *'A Woman With a Purpose.' The Diaries of Elizabeth Smith 1872–1884,* ed. Veronica Strong-Boag (Toronto: University of Toronto Press, 1980), pp. vii–xxxviii.

47. Elizabeth Smith Shortt, quoted in Gregory Clark, "Estate of Grey Owl may be near $100,000. Will probated soon," Toronto *Star,* June 30, 1938.

48. Yvonne's name and address appears in Grey Owl's Notebook "A" 1936, GREY OWL.

49. Handwritten note reporting the telegram message and dated November 22, 1936, FRASER.

50. Cy March to Arthur Stevens, dated November 26, 1936, FRASER.

51. Gregory Clark, "Estate of Grey Owl," Toronto *Star,* June 30, 1938.

52. The marriage registry of St. James United Church lists Grey Owl's name and parents in the following manner: "Archie McNeil, bachelor of legal age of Prince Albert, Saskatchewan, son of late Geo. McNeil of Arizona and his wife late Catherine Cochise." My thanks to Anne Donnelly, secretary of St. James United Church for this reference. As soon as he had arrived back in Canada after the first British tour, Grey Owl had begun publicly referring to himself as "Archie McNeil." See "Grey Owl at Halifax," Prince Albert *Herald,* February 21, 1936. The selection of "Cochise" as his mother's family name is an interesting twist. Cochise was a famous mid-nineteenth century chief of the Chiricahua band of Apaches, who lived to the southwest of the Jicarilla band. This new detail about his Apache past allowed Grey Owl to tell Yvonne that his "mother was a near relation of the great Indian Chief Geronimo" ("Grey Owl Indian, Says His Widow Denying 'Gossip'," Regina *Leader-Post,* April 20, 1938). Geronimo was also a celebrated Chiricahua leader.

53. The only surviving copy of Arthur Stevens' reply is in the Grey Owl file of the news morgue of the North Bay *Nugget,* North Bay, Ontario. It is dated December 26, 1936, and addressed to A. C. March. A slightly altered version appeared in the Toronto *Star,* April 16, 1938, in the article by Claud Pascoe.

54. "Grey Owl Indian, Says His Widow Denying 'Gossip'," Regina *Leader-Post,* April 20, 1938.

55. Grey Owl's telephone message to Hugh Eayrs, February 3, 1937, McMASTER. Sheilagh S. Jameson, *W. J. Oliver, Life Through a Master's Lens* (Calgary: Glenbow Museum, 1984), p. 80.

56. Hugh Eayrs to Lovat Dickson, dated February 24, 1937, and March 5, 1937, McMASTER; Lovat Dickson to Hugh Eayrs, dated February 19, 1937, McMASTER.

57. Interview by telephone with Mort Fellman, North Bay, Ontario, March 23, 1988.

58. B. J. Bach to Hugh Eayrs, dated April 26, 1938, McMASTER. B. J. Bach met Grey Owl in North Bay on March 4, 1937. See Grey Owl's telegram to Hugh Eayrs, dated Sioux Lookout, March 3, 1937, McMASTER. By March 5, 1937, Bert Bach had returned to Toronto. See Hugh Eayrs to Lovat

Dickson, dated March 5, 1937, McMASTER. The date of Grey Owl's interview with Mort Fellman (for which Bert Bach was present) was then Thursday, March 4, 1937.

59. "Publisher's Note," in Grey Owl, *Men*, p. v.
60. Jim Graham to Donald B. Smith, dated Troon, Scotland, March 14, 1989.
61. Britt Jessup to Donald B. Smith, dated May 17, 1971; Britt Jessup to Donald B. Smith, dated April 15, 1988.
62. Further details on the lives of both Ed Bunyan and Mort Fellman can be obtained from their obituaries: "Edward H. Bunyan of the Journal Dies at his Home," Ottawa *Journal*, December 5, 1952, p. 24; and "Mort Fellman, first reporter to tell world of Dionne quints," Toronto *Sunday Star*, November 13, 1988, p. A24 (my thanks to J. Patrick O'Callaghan for this reference).
63. Michiel Horn, "The Great Depression: Past and Present," *Journal of Canadian Studies*, 11, no. 1 (February 1976): 41.

Chapter Fifteen. The Summer of 1937

1. Grey Owl to Hugh Eayrs, dated January 27, 1937, McMASTER.
2. Grey Owl to Betty Somervell, early 1937, GREY OWL.
3. Ellen Elliott to Lovat Dickson, dated April 14, 1937, McMASTER.
4. Ibid.
5. Ibid.
6. Grey Owl to W. A. Deacon, dated May 13, 1937, DEACON.
7. Ibid. The moose's name appears in Anahareo, *Deerskins*, p. 154.
8. Grey Owl, *Tales*, p. 235.
9. Grey Owl to Lovat and Marguerite Dickson, dated May 4, 1936, McMASTER.
10. Grey Owl to Hugh Eayrs, dated May 14, 1937, McMASTER.
11. Grey Owl and Yvonne signed the visitors' register at the Bisco school on June 8, 1937. Mary Kohls showed me this in Bisco on June 5, 1973. At this time he gave three of his books to the school. See "People of Biscotasing Friends of 'Grey Owl'," Ottawa *Citizen*, April 18, 1938. This same article states that their canoe trip lasted two weeks.
12. Grey Owl described the best time for canoeing the Mississagi in the letter to Lovat and Marguerite Dickson, dated May 4, 1936, McMASTER.
13. Grey Owl to Lovat and Marguerite Dickson, dated May 4, 1937, McMASTER. Alex had died on August 9, 1936. Interview with Jane Espaniel McKee, Toronto, September 29, 1987.
14. On October 4, 1935, he had sent a telegram to Ellen Elliott from Biscotasing, "Not Passing Toronto Sorry Regards," McMASTER.
15. Grey Owl, *Tales*, pp. 168–69.
16. Ibid., p. 174. In reference to footnotes 16, 17, and 19, Ken Conibear wrote in August 1989 in his evaluation of my manuscript: "I'm glad you've included these passages from *Tales of an Empty Cabin*. They're Archie at his best— and as I remember him."
17. Ibid., pp. 179–80. After meeting Harry again, Grey Owl scribbled in his notebooks that he must send him all his books as well as clippings on his British tour. Grey Owl, Notebooks 'A' and 'B', 1936, GREY OWL. He so wanted to impress the "Compleat Police Officer."

18. Interview with Jim Espaniel, Estaire, Ontario, March 25, 1972; Jim Espaniel, interviewed by Vince Crichton July 6, 1947, in Vince Crichton, "Grey Owl."

19. Grey Owl, *Tales*, pp. 176–77.

20. Jane Espaniel McKee, Notes about Grey Owl, written for me in early February 1989, SMITH.

21. Interview with Jane Espaniel McKee, Toronto, June 18, 1973. Jane's certificate states that she "has complied with the requirements of the Department of Education for admission to a Collegiate Institute, High School or Continuation School." It is dated Sudbury, June 15, 1926. In the possession of Jane Espaniel McKee.

22. Grey Owl to Anahareo, dated June 29, 1933, GREY OWL.

23. A photograph of the inscription is reproduced in the North Bay *Nugget* and Sudbury *Star*, April 18, 1938.

24. "Bisco People Identify Grey Owl as A. Belaney with Wife at Temagami," North Bay *Nugget*, April 18, 1938. The Sudbury *Star* (on that same day) also published this article.

25. Grey Owl, *Pilgrims*, pp. 43, 38.

26. Ibid., p. 216.

27. Interview with Jane Espaniel McKee, Toronto, September 29, 1987.

28. Grey Owl, *Pilgrims*, p. 42.

29. Ibid., p. 43.

30. Milan Novak, "Beaver," in *Wild Furbearer Management and Conservation in North America*, ed. by Milan Novak et al. (Toronto: Ministry of Natural Resources, 1987), p. 295. My thanks to Mike Buss, Fish and Wildlife Specialist, Leslie M. Frost Natural Resources Centre, Dorset, Ontario, for his comments on this point. Letters to Donald B. Smith, March 16 and October 16, 1989.

31. Interviews with Jane Espaniel McKee, Calgary, January 3, 1989 and February 13, 1989.

32. Interview with John Jero, Thunder Bay, Ontario, December 6, 1974. Discharge of Pupils, Chapleau Indian School, June–September 1933, RG 10, volume 6193, file 462–10, part 1, NAC. My thanks to Jim Miller for this reference. Carolyn Hryhorchuk, principal of the Chapleau High School, sent his school record to me, in a letter dated May 9, 1988.

33. Interview with Gordon Langevin, Biscotasing, September 29, 1970.

34. Grey Owl, "Preface to the Special Tour Edition," *The Men of the Last Frontier.* Tour Edition 1937 (London: *Country Life*, 1937), p. xii.

35. William Arthur Deacon, "Friends Sure of Half-Breed in Grey Owl," Toronto *Globe and Mail*, April 16, 1938; interview with Jim Espaniel, CBC documentary, Biscotasing, mid-August 1971.

36. "Hold Folk Dance at Biscotasing. Grey Owl Sponsors Indian Display on Return," Sudbury *Star*, July 12, 1937.

37. Grey Owl, *Men*, p. 226.

38. Interview with Adam Espaniel and Jane Espaniel McKee, Calgary, February 13, 1989.

39. Ellen Elliott to Lovat Dickson, dated August 11, 1937, McMASTER. During the film editing of the Winter or Abitibi film in late March and early April

1937, Grey Owl and Yvonne had stayed at the Ford Hotel. See Ellen Elliott to Grey Owl, dated May 20, 1937, McMASTER. For her comments on his drinking there, see Ellen Elliott to Lovat Dickson, dated April 14, 1937, McMASTER.

40. Enos T. Montour, *The Feathered U.E.L.'s* (Toronto: United Church of Canada. The Division of Communications, 1973), p. 127. On the history of the border crossing see Barbara Graymont, ed., *Fighting Tuscarora. The Autobiography of Chief Clinton Rickard* (Syracuse: Syracuse University Press, 1973), pp. xxiv–xxvi, 88–89. Chief Clinton Rickard, a Tuscarora Indian from New York State, founded the Indian Defense League of America in 1936.

41. (Copy) Chief Clinton Rickard, Grand President; Raymond Fadden, President Executive; Melvin Johnson, Secretary; Indian Defense League of America, Resolution dated May 19, 1938, St. Regis Reservation, Hogansburg, New York, RG 84, vol. 1770, file PA–272–NC, NAC.

42. "Colorful Is Parade. Huge turnout marks tenth celebration of the restoration. Grey Owl Leads," Niagara Falls (Ontario) *Evening Review*, July 19, 1937.

43. "Grey Owl Indian, Says His Widow Denying 'Gossip'," Regina *Leader-Post*, April 20, 1938.

44. Mrs. Wilhelmine Davidson to Donald B. Smith, dated Brampton, August 5, 1988. A plaza, named Bramrose, is now on the site of the Davidson farm on Queen Street West and Highway 410. The "pow wow" took place on the front lawn of the farm. Brampton, which had a population of about 5,000 people in the late 1930s, now has nearly a quarter-of-a-million. For coverage of the event, see "Tom-toms, Whoops Fill Air at Brampton's Pow-wow. Four White Men Initiated into Cayugas to Ancient Chanting. Robbins takes part," Toronto *Star*, July 20, 1937, p. 6; and "Indian Whoops Heard First Time in Years. Historic War Dance Staged as Iroquois Celebrate Council Ceremonies on Farm near Brampton," Toronto *Globe and Mail*, July 20, 1937, p. 4.

45. "City's Paleface Mayor Receives Indian Honors," unidentified Toronto newspaper clipping, March 25, 1937, City of Toronto Archives, SC 200, Box 1, file 5 (W. D. Robbins, 1932–35). For background information on Jasper Hill, see "About a Man Called 'Wapi-Gok-Hos' or Big White Owl," *Tekawennake*, October 19, 1977. The Ken Kidd Collection of clippings on Indian Affairs in Canada contains an article, "Indian Council's Formation Takes Foothold in European Cities," the date given is July 7, probably 1937. The article, most likely from a Toronto paper, mentions that the council's laws and regulations were founded on Seton's *Woodcraft and Indian Lore*. Trent University Archives, Peterborough, Ontario.

46. "Four Chieftains Inducted at Indian Pow-Wow Monday," Brampton *Conservator*, July 22, 1937.

47. Grey Owl had asked Hugh Eayrs to send Chief Big White Owl a copy of *Pilgrims of the Wild*, in a letter dated December 16, 1934, McMASTER. On March 3, 1936, Grey Owl met him in Toronto. See Betty Somervell's diary for that date and also the section at the end of the diary, "Books to read," where the entry, "The Indians of Canada by Jenness, recommended by Big White Owl," appears.

48. Jasper Hill to Donald B. Smith, dated Keswick, Ontario, February 25, 1971. Interview with Jasper Hill, Moraviantown, June 10, 1988.
49. *The Indian Speaking Leaf*, 1, 3 (June/July/August 1938). Barnabas Shiuhushu's title is listed on the letterhead of the organization. See for example his letter to Philip H. Godsell, dated 18 Suns, 1938 Great Suns. The Heat Moon [July 18, 1938], in P. H. Godsell Papers, Glenbow Museum Archives, Calgary, Alberta, Box 7, folder 65 (Indian Association of America, 1937–39). My thanks to Ian Getty for this reference.
50. "Grey Owl Won't Be Paleface," *The Daily Mirror* (London, England), September 20, 1937, p. 5. Grey Owl also told a Canadian reporter, Irene Moore, in August 1937 that "he has been made a councillor of the Indian Association of America, on the executive of which are noted doctors, lawyers, scientists and men of letters." See Irene Moore, "Grey Owl is Ambassador of Great Northland," Regina *Leader-Post*, January 6, 1938, a copy in RG 84, volume 1770, file PA–272–NC, part 1, NAC. Grey Owl had been fooled by Shiuhushu's own publicity. Interview with Jasper Hill, Moraviantown, Ontario, June 10, 1988. On Shiuhushu's real identity, see Hazel Hertzberg, *The Search for an American Indian Identity* (Syracuse: Syracuse University Press, 1971), pp. 214–15. Barnabas also went by a number of other names, Red Fox James being the one most frequently used.
51. "Grey Owl to Open the Fair," North Battleford *News*, July 29, 1937, p. 1.
52. Stan Cuthand was not present, but his uncle, Sam Baunais of the Little Pine Reserve, later told him about Grey Owl's performance. Telephone interview with Stan Cuthand, Saskatoon, August 9, 1988. The North Battleford *News* said nothing of his dancing abilities in its story, "Record Attendance the Second Day of the Fair," North Battleford *News*, August 5, 1937.
53. Grey Owl to Hugh Eayrs, dated August 26, 1937, McMASTER.
54. Irene Moore, "Grey Owl is Ambassador of Great Northland," Regina *Leader-Post*, January 6, 1938; "Famed Author-Naturalist Passes Away," Prince Albert *Herald*, April 13, 1938.
55. Hugh Eayrs to Lovat Dickson, dated September 20, 1937, McMASTER.

Chapter Sixteen. The Greatest Triumph

1. "Beaver Authority Goes to England. Grey Owl Sails Prior to Giving Lectures in Old Country," Montreal *Star*, September 10, 1937; interview with Yvonne Perrier Clare, Ottawa, May 10, 1971. (His hair was all white. She dyed it every two to three weeks.)
2. Yvonne Perrier Grey Owl to Elizabeth Smith Shortt, dated on board the Canadian Pacific Steamships, September 15, 1937. Adam and Elizabeth Smith Shortt Papers, Queen's University Archives, Kingston, Ontario.
3. Jack Shadbolt to Donald B. Smith, letters received July 1980 and mid-November 1989. For details on his life see George Swinton, "Jack Leonard Shadbolt," *The Canadian Encyclopedia* (2nd ed., Edmonton: Hurtig, 1988), p. 1986.
4. Jack Shadbolt to Donald B. Smith, letters received July 1980 and mid-November 1989.
5. Lovat Dickson to Grey Owl, dated May 11, 1937, McMASTER.
6. Lovat Dickson to Grey Owl, dated August 11, 1937, McMASTER.

7. The published itinerary for "Grey Owl's Second United Kingdom Lecture Tour, October to December 1937," specifically states: "New films have been made for the purpose of this Tour, and Grey Owl's Lecture material will also be new."

8. Autobiographical notes written by Ken Conibear, Hastings, Sussex, September 21, 1988 (3 pages); interview with Ken Conibear, Vancouver, July 9, 1971.

9. For information on Frank Conibear, see "Canadian Discoveries and Inventions," *Horizon Canada,* number 71 (1986), third cover; and Angie Bevington, "Frank Ralph Conibear (1896–)," *Arctic,* 36, 3 (September 1983): 386–87.

10. Ken enjoyed his three years at Exeter College, but the would-be writer has one everlasting regret. His tradition-bound professors at Oxford then believed that true English literature only existed before 1832, hence the curriculum ended there. As Ken recalled half-a-century later, thus we "were spared the Americans and I was denied the novelists I most wanted to study." Ken Conibear to Donald B. Smith, dated March 22, 1988.

11. Ken Conibear's diary entry for October 29, 1935, copied in letter from Ken Conibear to Donald B. Smith, December 5, 1987: "October 29, 1935 (Tues) Hampstead. Get note from Mrs. Nelson, as result of which go to hear Grey Owl, who is very good. Met Lovat Dickson there." Ken mentions the nostalgia he felt after smelling moosehide, in his notes for his lecture, "Abroad with Grey Owl," written May 16, 1950, GREY OWL.

12. Ken Conibear's talk at Prince Albert National Park, Waskesiu, Saskatchewan, August 10, 1988. His novelist friend, who introduced him to Lovat Dickson in London, was the Canadian novelist, Alan Sullivan (1868–1947), who then lived in England.

13. Lovat Dickson to Hugh Eayrs, dated September 30, 1937, McMASTER.

14. Ken Conibear, "Grey Owl in England," eight-page typed manuscript, completed in early 1938 before Grey Owl's death on April 13, 1938, GREY OWL.

15. For his appearances see "Grey Owl's Second United Kingdom Lecture Tour October to December 1937, Country Itinerary." The description of Roedean School is taken from Lovat Dickson's letter to Hugh Eayrs, dated May 11, 1937, McMASTER.

16. "An Indian looks at England. Grey Owl's lecture at the Pump Room," Bath *Chronicle and Herald,* November 6, 1937.

17. Charles Camsell, *Son of the North* (Toronto: Ryerson, 1954), pp. 2–3.

18. For information on the Camsell family, I am endebted to Shirlee Anne Smith, Keeper, Hudson's Bay Company Archives, Provincial Archives of Manitoba, for her letters of June 2 and June 23, 1988.

19. Grey Owl to *Country Life,* quoted in "A Bookman's Diary," *John O'London's Weekly,* April 29, 1938.

20. Dickson, *House of Words,* p. 163.

21. Ken Conibear, notes for his lecture, "Abroad with Grey Owl," May 16, 1950, GREY OWL.

22. Ken Conibear to Donald B. Smith, dated February 27, 1988 and March 22, 1988.

23. Ken Conibear to Donald B. Smith, dated October 13, 1987.
24. "'Grey Owl' at Bexhill, Canadian Indian Charms Great Audience. Blood Sports a Blemish on Britain's Name," Bexhill *Observer,* December 4, 1937. Grey Owl spoke in Bexhill on November 29, 1937.
25. *The Listener,* November 6, 1935, published his first talk given on October 26, 1935. This was "his first appearance before the microphone either in this or any other country." On the 1937 tour he also spoke on the national program, "ABC," October 2nd. My thanks to Margaret Horsfield for this information.
26. "Grey Owl on England," *The Listener,* November 24, 1937, p. 1123. The text published in *The Listener* was slightly edited. Here I follow Grey Owl's exact words as recorded on the original BBC tape, BBC Archives, London. A two-minute film clip of an interview with Grey Owl at the time of his British tour of 1935–36 has also survived. It can be seen on the 1972 CBC documentary "Grey Owl," now available on video (program number X4J 7204) from CBC Enterprises, Toronto. In the film clip Grey Owl speaks, in his natural voice, exactly as he did in his lectures, but in the radio interview his voice is slightly different, due to the fact that he was apparently reading a text. Ken Conibear kindly pointed this out.
27. Leonard had worked for a little over a year for the Hudson's Bay Company at Moose Factory, Ontario, 1929–30. Maureen Dolyniuk, Assistant Archivist, Hudson's Bay Company Archives, to Donald B. Smith, May 31, 1982. See also the letter of the secretary of the Hudson's Bay Company to Lovat Dickson, dated June 23, 1938, DICKSON. He later left the company and moved to the Mackenzie River Delta. In February 1932 he was in Aklavik, and served as a member of the inquest jury into the death of Albert Johnson (the "Mad Trapper"). See Dick North, *The Mad Trapper of Rat River* (Toronto: Macmillan, 1972), p. 134. Leonard was back in England by the spring of 1938. See Lovat Dickson to Superintendent James Wood, dated April 28, 1938, McMASTER.
28. Lovat Dickson provides an excellent description of Kittie Scott-Brown (as he recalled her from their meeting after Grey Owl's death) in *Wilderness Man,* p. 21.
29. Kittie Scott-Brown to Lovat Dickson, dated Boscombe, June 11, 1938, SCOTT-BROWN.
30. Ken Conibear to Donald B. Smith, dated Vancouver, January 9, 1988; talk by Ken Conibear, Waskesiu, Saskatchewan, August 10, 1988.
31. Kittie Scott-Brown to the Misses Belaney, dated Crediton, Devon, quoted in "Parentage of Grey Owl," London *Times,* April 21, 1938.
32. Ken Conibear to Donald B. Smith, dated Vancouver, January 9, 1988.
33. Kittie Scott-Brown to Lovat Dickson, dated Boscombe, June 11, 1938, SCOTT-BROWN.
34. Kittie Scott-Brown to Lovat Dickson, dated Boscombe, June 13, 1938, SCOTT-BROWN.
35. Kittie Scott-Brown to Betty Somervell, dated Boscombe, "Saturday, 21–38" [June 21, 1938], SCOTT-BROWN.
36. Geoffrey Turner's diary, entry for November 30, 1937. The excerpt was kindly provided to me by his widow, Monica Turner.

37. Kittie Scott-Brown to the Misses Belaney, dated Crediton, Devon, quoted in "Parentage of Grey Owl," London *Times*, April 21, 1938.

38. "'Grey Owl'. Held Up by Accident, Condemnation of Blood Sports," Southport *Guardian*, December 4, 1937, p. 9. Lord Street is written "Lord-street" in the original passage.

39. Buckingham Palace confirmed the invitation on November 19, 1937. See Captain Richard Streatfeild, Private Secretary to The Queen to Vincent Massey, Canadian High Commissioner, dated November 19, 1937, RG 25, A–5, vol. 382 (Grey Owl), NAC.

40. Lovat Dickson to Hugh Eayrs, dated May 9, 1938, McMASTER.

41. A. F. Lascelles, secretary to the governor-general, to the Deputy Superintendent-General of Indian Affairs, dated July 13, 1935, RG 10, vol. 7995, 1/1–15–2–4, NAC.

42. Elizabeth Motiess[?] to Admiral Mark Kerr, dated Buckingham Palace, October 28, 1935, DICKSON.

43. Diary of Queen Mary, entry for December 10, 1937, The Royal Archives, Windsor Castle. The quotation is printed with the gracious permission of Her Majesty The Queen.

44. Lovat Dickson to Hugh Eayrs, dated December 13, 1937 (Confidential), McMASTER. Vincent Massey also later recorded his impressions of the Royal Command Performance in *What's Past is Prologue. The Memoirs of Vincent Massey* (Toronto: Macmillan, 1963), pp. 254–55.

45. "Baffling Riddle of Grey Owl's Identity," Hastings *Observer*, April 23, 1938.

46. "Grey Owl's Second United Kingdom Lecture Tour. October to December 1937. Country Itinerary." Copy of the 1937 tour itinerary is in SMITH.

47. Kate Holmes, "Grey Owl's Travelogue," Hastings *Observer*, December 24, 1937, p. 8.

48. "Grey Owl Attacks Blood Sports. 'Encouraging Pugnacity and Brutality'," Hastings *Observer*, December 18, 1937, p. 16.

49. Interview with Lillian Hazell O'Nions, Hastings, Sussex, England, September 20, 1988.

50. Mary McCormick Champness quoted in, "Baffling Riddle of Grey Owl's Identity," Hastings *Observer*, April 23, 1938.

51. Interview with Bob Overton, Hastings, October 10, 1971 (taped interview) and December 5, 1972.

52. The Misses Belaney's neighbour at 26 Wellington Road, Mrs. Dolly Head, by chance happened to see Grey Owl enter the Misses Belaney's house that morning—it was such an unusual sight, a Red Indian calling on these elderly ladies, who were almost total recluses. Interview with Dolly and George Head, Hastings, Sussex, September 21, 1971 and December 5, 1972. For the weather that day in southeastern England, see "Forecasts for Today," London *Times*, December 15, 1937, p. 18.

53. Ken Conibear to Donald B. Smith, dated February 27, 1988.

54. Interview with Yvonne Perrier Clare, Ottawa, May 10, 1971.

55. "Hastings Grammar School, Annual Prize Distribution," Hastings *Observer*, December 26, 1903. "Grey Owl could understand more French than he himself could speak," interview with Yvonne Perrier Clare, Ottawa, May 10, 1971.

56. Interview with Ivy Holmes, Waverley Abbey House, Farnham, Surrey, December 13, 1972. Lovat Dickson provides a description of the Misses Belaney's parlour in which he also sat (after Grey Owl's death). He visited the Misses Belaney for two hours on April 27, 1938. See the Hastings *Observer*, April 30, 1938. His description of the parlour appears in the manuscript copy of "Half-Breed," pp. 84–85, DICKSON, vol. 9. Grey Owl mentioned how much he detested shoes, suits, and starched collars in an interview with the Saskatoon *Star-Phoenix* on the eve of his first British Tour. See "Noted Canadian Naturalist, Grey Owl to Visit England," Saskatoon *Star-Phoenix*, October 1, 1935.

57. Interview with Ken Conibear, Vancouver, July 9, 1971.

58. I am speculating about his accent. The meeting with the women (whom Yvonne learned after Grey Owl's death were his aunts) made no impression on her. Interview with Yvonne Perrier Clare, Ottawa, May 10, 1971. If Grey Owl had suddenly began speaking with the same accent as the Misses Belaney, this would have indeed made an impression, one she would have remembered forty or so years later. I am certain he spoke to his aunts in his Canadian accent.

59. Dickson, *Wilderness Man*, p. 8. On September 21, 1971, Dolly Head kindly gave me one of the books from the bookcase, *The Hundred Days of Napoleon*, by Grey Owl's grandfather, Archibald Belaney. Carrie Belaney gave it to her after Ada's death in 1946. I donated the book to the Archives of Ontario in Toronto.

60. After Aunt Ada died, the semi-grand piano sold for only £10. Interview with Dolly Head, Hastings, Sussex, England, September 21, 1971. The aunts also had a wonderful chess set.

61. The Misses Belaney, quoted in the Hastings *Observer*, April 30, 1938.

62. H. Clifford Smith, *Buckingham Palace, its furniture, decoration and history* (London: 1930), pp. 146–47. My thanks to Stephen J. Patterson, Assistant Bibliographer, Royal Library, Windsor Castle for this reference.

63. Hazel Canning, "Grey Owl's Death Recalls His Talk Before Royalty," Toronto *Star*, April 16, 1938. One mistake appears in the article; the date of the Command Performance is given as Jan. 10, 1938—this should read December 10, 1937. Hazel Canning visited him in early February as she mentions in her article on his recent talk at the Harvard Club in New York City, which occurred on February 1, 1938.

64. Lovat Dickson to Hugh Eayrs, dated December 17, 1937, McMASTER.

65. Grey Owl quoted in "'Grey Owl' at Norwich," *The Journal* (Norwich), December 25, 1937; see also his similar comments at Ipswich, reported in the *East Anglian Daily Times* (Ipswich), December 16, 1937, in the article, "Modern Hiawatha at Ipswich." "Civilisation said Nature belongs to man: the Indian said man belongs to Nature." Grey Owl obtained support for this idea from his memory of talks with Indians in northern Ontario and Quebec and from his readings. A favourite book was John C. Gifford's *Billy Bowlegs and the Seminole War* (Coconut Grove, Florida: The Triangle Company, 1925). Two quotations in particular greatly influenced Grey Owl, who included them in *Pilgrims of the Wild* (p. xiv). The first was Gifford's statement

(*Seminole*, p. 10) that the Indian "rarely dominated the things around him. He was part of Nature and not its boss." Gifford's citing of an author named Hewitt on the Pueblo Indians of the American Southwest also impressed him (*Seminole*, p. 28). "In his own Southwest he is a harmonious element in the landscape that is incomparable in its nobility of color and mass and feeling of the Unchangeable. He never dominates it, as does the European his environment, but belongs there as do the mesas, skies, sunshine, spaces, and the other living creatures. He takes his part in it with the clouds, winds, rocks, plants, birds and beasts, with drum beat and chant and symbolic gesture, keeping time with the seasons, moving in orderly procession with nature, holding to the unity of life in all things, seeking no superior place for himself but merely a state of harmony with all created things—the most rhythmic life, so far as I know, that is lived among the races of men." Another favourite author was the Sioux writer Luther Standing Bear. In Grey Owl's copy of *Land of the Spotted Eagle* (Boston: Houghton Mifflin Company, 1933) he marked a line on page 196 with his pen. Chief Standing Bear, in this passage, distinguishes between the faith of the Indian and the whiteman. "Indian faith sought the harmony of man with his surroundings; the other sought the dominance of surroundings." Dawn Richardson showed me her father's copies of both *Billy Bowlegs and the Seminole War* and *Land of the Spotted Eagle*.

66. Grey Owl, "Grey Owl's Farewell," in Dickson, ed., *The Green Leaf*, p. 106.
67. J. W. Fitzwilliam, Secretary British Field Sports Society, "Grey Owl: A Correction," Birmingham *Gazette*, August 9, 1938. A copy of this article is in DICKSON, vol. 5.
68. "'Grey Owl' at Norwich," *The Journal* (Norwich), December 25, 1937.
69. The London *News Chronicle* has paraphrased the passage somewhat, "Grey Owl Refused to 'Scalp' Broadcast," *News Chronicle*, December 20, 1937. For the full text of this section see "Grey Owl's Farewell" in Dickson, ed., *The Green Leaf*, p. 105.
70. Dickson, ed., *The Green Leaf*, pp. 23–24.
71. Dickson, *Half-Breed*, p. 330; Dickson, ed., *The Green Leaf* (the figure of 50,000 appears on the inside of the dust jacket); "Grey Owl's Undelivered Lecture," *The Times*, December 31, 1937.
72. Talk by Ken Conibear at Prince Albert National Park, Waskesiu, Saskatchewan, August 10, 1988.
73. Ken Conibear to Donald B. Smith, dated December 5 and 8, 1987.
74. Editorial, *The Mountaineer* (published by Green Mountain College, Poultney, Vermont), January 14, 1938. My thanks to Major Benton for this reference.

Chapter Seventeen. The Exposé

1. Grey Owl's talk is listed in the 1937–38 program of lectures sponsored by the Academy of Science and Art of Pittsburgh. The talks were all held in the city's Carnegie Music Hall, Forbes Street at Schenley Park.
2. "Peterborough," *The Encyclopedia Americana*, Canadian Edition (Montreal: Americana Corp. of Canada, 1951), vol. 21, p. 662.
3. Mary Strickland Rogers, "The Peterborough Canoe," in Ronald Borg, ed.,

Peterborough Land of Shining Waters. An Anthology (Toronto: University of Toronto Press, 1967), pp. 233–35.

4. Lovat Dickson in *The Green Leaf* mentioned that he had given 138 lectures in Britain in 1937 (p. 16). During the subsequent North American tour he had lectured at least 20 to 25 times from January to early March 1938.

5. Jack Peterson, "Indian Boy Who Lost His Leg Is Visited By Grey Owl," Peterborough *Examiner,* March 12, 1938.

6. Interview with Gerald Johnston, Burleigh Falls, Ontario, June 17, 1971. Jack Peterson later gave Gerald Johnston a copy of the photo that he took of him with Grey Owl. The print that I had made of this photo now appears as an illustration in this book.

7. "Grey Owl's Prophecy Comes True With His Death at Prince Albert," Peterborough *Examiner,* April 13, 1938; "Wild Animals Will Not Attack Unless Molested Grey Owl Tells Trinity Audience. Holds Audience Spellbound As He Lovingly Told of His Friends The Animals," Peterborough *Examiner,* March 12, 1938.

8. Grey Owl, *Tales,* p. 149.

9. Ibid., p. 325.

10. Grey Owl to Ellen Elliott, dated July 20, 1934, McMASTER.

11. Hugh Eayrs, "Preface," *Book of Grey Owl,* pp. xv–xvi.

12. Hugh Eayrs to Lovat Dickson, dated December 4, 1936, McMASTER.

13. Gray, *Fun,* p. 215. Grey Owl's American agency was W. Colston Leigh, Inc.

14. Extracts from United States Declaration Form signed by Grey Owl in December 1937, DICKSON, vol. 8. Grey Owl seems to have chosen Hermosillo, Mexico, as his birthplace in 1934—when he filled out his Canadian naturalization papers. See file 8154, "Owl, Grey (Belaney)," Naturalization, Dept. of the Secretary of State. In his application prepared on April 5, 1934, Grey Owl states that he was born "near Hermosillo Mexico in Indian encampment, State of Sonora, Mexico." A photostat of the file was supplied to me on June 16, 1971, by the registrar, Canadian Citizen Registration Branch, Dept. of Secretary of State, Ottawa; Ken Conibear to Donald B. Smith, dated December 8, 1987.

15. Grey Owl, quoted in Hazel Canning, "Grey Owl's Death Recalls His Talk Before Royalty," Toronto *Star,* April 16, 1938.

16. Interviews with Jack Leve, Toronto, in mid-January 1972 (interview for the CBC documentary) and January 22, 1972; Yvonne Vickers, "The Return of Trader Jack," Cochrane *Northland Post,* October 14, 1971.

17. "Grey Owl Hushed," *Time,* January 3, 1938, p. 17.

18. Grey Owl quoted in "May Be 'Grey Owl' Abroad. Just 'Fatty Face' to Wife," Toronto *Star,* March 14, 1938.

19. Grey Owl to Maxwell Perkins, dated April 1937, SCRIBNER'S.

20. Maxwell Perkins to Grey Owl, dated January 17, 1938, SCRIBNER'S.

21. E. H. Morrow to J. C. Stead, dated January 20, 1938, RG 84, vol. 1770, file PA–272–NC, Bellaney, vol. 2, NAC; Harvard Club of New York City, Annual Report of the Board of Managers, December 31, 1938. Grey Owl spoke there on February 1 on "The Trails of Canada"; New York Auxiliary, *Delta Sigma Delta Desmos,* 44, 2 (May 1938), p. 118. He spoke to them on February 2.

22. Interview with Yvonne Perrier Clare, Ottawa, May 10, 1971. "Grey Owl wore false teeth, had a bridge, not a complete set."
23. "Grey Owl to Give Third Lecture," Montreal *Gazette*, January 14, 1938.
24. "Grey Owl Fears Losing Simplicity," Montreal *Star*, January 14, 1938.
25. Jean-Charles Harvey, "Un Apache au pays des Hurons," *Le Jour* (Montréal), le 22 janvier 1938.
26. Haddow Keith to Donald B. Smith, dated November 22, 1988.
27. Mrs. Peck's son Richard wrote me on October 19, 1988: "Yes indeed my mother was there filled with joy on account of Grey Owl's success. On her return disappointment showed on her face and when I asked her what was wrong she told me that when she went backstage to offer congratulations she found that Anahareo, of whom she was very fond, had been replaced by another woman."
28. A rough itinerary for the North American Tour is contained in the Macmillan Archives, McMASTER. See the correspondence for early 1938.
29. Ellen Elliott to Hugh Eayrs, dated January 25, 1938, McMASTER; "Education Best Means for Saving Wild Life," Hamilton *Spectator*, January 25, 1938.
30. D. K. P. "Mixed Cargo," Cobourg *World*, April 21, 1938. Grey Owl spoke to the students of Trinity College School.
31. Thomas R. Brophey, "The Roving Reporter," Windsor *Star*, February 15, 1938.
32. Yvonne to Ellen Elliott, dated February 17, 1938, McMASTER.
33. Grey Owl, *Tales*, p. 333.
34. "Noted Indian Lectures Here," Kenosha *Evening News*, February 19, 1938.
35. "Indian Tells His Crusade to Protect British Foxes," Milwaukee *Journal*, February 20, 1938.
36. "Indians Forsake Desire for War, Speaker Asserts," *Illinois State Journal* (Springfield), February 22, 1938.
37. "De Grey Owl," *L'Action catholique* (Québec), le 4 mars 1938. My thanks to Fernand Harvey for this article; "'Preserve Wild Animal Life', is Plea of Naturalist Here," Quebec *Chronicle-Telegraph*, March 4, 1938. My thanks to Betty Brehaut for this article, written by her husband, Judd Brehaut; "Grey Owl An 'Ill Bird'," Quebec *Chronicle-Telegraph*, March 5, 1938.
38. "Grey Owl Suggests Design He Thinks Suitable For Flag," Ottawa *Citizen*, March 9, 1938.
39. Diamond Jenness, *Indians of Canada* (Ottawa: King's Printer, 1932), p. 264; Marius Barbeau, "Our Indians—their disappearance," *Queen's Quarterly*, 38 (1931), p. 695; Grey Owl himself had believed this, see Grey Owl, *Men*, pp. 210, 220–21.
40. Thomas Crerar, quoted in the Debates, House of Commons, Session 1938, vol. 4, p. 3792 (Entry for June 13, 1938); Grey Owl refers to their meeting in "Grey Owl Suggests Design He Thinks Suitable For Flag," Ottawa *Citizen*, March 9, 1938.
41. Grey Owl to Hugh Eayrs, telegram, dated March 4, 1938, McMASTER.
42. Evelyn B. Scrivens to Donald B. Smith, December 18, 1988.
43. Marilyn Legge Godfrey to Donald B. Smith, February 11, 1971.
44. "Grey Owl's Prophecy Comes True With His Death at Prince Albert," Peterborough *Examiner*, April 13, 1938. His description of Jim Espaniel appears in *Tales*, p. 176.

45. Hugh Eayrs, quoted in Dickson, ed., *The Green Leaf*, p. 25.
46. Dickson, ed., *The Green Leaf*, p. 25; Massey Hall (since 1933) has had seating for 2,765 people, see Adrian Waller, "Massey Hall. Grand Old Lady of Shuter Street," *City & Country Home*, December 1985, p. 162.
47. A card giving Grey Owl's Railway Timetable for March 26, 1938, McMASTER; Ellen Elliott to Grey Owl, dated March 3, 1938, McMASTER.
48. James Wood to F. H. H. Williamson, March 16, 1938, PANP.
49. "Grey Owl is Glad to be Back in Canada," Prince Albert *Herald*, March 31, 1938; interview with Yvonne Perrier Clare, Ottawa, May 1971.
50. Ellen Elliott to Colston Leigh, April 19, 1938, McMASTER.
51. Superintendent James Wood to Lovat Dickson, reprinted in *The Green Leaf*, ed. Dickson, pp. 29–30. See also James Wood to Lovat Dickson, dated June 11, 1938, McMASTER.
52. Stan Winters identified Bill Houghton for me, in a letter dated November 5, 1989.
53. Bill Houghton to Mrs. Somervell, May 30, 1938, GREY OWL. See also his letter of May 23, 1938, to her.
54. Gregory Clark, "Grey Owl Really an Englishman, Old Friends Insist," Toronto *Star*, April 14, 1938. Claud Pascoe, "Witnesses Describe Grey Owl's Wedding to Temagami Woman," Toronto *Star*, April 16, 1938. Matthew Halton's articles appeared in the Toronto *Star* on April 19 and 20, 1938.
55. "English Continue Controversy," Toronto *Star*, April 20, 1938.
56. H. A. R. Cawkell to Donald B. Smith, dated October 27, 1988.
57. "Missing Toe May Help Solve Mystery," Prince Albert *Herald*, April 20, 1938.
58. "'Red Indian' Grey Owl Was A Native of Hastings," *Daily Express*, April 20, 1938.

Chapter Eighteen. Grey Owl's Legacy

1. Elizabeth Shortt quoting Grey Owl in Gregory Clark, "Estate of Grey Owl May be Near $100,000. Will Probated Soon," Toronto *Star*, June 30, 1938. Dr. Shortt recalled that their talk had taken place in January, but March—the time of Grey Owl's talk in Ottawa—is probably the correct date.
2. "Grey Owl Hushed," *Time*, January 3, 1938, p. 17.
3. "'Grey Owl' Abroad. Just 'Fatty Face' To Wife. Lecturer back from London. Airs Views on Royalty and Other Matters. Explains Fight," Toronto *Star*, March 14, 1938.
4. Tom Saville to T. Godfrey, Indian Agent at Chapleau, dated Shining Tree, March 4, 1938, RG 10, vol. 7995, 1/1–15–2–4, NAC.
5. Angele Belaney, testimony given at the Examination for Discovery, June 12, 1939, p. 13, FRASER.
6. R. B. Somervell, "In Defence of Grey Owl," Westmorland *Gazette*, April 30, 1938. Ken Conibear had returned to the Northwest Territories and could not be reached until several weeks after Grey Owl's death. He was out in the bush, trapping with his brother Frank. On April 21, 1988, Ken mentioned this to Peter Gzowski on CBC Radio's "Morningside."
7. James Wood to Lovat Dickson in *The Green Leaf*, pp. 30–31.
8. "Indian, or Englishman?" Ottawa *Citizen*, April 16, 1938; "The Grey Owl

Story," Ottawa *Citizen*, April 23, 1938; "Grey Owl or Archie Belaney," Prince Albert *Herald*, April 19, 1938; "Evidence in Conflict," Prince Albert *Herald*, April 21, 1938; "Fun to be Fooled," Winnipeg *Tribune*, April 20, 1938 (reprinted in the Ottawa *Journal*, April 23, 1938); "Grey Owl's Ancestry," Calgary *Herald*, April 21, 1938; "Grey Owl's Secret," Windsor *Star*, April 21, 1938; "The Fuss About Grey Owl," Ottawa *Journal*, April 22, 1938 (reprinted in the Calgary *Herald*, April 28, 1938); "Grey Owl," Saskatoon *Star-Phoenix*, April 23, 1938; "The 'Grey Owl' Mystery," Regina *Leader-Post*, April 23, 1938.

9. Anahareo, *Deerskins*, p. 180.
10. "Grey Owl's Ex-Wife Keeps Her Secret. Sails for Home," London *Sunday-Dispatch*, September 14, 1938.
11. Anahareo, *Deerskins*, p. 187.
12. Victor B. Scheffer, "Introduction to the New Edition," *Pilgrims of the Wild* by Grey Owl (New York: Charles Scribner's Sons, 1971), p. xiv.
13. Grey Owl to Ellen Elliott, dated July 20, 1934, McMASTER.
14. Grey Owl to Betty Somervell, quoted in *The Green Leaf*, ed. Dickson, p. 12.
15. Grey Owl, *Pilgrims*, p. 244. He also mentions the same essay in *Tales*, p. 8.
16. "Plaque in Memory of Famed Grey Owl," Toronto *Telegram*, July 31, 1959.
17. Shirley Dawn Bruce to John Gray, April 3, 1967, McMASTER.
18. Dr. W. G. N. van der Steen to R. A. Gibson, dated June 26, 1939, PANP. Bill Waiser reviews the Park's treatment of Grey Owl's memory in *Saskatchewan Playground*, pp. 84–85.
19. Kathleen Strange, "The Story of Grey Owl—Canadian Legend," *Family Herald and Weekly Star*, July 5, 1951.
20. Margery Wilder quoted in "Americans Preserve P.A. Park," Saskatoon *Star-Phoenix*, August 11, 1988. At the beginning of the 1990s it appears that other Americans are becoming aware of Grey Owl. In the January 1990 issue of *The Atlantic* Kenneth Brower contributed a review of Grey Owl's life and assessed his contribution to the environmental movement. Brower, a writer who specializes in wildlife and ecological issues, observes: "No man was more important to Canadian environmental consciousness, or to the environmental consciousness of the entire British Commonwealth, for that matter. If his deeds had been done at a slightly lower latitude, we all would have heard of him. In the pantheon Grey Owl belongs with Henry David Thoreau, John Muir, Aldo Leopold, and Rachel Carson—or perhaps with Lewis Mumford and Joseph Wood Krutch, on the level just below." See his article, "Grey Owl," *The Atlantic*, January 1990, pp. 74–84.
21. Grey Owl, *Pilgrims*, pp. 280–82.

Bibliography

This bibliography is divided into sections:
I. Grey Owl's Works
   A. Books by Grey Owl
   B. Articles by Grey Owl
   C. Films of Grey Owl
II. Published Reminiscences of Grey Owl
III. Studies of Grey Owl, or books containing brief references to him
IV. Manuscripts and Unpublished Reports about Grey Owl
V. Archival Collections on Grey Owl
VI. Interviews with individuals who knew Archie Belaney in Hastings, England, and in Canada
VII. Periodicals Checked
VIII. Useful Background Works

I. Grey Owl's Works (in chronological order)

A. Books by Grey Owl

The Men of the Last Frontier. London: Country Life, 1931.
Pilgrims of the Wild. Toronto: Macmillan, 1934.
The Adventures of Sajo and her Beaver People. London: Lovat Dickson & Thompson Limited, 1935. (Published by Scribner's in the United States under the title *Sajo and the Beaver People.*)
Tales of an Empty Cabin. London: Lovat Dickson Limited, 1936.
The Tree. London: Lovat Dickson Limited, 1937. (*The Tree* previously appeared as one of the stories making up *Tales of an Empty Cabin.*)
Reynolds, E. E., ed. *A Book of Grey Owl. Pages from the Writings of Wa-Sha-Quon-Asin.* With Preface by Lovat Dickson. London: Peter Davies, 1938.

B. Articles by Grey Owl

"The Passing of the Last Frontier," *Country Life,* March 2, 1929, pp. 302–5.
"The Vanishing Life of the Wild," *Canadian Forest and Outdoors,* June, 1930, pp. 321–23, 361–64.
"Little Brethren of the Wilderness, Part One," *Canadian Forest and Outdoors,* September, 1930, pp. 499–501.

"Little Brethren of the Wilderness, Part Two," *Canadian Forest and Outdoors,* October, 1930, pp. 573–74.

"The Fine Art of the Still Hunt," *Canadian Forest and Outdoors,* November, 1930, pp. 624–26, 666.

"King of the Beaver People," *Canadian Forest and Outdoors,* December, 1930, pp. 683–86.

"King of the Beaver People," *Canadian Forest and Outdoors,* January, 1931, pp. 13–15.

"Who Will Repay?", *Canadian Forest and Outdoors,* March, 1931, pp. 119–22.

"A Day in a . . . Hidden Town," *Canadian Forest and Outdoors,* April, 1931, pp. 177–80.

"More about 'Game Leaks.' The Indian's Side of the Question," *Canadian Forest and Outdoors,* April, 1931, p. 195.

"A Mess of Pottage," *Canadian Forest and Outdoors,* May, 1931, pp. 243–46.

"Comments on Mr. Godsell's Article by Grey Owl," *Canadian Forest and Outdoors,* July, 1931, pp. 343–44.

"White Water!" *Canadian Forest and Outdoors,* August, 1931, pp. 393–96.

"Little Indians," *Country Life,* August 22, 1931, pp. 196–200.

"The Perils of Woods Travel," *Canadian Forest and Outdoors,* September, 1931, pp. 9–13.

"And a Little Child Shall Lead Them," *Canadian Forest and Outdoors,* October, 1931, p. 40.

"Indian Legends and Lore," *Canadian Forest and Outdoors,* October, 1931, pp. 23, 32.

Lascelles, Tony, in collaboration with Grey Owl, "A Philosophy of the Wild," *Canadian Forest and Outdoors,* December, 1931, pp. 15–17.

"Unto . . . the Least of These," *Canadian Forest and Outdoors,* March, 1932, pp. 89–91, 94.

"Secrets of the Beaver Family," *Western Motordom,* July, 1932, pp. 8–10.

"Re-builder of the Wilderness. Part One," *Canadian Forest and Outdoors,* August, 1932, pp. 289–92, 304.

"Re-builder of the Wilderness. Part Two," *Canadian Forest and Outdoors,* September, 1932, pp. 335–38, 349.

"The Beaver Family Migrates," *Canadian Forest and Outdoors,* September, 1933, pp. 229–31, 256.

"Private Interest vs. the People," manuscript prepared in 1934 and never published. The Macmillan Archives, The William Ready Division of Archives and Research Collections, McMaster University Library, Hamilton, Ontario, Box 101, folder 2.

"The Beaver Babies," *Canadian Forest and Outdoors,* January, 1934, pp. 368–70, 378–80.

"A Description of the Fall Activities of Beaver, with some remarks on Conservation," in *Grey Owl and the Beaver* by Harper Cory. London: Thomas Nelson, 1935, pp. 110–31.

"Getting Lost in the Woods," *Canadian Forest and Outdoors,* May, 1935, pp. 859–60, 868–70.

"The Indian's Code of the Wild," *Canadian Forest and Outdoors,* June, 1935, pp. 883–84.

"Author's Special Preface to his English Readers, October, 1935," in *Pilgrims of the Wild*. London: Lovat Dickson & Thompson Limited, 1935, pp. iii–vi.
"Message of Good Will." *The International Journal of Animal Protection*, November, 1935.
"The Fine Art of the Still Hunt," *Canadian Forest and Outdoors*, November, 1935, pp. 1048–50.
"Grey Owl Speaks his Mind. An entertaining interview with the famous friend of the Beaver Kingdom," *Canadian Forest and Outdoors*, September, 1936, pp. 269–70, 282.
"A Plea for the Canadian Northland," in *Empire Club of Canada. Addresses delivered to the members during the year, 1936–1937*. Toronto: Printers Guild, 1937, pp. 90–102.
"Preface to Special Tour Edition," in *The Men of the Last Frontier*. London: Country Life, 1937, pp. ix–xiii.
"My Mission to My Country," *Canadian Forest and Outdoors*, February, 1938, pp. 37–38, 52.
"A Message from Grey Owl," in *My Weekly Reader. The Junior Newspaper*, May 2–6, 1938, pp. 129–30.

C. Films of Grey Owl (with the names of the filmmakers)

National Parks Board
Beaver People. Shot at Cabano, Summer 1930.
Beaver Family. Shot at Riding Mountain National Park, 1931. W. J. Oliver.
Strange Doings in Beaverland. Shot at Prince Albert National Park, 1932. W. J. Oliver.
Grey Owl's Neighbours. Shot at Prince Albert National Park, 1933. W. J. Oliver.
Pilgrims of the Wild. Shot at Prince Albert National Park, 1935. W. J. Oliver.

Associated Screen News
Grey Owl's Little Brother. Canadian Cameo Series, 1932. Gordon Sparling.
Grey Owl's Strange Guests. Canadian Cameo Series, 1934. Gordon Sparling.

Produced by Grey Owl
The Trail—Winter. Shot in Abitibi, Quebec, near Doucet, Winter, early 1937, by B. J. Bach.
The Trail—Summer. Shot in the Mississauga Forest Reserve, Summer, 1937, by B. J. Bach.

II. Published Reminiscences of Grey Owl

Anahareo. *My Life With Grey Owl*. London: Peter Davies, 1940.
Anahareo. *Devil in Deerskins. My Life with Grey Owl*. Toronto: New Press, 1972.
Cockerell, T. D. A. "A Visit with Grey Owl," *Natural History*, 37, 3 (1936): 223–30.
Dickson, Lovat. "Grey Owl, Man of the Wilderness," *Strand Magazine*, May, 1936, pp. 64, 73–74.
Dickson, Lovat. *The House of Words*. Toronto: Macmillan, 1963.
Diefenbaker, John. *One Canada. Memoirs of the Right Honourable John G. Diefenbaker. The Crusading Years, 1895 to 1956*. Toronto: Macmillan, 1975.
Doolittle, Ken. "A Day with Grey Owl," *The Fish and Game Sportsman*, 8, 4 (Winter Edition 1976): 31–36.

Draper, Bill. "Early Friend of Grey Owl Tells of Experiences with Noted Naturalist," Chapleau *Post* (Chapleau, Ontario), April 22, 1938.

Eayrs, Hugh. "Preface," *A Book of Grey Owl. With an Introduction by Hugh Eayrs.* Toronto: Macmillan, 1939, pp. ix–xxi.

Garland, Anne [Kathleen Garland]. "My Visit to Grey Owl," *Canadian Forest and Outdoors,* March, 1935, pp. 790–91.

Gray, John Morgan. *Fun Tomorrow, Learning to be a Publisher, & Much Else.* Toronto: Macmillan, 1978.

Harvey, Jean-Charles. *Des bois . . . Des Champs . . . Des bêtes.* Montréal: Les Editions de l'homme, 1965.

Massey, Vincent. *What's Past is Prologue.* Toronto: Macmillan, 1963.

M. M. [Margaret McCormick]. "Grey Owl. Recollections of his boyhood," *West Australian* (Perth, Australia), April 30, 1938.

Sparling, Gordon. "Grey Owl's 'Little Brothers'," *Canadian Forest and Outdoors,* July, 1932, pp. 260-61.

Van der Sleen, W. G. N. *Canada. Met Vier en Twintig Fotopagina's.* 2nd Revised Edition. Tilburg: Nederland's Boekhuis, 1947.

III. Studies of Grey Owl, or books containing brief references to him

Adams, John Coldwell. *Sir Charles God Damn. The Life of Sir Charles G. D. Roberts.* Toronto: University of Toronto Press, 1986.

Addison, Ottelyn. *Early Days in Algonquin Park.* Toronto: McGraw-Hill-Ryerson, 1974.

Cory, Harper. *Grey Owl and the Beaver.* London: Thomas Nelson and Sons, 1935.

Dickson, Lovat. *Half-Breed. The Story of Grey Owl.* London: Peter Davies, 1939.

Dickson, Lovat. *Wilderness Man. The Strange Story of Grey Owl.* Toronto: Macmillan, 1973.

Dickson, Lovat, ed. and arranged by. *The Green Leaf. A Tribute to Grey Owl.* London: Lovat Dickson Limited, 1938.

Jameson, Sheilagh S. *W. J. Oliver: Life Through a Master's Lens.* Calgary: Glenbow Museum, 1984.

Lucas, Alec. "Nature Writers and the Animal Story," in *Literary History of Canada. Canadian Literature in English,* ed. Carl F. Klinck. Toronto: University of Toronto Press, 1965, pp. 364–88.

McCourt, Edward. *Saskatchewan.* Toronto: Macmillan, 1968.

Mitcham, Allison. *Grey Owl's Favourite Wilderness.* Moonbeam, Ontario: Penumbra Press, 1981.

Pink, Hal. *Bill Guppy, King of the Woodsmen, life-long friend and tutor of "Grey Owl."* London: Hutchinson & Co. [1940].

Polk, James. *Wilderness Writers.* Toronto: Clarke, Irwin & Co. Ltd., 1972.

Raddall, Thomas. "Grey Owl," in *Footsteps on Old Floors.* Garden City, N.J.: Doubleday, 1968, pp. 95–156.

Rashley, R. E. "Grey Owl and the Authentic Frontier," *The English Quarterly,* 4, 3 (Fall 1971): 58–64.

Scheffer, Victor B. "Introduction to the New Edition," *Sajo and the Beaver People. Written and illustrated by Grey Owl.* New York: Charles Scribner's Sons, 1971, pp. xi–xiv.

Scheffer, Victor B. "Introduction to the New Edition," *Pilgrims of the Wild. Written and illustrated by Grey Owl*. New York: Charles Scribner's Sons, 1971, pp. xi–xviii.

Sluman, Norma and Jean Goodwill. *John Tootoosis. Biography of a Cree Leader.* Ottawa: Golden Dog Press, 1982.

Smith, Janet Adam. *John Buchan. A Biography.* London: Rupert Hart-Davis, 1965.

Thomas, Clara and John Lennox. *William Arthur Deacon. A Canadian Literary Life.* Toronto: University of Toronto Press, 1982.

Waiser, Bill. *Saskatchewan's Playground. A History of Prince Albert National Park.* Saskatoon: Fifth House Publishers, 1989.

IV. Manuscripts and Unpublished Reports about Grey Owl

Chester, Philip. "Grey Owl: Knight Errant of the Canadian Wilderness." Independent Study Essay (English 498), Department of English, Carleton University, Ottawa, 1988.

Conibear, Kenneth. "Grey Owl in England." Manuscript prepared in early 1938, before Grey Owl's death on April 13, 1938, 8 pages.

Conibear, Kenneth. "A Lecture Abroad with Grey Owl," January 1, 1950. Notes prepared for a talk on Grey Owl, 6 pages.

Crichton, Vince. "Archie Belaney (Chief Grey Owl)," 28 pages.

Legace, Ferg. "Memoirs" [Written out in longhand, 1972].

MacDougall, Stuart L. "More About Grey Owl," 5 pages.

Martin, Francis Mildred. Typescript of the interview with Francis Mildred Martin, completed by Jackie Keesey, 1986. Copy at Prince Albert National Park Library, Waskesiu, Saskatchewan.

Roberts, Lloyd. "Grey Owl—the Man." Prepared in 1937, 8 pages.

Roberts, Lloyd. "Brother to the Beaver." Manuscript about 40,000 words in length, prepared in 1950.

Roberts, Lloyd. "Grey Owl: Beaver Man," 13 Radio Scripts for CBC. Prepared in 1950.

Short, Georgean C. "Report on Investigations 'The Grey Owl Project'," November 30, 1971. Copy at Prince Albert National Park Library, Waskesiu, Saskatchewan. (This report contains the transcripts of many useful interviews about Grey Owl at Prince Albert National Park.)

Shortt, James. "A Structural and Furnishings History of the Grey Owl Cabin Site, Ajawaan Lake, Prince Albert National Park," Parks Canada, Manuscript Report Number 264 (1978).

Shortt, James. "A Study in Conviction and Fantasy: A. S. Belaney and Grey Owl, 1888–1938," Parks Canada, Manuscript Report Number 378 (1980).

Somervell, Betty. Letters to her daughter at school, aged twelve. Written in 1953.

Somervell, Betty. Diary, February 14–March 7, 1936; and September 10–October 7, 1936.

Tabulenas, D. T. "A Narrative Human History of Riding Mountain National Park and Area: Prehistory to 1980," Parks Canada, Microfiche Report Series 102 (1983).

V. Archival Collections on Grey Owl

American Philosophical Society, Philadelphia, Pennsylvania.
   Speck, Frank G. Algonquian Field Notes.

Archives of Ontario, Toronto.
   Grey Owl Collection, assembled by Donald B. Smith. Photostat copies of letters
      by Grey Owl to Lloyd Acheson (August 1, 1934), and Bill Oliver (April 5,
      1933).
   "Grey Owl," John Fisher Papers. Research Files in the Archives of Ontario,
      MU 4179.

Dalhousie University Archives, Halifax, Nova Scotia.
   Raddall, Thomas. Collection of Materials on Grey Owl, including a microfilm
      reel from the National Archives of Canada containing: Confidential Papers
      of Archie Belaney (his park employment record—civil service personnel
      file); Regimental Documents of Archie Belaney; Confidential War Diaries
      of 13th Canadian Infantry Battalion, October 1915–April 1916.

Department of Indian Affairs. Departmental Library, Hull, Quebec.
   "Grey Owl File, 1931–1938."

Environment Canada, Parks, Ottawa, Ontario.
   Parks Board Beaver File, PA 272, volume 1.
   Prince Albert National Park, March 1928 to November 1948.
   Beaver. Examined in 1971—this file has not been relocated.

Glenbow Museum Archives, Calgary, Alberta.
   P. H. Godsell Papers, Box 7, folder 65. Personal correspondence.
   Indian Association of America, 1937–1939.

McMaster University, Hamilton, Ontario.
   The William Ready Division of Archives and Research Collections, McMaster
      University Library, Hamilton, Ontario: Box 13, folders 1–3. Correspondence
      of Hugh Eayrs with Lovat Dickson, 1934–1940; Box 14, folders 2–3.
      Correspondence of Hugh Eayrs with Ellen Elliott, his secretary, 1936, 1938;
      Box 20, folder 5. Toronto Book Fair, 1936; Box 47, folder 6. Hugh Eayrs—
      Obituaries; Box 99, folders 3–9. Grey Owl materials; Box 100, folders 1–13.
      Grey Owl materials; Box 101, folders 1–2. Grey Owl materials; Box 102.
      Press clippings about, and photographs of Grey Owl.

National Archives of Canada, Ottawa, Ontario.
   Conibear, Ken. Grey Owl Collection.
   Dickson, Lovat. Papers on Grey Owl, MG 30, D 237, volumes 8–11, 24.
   External Affairs. Grey Owl, 1935–1938, RG 25, A 5, volume 382.
   Grey Owl Collection. MG 30, D 147: Vol. 1. Grey Owl's Notebooks, 1927–1937;
      Vol. 2. Grey Owl's correspondence with Anahareo, and letters to Mrs. Ettie
      Winters; Vol. 2, 3, 5. Articles written by Grey Owl, and clippings about him;
      Vol. 4–5. Material collected by Mrs. Betty Somervell about Grey Owl,
      including Anahareo's memoirs, written 1939–1940, in seven notebooks.

   Indian Affairs.
   Grey Owl. Departmental Correspondence. RG 10, vol. 7995, file 1/1–15–2–4.

Militia and Defence.
Confidential War Diary of 13th Canadian Infantry Battalion, August 1915–April 1916. National Archives of Canada. RG 9, III, vol. 4921.
Moses, Elliott. MG 30, C 169, vols. 1–2.
Newton-White, Ernest. MG 30 A 54.
King, William Lyon Mackenzie. MG 26, J, Correspondence about Grey Owl, 1936: J1, vol. 216, p. 186259; J1, vol. 217, pp. 187266–72; J4, vol. 170, file 1579, p. C121314.

Parks Canada.
Prince Albert National Park files: RG 84, volume 1770, file PA 272NC, pt. 1. Clippings and Correspondence 1931–1938; File PA 272NC, pt. 2. Correspondence 1938–1961; volume 1771, file PA 272NC, pt. 3 & pt. 4 (reconstruction of Grey Owl's cabin).
Grey Owl's Civil Service Personnel File, RG 32, volume 18.

Personnel Records Centre, Ottawa, Ontario.
Archibald Belaney, Attestation Papers, Canadian Over-Seas Expeditionary Force, May 6, 1915.
Service Record of Archibald Belaney.

Prince Albert National Park, Waskesiu, Saskatchewan.
Beaver Files: PA 61. To March 31, 1933; PA 61. April 1, 1933 to March 31, 1935; PA 61. April 1, 1935 to March 31, 1938; PA 61. April 1, 1938 to Dec. 31, 1944.

Princeton University Library, Princeton, New Jersey.
Grey Owl's Correspondence with Charles Scribner's Sons, with Related Papers.

Riding Mountain National Park, Wasagaming, Manitoba.
Grey Owl Correspondence File, 1931. (Photostated and sent to me by mail.)

Saskatchewan Archives Board, Regina, Saskatchewan.
Isa Murray (Whiteford) Papers.

Saskatchewan Archives Board, Saskatoon, Saskatchewan.
H. J. Fraser, Q.C. Papers: Re Grey Owl Estate, 1934–1953, microfilmed by Saskatchewan Archives Board, May, 1970.

Toronto Star, Toronto, Ontario.
The library's clipping file on Grey Owl.

Trent University Archives, Peterborough, Ontario.
Keneth Kidd Clipping Books.

University of Alberta Archives.
S. M. Blair Papers (see Karl Clark's letter of November 16, 1932, about his visit to Beaver Lodge, 85-31: 46/2/2/1/3).

University of Toronto, Toronto, Ontario.
Thomas Fisher Library
William Arthur Deacon (Grey Owl Correspondence).

Veterans' Affairs, Tunney's Pasture, Ottawa, Ontario.
Archibald Belaney's War Pension File (since misplaced).

VI. Interviews with individuals who knew Archie Belaney in Hastings, England, and in Canada

Taped interviews are indicated by an asterix. The tapes are deposited in the Moving Image and Sound Archives, Historical Resources Branch, National Archives of Canada, Ottawa, Ontario. At the end of each listing I have indicated Archie's relationship with the individual interviewed.

Hastings, England, 1900–1906

Henry Hopkin, Cowes, Isle of Wight, England, May 21, 1975* and London, July 29, 1976. BOYHOOD FRIEND.

Ivy Holmes, Farnham, Surrey, England, September 29, 1971; December 13, 1972; December 20, 1972; June 8, 1975. BOYHOOD FRIEND.

George McCormick, Maidstone, Kent, England, December 2, 1972*, December 11, 1972*, December 18, 1972; May 24, 1975. BOYHOOD FRIEND.

Percy Overton, Hastings, Sussex, England, October 6, 1971; December 5, 1972*; August 1, 1976. BOYHOOD FRIEND.

Temagami, Northern Ontario, 1907–1912

Ted and Molly Guppy, Temagami, August 3, 1970*. ACQUAINTANCES.

Donald Mackenzie, Bear Island, Lake Temagami, August 13, 1971; May 16, 1974*. ACQUAINTANCE.

Charlotte McLean Morrison, Temagami, August 3, 1970; September 26, 1970*; August 3, 1975. ACQUAINTANCE.

Charlie Potts, Temagami, August 12, 1971; March 16, 1972. ACQUAINTANCE.

Tom Potts, North Bay, February 10, 1973. ACQUAINTANCE.

Eliza Neveu Saville, North Bay, March 17, 1972*. ACQUAINTANCE.

John Stewart, Victoria, B.C., August 26, 1982. ACQUAINTANCE.

Biscotasing, Northern Ontario, 1912–1914

Célina Legace Barnes, Thunder Bay, Ontario, July 14, 1971. DAUGHTER OF MRS. LEGACE, HIS LANDLADY IN BISCO.

Maurice Kingsford, Queensborough, Ontario, August 1, 1972*; August 10, 1972*. FELLOW FOREST RANGER, SUMMER 1912.

Ferg Legace, Owen Sound, Ontario, June 12, 1971; Petawawa, Ontario, August 5, 1972. SON OF MRS. LEGACE, HIS LANDLADY IN BISCO.

Colin Phillips, Biscotasing, September 29, 1970; February 5, 1971. ACQUAINTANCE.

Elizabeth Miller Robinson, North Bay, Ontario, February 7, 1973*. ACQUAINTANCE.

Robert H. Wilson, Windsor, Ontario, July 10, 1973. FELLOW FOREST RANGER, SUMMER 1914.

In the Canadian Army, 1915–1917

Albert Chandler, Melfort, Saskatchewan, September 21, 1974*. FELLOW SOLDIER IN THE 13TH BATTALION.

In England, 1916–1917

Ivy Holmes, Farnham, Surrey, England, September 29, 1971; December 13, 1972; December 20, 1972; June 8, 1975. HIS ENGLISH WIFE.

Geoffrey McCormick, Hastings, Sussex, December 12, 1972*. ACQUAINTANCE.

Leonard Scott-Brown, Knoff Lake, B.C., July 19, 20, 1980; Vancouver, August 25, 1982. HALF-BROTHER.

Biscotasing, Northern Ontario, 1917–1925
Keith Acheson, interview by telephone, Toronto, June 29, 1970; Toronto, January 27, 1971; January 18, 1973*. ACQUAINTANCE.
Tom Bain, Chapleau, Ontario, February 5, 1971. ACQUAINTANCE.
Hector Bléau, Sudbury, Ontario, August 25, 1971. ACQUAINTANCE.
Art Boice, Thessalon, Ontario, December 6, 1970. ACQUAINTANCE.
Vince Crichton, Chapleau, Ontario, September 29, 1970*; March 19, 1972; June 4, 1973. ACQUAINTANCE.
Ted Cusson, Monetville, Ontario, August 3, 1970; December 6, 1970; Toronto, January 16, 21, 31*, 1971; Monetville, December 18, 19, 1971; Toronto, January 16, 17, 18, 19*, 22, 1972; Monetville, March 25, 1972; April 1, 1973. FRIEND IN BISCO AND ABITIBI.
Adam Espaniel, Calgary, February 13, 1989. ACQUAINTANCE.
Jim and Susan Espaniel, Estaire, Ontario, August 2, 1970; September 27, 1970*; December 6, 1970. Biscotasing, August 18, 22, 23, 1971; Estaire, December 18, 1971; March 25, 1972; October 31, 1972; March 29, 1973; Levack, Ontario, January 15, 1974; August 5, 1974; December 10, 1974; August 6, 1977. GOOD FRIENDS IN BISCO.
Gordon Gouett, Sudbury, Ontario, September 20, 1972*. ACQUAINTANCE.
John Jero, Thunder Bay, Ontario, December 6, 1974. SON BY MARIE GIRARD, OR JERO, BORN IN 1915.
Haddow Keith, Rochester, Minnesota, May 24, 1976*. FELLOW FOREST RANGER, SUMMER 1920.
Harry and Katie Phillips Kohls, Biscotasing, July 15, 1971; August 21, 1971; March 20, 1972; November 2, 1972; June 4, 1973; December 9, 1974; May 3, 1975. ACQUAINTANCES.
Bill Langevin, Biscotasing, July 16, 1971; December 16, 1971; November 2, 1972; April 22, 1973. ACQUAINTANCE.
Gordon and Hilda Kohls Langevin, Biscotasing, September 29, 1970; February 4, 5, 1971; July 15, 16, 1971; August 21, 1971; December 15, 16, 17, 1971; March 19, 1972; August 8, 1974; December 7, 1974. ACQUAINTANCES.
Ferg Legace (see entries under "Biscotasing, 1912–1914").
Jack Leve, Toronto, February 28, 1971*; April 26, 1971*; May 7, 1971*; October 28, 1971; January 6, 22, 1972; February 21, 1972; April 13, 1972*; May 15, 1972*; June 22, 1972. FRIEND.
Sam Luke, Timmins, Ontario, May 5, 1973*. ACQUAINTANCE.
Stuart MacDougall, Toronto, July 22, 1975*. FELLOW WORKER ON A SURVEY PARTY, SUMMER 1919.
Madeline Woodworth McLeod, Biscotasing, September 29, 1970; November 1, 1972. FRIEND.
Jane Espaniel McKee, Toronto, June 2, 1973; June 11, 1973; June 18, 1973; July 29, 1973; September 3, 1973; September 30, 1973; February 10, 1974; December 31, 1979; September 9, 1982; September 29, 1987; Calgary, January 3, 1989; February 13, 1989; June 26, 1989. FRIEND.
Robert McWatch, Chapleau, Ontario, February 6, 1971. ACQUAINTANCE.

Colin Phillips (see entries under Biscotasing, 1912–1914).

Rueben Phillips, Creighton Mine, Ontario, November 4, 1972. ACQUAINTANCE.

Ed and Charlotte Phillips Sawyer and Libby Sawyer, Sudbury, February 6, 1971*; Biscotasing, July 16, 1971; August 20, 21, 22, 1971; Sudbury, March 17, 22, 25, 1972; November 3, 1972; November 18, 1972; April 21, 22, 1973; Biscotasing, August 7, 1974; Sudbury, December 9, 1974; May 3, 1975; January 2, 1976. FRIENDS.

Irene Shaughnessy, Toronto, July 20, 1972*; November 8, 1972*; April 12, 1973. SCHOOLTEACHER IN BISCO.

Charles Sykes, Barrie, Ontario, January 22, 1972; May 19, 1972. ACQUAINTANCE.

Jack Woodworth, Cartier, Ontario, July 17, 1971; December 14, 1971; March 23, 24, 1972*; November 4, 5, 1972; April 20, 1973. FRIEND.

Temagami, Northern Ontario, 1925

Anahareo, Kamloops, B.C., July 5, 6, 7, 8, 1971. WIFE AND HEROINE OF *PILGRIMS OF THE WILD.*

Dewey Derosier, Temagami, September 26, 1970*. ACQUAINTANCE.

Agnes Belaney Lalonde, Temagami, August 3, 1970; December 5, 1970; May 9, 1971*; North Bay, March 16, 1972; January 1973*; February 8, 1973*; April 29, 1973; May 16, 1974; January 2, 1975; August 4, 1975; October 1, 1987; Calgary, July 2, 1988. DAUGHTER OF ARCHIE BELANEY AND ANGELE EGWUNA, HIS FIRST WIFE.

George Le Duc, Temagami, April 26, 1972*. ACQUAINTANCE.

Isobel Le Duc, Temagami, March 15, 1972; April 26, 1972*. ACQUAINTANCE.

Madeline Katt Theriault, North Bay, February 8, 1973*; January 2, 1976. ACQUAINTANCE.

Abitibi, 1925–1928

Anahareo (all entries under Temagami, 1925).

Bill Cartier, Monetville, Ontario, March 25, 1972*. ACQUAINTANCE.

Ted Cusson (see entry under Biscotasing, 1917–1925).

Témiscouata, 1928–1931

Joseph Bérubé, Cabano, Quebec, April 14, 1971*. ACQUAINTANCE.

John Bovey, Canmore, Alberta, August 26, 1988*. ACQUAINTANCE.

Lorenzo Charest, Cabano, Quebec, April 14, 1971*. ACQUAINTANCE.

Gertrude Côté, Cabano, Quebec, April 14, 1971*. ACQUAINTANCE.

Msgr. Jean-Philippe Cyr, Cabano, Quebec, April 14, 1971. ACQUAINTANCE.

Bernie Graham, Campbellton, New Brunswick, April 4, 1972*. FRIEND.

Yvon Lavoie, Ottawa, Ontario, December 31, 1972. ACQUAINTANCE.

Adélard Leblanc, Cabano, Quebec, April 14, 1971. ACQUAINTANCE.

Richard Peck, telephone interview, Ste.-Agathe-des-Monts, Quebec, October 12, 1988. ACQUAINTANCE.

Frank and Alice Graham Richardson, Campbellton, New Brunswick, April 2, 1972*. FRIENDS.

Walter Strong, Outremont, Quebec, April 6, 1972*. ACQUAINTANCE.

Riding Mountain National Park, 1931
> Hubert Green, Banff, Alberta, July 21, 1988. HIS FATHER, TONY GREEN, WAS A FRIEND OF GREY OWL AT RIDING MOUNTAIN.

Prince Albert National Park, 1931–38
> Adam Cuthand, interview by telephone, North Battleford, August 14, 1988. HEARD HIM SPEAK AT FORT CARLTON, AUGUST 1936.
> Stan Cuthand, Brandon, Manitoba, November 5, 1981; interview by telephone, Saskatoon, Sask., August 9, 1988. HEARD HIM SPEAK AT FORT CARLTON, AUGUST 1936.
> Wally Laird, Calgary, August 30, 1988, RCMP SPECIAL CONSTABLE, WASKESIU DETACHMENT, PRINCE ALBERT NATIONAL PARK, 1932–38.
> Francis Mildred Martin, interviewed by Jackie Keesey, 1986, taped interview at Prince Albert National Park Library, Waskesiu, Saskatchewan. ACQUAINTANCE.
> Dawn Richardson, Prince Albert, Saskatchewan, June 29, 1971; Toronto, June 10, 1972; Kamloops, B.C., March 16, 1975; September 20, 1980. DAUGHTER OF GREY OWL (ARCHIE BELANEY) AND ANAHAREO.
> Hazel Sorenson Schmitz, Calgary, Alberta, October 17, 1989. ONE OF HIS NURSES DURING HIS FINAL ILLNESS, HOLY FAMILY HOSPITAL, PRINCE ALBERT, APRIL 1938.
> Ettie Winters, Prince Albert, Saskatchewan, June 21, 1971. FRIEND.
> Herbert Winters, interviewed by Ron Dutcher, Prince Albert, Saskatchewan, March 25, 1970. Tape in the Prince Albert National Park Library, Waskesiu, Saskatchewan. FRIEND.
> Margaret Winters Charko, Ottawa, March 13, 1972. TYPED *TALES OF AN EMPTY CABIN*.
> Stan Winters, Prince Albert, July 2, 1971. HELPER WITH THE BEAVER, SUMMER 1936.
> John Tootoosis, Poundmaker Reserve, Cutknife, Saskatchewan, October 20, 1974; Calgary, March 23, 1976*; Calgary, March 17, 1978. FRIEND— "BROTHER" BY ADOPTION.

First British Lecture Tour, 1935–36
> Ted Blackmore, Eastbourne, Sussex, England, May 19, 1975; August 1, 1976; January 17, 1981. HEARD HIM LECTURE IN EASTBOURNE, AND HE LATER HELPED TO MAKE HIS WAR BONNET.
> John Burton, Hastings, Sussex, England, by telephone, September 21, 1988. HEARD GREY OWL SPEAK IN HASTINGS, 1935.
> Lovat Dickson, Toronto, February 28, 1970; February 3, 1971; March 1, 1971; November 22, 1971; January 25, 1972; June 25, 1972; November 14, 1972; November 27, 28, 1972; January 10, 1973; March 23, 1973; May 21, 1976; January 5, 1979. GREY OWL'S PUBLISHER IN ENGLAND, SPONSOR OF THE TWO BRITISH TOURS, AND FIRST BIOGRAPHER (1939).
> Laya Rotenberg Kurtz, Paris, France, December 9, 1972. GREY OWL'S SECRETARY ON THE FIRST BRITISH TOUR, January–February 1936.
> Betty Somervell, Toronto, October 12, 1971*; Kendal, Westmorland, England, December 16, 17, 1972; June 1, 1975. FRIEND.

Michael Wilson, Calgary, June 25, 1982. HEARD HIM LECTURE IN LEEDS, ENGLAND IN 1935 AND 1937.

Those Who Met Him on Eastern Canadian Visits, 1935–1938

John Gray, Toronto, February 23, 1970. ACQUAINTANCE AT MACMILLAN (HIS PUBLISHERS).

Maurice Hackman, Peterborough, November 13, 1989. HEARD HIM LECTURE IN HAMILTON, IN 1938.

Jasper Hill (Big White Owl), Moraviantown, Ontario, June 10, 1988. MET HIM SEVERAL TIMES IN TORONTO.

Gerald Johnston, Burleigh Falls, June 17, 1971. GREY OWL VISITED HIM IN HOSPITAL IN PETERBOROUGH IN 1938.

Ken Kidd, Peterborough, Ontario, June 18, 1971; July 26, 1987. MET HIM WHILE WORKING AT THE ROYAL ONTARIO MUSEUM.

Hoyes Lloyd, Ottawa, November 6, 1973. MET HIM IN OTTAWA.

Ellen Elliott McKanday, interview by telephone, Toronto, January 1, 1971. SECRETARY TO HUGH EAYRS, GREY OWL'S PUBLISHER IN CANADA (MACMILLAN).

The North Bay *Nugget*'s discovery of Angele Belaney in Temagami, 1935–1937

Mort Fellman, interviewed by telephone, North Bay, Ontario, March 23, 1988. MET HIM IN MARCH 1937.

Bert Jessup, interviewed by telephone, North Bay, Ontario, April 12, 1988. MET HIS WIFE ANGELE IN TEMAGAMI, 1935.

The Making of "The Trail—Winter," 1937 (the Abitibi film)

Yvonne Perrier Clare (see entry under Second British Lecture Tour).

The Making of "The Trail—Summer," 1937 (the Mississagi River film)

Antoine Commanda, Estaire, Ontario, September 27, 1970*. CANOEMAN ON THE MISSISSAGI TRIP, SUMMER 1937.

Second British Lecture Tour

Ken Conibear, Vancouver, July 8, 1971; March 14, 1975*; July 25, 1982; Knoff Lake, B.C., July 24, 1983; Vancouver, July 11, 1984; Waskesiu, Saskatchewan, August 10, 1988; Hastings, Sussex, September 18, 1988; Ken Conibear, interviewed by Phil Chester, May 23, 1988 (tapes donated to the Moving Image and Sound Archives, NAC). TOUR MANAGER.

Lovat Dickson (see entry under First British Lecture Tour).

George and Dolly Head, Hastings, Sussex, December 5, 1972*. DOLLY SAW GREY OWL ENTER HIS AUNTS' HOME, December 15, 1937.

Lillian Hazell O'Nions, Hastings, Sussex, September 20, 1988. HEARD GREY OWL SPEAK IN HASTINGS, 1937.

Yvonne Perrier Clare, Ottawa, May 10, 1971. WIFE AND SECRETARY, 1937 TOUR.

Ian West, Hastings, Sussex, September 18, 1988. HEARD GREY OWL'S LECTURE AT BEXHILL, SUSSEX.

Michael Wilson (see entry under First British Lecture Tour).

Additional Interviews

Gregory Clark, Toronto, November 4, 1970. EXPOSÉ OF GREY OWL AFTER HIS DEATH.

CBC Archives, Toronto. Tapes Recorded for Man at the Centre's television documentary on Grey Owl, 1971. Tapes and transcripts of interviews with Anahareo, Ted Cusson, Lovat Dickson, Jim Espaniel, Jack Leve, Lottie Phillips Sawyer.

VII. Periodicals Checked

Canadian Forest and Outdoors, 1930–1938.

Detroit *Free Press*, February 11–17, 1938.

Le Soleil (Quebec City) September 1–December 6, 1929; October 1– November 24, 1930.

Montreal *Gazette*, April 13–30, 1938.

Montreal *Standard*, April 16–30, 1938.

Montreal *Star*, January 13–17, 1938; April 13–30, 1938.

North Bay *Nugget*, April 13–30, 1938.

Ottawa *Citizen*, March 7–9, 1938; April 13–29, 1938.

Ottawa *Journal*, February 16–April 30, 1938.

Peterborough *Examiner*, March 5–18, 1938; April 13–30, 1938.

Prince Albert *Herald*, October 21–November 2, 1931; April 1–30, 1938.

Regina *Leader-Post*, April 13–30, 1938; June 15–23, 1938.

St. John *Telegraph-Journal* (St. John, N.B.), April 13–23, 1938.

Saskatoon *Star-Phoenix*, April 13–30, 1938.

Sudbury *Star*, April 13–29, 1938.

Toronto *Globe and Mail*, April 13–30, 1938.

Toronto *Star*, November 9–12, 1936; April 13–30, 1938.

Vancouver *Sun*, April 13–30, 1938.

Windsor *Star*, April 13–30, 1938.

Winnipeg *Free Press*, October 1–31, 1931; April 13–30, 1938.

Winnipeg *Tribune*, October 4–9, 1931; April 13–30, 1938.

VIII. Useful Background Works

Back, Brian. *The Keewaydin Way. A Portrait: 1893–1983*. Temagami: Keewaydin Camp, Ltd., 1983.

Baines, J. Mainwaring, J. R. Conisbee, and N. Bygate. *The History of the Hastings Grammar School, 1619–1966*. Hastings: Hastings Grammar School Foundation, 1967.

Barbeau, Marius. "Our Indians—Their Disappearance." *Queen's Quarterly*, 38 (1931): 691–707.

Berkhofer, Robert F. *The White Man's Indian. Images of the American Indian from Columbus to the Present.* New York: Vintage Books, 1979.

Campbell, Maria. *Halfbreed.* Toronto: McClelland and Stewart, 1973.

Camsell, Charles. *Son of the North.* Toronto: Ryerson, 1954.

Clifton, James A., ed. *Being and Becoming Indian. Biographical Studies of North American Frontiers.* Chicago: The Dorsey Press, 1989.

Cook, Helen and Lloyd. *Scrapper the Beaver.* New Liskeard, Ontario: Temiskaming Printing Company, n.d.

Crichton, Vincent. *Pioneering in Northern Ontario. History of the Chapleau District.* Belleville, Ontario: Mika Publishing Company, 1975.

Davidson, Malcolm. "History of the Native Peoples of the Treaty Nine Area to 1930," the first half of his forthcoming Ph.D. thesis in Canadian history for the University of Toronto.

Davidson, D. Sutherland. "The Family Hunting Territories of the Grand Lake Victoria Indians." *Atti del XII Congresso Internazionale degli Americanisti Roma—Settembre 1926,* volume 2, pp. 69–95.

Emerson, Ralph Waldo. *Essays and Representative Men.* London: Collins' Clear-Type Press, n.d.

Foster, Janet. *Working for Wildlife.* Toronto: University of Toronto Press, 1978.

Gossett, Thomas F. *Race: The History of an Idea in America.* Dallas: Southern Methodist University Press, 1964.

Hodgins, Bruce W. and Jamie Benidickson. *The Temagami Experience: Recreation, Resources, and Aboriginal Rights in the Northern Ontario Wilderness.* Toronto: University of Toronto Press, 1989.

Hummel, Monte, ed. *Endangered Spaces. The Future of Canada's Wilderness.* Toronto: Key Porter Books, 1989.

Jenness, Diamond. "Canada's Indians Yesterday. What of Today?" *Canadian Journal of Economics and Political Science,* 20, 1 (February 1954): 95–100.

Jenness, Diamond. *Indians of Canada.* Ottawa: King's Printer, 1932.

Keller, Betty. *Black Wolf. The Life of Ernest Thompson Seton.* Vancouver: Douglas & McIntyre, 1984.

Loram, C. T. and T. F. McIlwraith, eds. *The North American Indian Today, University of Toronto–Yale University Seminar Conference, Toronto, September 4–16, 1939.* Toronto: University of Toronto Press, 1943.

Miller, J. R. *Skyscrapers Hide the Heavens. A History of Indian–White Relations in Canada.* Toronto: University of Toronto Press, 1989.

Morantz, Toby. "Dwindling Animals and Diminished Lands: Early Twentieth Century Developments in Eastern James Bay." In *Papers of the Eighteenth Algonquian Conference,* edited by William Cowan, pp. 209–27. Ottawa: Carleton University, 1987.

Morrison, James. *Treaty Nine (1905–06): The James Bay Treaty.* Ottawa: Treaties and Historical Research Centre, Indian and Northern Affairs, Canada, 1986.

Nash, Roderick. *Wilderness and the American Mind.* New Haven: Yale University Press, 1967.

Novak, Milan. "Beaver." In *Wild Furbearer Management and Conservation in North America,* edited by Milan Novak et al, pp. 283–312. Toronto: Ministry of Natural Resources, 1987.

Potts, Gary and James Morrison. "The Temagami Ojibwa, Frank Speck and Family Hunting Territories." Paper presented to the American Society for Ethnohistory Conference, Williamsburg, Virginia, November 11, 1988.

Rowlands, John J. *Cache Lake Country. Life in the North Woods.* New York: W. W. Norton & Co., 1947, 1959.

Seton, Ernest Thompson. *Two Little Savages.* New York: Doubleday Page & Co., 1903; reprinted New York: Dover Publications, 1970.

Speck, F. G. *Family Hunting Territories and Social Life of Various Algonkian Bands of the Ottawa Valley*. Ottawa: Government Printing Bureau, 1915.

Speck, F. G. *Myths and Folk-lore of the Timiskaming Algonquin and Timagami Ojibwa*. Ottawa: Government Printing Bureau, 1915.

Suzuki, David. *Metamorphosis. Stages in a Life*. Toronto: General Paperbacks, 1988.

Theriault, Madeline. *Moose to Moccasins*. North Bay, Ontario: Printed by the author, 1985. Mimeographed.

Tiller, Veronica E. Velarde. *The Jicarilla Apache Tribe. A History, 1846–1970*. Lincoln: University of Nebraska Press, 1983.

Titley, E. Brian. *A Narrow Vision. Duncan Campbell Scott and the Administration of Indian Affairs in Canada*. Vancouver: University of British Columbia Press, 1986.

Wadland, John Henry. *Ernest Thompson Seton. Man and Nature and the Progressive Era 1880–1915*. New York: Arno Press, 1978.

Whitefield, Charles L. *Healing the Child Within. Discovery and Recovery for Adult Children of Dysfunctional Families*. Deerfield Beach, Florida: Health Communications, Inc., 1987.

Wilsson, Lars. *My Beaver Colony*. Translated from the Swedish by Joan Bulman. Garden City, New York: Doubleday, 1968.

Zaslow, Morris. *The Opening of the Canadian North, 1870–1914*. Toronto: McClelland and Stewart, 1971.

Zaslow, Morris. *The Northward Expansion of Canada, 1914–1967*. Toronto: McClelland and Stewart, 1988.

Index

A Note for the Paperback Edition

Since the publication of *From the Land of Shadows*, a number of people have asked me about the subsequent lives of the principal characters after Grey Owl's death, and have enquired about how I located them. Many, of course, had died by the time I began my research early in 1970: the Misses Belaney and Kittie Scott-Brown, for instance. Fortunately, however, Betty Somervell and Lovat Dickson had taken notes of their interviews with them in the weeks immediately following Grey Owl's death, and they kindly made them available to me.

I was successful in locating several of Archie Belaney's boyhood acquaintances. An enquiry letter to the Hastings *Observer* during my first English research trip in 1971 led me to Percy Overton, who in turn put me in touch with members of the McCormick family in Australia. Through their help I obtained the address of George McCormick, who had lived next door to the Belaneys seventy years earlier. I visited Mr. McCormick, a World War One veteran and a retired major in the British Army in India, at his home in Maidstone, Kent, in 1972. In 1971 I also located Ivy Holmes, who had remarried and lived in Farnham, Surrey. She supplied invaluable information about Archie Belaney's childhood in Hastings. In 1975, further research allowed me to contact Henry Hopkin, one of Archie's fellow students at the Hastings Grammar School. Mr. Hopkin had spent several decades working for English-language newspapers in Malaya and Singapore before he returned to work as a journalist in England.

In Canada I met many individuals who had known Archie Belaney or Grey Owl in Temagami, Biscotasing, Cabano, and Prince Albert National Park. Anahareo lived in Kamloops, B.C., when I interviewed her in the 1970s. She died in 1986, two years after the death of her daughter, Dawn. I met Grey Owl's son, Johnny Jero, in Thunder Bay in 1974. John, who had been seriously wounded and permanently handicapped during his service with the Canadian Army in World War Two, died in 1979. Of those of his children that I met, only one remains alive—Agnes Belaney Lalonde of North Bay, Ontario.

The late Lovat Dickson assisted me greatly from the year I began my research, 1970, to his death in 1987. The late Betty Somervell of Kendal, in England's Lake District, provided much assistance as well. Ken Conibear of Vancouver, Grey Owl's manager during the 1937 British lecture tour, was also a constant support. Ken is currently Associate Director in Continuing Studies at Simon Fraser University and he manages the university's senior citizens' program. At the very moment that I badly needed the final encouragement to finish my book, Jane Espaniel McKee, whose family had known Grey Owl so well at Biscotasing, moved to Calgary to join her son and daughter-in-law and their family.

I am delighted that Western Producer Prairie Books has decided to bring *From the Land of Shadows* out in paperback, thus making it available to a larger audience. I hope that in the years to follow, other researchers will make their own discovery of Grey Owl, a conservationist visionary. The Glenbow Archives in Calgary has agreed to store my collection of research notes on Grey Owl and they are open to future students of the man who wrote over half a century ago: "Remember you belong to Nature, not it to you."

DONALD SMITH
CALGARY
NOVEMBER 6, 1990